The Complete Conductor

The Complete Conductor

A COMPREHENSIVE RESOURCE FOR THE PROFESSIONAL CONDUCTOR OF THE TWENTY-FIRST CENTURY

Robert W. Demaree, Jr.
Indiana University South Bend

Don V Moses
University of Illinois at Urbana-Champaign

PRENTICE HALL, Upper Saddle River, NJ 07458

Library of Congress Cataloging-in-Publication Data

DEMAREE, ROBERT W.
    The complete conductor : a comprehensive resource for the
professional conductor of the twenty-first century / Robert W.
Demaree, Jr., Don V Moses.
        p.   cm.
    Includes bibliographical references (p.) and index.
    ISBN 0-13-173014-2 (hard cover)
    1. Conducting.   I. Moses, Don V.   II. Title.
MT85.D36   1994
781.45—dc20   93-48392
                                                  CIP
                                                  MN

Acquisitions editor: *Norwell Therien*
Editorial/production supervision
    and interior design: *Carole R. Crouse*
Copy editor: *Carole R. Crouse*
Cover designer: *Rich Dombrowski*
Production coordinator: *Bob Anderson*
Editorial assistant: *Kathy Shawhan*

© 1995 by Prentice-Hall, Inc.
A Pearson Education Company
Upper Saddle River, NJ 07458

Printed in the United States of America

10   9   8   7   6   5   4   3   2

ISBN 0-13-173014-2

Prentice-Hall International (UK) Limited,London
Prentice-Hall of Australia Pty. Limited, Sydney
Prentice-Hall Canada Inc., Toronto
Prentice-Hall Hispanoamericana, S.A., Mexico
Prentice-Hall of India Private Limited, New Delhi
Prentice-Hall of Japan, Inc., Tokyo
Pearson Education Asia Pte. Ltd., Singapore
Editora Prentice-Hall do Brasil, Ltda., Rio de Janeiro

Contents

Preface

TO THE PROFESSOR AND THE FUTURE CONDUCTORS

This comprehensive, innovative, and practical text is intended for *all* those who study conducting. Whether you are now a beginner, an advanced student, or a working professional, you should find it of direct help.

- It analyzes in detail every step you must take as a conductor, from your private study and preparation, through early rehearsals, to your final practice sessions and your performances.
- It identifies and deals with the technical skills you must develop, presenting effective exercises in a context of an evolving physical discipline.
- It emphasizes in an exceptional way the linkage between this technical discipline and the whole range of musical styles from the Medieval world to the present day. The bulk of *the music you need for this study of performance practice is presented in this volume in fine editions* based on the best current scholarship. (You should not need to compete for library copies or order stacks of scores.)
- It prepares you to conduct *all* serious repertoire, whether for choirs, instrumental ensembles, or the musical stage.
- It explores the special administrative and organizational problems characteristic of each of those circumstances.

The Diamond Design

This book is uniquely structured so that the professor can assign it for one or two semesters, at either the undergraduate or the graduate level, and it is constructed in modules that can be arranged to fit the professor's own syllabus. Please refer to the diagram on page xiv.

Exercises (especially in the early chapters) are kept brief so that *every student may conduct daily* and each chapter may be covered in a week (assuming a twice-weekly class of standard size). Thus, this text may be employed in the following settings:

- *Basic (introductory) Conducting* (one semester), using Part One extended with one or two chapters each from Parts Two and Three.

- *Introduction to Choral Conducting* (one semester), combining Parts One and Two into a twelve-to-fifteen-week course.
- *Introduction to Instrumental Conducting* (one semester), combining Parts One and Three into a twelve-to-fifteen-week course.
- A second-semester course in *Choral Conducting*, combining Part Two with most of Part Four.
- A second-semester course in *Instrumental Conducting*, combining Part Three with most of Part Four.
- A two-semester, comprehensive *Conducting I and II*, using the entire book, with Part One treated either as a necessary introduction or as review material for advanced students.
- A *Graduate Conducting* class, for which Parts Two, Three, and Four, with their emphasis on style study, will be quite appropriate.
- As a *general reference work for professional conductors*, this text—with its complete units on conducting theory, performance practice in the various style periods, and conducting technic—should be useful throughout one's career.

PART ONE
Linking the Mind and the Body

Eight chapters (seven or eight weeks, unless the class is merely reviewing this material) covering the physical and intellectual fundamentals of conducting. Exercises are brief, so that each student can conduct daily, if the professor so desires. Each step forward is carefully staged.

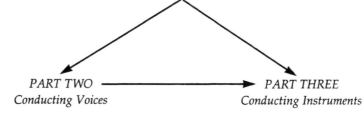

PART TWO	PART THREE
Conducting Voices	*Conducting Instruments*
Four chapters (four to eight weeks) on choral conducting, vocal factors, and choral methods in styles ranging from chant to today's music, always through masterworks.	Four chapters (four to eight weeks) on instrumental conducting, band, and orchestra considerations in musical styles from c. 1500 to today, always through masterworks.

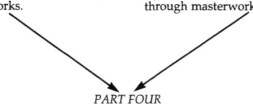

PART FOUR
Mastery and Management

Nine chapters (seven to fifteen weeks) dealing first with programming, preparation, rehearsal techniques, and performance considerations; then with the study and conducting of five full-length masterpieces—works for chorus, orchestra, concerto, band, and the opera stage from the Baroque era to the present day.

Specific Features

1. A virtual anthology of masterworks, each in an edition of proven scholarship, is incorporated into this volume. The reader is led through step-by-step analyses that consider the historical, theoretical, and conductorial aspects of each work. For the early chapters, brief musical examples illustrating specific problems have been specially composed.
2. Some sixty carefully designed practice exercises are included as technical drills.
3. Over fifty artfully drawn diagrams depict and clarify the beat patterns, cutoffs, and other conductorial gestures.
4. Some two dozen passages headed "More Conducting Theory" (listed at the beginning of the Index) provide conceptual and philosophical backgrounds for conducting traditions and practices.
5. Several dozen "Axioms" (conductorial "proverbs") have been printed in boldface in the text to emphasize their wide-ranging usefulness.
6. A substantial bibliography of important monographs, scores, and supplementary resources has been included.

A Credo for Conductors

We take the following as our "creed," and we ask you to join us in subscribing to these professional values.

- We believe that every conductor should be able to conduct both voices and instruments with virtually equal skill and understanding; thus, it follows that this book is intended for *conductors*, not just for "choirmasters" or "band directors." Our own professional experiences support that view.
- We believe that *conducting the music of a particular period is best approached through an understanding of the style of that era itself*, rather than by means of artificial, anachronistic excerpts. To spend months and years practicing technic without getting directly involved in great music and a knowledge of styles surely misses the goal!
- We believe that "conducting books" should prepare one for the music of the Medieval and Renaissance worlds, as well as more recent styles (although we make it possible for the teacher to skip over the Gregorian chant section in Chapter 10, as may seem best in a particular situation).
- We believe that "as much as possible should be shown in the right hand," and so we devote much of Part One to building first of all a secure right-hand technique.
- We believe that the ability to conceive, remember, and manage longer and longer musical structures is crucial for the young conductor, and thus, by Part Four, our studies evolve from short works to multimovement masterpieces.
- We believe conductors must be planners and managers, too, and thus we give careful consideration to the administrative aspects of our discipline.
- We believe that these attitudes are consonant with the new vitality conducting classes have earned in the college curriculum, and with the enhanced esteem schools of music are granting to those who bring consummate interpretive musicianship to this demanding vocation.

We hope you subscribe in philosophy, in advocacy, and in discipline to this creed.

The authors are grateful to the following reviewers for their advice and helpful comments: James Smith, Glen A. Yarberry, Herbert W. Fred, C. Lee Humphries, Robert H. Klotman, Joseph Labuta, Douglas Smith, and Christopher Gallaher. We express warm appreciation to all those who have been of particular help in the creation of this text, especially for the graphic design work of Mark Feckewitz, the professional insights of our colleague Dr. Michael J. Esselstrom, the research assistance of Donald Nally and Victoria Lynn Shively, the patient editorial guidance of Carole R. Crouse and Norwell ("Bud") Therien, and—most of all—the sympathetic support of our wives.

Don V Moses
Robert W. Demaree, Jr.

The Complete Conductor

CHAPTER *1*

The Intellectual Basis

Musician, scholar, coach, communicator, educator, diplomat, disciplinarian, executive, planner, budget manager, personnel officer, efficiency expert, advocate, publicist, guide, leader, visionary: The ideal conductor combines all these roles in an intricate vocation.

As an artist, the conductor is first among equals. Every musician needs an instrument. Trumpeters, clarinetists, singers, pianists, and all the rest use a mechanical or physical device to generate the musical ideas they want to convey to their listeners. Each musical instrument has special qualities, and each demands of the artist a highly disciplined technique. No pianist can make use of the full range of keyboard literature and the expressive possibilities of the piano itself without first having mastered the skills needed to play it well.

So it is with conducting. The "instrument" through which you the conductor express yourself will be your ensemble. You will need to study their special qualities, judge their expressive abilities, and work to help them sound their best. To do so, you yourself must build a technical discipline as a conductor equal to or better than their instrumental expertise, for no one can conduct simply by wanting to; it is through careful, thoughtful mastering of performance skills that the musician becomes a conductor.

At the same time, you must not limit your expressive opportunities. A fine clarinetist is not "just a band player" or "only an orchestral musician"; fine artists are capable of performing all the repertoire written for their instruments, whatever the ensemble. Plan now to be not merely a "band leader," a "choirmaster," or an "orchestra director," for those occupations are only subsets of the ideal. Be a *conductor*!

Talented people make the difficult look easy. Conductors are no exception. One watches a Herbert von Karajan and sees only evocative gestures (less flashy in size and sweep than one expects, perhaps). One rehearses with a Robert Shaw and watches him lead his choir or orchestra logically enough toward a result that seems—in the end—inevitable. One hears the performance of a choir trained by a Margaret Hillis and cannot imagine that any other set of sounds might have been produced. Seeing only the apparent grace and ease with which great music is achieved, one may take for granted the years great conductors spend achieving technical brilliance by long practice, building musical understanding through scholarship, and gaining judgment about musicians and ensembles in dozens of rehearsals and performances.

You are about to learn that there is quite as much justifiable pride in the art and discipline of the conductor as in the work of any other artist. That pride must be earned by serious preparation.

WHAT IS CONDUCTING?

Conducting is the act of communicating musical ideas to an ensemble through *gesture*. Although that skill itself can be made to look uncomplicated, or even easy, the totality of conducting is both complex and demanding. It is true that all performing media are taxing; yet, none requires a more comprehensive understanding of the work at hand, and none calls for a more highly developed technique.

Conducting is a very physical pursuit. It demands considerable bodily stamina, as you will find when you conduct a two-and-one-half-hour orchestra rehearsal or a complete opera; just to prepare and pace yourself so that your arm and shoulder muscles do not tighten up is a serious consideration, if you are not used to this length of work. But conducting is physically difficult in another way, as well: It necessitates a *subtlety* of gesture from the hands, arms, fingers, eyes, and face equivalent to the sophistication of movement present in the technique of an actor or a dancer. Properly conceived, each movement the conductor makes will mean something to someone in the ensemble (or in the audience) and will be necessary to the presentation of the music at hand.

Like other kinds of intricate bodily activity, the movements within the complex gestures made by the conductor can be isolated, examined, studied, and adjusted one by one. Efficiency and effectiveness can be enhanced by work on the detailed physical aspects of this discipline.

At the same time, conducting is an intense *intellectual* pursuit. A fine conductor studies musical works as exhaustively as a classics scholar scrutinizes ancient manuscripts, trying to bring them to life—the classicist for the reader, the conductor for musicians and an audience. The construction of music, the ways in which a particular work differs from other music, the attitudes of musicians and laypeople in the time it was written, and the traditional approaches to its performance in that day and at the present time are all matters for precise thought and analysis.

And there we define a need for careful attention to the psychological responses of both the musicians and the audience. How can you best utilize the talents of an ensemble, and how best communicate to them your own hopes for the performance of a given work? What can you do to convey the intentions the composer expressed in the score in a lively and telling way? How can you present new works in a light that will persuade audience members to understand, enjoy, and value them? How can you offer familiar music with freshness and vitality?

You must bring both physique and intellect to the podium. The nature of conducting is an expression of the ancient Greek ideal of an active mind in an agile body.

A TRADITION OF LEADERSHIP

The earliest conductors are seen in shadow, visible only through mythic recollections, ancient drawings, and modern inferences.

So long as a musical performer is an individual—a priest serving at an altar, a bugler calling troops into action, a minstrel serenading outside milady's window—there is no need for someone to conduct. In routine chanting of a ritual or in group singing of songs (hymns, perhaps, learned by rote in childhood and kept familiar by regular repetition), a body of people can make music together without a supervisor. That genre known as chamber music string quartets, madrigal groups, and small jazz units, for example—can be managed nicely without direction. It is when someone is needed to assign specific duties to single members of the group, to unify the variety of concepts present, to heighten by sensitive judgments the artistic and dramatic impact of the music, and (especially) to manage by signal the coordination of these values in the moment of performance that a central figure—the person we have come to call "the conductor"—emerges.

Hand signs seem to have been part of the discipline from ancient times. The early Christian church acquired from the Mediterranean World techniques of gesture that had served for the liturgies of the Middle East, applying them to the body of chant now called Gregorian.[1] By the Renaissance, the increasing complexities of rhythm and polyphonic counterpoint had led those known as *maestri di cappelle* to begin the use of a simple (vertical) beat pattern that made no effort to identify strong pulses.[2] During the Baroque era, leadership of an ensemble commonly came from the keyboard player; that convention continued through at least the time of Joseph Haydn, who directed from the harpsichord, we are told, as late as his London concerts in the 1790s. It was only during the nineteenth century that our modern notion of the conductor—a central authority, working with a baton from the advantage of a podium—became the standard image.

The nineteenth century also left us a body of names of great musicians known, for the first time, primarily as conductors, not as court composers or local musical executives. Levi, von Bülow, Richter, and (into the twentieth century) Toscanini became internationally famous in their own times. Like their twentieth-century successors, they were travelers, conducting concerts in Paris, London, and Vienna while preparing for opera performances in Milan and Bayreuth.

---

[1]These techniques are generally known as *chironomy*.

[2]This is the so-called *tactus*. In this technique, there apparently was no visual signal equivalent to our downbeat.

Today's star conductors are highly visible as they jet from continent to continent, but they are neither as numerous nor, ultimately, as important as the hundreds of conductors who serve in schools, churches, universities, town bands, small opera and musical theater companies, civic symphony orchestras, and similar posts. Their duties are, in essence, the same.

THE CONDUCTOR'S RESPONSIBILITIES

As a conductor, you must be, first of all, a superb *communicator*. Working with hands, body, face, and mind, you have to show your musicians what you believe is the whole nature and essence of the music before them. You also must be an excellent *listener*. You must learn to hear and evaluate everything you and your musicians produce, both in detail and as a whole, so that you can guide the overall interpretation.

Part of your duty to communicate is the responsibility to *persuade*. Conducting is not so much a matter of imposing authority as many laymen may believe. The more talented and imaginative the musicians who make up your ensemble, the more likely it is that strong differences of opinion over alternative interpretive choices will exist among them; you will find that your role is not so much to force them to accept a single viewpoint as to harmonize their varied but valid and often compatible artistic judgments.

How does one know which of these several opinions to honor at a particular moment? **Superior musicianship is the prime quality of a conductor.**[3] The perspective and judgment to identify an interpretation that can and should be adopted by all the members of an ensemble is the key requisite. To gain this capacity, you must be for all your life a serious student—a scholar—who is willing (even glad) to commit to the music at hand the hours of thoughtful examination from which well-grounded interpretive decisions come.

As the center of an organization, the conductor also is an *executive*. You must develop administrative skills. Especially, you will need the foresight of a planner, the judgment of a personnel officer, and the respect for well-spent time of an efficiency expert. There will come unhappy moments when a member of your ensemble will create problems for the other musicians; in such a circumstance, you may need the wisdom to discipline that individual in some appropriate way. All these management skills relate directly to your work in auditions, rehearsals, and performances.

But there is another aspect of administration to consider, too; as conductor, you are, in effect, a *public relations specialist*, often the primary spokesman for the needs of the ensemble, and you must develop the ability to "sell" your program to your superiors, whether they are college administrators, school principals,

[3]Throughout this volume, general concepts of compelling importance are styled "Axioms," and are denoted as is this one. See the Preface.

clergy, or board members of a major symphony orchestra. To buttress the arguments you make, you will have to have a certain knack for advertising, as well; your performances must be publicized, and no one will care more about that than you. And, having persuaded the authorities in charge to support you, you may find yourself responsible for overseeing the budget that provides for those needs.

THE CONDUCTOR AS MUSIC EDUCATOR

No matter what the level and circumstances in which you hope to conduct, the obligations to know the music, the performers, and the audience remain the same. *All conductors are music educators.* Our most basic objective is to take performers as they are and try to make them better. At the same time, the conductor takes the audience as it is, decides what repertoire is appropriate for the circumstances, and tries to help the listeners gain new insights. Both are educational processes.

As a conductor, you will introduce your musicians to repertoire unfamiliar to them. For the singers and the players, the immediate implications may be new technical demands, fresh uncertainties about phrasing, strange problems of tone and balance, and peculiar circumstances of other kinds. In the long run, however, their need for you to teach them to comprehend an unfamiliar style is likely to be your overriding concern.

It is not only the musicians you must educate. All we have been saying applies to the audience, too. New technical demands are placed on the listeners by your choices of repertoire. They, too, will experience uncertainty about phrasing, surprise over tonal innovations, and difficulty comprehending the structures they are hearing. They, too, need to be taught the special features of an unfamiliar style.

Frequently, neither the performers nor the audience *wish* to undergo this exercise, to give this mental and emotional effort; yet, it is only by confronting the unfamiliar that we grow and develop. How much new material can you introduce? How radical can these strange interpolations be? How much of the old, common, and comfortable should (or must) you include in your "assignments"? *How can you best present the repertoire you conduct so that it will bring fresh insight and exhilaration to both performers and listeners?*

These are all problems for the educator. You will find that **the rehearsal procedures and conducting methods you employ must be outgrowths of your musical purposes,** just as they have been for the great conductors of the past. How many ways can you think of to teach a given ensemble or audience a specific piece of music? One might argue that the best conductors, and the best music educators, are those who have the most imagination—who can think of (say) forty different ways of dealing with a particular instructional situation.

An Understanding of the Music

We have said that superior musicianship is the prime quality of a conductor. If you are to provide the sort of musical leadership we have been describing, you must be one of the very best students in your classes in music theory and music history, for it is in those studies that a firm foundation is laid for the analyses conductors must do. This is more than just a matter of acquiring terminology; you need to gain clear insights into the traditions of structure and style that extend through long periods of music history.

You need to be a solid, experienced performer in your own right on at least one instrument (or in voice). Before you conduct others, you need to face and deal with all the aspects of interpreting, preparing, and presenting both familiar and new works to an audience; moreover, it is in confronting the intimidating challenges of the concert hall yourself that you learn to understand and value good performers.

You should have a basic comprehension of many other instruments, as well; essentially, you should know something of the unique characteristics and special problems of the members of the brass, keyboard, percussion, string, and woodwind families. At the piano, you need more than a rudimentary facility; ideally, you should learn to read at the keyboard scores (choral and orchestral, complete with a variety of clefs and transpositions) with some fluency.

As a sight reader (and sight singer), you *must* be exemplary. Every score-reading error you make in a rehearsal will be a public one! (It is much more important to remember, however, that every such incident will lose you time, and cost your words impact.)

Ultimately, you should know everything there is to know about any work you are conducting. At first, this means you should know the work at hand in musical terms and have a thorough background in the history of the work; as you labor at your profession, you can expect to probe deeper into works, comparing and contrasting them with other compositions.

If you plan to conduct one work by Bach or Beethoven or Stravinsky, you will find great benefit in the study of other works by that composer, of works by others of his era, and ultimately of works by composers from earlier or later periods; this is what the great choral musicologist Julius Herford called "the spiral study," in which you work your way from the single piece of music under your hand back through other music literature, adding along the way a broader and richer consideration of the social, cultural, and political history and philosophy of the time. As any music is an expression of a certain time and world, so the conductor of that music must come face to face with the features and attitudes of its world. (Thus it is that serious conductors study two to six hours for a single one- or two-hour rehearsal.) A conductor's judgment about a particular composition grows out of a wealth of experiences in other music, but that judgment matures also through insights gained in literature and the other arts, in science, in society, and in all of life. Conductors learn to form general concepts of style in this way, and in the long run they tend to become—like many other artists—very broadly educated.

An Understanding of the Performers

Whether you are conducting a band, a chorus, a concert orchestra, a jazz organization, or an opera orchestra; whether your forces are high school students or well-paid professionals; whether the music before you is Richard Strauss or Richard Rodgers—*you are a conductor, and your work is important.* You still are concerned with pitches and rhythms, with well-shaped phrases, with balance and cleanness of ensemble, with an honest and sensitive rendering of the composer's intentions, and with bringing to your audience all of the power and beauty and meaning in the music. You still have the same research duties, too; you must trace the roots of the music you are conducting, whatever the instrumentation and style.

This is not to say that there are no distinctions between, say, work with a band and work with an orchestra. Each has its own special characteristics and problems, and each has—as a result—its own peculiar jargon. Singers in choirs expect to hear about "open" and "closed" vowels; string players want to know whether you want a passage "on the string" or off it; band players will ask you about the "stinger" at the end of a march. All need you to make specific decisions in precise terms about articulation. You must have a general competence in each of these technical "dialects."

You may have played in an orchestra but know little or nothing about bands. You may be a singer who never has needed to know a glockenspiel from a goldfish. Listening to a rehearsal, someone experienced in band music immediately recognizes the strengths and weaknesses of the playing. A singer finds it rather easy to identify the technical and musical virtues and shortcomings of a choir. As a *conductor*, however, you must have a broad enough knowledge of these parochial differences, and a wide enough experience in music literature, to be able to provide leadership to any body of musicians.

Where do you procure all this information and proficiency? We hope to deal directly with many of your needs in this book, and there are the other formal classes you have taken or will complete. These are not the only sources available to you, however. *Study is a lifelong occupation.* In colleges and universities, most of us devote ourselves almost exclusively to "assignments," tasks imposed on us by our teachers. In the world outside the schools, however, we become the ones who make the assignments—to ourselves—and the research we do is the basis for our further professional development. Learn, then, to find the sources—the books, the manuscripts, the historical sites, the concerts, the recordings—from which you can educate yourself.

Students can benefit from teachers and from books, but they *also can learn from each other.* Trombonists can be taught by sopranos, bassoonists by 'cellists, percussionists by pianists, and tenors by tuba players. Thus, the singer who takes the time to learn about pizzicato and about *martelé* bowing from a violinist can build toward a future spent conducting orchestras, and a trumpet player who learns that breath support is a concern for tenors can direct choirs. Any college or university is a vast storehouse of specialists, and the conductor (who must, by the nature of his or her responsibilities, be a generalist) can take good advantage of close contact with those experts, whether they are faculty members or students.

The basic ground rules for all conductors (the commitment to accuracy of pitch and rhythm, the focus on interpretation, the matters of cleanness of attacks and release in ensembles, tuning, tone, articulation, and so on) remain the same. Shifting from one type of ensemble to another is much like traveling in a foreign country: You may have to use a different language to communicate, but the need to find food for the day and shelter for the evening is the same as at home. Your unfamiliarity with that new language can make your first foreign trip either embarrassing or exciting; once you have learned the language, however, the richness of your experiences in a new land and culture are fine rewards. So it is with conducting: Once you step out of the provincialism of narrow experience into a broader concept of the nature of leadership, a whole new geography is open to you.

It is worth noting, too, that in strictly practical terms the more you choose to limit yourself—the less flexible you are as a conductor—the *fewer fine professional opportunities you will have.*

An Understanding of the Audience

You must learn to give careful consideration to the nature and background of the listeners for whom you are performing. What sort of audience is this? Is it composed primarily of regular concertgoers who know exactly what sort of repertoire to expect, and who are relatively experienced in listening to it? (Such people can be found at an opera, a jazz session, or a rock concert.) Is it made up of folk who are present largely because they feel an obligation to one or more of the performers, as is often the case at elementary or high school performances? Are they present for a reason unrelated to music, like the fans who watch a football halftime show? Are they there primarily to see some "star" who also is appearing? Or are they in their seats because they were thrilled with the performance you and your forces gave last week, or last month, or last year?

How much do they know of the style(s) of music you will be performing? Some unfamiliar repertoire you bring to your listeners may not seem strange to them, for it may resemble other works they know and like; if, however, you present a work by Bartók to an audience unfamiliar with contemporary music, they may feel disoriented by the dissonances, and they may blame you for it.

And what about the performance environment? If you become a church choirmaster, you may confront strong local or parochial traditions that limit your freedom to select repertoire. (Some deal with this problem by carefully scheduling works that are "old favorites" of the congregation on the Sundays immediately before and after performing a controversial anthem. This may prove a good approach in other settings, as well.)

Is it *your* responsibility to build an audience? (It almost always is; even in a church situation, an excellent music program, as its reputation spreads, can contribute to the growth of the congregation.) In all the performing arts, audience size and response are inextricably bound to such crucial concerns as budget, employment of personnel, and professional stature. A special group of artists can find sufficient support from a limited but enthusiastic audience. The reality is, nonetheless, that no conductor, in choosing repertoire, can afford to disregard entirely the nature, the experience, and even the preferences of the listeners, and that, moreover, for most of us it is important to actively seek new audience members.

Here we see the intricacy of thoughtful programming. Repertoire must be chosen to suit the capacity and experience of the conductor, the capabilities and developmental needs of the ensemble, and the nature and receptiveness of the audience. Programs must be balanced in content (in one way or another), both within a single concert and across an entire season. Careful judgments about timing factors must be made: How long until the first intermission? How long must the chorus stand, if there are to be no chairs on the stage? How quickly can the antiphonal brass group in the balcony make it back to their chairs within the band itself? How much music of unfamiliar style(s) is there in the overall program?

Some of the decisions you will take on such issues will be part of a long-range program you will keep in mind or on paper. Choosing repertoire is not just a matter of planning a single program or of filling the ensemble's folders for an academic year; a master conductor-educator has a comprehensive blueprint, based on policy and philosophy, that aims at the distant (as well as the immediate) future.

BEGINNING A THEORY OF CONDUCTING

In outlining the responsibilities of the conductor, we spoke of the need to unify, or coordinate, various interpretive possibilities created in the minds of the musicians. How does one do that?

The conductor must hold in his or her imagination (in a sort of "inner ear") a complete, complex, satisfying image of the work as he or she wishes to hear it performed. This image in the conductor's mind—a matrix that the philosopher Suzanne Langer has called "the commanding form"[4]—can be used, then, as a template against which all the musical occurrences in rehearsals and performances can be measured, judged, and accepted or corrected. (This process may sound a bit mysterious to you, but it need not be: "Hear" right now—the na-

---

[4]Suzanne K. Langer, *Feeling and Form* (New York: Scribner's, 1953), p. 129.

tional anthem or some other familiar tune; *almost* sing it, in the procedure reading teachers call subvocalizing; interrupt your progress through that melody right in the middle of a phrase, and then think—that is, imagine or "hear"—the *tonic* pitch you were using. You will realize that this capacity to "hear" with your imagination can be quite specific.)

To conceive and employ such a "conducting matrix," you need two primary abilities: (1) an adeptness and thoroughness at analyzing a score, and (2) unbroken concentration during study, rehearsals, and performances. Thoroughness at score analysis can come from another application of the principle of "spiral study."[5]

As for concentration, it is perhaps the most important hallmark of the fine conductor. It is achieved, like almost all good things, through preparation. Everything you have learned about the music before facing the musicians must be used to form the matrix, the "commanding form." *It is this already-formed matrix of expectations that you should compare against the reality of the moment* in rehearsal and performance.

The Sonorous Ideal

Pitches, rhythms, balances, and momentum must all be part of the sonorous ideal you are carrying with you, and your preferences (and those of the composer) must be communicated to the ensemble members. All great conductors have carried this mental, "subaural" *image of what the music should sound like* around with them, and each has used it to mold the sound and style of his ensemble. Each has insisted that his ensemble reach for this conceptual ideal, and each has chosen rehearsal techniques designed to reach toward that ideal.

One builds the experience and judgment to create this conducting matrix, this sonorous image, through careful study of scores and listening to rehearsals, performances, and recordings, as we have said, but those are not the only ways.

1. It is very important—much more so than it was a generation ago, perhaps—that you begin now a regular routine of reading source materials on performance practice (that is, on the ways in which a given piece of music was performed in the era of its composition). Whether or not you choose to imitate those historic performance approaches, you should know how the work was viewed by those who lived at the time it was composed.

2. It is just as important that you begin making lists—both mental and written—of what is crucial to each of the musical styles with which you come in contact. What are the common features of that style in formal and tonal structures, melodic and harmonic practices, metric and rhythmic characteristics, textural designs, tempos, ornamentation, instrumentation, dynamics, articulation, and the rest? Such listings help you force yourself to be specific about stylistic features, help you recognize, through similarities, parallel works and composers, and enable you to identify innovations and peculiarities that are not characteristic of a particular era or manner.

[5]See the discussion in Chapter 18.

You may have believed at first that conducting consists merely of knowing and using beat patterns and other hand gestures. You begin to realize now that such matters represent only the fundamental technical basis; skill with beat patterns, crucial as it is, has ultimately no more (and no less) to do with conducting a Brahms symphony or a Sousa march than dexterity in playing a C major scale with both hands has to do with playing a Beethoven piano sonata. The routine things in conducting, like the basic beat patterns, preparatory beats, releases, cues, and other gestures, must be practiced until they become automatic. Like the conscious mind of a fine football player, who weaves his way through tacklers toward the goal line without having to instruct his legs or arms just what to do at a given moment, the mind of the conductor must be free to devote itself fully to the sounds it hears, and to the imagined sounds it hopes to hear. The hands must be, in essence, independent of each other and must work without the attention and concentration of the conscious mind.

Watch a fully professional conductor. She or he may use much more economical gestures than other directors you have seen; that may be because the musicians in this situation, given their own training, do not need so many visual cues. You may be certain, however, that this master (this *maestro*) has learned all the basic patterns, all the special ways of communicating with the musicians, and all the procedures needed to shape a rehearsal or a program to her or his purposes.

Beginning conductors run into trouble here in three basic ways: with the technical discipline of the routine gestures; with the formulation of a clear aural ideal, or matrix; and with the communication of that ideal image to their musicians. *Most of them develop a further shortcoming, too; they limit themselves by background, study, and experience to one genre: band, chorus, or orchestra.* It is the purpose of this textbook to prepare you so that these shortcomings will not be yours.

IN PREPARATION TO CONDUCT

Thus, we are going to begin this study by addressing the physical fundamentals, the primary uses of the body, face, eyes, right hand, and left hand; in the process, we will deal with the basic beat patterns, preparatory beats, beat motions of various characters and sizes, adjustments to the speed of the beat, attacks, releases, cutoffs, cues, dynamics, and a great deal more having to do with technic.

We will speak about the qualities of leadership, and of the approaches you should use in supervising your musicians. We will consider ensemble management—dealing with groups, and with individuals within groups—and will itemize some basic rehearsal and performance methods available to you.

Two entire units of this text will orient and train you in the special considerations involved in conducting voices, on the one hand, and instruments, on the other. In each of these, we will make a thorough examination of the performance forces used in that kind of ensemble, of audition processes, of idiomatic rehearsal procedures, of technical problems, of sight-reading approaches, and of characteristic terminology. After that detailed discussion, we undertake performance analyses of specific works, each chosen from a historic style period (the Renaissance, the Baroque, and so on). The authors believe firmly that **conducting the music of a particular period is best approached through an understanding of the style of that repertoire itself, rather than by means of artificial and isolated excerpts.** We believe also that you should begin conducting fine music as soon as you know how to make the rudimentary gestures. When the time comes, your first complete work will be one by Bach.

Since conductors must be planners and managers, too, the final section of the book will cover at a *professional* level such crucial topics as programming, choosing soloists, preparing for rehearsals, guiding interpretation and ornamentation, managing dress rehearsals, preparing for performances, and conducting them.

Many of the very greatest masterworks are extended, elaborate musical structures. You must develop the abilities to conceive, remember, and conduct longer and longer designs, as your technical dexterity and your assurance increase; thus, the closing set of chapters also will present and analyze five major multimovement works (again from different style periods). Once you have studied these masterpieces, you should be equipped to conduct a broad repertoire with skill, confidence, and grace.

CHAPTER 2

The Physical Basis

Conductors must be capable of immediately translating Intention into Action thousands of times per hour. This demands disciplined bodily coordination, of course, but it also requires stamina. Physical condition is deceptively important, whether you conduct regularly for an hour per day, or weekly for twice that long. There can be a reward built into this activity, too: Extensive daily conducting is in itself an exercise regimen that can help keep its practitioner in excellent shape. (One thinks immediately of Toscanini and Böhm, both of whom were conducting regularly well into their eighties, and of Stokowski, who was on the podium halfway through his nineties. Nor are those isolated cases.) On the other side, long rehearsals and performances can be very strenuous for one who is not accustomed to them.

You may want to adopt a regular exercise program, if you do not have one already. At the very least, be aware constantly that what you are doing as a conductor is substantially physical in character, from the wrist motion in a cutoff to the way you stand onstage.

MORE CONDUCTING THEORY
Posture

For conductors, good posture is not just a goal in itself. **The purpose behind every physical act is effective and efficient communication, and anything that detracts from clear and accurate communication is a fault.** That applies to the stance we adopt.

This is not just a matter of your position on the podium. As you walk onto the stage, you make a vivid impression. This is the first visible contact between you and your audience, and their initial judgment about your manner and competence forms at this moment.

Your entrance has impact on your ensemble, as well. Their first glimpse of you creates an atmosphere, either of confidence or of uneasiness, of concentration or of casualness. The way you assume your place on the podium and the posture you maintain while the performance proceeds extend these initial impressions. There are many styles you can adopt; you can appear arrogant, humble, businesslike, friendly, shy, preoccupied, surprised at the initial applause, or confident. **A great conductor is (among many other things) a fine actor. You must use your whole body—not just your face and eyes—to establish a mood and convey meaning.**

Some may feel that this approach is not properly a part of their role onstage and that conductors should "let the music speak for itself." The reality is that human beings use *all* their senses in perceiving the world around them, and a performer must consider every factor that the listeners can apprehend. (We can say that virtually every great conductor has demonstrated an obvious, considerable concern for this ingredient in his or her work.)

DEVELOPING CONDUCTING POSTURE

It is very important that you begin by building your concept of good conducting on a foundation of excellent physical balance and posture. Consider each part of your body.

1. Start with your feet. Their placement should be comfortable, with your hips squared toward the ensemble. You may place one foot slightly in front of the other if that gives you a better sense of balance.
2. Your torso, shoulders, and head should be erect. (Some people like to imagine "a string, attached to the top of the head, pulling straight up," or "turning over the second button on one's shirt.")
3. Ankles, knees, hips, shoulders, neck, elbows, and wrists should feel loose and relaxed. Tension restricts your freedom of motion and, in times of stress, can make you light-headed.

To your ensemble, your posture must make you seem accessible. If you are consistently turned away from some of them, or if you are constantly bending over (with your head in the music, perhaps), you can seem to "close out" the ensemble. Your stance should "include" all your forces all the time.

Practice Exercise 2-1 *Posture*

To accustom yourself to a good conducting posture, stand with your feet slightly apart (6–8 inches, unless you are very tall) and *consciously relax the body*, bit by bit: Start with the feet and ankles; then move to the knees, then to the shoulders, arms, hands, and neck. As you do so, keep striving for an awareness of good balance, relaxation, and alertness.

In a physical activity—athletics, ballet, or whatever—good coordination of the upper body can be achieved only when good balance has been attained. With a proper postural foundation established, you are ready to move your arms into position. Formal conducting is done entirely with the upper body; even though rhythm is felt throughout the anatomy, the lower half must not become involved in actual physical movements. In general, the feet should remain still; you certainly may change positions, for comfort, so long as these changes do not become obvious or obtrusive. The upper body always faces the ensemble so that the arms can be the direct contact between you and the musicians.

Most of the movement made by a conductor takes place in the right arm, shoulder, and wrist. Bend the right arm at the elbow so that the lower arm forms a right angle to your body. Then raise the whole arm from the shoulder until it is approximately at shoulder height, moving it toward the left a bit so that it is slightly to the right of center of your body. (If your arm is at the correct height, you will find yourself looking at your ensemble *through* the upper part of your beat pattern.) The palm of the right hand should be turned down.

When you use your left arm, it should be positioned in a similar way but kept somewhat to the left (out of the way of the hand giving the beat). Face the palm of this hand to the right, turned slightly up, in a comfortable position.

Although every physique is unique in some way, and the stance that proves both comfortable and effective for you may vary slightly from that adopted by someone else, your basic posture should be very close to that shown in Figures 2-1 and 2-2. Do not trust yourself to move immediately into this conducting posi-

Figure 2-1 The basic conducting posture seen from the side

Figure 2-2 The basic posture seen from the ensemble itself

tion automatically. At first, it will be better for you to enter it in the stages we have just described; later, as you work at this discipline daily, finding the correct position will become habitual, so that even a tiny adjustment will feel strange or uncomfortable to you. Should you get into bad posture habits, it will prove very difficult to break them; and they will influence (or even form the basis of) other conducting difficulties.

Practice Exercise 2-2 *Arm Position*

Memorize these individual steps until moving into a good conducting position comes quickly and easily.

1. Repeat the process in Practice Exercise 2-1.
2. Raise the lower arms from the elbows, at right angles to the body. The palms of your hands should be down.
3. Lift the right arm from the shoulder until it is near shoulder height, moving it to a point slightly to the right of the center of your body.

Why Not the Left Hand?

Conducting is not—like handwriting or combing the hair—a one-handed skill; neither is it the sort of activity for which you can choose, almost unthinkingly, one hand or the other. By convention, the beat is given with the *right* hand. Performers expect it to be so.

Even if you are left-handed, you will grow accustomed rather quickly to this arrangement. With a bit of practice, the beat patterns become routine, and you will find that your right hand is very capable. Independence is the real problem: Too many students find not that one hand or the other will not maintain the beat pattern but that their "other hand" automatically "mirrors" that pattern, a practice to be avoided.

Actually, conducting resembles more closely the manual skills of a pianist or a violinist, in that *both* hands must act importantly and independently. The left hand makes *ad hoc* gestures, not routine ones, and these must be subtle, as well as specifically timed. (In the end, long after all the right hands in your class have accustomed themselves to the responsibility of maintaining the beat, the student who is left-handed will be found to have a real advantage: That left hand will be more naturally agile in making the special, impromptu gestures for cueing, shading, and emphasis that those who are right-handed find clumsy.)

THE BATON

"To baton or not to baton," Shakespeare might have said; "that is the question." There has been much controversy on this point, especially in America over the past century. *The baton is simply a flexible extension of the arm.* Some conductors (both choral and instrumental) have preferred to use the hand alone; others have insisted on employing a baton. The same is true today.

One thing is certain, or close to it. Like a baby with a spoon, or a pencil, no beginning conducting student finds using a baton comfortable or natural at first. The student fears dropping the stick and so grips it too tightly; thus, it becomes inflexible in the hand. If he loosens his hold, he does drop it, in all likelihood, and so grasps it even tighter thereafter.

A few months of *daily* use, however, and the baton becomes a familiar and handy tool, a device that many find more effective than conducting bare-handed.

But is the time spent adjusting to this foreign implement worth it? Why not just forget the baton?

All conducting students should learn to employ the baton skillfully, whether or not they intend to continue its use afterward. Consider the following.

1. Although some choruses are used to the baton and others are not, most instrumentalists *are* accustomed to it and may not respond to you as efficiently if you work without one.

2. Although many American conductors have not used batons in choral work in the past, that seems to be changing. One reason is the increase in programming voices *and* instruments in schools and colleges; since combined performances of this sort make the geographic separation between the conductor and the chorus greater than usual, employing a baton—precisely because it *is* an extension of the arm—can make good sense.

3. In the opera or musical theater pit (whether in a high school or a professional house), the distances involved—and the side angles in a long, narrow pit—make the baton virtually essential.

4. In any setting, it is realistic to say that beat patterns shown with a baton tip are clearer and more precise, both from the front and from the sides, than those formed without a stick; moreover, what is so for the beat itself is even more true for the smaller conducting gestures: Subdivisions of the beat, changes of articulation, dynamic contrasts, cutoffs, and subtleties of shading are all *more visible* when delivered with a baton.

5. Because the beat pattern with the baton is clearer and more visible than without it, its use tends to magnify and highlight flaws and bad habits in conducting; as a result, most of us are more careful and more accurate when employing it.

6. The most important point: We believe you should prepare yourself to compete for, and accept, the maximum number of conducting opportunities; since some of those are in the opera pit and on the oratorio stage, it would be limiting for you to avoid the baton.

Choosing a Baton

For a conductor, the choice of a baton is as important as picking out a pair of walking shoes. A bad choice can prove very uncomfortable, and it is unlikely that the cheapest model available will be the right one for you. Try several. Compare them. Be sure you know—*before* you break or lose it—what makes your favorite one superior to the others.

In our experience, the best-balanced and best-weighted batons are of wood.

Figure 2-3 A well-balanced baton of appropriate design

These come in two colors: natural wood finish and white. The latter are somewhat easier to see, especially in an opera pit or on large stages.

Batons range in length from ten inches or so to two feet or more. Short ones are ineffective (for the baton is supposed to effectively *extend the arm*), and very long ones are clumsy (or genuinely dangerous on a crowded stage or in the opera pit). A good rule of thumb is to choose one about equal to the distance from your half-curled fingertips to the inside of your elbow. Some conductors prefer a longer baton, however, and your own selection can be personal; comfort is decisive here.

There are various styles of handles: bulbous, skinny, tapered, wood, and cork. The issue here is grip: The less pressure needed to keep the baton comfortably secure in your hand, the less chance the muscles in your lower arm and hand will cramp, especially during long rehearsals and performances. Some conductors prefer a long handle, one that touches the palm of the hand; others hold the handle itself in their curved fingers. (This is a matter of personal preference.) Most handles will feel somewhat strange at first; find a likely one, and give your hand time to grow accustomed to it.

Balance is important. If you lay a baton across the top of your extended index finger, it should have a balance point between one-half and one full inch beyond the joint between the stick and the handle. If the balance point is farther down the stick, the baton will seem heavy to you after a time. Overall weight is not as critical, but the lighter the well-balanced baton, the better. (A good design is shown in Figure 2-3.)

Get used to having a baton handy, by the way—in your briefcase, or locker, or studio—and *do not get into the habit of using a pencil, or a pen, or a poorly weighted baton as a substitute for a good one,* or you will find you are having to relearn your beat pattern!

Holding the Baton

Watch someone pick up a baseball from a table. A small child will use the entire hand, wrapping all the fingers around it. A major league player—without thinking about it—will grip the ball between his thumb, index finger, and middle finger, rather than palming it. The difference in approach is not just a matter of hand size; the child has not yet grown accustomed to holding the baseball and has to think deliberately about how to grasp it; the professional automatically adopts his routine, efficient hand position.

Try to approach a baton in the same way. Take it from a tabletop, the butt end of the handle stuck back into the palm of your hand, and notice how you are holding it.

Your fingers should be curled slightly around the handle, the stick held lightly between the thumb and either the middle or the index finger, as shown in Figure 2-4; in any case, the index finger should rest on one side or the other (for if you keep it on top of the baton it will restrict the freedom of the stick). The base of the handle probably should *touch* (but not *press* against) the palm of the hand. The point of the baton should aim straight out from the hand and should not project at an angle (slightly to the left, for example). The thrust of the arm and the stick together should be slightly upward.

Let the baton have a life of its own in your hand. Hold it lightly (but not *loosely*) so that it can move freely. It is, as we have said, an extension of the arm, but your arm should not be rigid—its upper and lower segments, and your hand, assume various angles as you move—and the stick should have as much flexibility as the other parts. The hand need move only three or four inches, perhaps, while the baton is traveling a foot or more. This can help you avoid tension and maintain stamina.

As you stand holding the baton, remember what you have already learned about the physical basis of conducting. Be aware of your posture, and of the position of your right arm. Check yourself in a mirror. The grasp of the stick must be integral to your overall conducting stance.

You want all this to look and feel natural, of course, but it will not at first. Give the learning process time. Keep your baton with you. Handle it. Make it feel as much a part of you as your shoes or your watch.

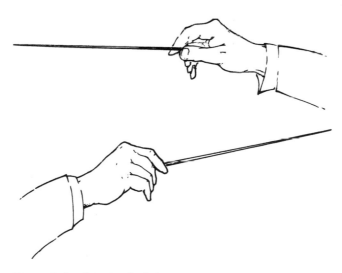

Figure 2-4 Gripping the baton

Practice Exercise 2-3 *Grasping the Baton*

1. Pick up the baton, holding it lightly between the thumb and one other finger.
2. Be certain the other fingers are lightly curled and that you are unaware of tension in the hand, wrist, or lower arm.
3. Check to see that the butt of the handle barely touches your palm and that there is a straight line from your elbow to the tip of the baton.
4. Now be certain you are assuming the posture and arm positions developed in Practice Exercises 2-1 and 2-2.
5. Repeat the entire process, step by step, several times.

PHYSICAL TENSION AND RELAXATION

The feeling of naturalness you are seeking—the sense of relaxed well-being—will prove very important to you. Anything you can do to minimize the muscular tension in your stance and movements will increase your ability to work through long rehearsals and performances.

Physical tension is a serious matter for the conductor. An opera or musical theater rehearsal may last more than three hours, with one or more short breaks, and two-and-a-half-hour orchestra calls are standard. A conductor's right arm makes many more "strokes" than does the arm of a pitcher or a tennis player over the same period of time! It is no wonder, then, that the physical problems common to such athletes (bursitis, "tennis elbow," muscular inflammation, and so on) are risks for conductors, as well. Pain from fatigue or muscle spasm can be damaging to your musical purposes, causing you to make unclear, ineffective gestures.

A regular conducting discipline can help. Rehearsal obligations of a constant length, on a daily basis, can build stamina. Even a high school orchestra director accustomed to this sort of regimen can run into trouble, however, over the sudden demands of a week of three-hour musical comedy rehearsals. (If you see such a responsibility coming, try to build up over a period of several weeks the amount of time you spend each day in conducting.) But even routine use of your physical system is no insurance policy if some element of tension or some type of excess motion represents a gradual abuse of your musculature. (Even great athletes sometimes are halted at the height of their careers by such problems.)

Make sensitivity to good physical condition a part of your conducting discipline from the start. You may find the following suggestions helpful.

1. Develop the habit of "body-scanning" whenever you are conducting. Every few pages of score, monitor how your shoulders feel, whether your neck is stiff, whether your baton grip is a light or a tight one. Try to be aware of developing problems so that you can head them off.
2. Do not let stress or nervousness change your normal stance or your conducting motions. Be careful not to tighten your grip on your baton: A bit of extra, unnecessary

pressure by the thumb or a finger can cause a lower arm muscle to cramp, and that can lead you (sometimes without realizing it in the activity of the moment) to change your shoulder motion; soon you have tight muscles everywhere. Know your conducting position and motion, and maintain it consistently.

3. Develop your own relaxation techniques, either by reading from available sources or by experience. These are mental processes, in part; sometimes, nothing more is needed than to imagine yourself for a moment in a favorite vacation spot. Relaxation methods can and should be practiced (on a daily basis if you are conducting professionally, for they are skills, and they benefit from repetition).

4. During a rehearsal or a performance, make use of practiced relaxation techniques to forestall problems.

5. If tightness or a spasm occurs, you will find you can gradually work through it, without stopping in most cases, but this can take a (painful) half-hour or more of endurance.

6. Should certain problems occur regularly, you may need to seek professional advice, of course. More and more sophisticated help is available these days, particularly in the orthopedic subfield known as sports medicine. (Major symphony orchestras and other arts organizations are sponsoring consultations for musicians with such specialists.)

THE CONDUCTOR'S STAND AND PODIUM

Your music stand should be positioned in such a way that you can refer to your music (only brief glances, not constant ogling) with minimal loss of eye contact. Consider where to place it so that you can manage the score efficiently. (One of the authors likes his stand straight in front of him; the other prefers it at a slight angle on the left so that he can turn pages easily with his left hand with little reaching across into the path of his right-hand beat.)

The height of the stand is important, too: It should not be so low that you must stoop to turn a page, but it should be as low as possible to avoid blocking the performers' view of you and to keep it out of the path of your beat pattern.

The stand you use must be a sturdy one and should have a good friction or screw-type device for adjusting the height. The size of the shelf and the nature of its support base depend on the size of the scores you are using; a standard music rack will do for choral parts, but a much larger one is needed for some band and orchestra scores. For opera or musical theater, a special "shadow box" (large enough for huge scores) with a light for your music and a frame around it to keep that light from glaring in the eyes of the pit players (and the audience) is the proper thing.

You may think it convenient to use a stand with a lower shelf so that more than one score can be kept within reach. (There are models on the market, in fact, that constitute rolling music cabinets, but these tend to build a wall between you and your ensemble.)

The conductor's podium is there only to give the performers a clear view of you. It must be sturdy and free of squeaks; it should have carpet to deaden sound from your feet and to prevent your slipping. The podium must be large enough for you to change positions as necessary.

For rehearsals, it is possible to use a high conductor's stool. Comfortably padded seats with backs are available, and a stool can be a great help while the ensemble is taking a break, during an extended opera rehearsal, or the like. We recommend strongly against your using them for one-hour rehearsals, however, for they encourage casual posture in the musicians, and—in changing your basic conducting posture—you risk developing bad conducting habits.

EYE CONTACT

Remember that you must know your scores thoroughly before you come to rehearsal. The copy on your music stand is there only so that you can check measure numbers, instrumentation, and the like; it is not there for you to follow, bar by bar. If you do so, you lose eye contact with the musicians.

This is crucially important to your performers. *Lost eye contact is awful for them.* They sense that you are intimidated by them or not interested in them, or—worst of all—that you do not know the music. They feel alone. Their attention wavers, and then leaves you. (You may have difficulty getting it back.)

You should be looking through your beat patterns at the performers. If you are doing so, you are maintaining good eye contact, and you are keeping your patterns in the proper position.

We will have more to say about eye contact when we speak of cueing techniques in a later chapter.

THE CONDUCTING FRAME

Imagine you have a rectangular picture frame 16 inches high and 20 inches wide hanging in front of your face and upper chest, the top of it approximately even with your forehead and the bottom two or three inches below the level of your sternum. This is the outlined, limited area within which all your beat patterns should be presented if you are to gain optimal visibility, clarity, and accuracy; remaining within it is basic to producing a clear, clean pattern. Ideally, as we will explain in the next chapter, the size of this area will depend on the dynamic level involved at a given moment, and your beats will touch (but not cross) the edges of this rectangle we call "the conducting frame." (This frame can move to either side and back with you as you pivot toward the various sections within your ensemble.)

This is the physical realm within which your right hand now can begin to conduct.

CHAPTER 3

The Right Hand: Commencing

Once we have established good posture, the right hand properly is our first concern, for its disciplined activity is primary in conducting. **The ideal is for everything you wish to communicate to your ensemble to be shown in your right hand.** (It is possible for someone who lacks a left arm to capably conduct a professional performance. There was, in fact, a macabre joke among musicians who knew the work of Fritz Reiner that Reiner had suffered some accident that had incapacitated his left arm. The reality was that he believed he did not need it much, and so he let it hang—apparently useless—at his side for most of each performance. He did not hesitate to employ it, of course, when he thought a left-handed gesture would help him express his ideas.)

Most conductors use the left hand a great deal, of course. Some of their gestures are appropriate and needed, some only duplicate what the right hand already is showing, and some are actually confusing. Sometimes, too, conductors whose right-hand technique is not skilled use the left hand to clear up the inaccuracies and inadequacies of the right.

You can learn to avoid these problems. Concentrate for now entirely on developing an efficient and effective right-hand technique. Work to make it clear, expressive, and accurate, and soon you will be able to communicate very well with it.

LEARNING BEAT PATTERNS BY WORKING WITHIN THE CONDUCTING FRAME

One often hears: "He's hard to follow," and "I can't tell where her beat is!" Most such difficulties arise from a sprawling, overblown beat pattern in which the individual pulses lack clear definition.

As you begin to learn the basic beat patterns and to make them routine, it is important, then, that you discipline both the shape and the size of your motions. Your gestures need to be consistent; if they are regular and unvarying, you will

not have to think about them, and your musicians will have no difficulty interpreting your wishes. This is not easy to do, however, for your conducting motions must signal to your forces all levels of tempo and dynamics, all sorts of articulation, and a variety of other effects.

Late in the last chapter, we introduced to you our concept of the "conducting frame." This can give you a clear working image of the shape and size your
movements should take.

For practice purposes, we urge you to cut out at least five rectangles in various sizes, as follows:

1. Obtain a single piece of stiff cardboard at least 24 by 28 inches in size, and thick
   enough for strength and durability. If you are careful, all five rectangles can be cut
   from this one source. (See Figure 3-1.)
2. On the cardboard, pencil in the outlines of the five "nested" rectangles, following
   the dimensions given in the following paragraphs. Each rectangle will have a border
   4 inches wide on all sides.
3. The largest of these frames should have an outside edge 24 inches high by 28 inches
   wide, and a 20-by-24-inch inner edge. Label this rectangle "ff."
4. That 20-by-24-inch inner edge becomes the outer edge of the next largest frame,
   which should have an inner edge of 16 by 20 inches. Label this one "f."
5. In a similar way, mark out a 12-by-16-inch rectangle for "mf," an 8-by-8-inch frame
   for "p," and a 4-by-4-inch unit for "pp."
6. Using a utility knife or a razor blade, cut out your rectangles, creating a set of five
   conducting frames.
7. Now obtain a couple of spring-loaded clothespins (or small clamps of some sort)
   and use them to clip the bottom edge of one of these frames securely to the top of a
   music stand.

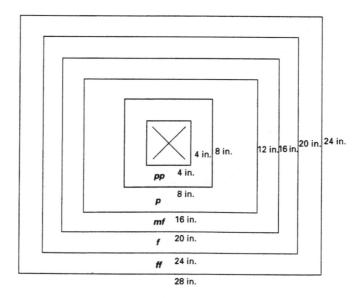

Figure 3-1 Cutting a nest of conducting frames for practice

In practicing the beat patterns that follow, you will want to stick your baton partway through the frame, using the inner edges to control the size and shape of your motions. The height at which you place the rectangle (atop the music stand) is crucial, of course. In general, the bottom *inner* edge of the *mf* frame should cross about two inches below your sternum; the smaller rectangles should be placed higher, and the larger ones lower. (Remember that the frame is always wider than it is high.) Obviously, your beat can be no larger than a given frame will permit; the motion could be even smaller than the sizes we have suggested, especially if you are working with a small ensemble, but these five rectangles are good representations of relative dynamics. We strongly urge that (at least until your studies are completed) *you use no larger beat patterns* than the ones we have suggested.

READINESS

Think of the beginning of a foot race. The starter calls out, at a deliberate pace, the words "Ready . . . Set . . . Go!" The runners get *two* warnings before the signal releases them for the race itself.

So it is with an ensemble. There are three signals.

1. The first is your stepping onto the podium (or, if there is no podium, your moving directly in front of your music stand); at this point, the members of the ensemble should adopt a position of readiness. With a band or an orchestra, for example, your players should bring their instruments up to playing position.

2. The second is your raising your baton. Note Figure 3-2: Near the right center edge is a box labeled "ATT" for "Attention!" (Thinking of your breastbone as aligned with the vertical line down the middle of the diagram, move your baton to a position straight out in front of your right shoulder.) Instrumentalists at this moment bring their mouthpieces to their lips or raise their bows directly over the strings, ready for the first stroke.

3. Then comes the all-important preparatory beat. (This sequence is shown in Figure 3-2.)

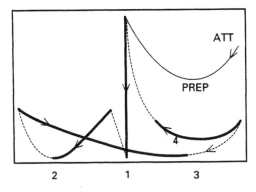

Figure 3-2 The basic four-beat pattern, including the Attention position and the preparatory beat

THE PREPARATORY BEAT

Many times the players of the Cleveland Orchestra had invited their conductor, the late, legendary George Szell, to join them for one or two postrehearsal beers at a pub near Severance Hall, but he always had declined. One day he accepted, and sat with them for a time; at length he excused himself. As he started for the door, one of the musicians called jocularly after him, "See you on the downbeat!" Szell spun around and retorted swiftly, "No! On the preparation!"[1]

This gives you an idea of the emphasis professionals place on the preparatory beat, the movement from the Attention position to the top center of Figure 3-2. This motion gives your musicians a sense of *the tempo, the dynamic level, the mood, the style of articulation, and the intensity.*

Unifying the ensemble, making them all concentrate together—and rhythmically so—is the vital issue here. They must all come to think and feel together. *Make them breathe with you, at least when you are new to them, and from time to time thereafter, until this process becomes routine for the musicians, too.* Train them to take this breath in rhythm, and, until your technique is solid, you breathe with them; this unison act can make an ensemble of them.

Make certain everything you do at this moment of attention and preparation is deliberate in manner, paced carefully in keeping with the mood. Be sure the ensemble has time to *anticipate* your next move.

Don't make a "sneak attack" on them, delivering the downbeat before they know it has happened; that can be disastrous! If you surprise them, you are likely to get a very rough attack, and (what is worse) it is likely to take you virtually the entire movement to get them back together. **Beginnings are irretrievable. For the musicians and the audience, the initial atmosphere affects everything that follows.**

You may find it useful (many students do) to think, or actually hum quietly, the subdivision of the pulse as you deliver the preparatory beat. This should make the tempo of your beat more dependable.

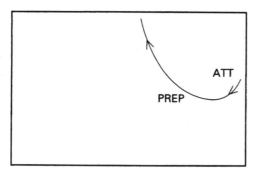

Figure 3-3 The position of attention and the preparatory beat

[1]Don V Moses, Robert W. Demaree, Jr., and Allen F. Ohmes, *Face to Face with an Orchestra* (Princeton, N.J.: Prestige Publications, 1987), p. 27.

Figure 3-3 isolates for you the position of attention and the preparatory beat. Notice the shape of the latter. The preparatory beat is *not just another upbeat.* It does not reach down to touch the bottom of the conducting frame, but curves slightly from the position of attention to the beginning of the downbeat at the top of the frame; in the process, it "ticks" one beat, in tempo, at the lowest point of its curve, and rebounds; thus, it shows the musicians the equivalent (in quadruple meter) of a fourth pulse on the way to the downbeat.

Practice Exercise 3-1   *Readiness and the Preparatory Beat*

Beginning each time by assuming the Attention position, practice *only* giving the preparation beat (through the downbeat) *at various tempos,* taking a breath with the preparation beat each time. Be aware of its shape, speed, direction, and clarity at each new pace. Do this fifty or more times, until it becomes as natural as the breathing.

We cannot stress this matter of preparation too much. A great many of the errors that occur in performances and rehearsals happen because of carelessness—either by the conductor or by one of the ensemble—about the preparatory beat.

THE ATTACK

After the preparatory beat comes the first half of the downbeat itself, the beat-stroke, which begins at the top center of the conducting frame and drops more-or-less forcefully straight down. The attack of your ensemble should occur at the precise moment when your beat touches the bottom of the frame, ending the beat-stroke. This moment must dovetail with the matrix in your mind so that you *expect* to hear that attack match exactly the arrival of your hand at the point of the beat. If you and your musicians are not precise about this, your ensemble will lead or trail you, and you gradually will lose your ability to get them to follow the baton.

THE REBOUND

After your hand "hits bottom" on the downbeat, it will rebound naturally. Your concern is to control the character and direction of that motion.

Rebounds are, essentially, connecting motions between a given pulse and the beat-stroke to the next pulse. The rebound of a standard downbeat moves a distance of 4–6 inches (at *forte*), or perhaps one-third of the height of the conducting frame, slightly to the left of the previous beat-stroke itself— that is, *in the direction of the beat to come*—and this is a part of the preparation of the second beat.

Practice Exercise 3-2   *The Downbeat and the Attack*

Repeat Practice Exercise 3-1 with some changes. Begin each time at the Attention position; give the preparation beat and the downbeat at various tempos, taking a breath with the preparation beat each time. Work for cleanness of attack by saying "dah" exactly at the moment your hand reaches the first pulse. Stay aware of the shape, speed, direction, and clarity of your beat at each new pace. Do this fifty or more times.

THE BASIC FOUR-BEAT PATTERN

As we begin learning the primary beat patterns, it is helpful for us to start with the basic four-beat format. Clip your 12-by-16-inch *(mf)* conducting frame to your music stand.

Consider Figure 3-2 again.[2] Within your conducting frame, the four-beat pattern begins with the baton at the lower right-hand corner of the rectangle. With a curving motion down to your left and then up, touch the top center of the frame; this is the *preparatory upbeat.*

Continue now, straight down, to the bottom center of the frame for the first pulse; this is the *downbeat,* and it is followed by a short rebound up and slightly to the left of the downbeat itself. (Note in Figure 3-4 that the whole "first pulse" is a downward stroke *and* a rebound.)

Now, move your baton on to the left, swooping down to touch the left lower center of the frame for pulse two and rebounding further left until your baton just touches the middle of the frame's left edge; this is the *second beat* (see Figure 3-5).

A very long stroke to the right, touching the lower right center of the frame for pulse three, and continuing on the rebound to the midpoint of the right edge, is the *third beat.* Note in Figure 3-6 that the rebound does not touch the frame at the same point as the original preparatory beat. (This helps keep the strokes separate in the eyes of your musicians.)

Finally, a movement down and to the left, touching a point on the frame for pulse four (a spot near your third beat), and rebounding to the top center of the frame, constitutes the *fourth beat* (shown in Figure 3-7). With your hand back at the highest point, you are ready now for another downbeat; this is the basis for the continuity of the four-beat pattern.

To summarize, the first measure of a work in four moves from a position of attention through four beats, each located on the plane that is the bottom edge of our conducting frame. Each of these beat-strokes is forecast by the previous beat, as a preparation, and each is followed by a rebound; the first rebound comes back into the center of the frame, but the second, third, and fourth rebounds touch, respectively, the left, right, and upper edges of the frame.

---

[2] The pattern shown in Figure 3-2 is the nonlegato version; there will be differences in the case of a staccato passage, or a legato one, as we will see shortly.

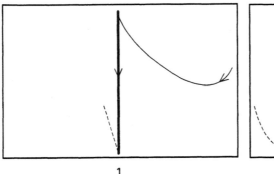

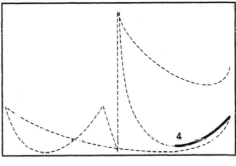

Figure 3-4   The whole downbeat: beat-stroke and rebound

Figure 3-5   The second beat: stroke and rebound

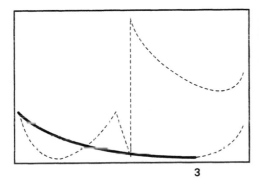

Figure 3-6   The third beat: stroke and rebound

Figure 3-7   The fourth beat: stroke and rebound

Move your hand through this basic format several times in an unbroken flow, judging the distance so that the baton just touches the frame each time (rather than bumping hard against it). Notice that each beat-stroke changes the previous direction of the baton, *and* that each rebound is a more-or-less obvious change of course, as well. Try to make your motion consistent each time you go through the whole pattern.

Now try the 4-by-8-inch *pp* frame. (You will need to move the music stand much higher *so that the exact center of this rectangle is at the same spot as the center of the larger one had been.* This will keep the center of your beat pattern in the same relation to your musicians.) The movements you use at *pianissimo* are much smaller and less sweeping, as you see, but *the pattern is exactly the same.* The same is true for all the other dynamic levels. The optimum point for the impact of the downbeat moves with the body. Generally, at *mf* it falls two or three inches below the sternum, but it will have to be adjusted at *pp, p, f,* and *ff,* and when you are dealing with forces that are either unusually large or unusually small.

Practice Exercise 3-3   *The Basic Four-Beat Pattern*

To accustom yourself to this format, "conduct" 100 measures or more of it, using the 16-by-20-inch *f* frame. When you find your gestures becoming more spontaneous, change to a frame of a different size; "conduct" at least 25 measures inside each of the other four frames. Do this daily until your next class meeting.

   Take care in practicing these patterns that there are no extra movements, no purposeless gestures, no ornamental flourishes.

MORE CONDUCTING THEORY
The Standard Beat Patterns

Why should we all use this standard format? Would our conducting not be somehow "more personal" if we employed any set of gestures we happen to choose in a given circumstance?

   There is much freedom in conducting—opportunity to modify this basic design in ways that express in some special motions the distinctive character of a unique passage of music. Nevertheless, the basic pattern itself is a convention all musicians depend upon, in rehearsals and in performances, and their dependence on its clarity and accuracy becomes a matter of habit. Personal idiosyncrasies can be seen in professional conductors; their peculiarity does *not* necessarily make them helpful, however; even great maestros may adopt eccentric conducting behaviors that inhibit the quality of their performances. You will do well to concentrate on communicating as *simply and directly* as you can.

   Why have conductors found over the years that this particular four-beat pattern works more effectively than some other format?

   Ask yourself exactly where the pulses occur. Where does the strongest beat (within the measure) occur? And the next strongest? The weakest?

   The preparation of the downbeat (important partly because it constitutes an invitation to the musicians to join in) has within it *two* directions: a tiny movement down and to the left, followed by a bigger movement up to the upper edge of the conducting frame.

   The downbeat hits "bottom," and thus is easy for the musicians to recognize; note that the width of the frame—greater than its height—makes *the first beat the only downward beat of the four.* The second beat (metrically weak) veers off to your left. The metric importance of the third beat (the next strongest, after the downbeat) is emphasized by its *reversal of direction.* Last comes the relatively weak fourth beat, which leads back to readiness for the downbeat.

   At the moment of each pulse, the baton should actually touch the bottom of the frame for each beat, making a tiny sound as it hits; then it should "rebound" in the direction indicated.[3] This bottom edge of the frame—the horizontal surface on which all the beats actually occur—we call the "conducting plane."

Recall our discussion of the "conducting matrix" in Chapter 1. As the leader of the ensemble, you carry in your mind a blueprint of the entire work. Obviously, you are to communicate that ideal image to the musicians as the piece evolves. Just as surely, you must do that for each note of music before they attack that note; if you indicate your interpretation of that particular spot as they are performing it, you already are too late. (And if you are not trying to communicate your interpretation at each moment, then you are only "beating time." They would be better off with a good metronome.) How are your ideas to reach them?

In a sense, **each beat in the pattern is a preparation** for the next one: You are responsible for **"hearing" the music before it sounds and signaling with your gestures the nature of that music one full beat before the musicians are to play it.** They read your intentions during a fourth beat, for example, and prepare to reproduce those ideas on the downbeat; during that downbeat, as they do so, you already are showing them with new gestures how you want the upcoming second beat to sound.

Thus, the pattern displays in your movements the relative importance of the four beats, and keeps them visually distinct.

GIVING PREPARATORY BEATS ON PULSES OTHER THAN THE FIRST

You will find that a substantial share of the music you study begins on some pulse other than "One." You will be confronted often with the need to begin a work (or a section of a work) on the second, third, or fourth beat (or whatever); not all preparatory beats, therefore, fall on the last pulse of the measure.

The rule for the procedure involved is a simple one: If the music actually sounds first on the second beat, the conductor delivers the first beat as a preparation, *providing only the beat-stroke of the downbeat*—starting with the tip of the baton pointed up, and then dropping straight down, to rebound off the conducting plane—as a signal of the tempo and dynamic level to come. *Be careful not to "prepare" the preparatory beat itself!* Show your ensemble *only* the beat-stroke. (See Figure 3-8.)

The danger here is that you will add a little "hook" to the start of the preparatory beat by raising the baton tip slightly before you deliver the downstroke. That "hook" will look to your musicians like a preparatory beat, and some of them will enter a beat early instead of waiting until the second pulse.

---

[3] If you must sometimes practice in front of a desk or a music stand, each beat should strike the surface, at least slightly. (Be certain the desk or stand is high enough, however, that you are not beating time at your waist.)

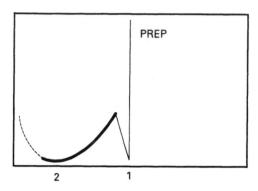

Figure 3-8 The preparatory beat on One (for spots in which the music first sounds on the second pulse)

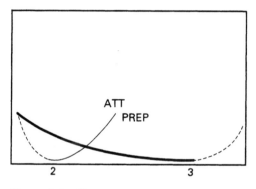

Figure 3-9 The preparatory beat on Two (for spots in which the music first sounds on the third pulse)

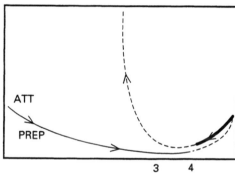

Figure 3-10 The preparatory beat on Three (for spots in which the music first sounds on the the fourth pulse)

Similarly, when the music first sounds on the third, the fourth, or some later pulse, your preparatory beat should be delivered one pulse earlier, and should begin with the beat-stroke itself (and its rebound). (See Figures 3-9 and 3-10.)

Practice Exercise 3-4 *Starting Preparatory Beats on a Variety of Pulses*

Facing a mirror, conduct several measures of the basic $\frac{4}{4}$ pattern until it feels comfortable to you. Then (thinking in quarter notes) "conduct" yourself in the singing of a major scale. Start the scale (1) on the downbeat, (2) on the third beat, (3) on the final beat, and (4) on the second beat. Make certain each time to give a clear preparation, and avoid extraneous motions.

THE OTHER SIMPLE METERS: THREE, TWO, AND ONE

Let us now turn to beat patterns other than four. The basic three-beat pattern is shown in Figure 3-11. Note that it resembles in some respects that four-beat pattern you already know.

1. The Attention position is essentially the same.
2. The preparatory beat is unchanged.
3. The downbeat and its rebound are virtually the same.
4. The third beat (the final one) here looks much like the final beat of the four pattern.

Only the new second beat is completely different. It begins at the peak of the downbeat rebound, curves down to touch the conducting plane halfway between the midpoint and the right edge of the frame, and then bounces to a point halfway up that right edge, where the pattern repeats. Figure 3-11 is, in short, much like the right half of Figure 3-2.

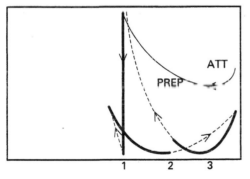

Figure 3-11 The basic three-beat pattern, including the Attention position and the preparatory beat

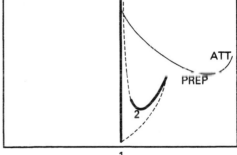

Figure 3-12 The basic two-beat pattern, including the Attention position and the preparatory beat

---

Practice Exercise 3-5 *The Basic Three-Beat Pattern*

To accustom yourself to this format, "conduct" 25 or more measures of it, using the 16-by-20-inch *f* frame. When you find your gestures becoming more spontaneous, change to a frame of a different size; "conduct" at least 25 measures inside each of the other four frames. Do this daily until your next class meeting.

The basic two-beat pattern is shown in Figure 3-12. Once again:

1. The position of attention is the same.
2. The preparatory beat is unchanged.

But with the downbeat, this time, the rebound is *to the right* of the downward stroke itself (about the same difference from the beat-stroke as with the rebound of the downbeat in the four-beat pattern). The second beat, then, begins at the tip of that rebound, curves downward slightly (but *not as far as the conducting plane*), and turns up to the top center of the frame to repeat the pattern.

This is the first time we have recommended that a primary beat *not* touch the conducting plane; it is an important factor in this case, for the first and second beats can look too much alike (seen from either side, for example, in a large orchestra). Making a clear difference in the tip of the two rebounds, and in the height of the two pulse points—together with enough horizontal motion in the first-beat rebound—can make this pattern much clearer.

Practice Exercise 3-6   *The Basic Two-Beat Pattern*

To accustom yourself to this format, "conduct" 25 measures or more of it, using the 16-by-20-inch *f* frame. When you find your gestures becoming more spontaneous, change to a frame of a different size; "conduct" at least 25 measures inside each of the other four frames. Do this daily until your next class meeting.

The one-beat pattern is peculiar (see Figure 3-13); again, the position of attention and the preparatory beat are essentially unchanged, but this time the downbeat rebounds straight up, and that rebound returns all the way to the top center of the conducting frame, where it connects to the repeat of the downbeat. (Be certain that your rebound really bounces high enough that your beat-stroke does not gradually get shorter.)

Practice Exercise 3-7   *The Basic One-Beat Pattern*

To accustom yourself to this format, "conduct" 25 measures or more of it, using the 16-by-20-inch *f* frame. When you find your gestures becoming more spontaneous, change to a frame of a different size; "conduct" at least 15 measures inside each of the other four frames. Do this daily until your next class meeting.

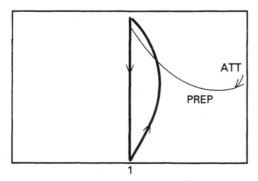

Figure 3-13 The basic one-beat pattern, including the Attention position and the preparatory beat

Practice faithfully! These are simple exercises, they are fundamental, and they must be *mastered thoroughly in a short time* if you are to make progress with other matters. Learn the one- , two- , three- , and four-beat patterns until they become second nature. Remember to try subvocalizing the metric subdivisions. And take care not to confuse your musicians with extraneous gestures.

ARTICULATION AND THE CHARACTER OF THE BEAT

The baton movements you have been learning to this point have been nonlegato in character; not all music is nonlegato, of course. Since your beat must communicate everything to the musicians, your gestures must reflect every type of articulation.

How does the beat pattern change for other styles of articulation? Let us consider several of the most common types.

Since *legato* implies very smooth connections between individual notes, you can express that in your beat pattern by avoiding abrupt motions of any kind, and especially by *making the rebound after each beat flow more evenly.* (See Figure 3-14.) A liquid wrist motion helps here: Let your wrist "lead" the baton slightly in each new direction during a legato pattern. Try imagining that your baton hand is moving through water as you conduct legato![4]

Staccato implies light, rather short notes, with a great deal of silence between them. Figure 3-15 shows a light staccato, at *pp*, signaled to the musicians by making the baton *stop* briefly on each rebound. One uses only the wrist to produce the stick movement. For a louder staccato—*mf* or higher—one uses the whole arm, but with some wrist action and with the stick still stopping on the rebound.

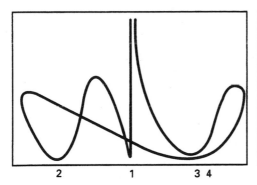

Figure 3-14 The four-beat pattern in legato articulation

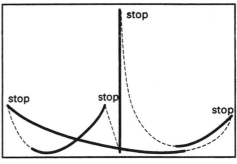

Figure 3-15 The four-beat pattern in staccato articulation

[4]Some conducting teachers have taught students to conduct legato by taking them to swimming pools.

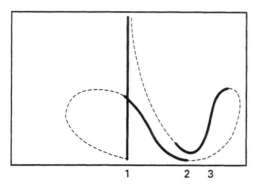

Figure 3-16   The three-beat pattern in an espressivo articulation

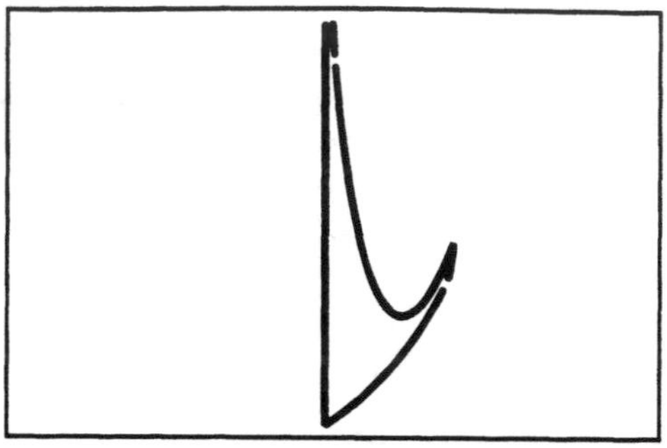

Figure 3-17   The two-beat pattern in a tenuto articulation

Espressivo indicates very liquid, free (even rubato) connections between notes. Again here, as Figure 3-16 illustrates, rebounds are the key to showing the difference: They can be larger and more sweeping as they connect the previous beat to the next preparation. Your pulse points should still fall on the conducting plane (that is, on the bottom of the conducting frame).

The word *tenuto* is used in two different senses. It can be ametric, involving a temporary suspension of the meter itself, rather like a fermata; that is not the meaning with which we are concerned here.[5] It often (perhaps more often) also can connote the *metric* lengthening of a nonlegato note; that is, given a standard nonlegato articulation, with audible separations between notes, one or more pitches may be given greater length (and therefore shorter separations) by use of tenuto articulation. This often is represented by a dash over the note (with or without the word *tenuto* itself) or by a dash with a dot over it.

For the word *tenuto,* or for the dash marking, the stick suddenly moves more slowly through the duration involved (see Figure 3-17). For the notation of a dot over a dash, the slower movement can be followed by a quick gesture—

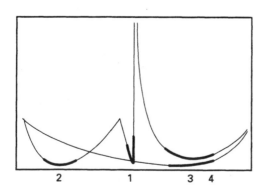

Figure 3-18   The four-beat pattern in a marcato articulation

[5]For a discussion of the "ametric" tenuto, see Chapter 5.

involving a flick of the wrist—that signals to the ensemble both the release of the sustained sound and a return to the regular pulse.

Marcato instructs musicians to stress emphatically the notes so marked. You can communicate this in your beat by using the whole arm and by marking the point of the beat with vigorous wrist action (though perhaps less than in a loud staccato). Do not stop the arm after each rebound (thus creating what is sometimes called a "bounce beat"), for it is important to the flow of the musical line that you keep the arm moving. (See Figure 3-18.)

Example 3-1   Six types of articulation[6]

Practice Exercise 3-8   *Conducting Various Articulation Types*

Conduct Example 3-1, observing the articulatory markings in each measure. (Remember, the first bar is a standard nonlegato.) *The change in articulation must be shown to the musicians one beat before they begin to do it!* Work to show clearly in your baton distinct differences between the articulatory types.

Observe the repeat sign again and again, until you feel confident; then, having memorized the musical example, watch yourself do this exercise before a mirror. Would you be able to "read" your own articulation signals?

Example 3-2   Articulation types in changing meters

Practice Exercise 3-9   *Conducting Various Articulation Types*
                            in Changing Simple Meters

Conduct Example 3-2, observing the articulatory markings in each measure. (Remember, the first bar is still a standard nonlegato.) *Continue to be certain that you show the articulation type to the musicians one beat before they have to perform it.*

Observe the repeat sign as many times as necessary, as you did in Practice Exercise 3-8. Work in front of a mirror.

[6]Most musical examples in the early chapters can be easily sung by an individual or a class. Varied clefs and key signatures are used deliberately.

DEVELOPING "AN EAR FOR TEMPOS"

This is a good moment for you to begin familiarizing yourself with different tempos. **As a conductor, you must come to have great confidence in your own ability to choose a good tempo, remember it from day to day, and "find" it again at the moment you need it.** That can be difficult, especially if you must remember exactly an upcoming tempo while the previous section of the work is in progress.

Use a metronome for practice. It can act like a teacher standing by your side, keeping you "on the beat" rhythmically. Monitor yourself constantly, making certain that your hand reaches the pulse points on your conducting frame at exactly the same moment the metronome does. Use varying speeds right from the start, for this will help you understand the effect different tempos have on the motion of your beat pattern.

If you do not own a good metronome, this is the time to obtain a fine one, for you are going to be using this professional tool steadily from now on. There are excellent models on the market, including pocket versions (some fueled by a battery and some operated by a clockwork mechanism). Many of them have special features, like tone generators that produce an A-440; most of the electrical type offer two kinds of signals: a flashing light and an audible click.[7]

Using your metronome, start learning now (in your mind, or "inner ear") to find certain "key" tempos—60 beats per minute, or 120, or 90—quickly. Play a daily game with yourself: How close can you come to "remembering" each of these? (This is rather like so-called perfect pitch. Some people can recall tempos easier than others. They seem to "have an ear" for it. As with "relative pitch," however, all of us get better with practice.)

You need not learn to remember *every* tempo you conduct, for you can use arithmetic relationships to "modulate" from a known tempo to another one: If one imagines 60 beats per minute in quarter notes, for example, then the eighth notes within those quarters give one 120, and the triplet-eighths are at 180; further, if one ties those triplet-eighths together in pairs, one has 90 beats per minute, and 45 is two pulses at 90 tied together. Thus, in finishing one movement of a work, one can look for a simple mathematical relationship between that (known) tempo and the pace of the coming movement; this eliminates the risk of trusting entirely one's memory (which may be fallible, especially under the influence of the adrenalin stimulated by performance pressures).

For recalling certain standard tempos, some conductors use "associative repertoire"; that is, confident that they *can* recall the exact tempo they like for a particular piece of music, they exploit that confidence, setting from it tempos for other works. For example, if they find that they can imagine a certain Strauss waltz at 60 beats per minute with almost infallible accuracy, that ability gives

---

[7]Toscanini, who was said to have an excellent sense of tempo, never used a mechanical metronome, we are told. He preferred to carry a weight tied to a measured length of string; this implement gave him more than just the sound of a momentary impact—it presented an *image of movement*, as well.

them a means of "finding" tempos like 60, 120, 90, and 180 just by using a little arithmetic. If you have half-a-dozen varied paces that you can recall *dependably* by this method of associative repertoire, you have the means of calculating mathematically perhaps two dozen tempos.

Practice Exercise 3-10   *Finding Tempo Relationships*

Using your metronome (or the second hand of your watch), establish a tempo of ♩ = MM60, and conduct 4 measures of $\frac{4}{4}$ at that pace; as you reach bar 3, begin to speak eighth notes (using "dah-dah" syllables). On the fifth downbeat, shift to conducting at ♩ = MM120. Then, in a similar way, make transitions directly from ♩ = MM60 to 180, to 90, and to 45. Start again at 60 and shift to 120, 40, and 80.

Working on the same principles, establish a tempo of ♩ = MM50, and use it to find 100, 150, and 75. Then, establish ♩ = MM80 and use it to find 160, 40, 120, and 60.

A WORD ABOUT PRACTICING

Any physical skill, including conducting, must be practiced if it is to become efficient. We know that physical acts repeated many times become easier because smoother connections gradually evolve between nerve endings; it is almost as if the signals we send from the brain slowly wear grooves, through repeated practice, and the once-difficult becomes manageable. Thus, certain kinds of movements can become routine and semiautomatic.

That is exactly what a conductor needs to develop. Your use of your right hand must become "second nature"; the hand must move for you, without your using your attention and concentration to consciously tell it what to do. *Your right hand must become the robotic expression of your musical intentions.*

Persuade yourself now that the practice time you must give to achieve this discipline will be worth it.

CHAPTER *4*

The Right Hand: Continuity

Once music has been set in motion, the continuity that follows has a flow like that of a running stream. There are things you can do to speed or slow the pace of that forward motion; for the moment, however, we are going to maintain a constant velocity—a steady rhythm. In future chapters, we will learn how to alter that flow, and eventually to stop it.

You have studied the conducting of the simple meters, and you are ready to attempt more complicated patterns. First, however, to lay a foundation for intricate formats, we need to speak about some theoretical concepts.

MORE CONDUCTING THEORY
Meters and Patterns

By convention, we speak of simple, compound, and complex meters, although the boundaries between these types are somewhat arbitrary.

In a *compound* meter, the beats articulate two separate metric strata—a lower level of pulses and a "super-meter." In $\frac{6}{8}$, for example, that "super-meter" is duple, made up of dotted quarters; below that duple beat is a pattern of six eighth notes per measure; that is, the eighths, form a triple subdivision of the dotted quarters on the high level. So it is with meters of nine and twelve beats; just as $\frac{6}{8}$ is a superstructure of two dotted quarters superimposed on triplet-eighths, $\frac{12}{8}$ is likely to be a compound of *four* dotted quarters and triplet-eighths, as we see in Figure 4-1.

A *simple* meter is one in which only one metric level is present in the beats themselves. $\frac{2}{4}, \frac{3}{4}$, and **1** are examples of this species. By convention, again, we regard $\frac{4}{4}$ as a simple meter, also, although in a sense the four-beat pattern we stud-

40

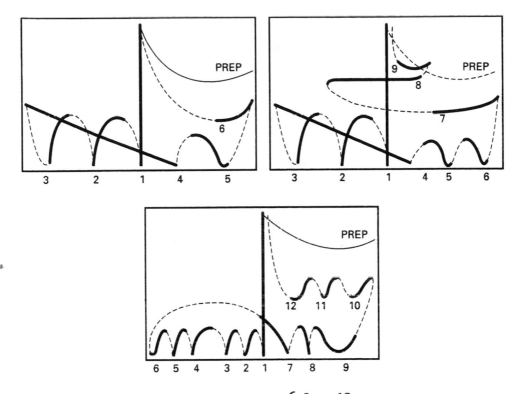

Figure 4-1 The subdivisions that make $^6_8$ $^9_8$ and $^{12}_8$ compound meters

ied in the last chapter—whether $\frac{4}{4}$, $\frac{4}{8}$, $\frac{4}{2}$, $\frac{4}{16}$, or whatever—is virtually a compound duple meter. (That is, $\frac{4}{4}$ is constituted a super-meter of two half notes, each subdivided by pairs of quarters.)

Complex meters are generally compound in type but asymmetrical in subdivision; a fast $\frac{5}{8}$, for instance, often is a compound duple meter with one beat subdivided into a pair of eighths, and the other into three. (See Figure 4-2.)

All this sounds very neat and precise. There are several problems, however.

1. The distinctions that make up these definitions are not always precise. In a sense, for example, both $\frac{2}{4}$ and $\frac{3}{8}$ are subdivisions of one (just as $\frac{4}{4}$ and $\frac{6}{8}$ are compounds of two).

2. The super-meter itself can vary: Six, for example, can be either a duple or a triple compound. By custom, we speak of $\frac{6}{8}$ as duple (*two* dotted quarters, each subdivided by *three* eighth notes) and $\frac{6}{4}$ as triple (*three* quarter notes, each subdivided by *two* eighth notes), but this is just a matter of tradition; a composer is free, as we see in Figure 4-3, to treat $\frac{6}{8}$ as compound triple and $\frac{6}{4}$ as compound duple.

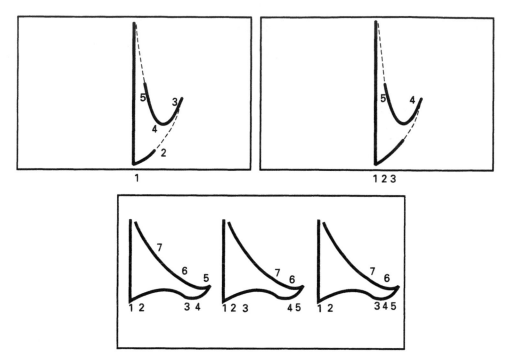

Figure 4-2 The asymmetrical subdivisions that make both $\frac{5}{8}$ and $\frac{7}{4}$ complex meters

Figure 4-3 $\frac{6}{4}$ illustrated both as compound duple and as compound triple

3. Some of these theoretical distinctions are not audible. No one can actually *hear* the notated difference between a standard $\frac{12}{8}$ and a $\frac{4}{4}$ written with a triplet subdivision, for example. Schumann, Brahms, and others have written passages full of "two-against-three" ($\frac{4}{4}$ subdivided with simultaneous, conflicting eighths and triplet-eighths).

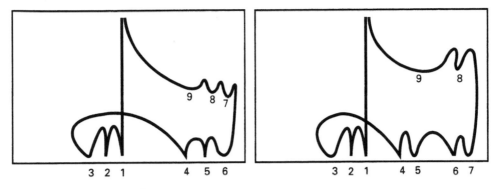

Figure 4-4 $\frac{9}{4}$ shown both as the standard (3 + 3 + 3) and as (3 + 2 + 2 + 2)

4. In more recent music, it is common for composers to use subdivisions other than the traditional ones, often marking at the beginning of such passages indications of their wishes ($\frac{9}{4}$ = 3 ǀ 2 ǀ 2 ǀ 2). (See Figure 4-4.)

5. These classifications are not always useful. Conductors do not always employ a four-beat pattern for $\frac{4}{4}$; they may take a given passage in two beats per bar, or in one, or in a subdivided four that amounts almost to an eight. $\frac{3}{4}$ is often conducted "in one," and $\frac{6}{8}$ "in two." Even a complex meter like $\frac{5}{8}$ may be taken in an asymmetrical "two." So you have seen in your own performances.

All this may seem to you very abstract. Nonetheless, it must be one of your primary concerns in preparing to direct your ensembles. **Nothing is more important to a conductor than a clear understanding of the metric and rhythmic substance of the music, and of the choices of gesture that make that metric and rhythmic foundation visible to the musicians.** The beat pattern you choose to use in a given work is not based on the notated meter; your choice must reflect the tempo, the mood, the rhythmic stresses, the melodic line, the accompanimental patterns, and all. For convenience, we will make use of the "simple–compound–complex" meter classification system, but as this chapter proceeds we also will examine subdivision of the pulse, and in later chapters we will discuss conducting certain passages in beat patterns that differ from the notated meter.

THE COMPOUND METERS

In the basic six-beat format shown in Figure 4-5 (especially useful in slower tempos), the position of attention and the preparatory beat are treated in the usual way. Otherwise:

1. The downbeat is standard, but its rebound curves to the left.
2. The second beat is a short, curving stroke down to the conducting plane about one-

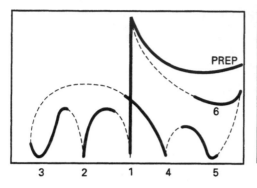

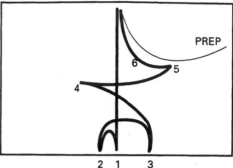

Figure 4-5 The basic six-beat pattern, including the Attention position and the preparatory beat

Figure 4-6 An alternative six-beat pattern, including the Attention position and the preparatory beat[1]

third of the way from the downbeat to the left edge of the frame. Its rebound curves a short distance up and, again, to the left.

3. The third beat-stroke is just like the previous one, touching the conducting plane near the corner of the frame.

4. The fourth beat, then, is a long stroke (emphasizing that this pulse and the downbeat are the two strong beats in six); it crosses all the way from the left edge of the frame to a point perhaps one-third of the way between the downbeat and the *right* edge of the frame. Its rebound curves up a short distance to the right.

5. The fifth beat—like a mirror image of the third—is a short stroke curving down to the conducting plane at a point perhaps two-thirds of the way to the right edge, and then rebounding up to touch that edge near its midpoint.

6. We offer you two alternatives for the final beat: It can return all the way back to the conducting plane near the point of the fifth beat, rebounding to the top center of the frame, or it can curve just below the original preparatory beat, creating a pulse within the frame (not on the conducting plane), and then rebound to prepare the downbeat. Which of these you choose may depend primarily on your tempo; a quicker pace may make the first choice—with its long, descending curve—look too awkward or too important.

Figure 4-6 shows you an alternative six-beat pattern, which is convenient especially for faster tempos, when elongated strokes look or feel clumsy. For reasons that are obvious from the sketch, many people call it the "Christmas Tree Six."

1. The downbeat is standard. The next two strokes, then, fall very close to it, just to the left a bit.

2. The fourth stroke crosses to the left edge of the frame, staying well above the conducting plane. (The fourth pulse occurs in the mid-left area of the frame.)

---

[1]For simplicity and clarity, the position of attention and the preparatory beat are not notated on the beat-pattern diagrams from this point on. Remember, however, that these always are located in the same vicinity, whatever the pattern.

3. The fifth beat *reverses direction*, swinging back to the right of the downbeat. Its pulse point rises still farther above the plane, and rebounds *toward* the right edge.
4. Stopping in the mid-right part of the frame, the baton turns back to create a sixth pulse just to the right of the downbeat stroke, as part of a curve from the fifth-beat rebound to the top center of the frame.

These patterns are more complicated than the ones you have already tried. (It is harder to tell your hand to move *twice* to the left, and then twice to the right.) Drill them dutifully.

Practice Exercise 4-1   *Alternative Six-Beat Patterns*

Conduct 25 measures or more of the standard six-beat pattern shown in Figure 4-5, using your 12-by-16-inch *mf* frame. Then, try 25 or more measures of the alternative version shown in Figure 4-6.
  Next, conduct 50 measures, alternating between two bars of Figure 4-5 and two of Figure 4-6.

The nine-beat pattern shown in Figure 4-7 obviously bears resemblances to both the basic three-beat format of Figure 3-11 and the six-beat pattern of Figure 4-5. All of the more intricate matrices, in fact, are elaborations of one of the *five basic patterns (one, two, three, four, and six beats) we have given you*. In the case at hand:

1. The first five pulses of the pattern imitate Figure 4-5, but the sixth still moves to the right; its rebound, then, bounces up to touch the frame's right edge.
2. The seventh and eighth beats fall on the plane near the fourth and fifth ones. Then the ninth beat curves down toward the frame near its midpoint and rebounds to the top center, preparing the next downbeat.

Note that the primary beats of this "super-three"—the first, fourth, and seventh—get changes of direction, strong rebounds, and more length than the sec-

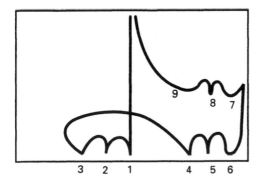

3 2 1   4 5 6   **Figure 4-7** The nine-beat pattern

ondary beats; thus, they help keep your ensemble oriented through this knotty pattern.

Here we see the "compound" character of these meters expressed in the beat format: Just as $\frac{9}{8}$, for example, is essentially $\frac{3}{4}$ with a triplet subdivision, so the pattern you conduct shows both three-beat and nine-beat aspects.

Practice Exercise 4-2 *The Nine-Beat Pattern*

To accustom yourself to this format, "conduct" 25 measures or more of it, using the 16-by-20-inch *f* frame. When you find your gestures becoming more spontaneous, change to a frame of a different size; "conduct" at least 15 measures inside each of the other four frames.

Similarly, the most common twelve-beat pattern is a compound elaboration of the basic four-beat format, as we see in Figure 4-8.

1. A standard downbeat, with smaller second and third beats grouped just to its left
2. A longer stroke to the fourth beat, with smaller fifth and sixth pulses grouped to its left, the rebound of the latter touching the left edge of the frame
3. A reversal of direction and a long cross-stroke leading to the seventh beat, on the right side of the frame, just past the downbeat, with eighth and ninth pulses grouped just to its right (the rebound of the latter touching the right edge)
4. Another reversal of direction leading back to the left to tenth, eleventh, and twelfth beats, with a long rebound from the twelfth beat leading up to the midpoint of the frame

Again we see primary beats given emphasis by reversals of direction, longer strokes, and stronger rebounds.

Next we have another "Christmas Tree" design, a possible alternative shown in Figure 4-9. Here, the first nine pulses are identical to Figure 4-8, but

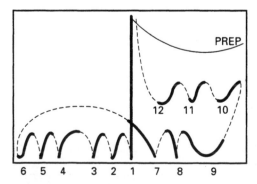

Figure 4-8 A twelve-beat pattern

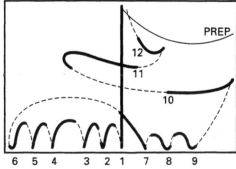

Figure 4-9 An alternative twelve-beat pattern

after the rebound of the ninth beat,

1. The tenth beat falls near the downbeat line and rebounds to the left half of the frame.
2 The eleventh beat swings back again, rebounding to the right side of the center line.
3. The twelfth pulse comes near the center, as its rebound curves up to the top center of the frame.

Practice Exercise 4-3   *Alternative Twelve-Beat Patterns*

Conduct 50 measures or more of the standard twelve-beat pattern shown in Figure 4 8, using your 12-by-16-inch *mf* frame. Then, try 25 or more measures of the alternative version shown in Figure 4-9.
   Next, conduct 50 measures, switching between two bars of Figure 4-8 and two of Figure 4-9.

MORE CONDUCTING THEORY
Clarity from Every Angle

It is a primal principle of conducting that each beat and pattern must be easily distinguishable from the others. Remember the problem with the second stroke of the two-beat pattern? That gesture, we said in Chapter 3, must be shallower in curvature, as well as somewhat to the right of the downbeat, so that it can be distinguished from the downbeat by the musicians.

Not all the members of your ensemble stand or sit directly in front of you in rehearsal and performance. Their viewing angles vary; consequently, your beat looks different to each of them. In an orchestra, for example, those farthest to your left and right see a very "flat" image of your beat. From the back stand of the 'cellos, one can see the depth of the downbeat clearly, but the second and third beats (in $\frac{4}{4}$) can look very much alike (for only the player's depth perception can tell them apart). Now consider $\frac{12}{8}$: If the first violins have a problem distinguishing your second beat from your third in $\frac{4}{4}$, what will they do when you are beating only two easily recognizable strokes out of twelve per bar—the downbeat and the final upbeat?

Consider the clarity of your beat from all angles. On the horizontal strokes—two and three in $\frac{4}{4}$, for instance—let your hand naturally turn somewhat to the left and right in turn; this lets players in the extreme seats glimpse the front and back of your hand; here, the point of the baton on a second beat actually turns partway toward the first violins, and that makes their judgment about your beat much easier.[2]

---

[2]This is one more argument for using a baton: Small gestures on your part become more visible, especially when you permit the tip of the baton to turn up, down, and sideways a bit on beat strokes.

For a given tempo, we use the simplest, most visible beat pattern we can adapt to the needs of the music before us.

And just as we use the fewest beats that will be effective in a certain musical context, so we sometimes must use *more* gestures than the basic beat pattern provides to make clear some of the rhythmic nuances of a particular passage. For this purpose, it is possible for us to *subdivide* the beat, breaking it into mathematically equal "subbeats." This technique can be especially useful in conducting tempos *almost* too slow for the beat pattern, in controlling dotted rhythms and other rhythmic complexities, and in managing changes of tempo—ritards, accelerandos and decelerandos, and the like.

SUBDIVIDING THE BEAT

Subdivide the beat when the pattern you are using is not sufficient to show to your musicians some subtlety or some change in the rhythmic flow of the music. Keep the subdivisions metric. They should be as precise and proportional as the beat-strokes themselves.

When subdividing, use the standard beat pattern, of course (that is, use four for a subdivided four), keeping the subdivision-strokes relatively small and close to the main pulse points. This will maintain the clarity of your overall pattern. Subdivision is intricate; at least until you have mastered the technique, keep the beats and the subdivisions located just where they belong and be certain exactly which stroke you are delivering. The ensemble finds subdivision complicated, too, and must be able to tell precisely where you are at all times. Use no vague motions! Do not let the subdivisions wander loosely between the main beats!

There are *many* gestures one can use in subdividing the beat. One may, while keeping the stick moving, tap the point of the previous pulse again, permitting only a short rebound this time; one may bring the original beat to a complete stop at the peak of its rebound, and then restart the hand before tapping the subdivision on the conducting plane. These are the extremes, and subtler procedures lie between them. What motion you choose will depend, of course, on the musical circumstance: Is this subdivision needed to signal a tiny ritard, to pace a transition into a new tempo, or to clarify a rhythmic characteristic?

Your rebounds have to change here. As Figure 4-10 illustrates, the rebound after each main beat-stroke must keep your hand in the area of that pulse so that the subdivision-stroke can tap that spot again. It will be the rebound *after the subdivision-stroke* that will move on in the way you have learned. In the four-beat pattern, for example, the second beat touches the conducting frame halfway to the left side and then rebounds to touch the midpoint of that edge; in a subdivided four, however, the rebound after the second beat must be shorter and more vertical; the subdivision-stroke after the second beat taps almost the same spot on the conducting plane and *then* bounces over to brush the left edge of the frame. So it is with the other pulses, and with other beat patterns.

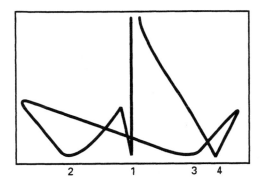

2   1   3 4

Figure 4-10 A nonlegato subdivision of the four-beat pattern

Subdividing the beat is a precise technique, and a rather dangerous one. It should be used only when a specific musical need demands it. **Do not get into the habit of trying to show your musicians every minor rhythmic event.** Your duty is to provide what is essential in pulse, articulation, dynamic, phrasing, and nuance; if you attempt to show them too much, they will not be able to separate the important from the trivial.

Practice Exercise 4-4   *Subdivision in a Four-Beat Pattern*

Using your 4-by-8-inch *pp* conducting frame, conduct at least 25 measures of Figure 4-10 at a moderately slow tempo. Be certain you keep each subdivision-stroke near the previous pulse point and that the succeeding rebound ends in the proper spot.

Now, try 25 measures of the same diagram within your 16-by-20-inch *f* frame. Be just as precise as before.

AUTONOMOUS RESPONSES WITH THE BATON

It is necessary for your right hand to operate virtually "on its own," as we have said before. In this chapter, you have seen most of the gestures the right hand must "remember to make"; beyond these beat patterns, subdivisions, and the like remain cutoffs, fermatas, cues, and refinements of the beat-stroke for dynamics, articulation, and other interpretive shadings. Soon you will be using them.

You also must be able to switch back and forth from one beat pattern to another. As quickly as your eye sees that the meter has changed—say, from $\frac{4}{4}$ to $\frac{6}{4}$— your brain must be able to transmit to your hand the single command "Six!" and have your baton carry out the whole six pattern by habit. (Ideally, then, in an irregular series of meter changes, you send one such command to your hand each time the meter shifts, devoting most of your attention to other concerns.)

Achieving this skill requires a great deal of practice, until it is no longer necessary for you to tell your hand which way to go at a given moment for a certain beat.

In practice, you can check what your baton hand is doing by stopping to look at it any second. Keep it properly oriented spatially; that is, make certain that the pulse points themselves are falling where they should in relation to your body and to the conducting frame.

Practice Exercise 4-5 *Changing Meters Rapidly with a Constant Hand Speed*

Repeat the following metric succession ten times, using your 16-by-20-inch *f* frame. Assume that the quarter note is the beat in each meter (so your hand speed will remain constant throughout). Use a moderate tempo for your first five repetitions, and then vary the pace each time.

Now repeat the succession two or three times (again at varying tempos) within each of your other conducting frames.

$\frac{4}{4}$ — | — | $\frac{3}{4}$ – | — | $\frac{4}{4}$ — | $\frac{2}{4}$ – | — | $\frac{4}{4}$ — | $\frac{1}{4}$ | $\frac{3}{4}$ — | $\frac{1}{4}$ |

$\frac{2}{4}$ – | $\frac{3}{4}$ — | $\frac{1}{4}$ | $\frac{3}{4}$ — | $\frac{6}{4}$ — | $\frac{2}{4}$ – | $\frac{6}{4}$ — | $\frac{3}{4}$ — | $\frac{6}{4}$ — |

$\frac{1}{4}$ | $\frac{12}{4}$ — | $\frac{9}{4}$ — | $\frac{2}{4}$ – ||

GIVING THE PREPARATORY BEAT FOR SHORT PICKUP NOTES

In the previous chapter, you learned to deliver preparatory beats one full pulse before the music first sounds. There are circumstances, however, in which a pickup beat *shorter than the pulse* (that is, an eighth note in $\frac{4}{4}$ meter, a sixteenth in $\frac{6}{8}$, and so on) is the first sound. Such a pickup usually represents the subdivision of the pulse (or sometimes half of the metric subdivision).

In these situations, the *duration* of your preparatory beat does not change! If the first sound heard in a $\frac{4}{4}$ passage is to be an eighth note on the last half of the fourth pulse, your preparation still begins with a full fourth beat. You are depending, in this case, on the musicians who have the eighth-note pickup to enter exactly halfway through your preparatory beat. Not all of the ensemble are likely to have the pickup; the melodic line may begin with the eighth note, for example, whereas the accompanying instruments or voices enter on your downbeat. These latter folk are entitled to a proper preparatory beat in this circumstance—a full-length one a pulse ahead of time—just as they would be were the short pickup note not present.

You may encourage those performing the pickup by making your preparatory beat curve slightly deeper than usual before it moves on to the start of the next beat-stroke. Be certain that you *hear the metric subdivision in your mind at least one full pulse before your preparatory beat.*

Short pickups to pulses other than the downbeat are handled in exactly the same way.

There are *rare* circumstances in which (because of a difficult rhythm or tempo shift) it is permissible (and may be necessary) to give *two* preparatory beats. In such a case, one must be careful to warn the ensemble in rehearsal that one is going to deliver an "extra beat" at that spot. (Since ensemble reaction to a clear preparatory beat is almost reflexive, even with this sort of prior verbal warning, the giving of two preparatory beats is a risky procedure and should be avoided whenever possible.)

Example 4-1   Preparatory situations involving short pickup note(s)

Practice Exercise 4-6   *Preparing Entrances that Begin with Short Pickup Notes*

Conduct each of the phrase beginnings in Example 4-1 several times, singing the subdivision beforehand for the full measure leading up to the pickup note(s). Be certain you "hear" the pickup(s) match the subdivision you are singing. Be sure also that the motion of your preparatory beat itself is not affected: Do *not* subdivide the beat. (You may employ a slightly deeper prep beat, however.)

CHAPTER 5

The Right Hand: Changing the Flow

In Chapters 3 and 4, you began to conduct the basic simple and compound patterns, two of the three metric categories you must study. Now it is time for you to begin work on the third species.

THE COMPLEX METERS

We have said that complex meters tend, by nature, to be compound; their rhythms generally create two or more primary pulses, around which secondary beats are grouped asymmetrically. One of your responsibilities is to decide where those primary pulses are. Is the $\frac{8}{8}$ before you basically a 2 + 2 + 2 + 2 subdivided four, for example, or is it really a 3 + 3 + 2 compound, or a 3 + 2 + 3, or something else? Is that relationship of primary beats consistent, or does it vary?

If it varies, then you may want to alternate the beat pattern you use, as well. Figures 5-1 and 5-2 exhibit parallel five-beat patterns; master both of them, and learn which to use in given musical circumstances.

In quintuple meter with a 3 + 2 subdivision, it makes sense that the strongest beat after the first should be the fourth; thus, those two beats emphasize the primary pulses. Figure 5-1 illustrates a beat pattern for that situation. Essentially the same as our basic six, but with the next-to-last pulse deleted, this format has its motion to the left reversed for a long fourth beat. Everything else is standard.

With a 2 + 3 subdivision, on the other hand, the first and third pulses are the primary ones. Figure 5-2, which resembles our basic four-beat pattern, has a reversal of direction after a weak second pulse, so the third stroke is long and strong. An additional beat, small in size, comes next, and the fifth stroke returns us to the top center of the frame in the usual way.

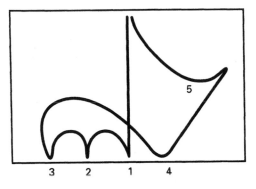 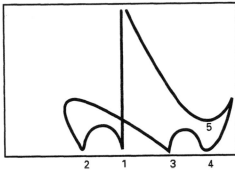

Figure 5-1 A five-beat pattern built on a 3 + 2 subdivision

Figure 5-2 An alternative five-beat pattern built on a 2 + 3 subdivision

Learn both these patterns well enough that you can shift fluently back and forth from one to the other in the middle of a work. You will need them, especially in twentieth-century music.

Practice Exercise 5-1   *Alternative Five-Beat Patterns*

Conduct 25 measures or more of the 3 + 2 pattern shown in Figure 5-1, using your 16-by-20-inch *f* conducting frame. Then try 25 or more measures of the 2 + 3 version shown in Figure 5-2.

Finally, conduct 50 measures in five, alternating *every measure* between Figures 5-1 and 5-2.

In the same way, meters of seven pulses usually can be divided into 4 + 3 or 3 + 4. Figures 5-3 and 5-4 present patterns for these two possibilities.

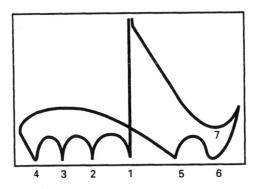 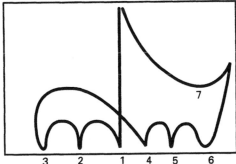

Figure 5-3 A seven-beat pattern built on a 4 + 3 subdivision

Figure 5-4 An alternative seven-beat pattern built on a 3 + 4 subdivision

Figure 5-3 shows us a matrix much like our basic six-beat format, with an additional weak beat on the left side of the frame. Here, the first and *fifth* strokes are the long, strong ones, just as we would wish for a 4 + 3 subdivision.

Figure 5-4 presents again a relative of the six-beat pattern. This time, the weak added pulse appears on the right side. In this design, the first and *fourth* strokes give the proper visible emphasis to the 3 + 4 subdivision.

Another possibility: Sometimes a very strong tripartite division of seven can be found (3 + 2 + 2, or 2 + 2 + 3, or whatever). In such cases, a pattern related to our basic three-beat format is useful, for it will emphasize *three* primary beats, grouping the secondary pulses around them; the longest of the three "super-beats" should be employed (for visual clarity) to cover the triple grouping wherever it occurs in the measure.

Practice Exercise 5-2   *Alternative Seven-Beat Patterns*

Conduct 25 measures or more of the 4 + 3 pattern shown in Figure 5-3, using your 12-by-16-inch *mf* frame (to limit and discipline the size of your motions). Then try 25 or more measures of the 3 + 4 version displayed in Figure 5-4.

Now try inventing exercises, built on the basic *three-beat* pattern, that involve 2 + 2 + 3, 2 + 3 + 2, and 3 + 2 + 2.

USING THE LEAST COMPLICATED
BEAT PATTERN NECESSARY

In general, the faster the tempo, the simpler the gestures. The slower the pace, the more elaborate the pattern should be, for the musicians need to see a constant flow from you—even in a Largo or a Grave.

Patterns with many beats—five or seven, nine or twelve, or even four in a very bright tempo—can get clumsy. Therefore, it is a rule one rarely should override that *the beat pattern to be used is the one with the fewest beats possible for the circumstance.* Where certain rhythmic features occur—short note values, dotted rhythms, or the like—it is necessary to show more pulses; where rhythmic relationships are simple and note values are long, uncomplicated beat patterns are best. *Never* use an elaborate format pretentiously. It gets in the way of communication.

In later chapters, we will have opportunities to weigh options in choices of tempos and beat patterns. For the moment, let us look at the effect of bright tempos on asymmetrical meters.

If we need to take a $\frac{6}{8}$ passage quickly, we conduct in two, not six, of course; but what is to be done when the meter is five?

If the tempo is too bright to use a five-beat pattern, and too slow to be taken in one, we conduct it in two. In a $\frac{5}{8}$ situation, one of the two beats must be two

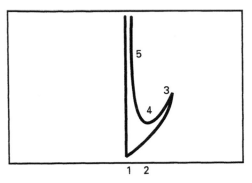

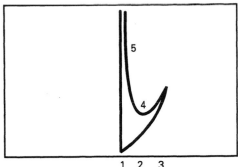

Figure 5-5 A five-beat pattern for a fast tempo, with a 2 + 3 distribution

Figure 5-6 A five-beat pattern for a fast tempo, with a 3 + 2 distribution

eighth notes long, and the other three. (That means, since the length of the first and second beats is about the same, that the baton must move faster for one beat—the one with the fewer eighth notes—than for the other.) Which beat covers the most eighth notes depends upon the subdivision within the music, as we have said.

Figure 5-5 shows you how to conduct quintuple meter in a fast tempo when the subdivision is 2 + 3. Here we see a basic two-beat pattern, much like Figure 3-12. If the meter is $\frac{5}{4}$, then two quarter notes will occur during the downbeat; that means that the upbeat must be "stretched" longer (in time, not in space) so that three quarters can fit within it.

Figure 5-6, on the other hand, displays a 3 + 2 subdivision in the same tempo. Here, it is the downbeat that must be "stretched" to cover three notes.

The preparatory beat used to introduce either of these two patterns should be consistent with the duration of the downbeat: If a downbeat is two eighth notes long, for instance, the preparatory beat should also be a quarter note in length, unless the nature of the pickup note(s) dictates something special. In the case of Figure 5-5, on the other hand, the preparatory beat should be three quarter notes in duration.

Practice Exercise 5-3 *Alternative Patterns for Five in a Fast Tempo*

Conduct 25 measures or more of the pattern shown in Figure 5-5 (as if the meter were $\frac{5}{8}$), using your 12-by-16-inch *mf* frame. Then shift to Figure 5-6, doing at least 25 more measures. *In both cases,* sing ("dah-dah") five eighth notes per bar (to keep your beat even).

   Next, conduct 50 measures, alternating each measure between patterns 5-5 and 5-6. Continue singing the eighth notes, but this time accent either the third or the fourth one in each bar, depending on the 3 + 2 or 2 + 3 subdivision.

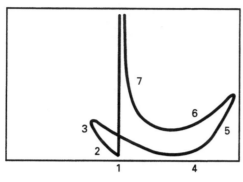

Figure 5-7 A seven-beat pattern for a fast tempo, with a 3 + 2 + 2 distribution

Any of the asymmetrical meters, if taken in a bright tempo, will require that you handle one of the basic beat patterns in a way similar to the preceding five-beat formats. Look at Figure 5-7. Here is a pattern for use with a fast seven: In the diagram, which assumes a 3 + 2 + 2 subdivision, the first beat is lengthened in duration so that it can cover three notes (quarters, eighths, halves—whatever carries the subdivision).

Should the distribution be different (2 + 2 + 3, for example), or should the rhythmic patterns vary during the work, any of the three primary beats can be "stretched" to cover the longer unit.

Practice Exercise 5-4   *A Pattern for Seven in a Fast Tempo*

Conduct at least 25 measures, using Figure 5-7, within your 12-by-16-inch *mf* frame. Sing eighth notes in $\frac{7}{8}$ (as in Practice Exercise 5-3), keeping a 3 + 2 + 2 subdivision. Accent the first, fourth, and sixth notes as you sing.
    Then try 25 measures of a 2 + 2 + 3 distribution, and 25 more of 2 + 3 + 2, changing the accent pattern you sing each time.

Now that you know the process, you can conduct other complex meters in fast tempos by adapting basic beat patterns. $\frac{8}{8}$ subdivided as 3 + 3 + 2 can be conducted with the basic three-beat pattern: three eighths under each of the first two beats, but only two covered by the quicker third stroke. $\frac{9}{8}$—if not simply 3 + 3 + 3, which you have already studied—can be adapted (to a four-beat format for a 3 + 2 + 2 + 2, for example), as can $\frac{11}{8}$; it is just a matter of allowing for the asymmetrical element by making one stroke of a basic beat pattern longer or shorter and quicker or slower than the others.

SUMMARY OF THE BEAT PATTERNS

What principles can we draw from the general similarities between these beat patterns?

The position of attention is always the same, no matter what the meter; that means that the preparatory beat (which varies a great deal, of course, in speed and length, depending on the tempo and the dynamic) always comes from the same direction—the conductor's right.

The downbeat itself always begins at the top center of the frame and invariably comes *straight down* to strike the conducting plane dead in the middle, before it rebounds slightly to one side or the other.

The stroke *before* the downbeat (the final beat of the pattern) comes from the conductor's right in every case. Even in the most complicated metric patterns, this upbeat from the right is an unmistakable signal to your ensemble that the downbeat of the measure will be next.

"Strong beats" (those stressed by the meter) tend to begin with a change of direction, and get longer strokes than do "weak" ones.

The smoothness of connections between beats, and the nature of the rebounds, should tell your musicians what style of articulation you want. Dynamics are shown best in the beat's size.

For *simple meters*, we use one of the *basic* beat patterns. For *compound meters*, in general, we elaborate one of these basic formats; its strokes become the *strong* beats of the design, and the weak beats are interposed between them. For *complex meters* (whatever the tempo), we again use one of the basic patterns, choosing a design whose strong beats *match the primary beats implicit in the music at hand*, and adding or subtracting a *weak* beat somewhere to make the number of pulses right. We speed up or slow the baton, as necessary, to allow for uneven numbers of pulses per stroke in these asymmetrical meters.

As you have seen in our discussion of the complex meters, not every beat in an asymmetrical pattern can be the same speed. Changes of the note value denominating the pulse mean changes in speed of stroke, as well. Practice Exercise 5-5 requires that your hand make shifts in speed as well as in pattern.

Practice Exercise 5-5 *Shifting Meters Rapidly*
with Changing Hand Speed Required

Repeat the following metric succession ten times, using your 16-by-20-inch *f* frame. Assume that the lower number in each time signature is the beat (which means that your hand speed will have to change almost as often as the meter shifts). Use a moderate tempo for your first five repetitions, and then vary the pace each time. Next, repeat the exercise two or three times (again at varying tempos) within each of your other conducting frames.

$\frac{4}{4}$ —— | $\frac{3}{4}$ — | —— | $\frac{6}{8}$ —— | $\frac{3}{4}$ — | $\frac{5}{4}$ —— | $\frac{1}{4}$ | $\frac{4}{4}$ —— | $\frac{2}{2}$ —— |

$\frac{3}{4}$ — | $\frac{5}{8}$ — | $\frac{1}{4}$ | $\frac{5}{8}$ —— | $\frac{2}{4}$ - | $\frac{7}{4}$ —— | $\frac{7}{8}$ —— | $\frac{2}{4}$ - | $\frac{3}{8}$ - | $\frac{6}{4}$ —— |

$\frac{3}{2}$ —————— | $\frac{1}{4}$ | $\frac{6}{8}$ —— | $\frac{7}{8}$ — | $\frac{1}{8}$ | $\frac{2}{4}$ - | $\frac{3}{8}$ - ||

MAINTAINING A CONSTANT PULSE

At the end of Chapter 4, you were conducting through sequences of rapidly changing meters. In this chapter, before we can speak of changing the "flow," or pace, of the music at hand, we must be certain we know what that flow is, and that we are able to control it. This demands of you a sure sense of rhythm.

This "sure sense of rhythm" depends primarily on one of the most important skills you must possess: the ability to sense and maintain a steady pulse. Music is one of the arts that take place in Time, and in music the passage of time must be *strictly* controlled. Some students have been given the impression that pitch must be precise, and that one can be exactly right or wrong about intonation, but that rhythmic precision is either impossible or not very important.

The truth is that the shape of everything you conduct—one measure, one phrase, a section, a movement, or a lengthy work—depends on the steadiness of the pulse and on your ability to sustain that pulse metronomically, speeding it up or slowing it down *only* when you intend to and *only* when you know precisely toward what new tempo you are headed.

To hold on to a particular pulse, you must "hear" it—almost audibly—in your mind. You must be able to measure mentally the difference between that desired tempo and any other metric flow around you. If your ensemble is "rushing" or "dragging," you must determine what is causing the unsteadiness and act to stabilize the pulse again.

USING METRIC SUBDIVISIONS

To hold a tempo in your mind, even with the help of your baton hand, is not easy, and it can be particularly difficult in slower passages. You will find it helpful to "hear" the basic subdivision of the beat, as well as the pulse itself; when conducting a slow $\frac{6}{8}$ in two, for example, you should be thinking the eighth notes

---

Practice Exercise 5-6   *Dealing with Subdivisions of the Beat*

Conduct, as shown below, two measures each of a sequence of meters; at the same time, sing alternately on the syllable "dah" both the duple and the triple subdivisions of the meter; that is, in $\frac{4}{4}$ sing first a measure of eighths and then a measure of triplet-eighths, and so on. (Assume a constant quarter at about MM = 60.)

$\frac{4}{4}$ ----| ---- | $\frac{3}{4}$ --- | --- | $\frac{2}{4}$ -- | -- | $\frac{1}{4}$ - | - | $\frac{3}{4}$ --- | --- |

$\frac{2}{4}$ -- | -- | $\frac{4}{4}$ ---- | ---- | $\frac{1}{4}$ - | - | $\frac{5}{4}$ ----- | ----- | $\frac{1}{4}$ - | - ||

Now reverse the procedure, performing the triplets first and then the duplets in each pair of measures.

Next, try the same exercise at different tempos: MM = 80 and MM = 120, for example.

as well as the dotted quarters. This constant sense of the subdivision will make it easier to measure exactly the duration of each dotted quarter; in addition, it will facilitate whatever eventual ritards or transitions occur as the flow continues.

Concentration is important here. You cannot maintain this inner sense of subdivided pulse intermittently. You must be aware of it at every moment.

ALTERING THE PULSE

In the next chapter, we will be concerned with halting the forward motion of the music—bringing the pulse to a stop. For the moment, however, we need to consider alterations of pace *within* a work.

As you know, tempo changes are frequent in music. Some are abrupt, moving suddenly at a double bar from an Allegretto to a Presto, for example; some are gradual, developing through perhaps an accelerando or a rallentando of dozens of measures, and arriving finally at a new, steady tempo. There is variety, too, in the duration of tempo changes: Some shifts determine the pace for the remainder of a long movement; other changes are transient, in effect interrupting an established tempo for a few measures.

Recognize that all these shifts have something in common: *Each involves an alteration of the pulse.* In each case, you must know (1) exactly when to depart from the old pace, (2) what gestures will show that departure clearly, (3) how gradual the shift will be, (4) how long it will be before the new tempo is established, (5) what gestures to use to control that gradual or abrupt transition, (6) exactly where the new tempo is to begin to function, and (7) what gestures to employ to establish a steady beat at the new pace.

Conducting a Tempo Change

Exactly what should you do in the case of a rallentando into a new tempo?

1. Be certain you are thinking the subdivision of the pulse as you approach the transition point.
2. About one full beat *before* you want your musicians to actually begin changing the tempo, show them a "stretched" pulse by enlarging the beat pattern.
3. Control the speed of change by continuing to alter the size and pace of the pattern (always one beat ahead of the musicians' arrival at that tempo).
4. Stabilize the new pulse by showing your ensemble a steady beat pattern in a size that reflects the dynamic level you want.

The Ritard

Probably the most common type of tempo change is the *ritardando,* or the ritard. Some ritards are quite subtle and brief, meant only to stretch the end of a phrase; some skid sharply into cadences, preparing a new tempo; others extend over many measures and pull down the whole momentum of a movement. Each variety presents different technical problems for you.

Musicians sometimes say they "feel" a ritard, conveying the idea that ritards are natural and commonly perceived as needed at a given moment; but an ensemble of sixty players is likely to have sixty different ideas of how a particular ritard should progress, how abrupt it should be, and how extensive. You must fashion these disparate ideas into a unified result.

Anytime you change an established pulse, you risk a muddle, a loss of clean ensemble work. All your musicians know "where" the beat is in a steady tempo, but if your wishes are not absolutely clear in your baton, the performers will fall back on their personal feelings, and those sixty different ideas of how a given ritard should proceed will become audible. You must conduct at such moments with precise clarity and apparent confidence.

In a simple ritard (especially a short one), show your intention one beat early by suddenly enlarging the pattern. (Example 5-1 presents such a circumstance.) If the ritard is a lengthy one, continue to enlarge your beat throughout it, until you reach the point—again one beat early—at which you can establish your next tempo.

Example 5-1 Conducting a ritard

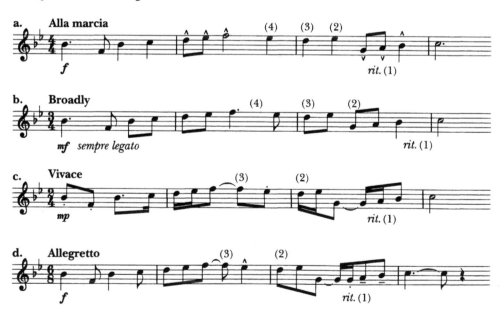

Practice Exercise 5-7 *Conducting Ritards*

Conduct Example 5-1, beginning a ritard on the third beat of bar 3, as marked. Then do it again, starting the ritard one beat earlier (at number 2). As you continue to repeat the example, move the ritard earlier (following the numbers) each time. As you conduct, sing the duplet subdivision (the eighth notes) on "dah" each time.

Now change to another meter—$\frac{3}{4}$, then $\frac{2}{4}$, then $\frac{6}{8}$ (in six)—and repeat the exercise several times in the same way. Always sing the subdivision for that meter.

In more complicated situations (particularly more substantial tempo changes), you often will find it helpful to subdivide the beat. Shifting to a lower metric level gives you more frequent subbeats with which to show the pulse to your musicians, increasing your control over the situation. Most mistakes in this circumstance come from a failure on the part of the conductor to actually think the subdivisions. Thus, the precise pace and extent of the ritard is not made clear.

In this procedure, one begins showing subdivisions about one beat before beginning the ritard, and then enlarges the beat to display and guide the unfolding of the ritard.

Example 5-2 Conducting a ritard involving a metric subdivision

Practice Exercise 5-8 *Conducting Subdivided Ritards*

Conduct Example 5-2 in three, subdividing one beat before the ritard. Repeat, moving the ritard back, number by number. Then practice each of the rhythmic lines below.

The Accelerando

A similar case, if a somewhat more difficult one, is the *accelerando*. The process is much the same: You begin by suddenly decreasing the size of the pattern about one beat before the point at which you want the accelerando to commence. Then you continue to make the beat smaller until the point at which you want to stabilize a new tempo.

Ensembles generally have more problems with this than with the ritard, because the conductor is asking the musicians to increase speed while the size of the beat is decreasing.

Example 5-3   Conducting an accelerando

Practice Exercise 5-9   *Conducting the Accelerando*

Conduct Example 5-3 in four. Then practice each of the rhythmic lines below, beginning to decrease the size of the beat at the marked accelerando.

Just as you may subdivide the beat to control a ritard more effectively, you may *decrease* the number of beats through an extended accelerando. A passage that begins in $\frac{4}{4}$ and accelerates to a markedly faster tempo, for example, may change to $\frac{2}{2}$ at a convenient point along the way. Your musicians need to know in advance that you will shift to the new pattern at a precise point in the music. In your mind, the old pulse becomes the *subdivision* of the new meter.

The process is this: You begin the acceleration in the usual way and continue to decrease the size of your pattern until the point of the meter change, at which time you adopt a somewhat larger beat, keyed to the dynamic level you want at that moment. Having changed meters, you now may continue to accelerate, if need be, to the point at which you wish to stabilize a new tempo. Like any change of pulse, this is a dangerous technique and must be carried out with clarity and confidence.

Example 5-4   Conducting an accelerando involving a shift of meter

Practice Exercise 5-10   *Conducting an Accelerando*

Master the problems in Example 5-4, starting it in four. Then try the rhythmic lines below.

Allegro   Vivace

Langsam (in 9)   Andante con moto

Allegretto (in three)   Presto (in one)

The "Ametric" Tenuto

As an expressive device by which a single note or chord can be sustained momentarily, the *tenuto* is another interruption of the pulse frequently used by conductors. We have already discussed its use *within* the meter in Chapter 3.

You will find moments when a composer asks specifically for a tenuto, and you will have to decide whether or not he or she intends that the meter be affected; but there will be other times when you will wish to lend a bit of emphasis to a musical event by extending or sustaining its duration a bit. (This is well within your interpretive authority as a conductor.) The technique one uses to produce this sort of tenuto is much like that of the fermata. (See Chapter 6.)

The "Breath Mark"

Commas (casually called "breath marks") are notated in music in many places, especially to denote phrasing in choral groups, in orchestra winds, and in string parts where it is necessary that they match their own releases to singers or winds.

These have virtually the same effect as the ametric tenuto we have just discussed. The baton travels more slowly, and in a little larger gesture, until the release point, at which time it moves more quickly through the preparation of the next entrance. Again, a slight wrist movement is involved.

Practice Exercise 5-11   *Conducting the "Breath Mark"*

Have a friend hold a single pitch, singing the syllable "dah." Conduct a $\frac{4}{4}$ pattern as he or she does so, and—without saying anything, and keeping the pulse constant throughout—add "breath marks" on occasional beats clearly enough that your friend releases, breathes, and attacks the pitch again without being told to do so.

The Rubato

An alternation of brief ritards and accelerations continuing through a musical passage, thus creating for expressive purposes an unsteady pulse, is called a *rubato*. (It is usually said that in a rubato, anything taken away for a ritard must be given back in an accelerando, and vice versa; thus, a kind of balance preserves the basic overall pace, even though the pulse is unsteady at any given moment.)

From the conductor's point of view, the technique of the rubato consists simply of managing a series of ritards and accelerandos, using the procedures you have already studied.

Example 5-5   Conducting a rubato passage

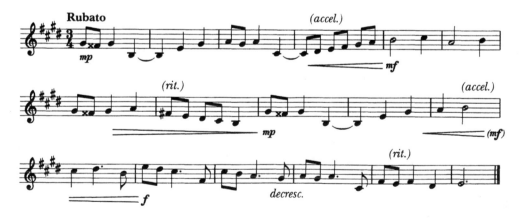

Practice Exercise 5-12   *Rubato Conducting*

Conduct Example 5-5 in three, observing the bracketed markings, which represent one possible rubato approach here. Keep the first accelerando and the first ritard in proportion, so that bar 9 comes naturally back to the original tempo. Your beat must show the final decrescendo.

Conducting Transitional Passages

In passages in which the pulse is clearly established, cues, releases, and nuances are your immediate concerns. It is when one section of a passage ends and another begins that you are most needed, especially if the transition involves a temporary or permanent change of tempo. These transitional passages (or "seams")—because they may involve a complex merging of releases, entrance cues, a ritard, a tenuto or a fermata, and the setting of a new tempo—require the most careful planning and preparation.

The examples that follow give you opportunities to practice these problems. In Example 5-6, you test your new skills with the ritard and the breath mark. The release of the latter is timed to maintain your original tempo.

Example 5-6   Conducting a ritard, a breath mark, and continuation of the same tempo

Practice Exercise 5-13   *Conducting a Return to Tempo*

Try Example 5-6, showing the breath mark as a brief interruption in the line. (You'll learn cutoff gestures in the next chapter. Just use a flick of the wrist for now.) Slow your beat for the ritard; move immediately back to the original tempo. Make certain your beat pattern in measure 5 (after the crescendo and the diminuendo) is the same size it was at first.

Example 5-7 is much the same, but it requires that you establish a new tempo after the second breath mark instead of returning to Tempo I. (In this case, the release of the breath mark must be at the right speed and of the right size to signal the new tempo; that is, that release must be the *preparation beat* for that new pulse.)

Example 5-7   Conducting a transition with a ritard, a breath mark, and a shift to a new tempo

Practice Exercise 5-14   *Conducting at a "Seam"*

First try keeping this passage in two, taking a modest ritard without subdividing it; then conduct it with a subdivision beginning on the last note in measure 3, and a big ritard. (Both circumstances occur in real works.) Make certain the new tempo you set at the Allegro is firm.

Example 5-8 presents an abrupt tempo change, which must be accomplished without making a substantial ritard. Here, you should maintain a steady pulse *through* the last beat before the tempo shift; in spite of the change, the length of that beat must be consistent with the old pace. *The change of tempo must come exactly on the first beat of the Vivace, with no ragged edges before it.* How can this be managed?

1. If the new tempo is a *faster multiple* of the old one, subdivide the last beat before the change, creating a preparatory beat on the last eighth in the bar. That eighth will equal a quarter in the new tempo.
2. If the new tempo is slower or is not a multiple of the old one, it is virtually impossible to show the new tempo before its first beat. The tempo must change *within* the downbeat.

Example 5-8   Conducting a transition with an abrupt change of meter and tempo

Practice Exercise 5-15   *Conducting an Abrupt Tempo Change*

Try this two ways, as well: (1) Start the Lento in three, and take the Vivace in four; subdivide the last half of the C-sharp in bar 4 (thus showing two eighth notes); the subdivided eighths will equal a quarter note in the new tempo. Don't ritard! (2) Without subdividing, make the shift directly from Lento in three to Vivace in *two*. Again, don't hesitate at the "seam."

This procedure might seem to be a violation of our rule that every change must be signaled by a full-length preparatory beat, but it may not be. In a tempo change, exactly where is the change effective? Not on the downbeat, although that is what we usually assume. Actually, it cannot be articulated (or heard by the listener) until the *next note after the downbeat*. It is the moment that your baton strikes the *second* pulse of the new tempo (which may be on, before, or after that "next note," of course) that the tempo shift is defined precisely.

Slowing down is more dangerous than speeding up in such cases. In a shift to a faster tempo, your stick will show the second pulse sooner than it would have occurred at the old pace, and thus you are "ahead" of the ensemble; if you are decreasing speed, on the other hand, there is a real danger your musicians will articulate an "old" second beat before you show them the "new" one.

In the next chapter, we will be discussing the technique of the fermata. At points like this, a "bird's-eye" on the last beat before the change—providing your interpretation of the music permits one—would allow you to show a full preparatory beat (as the release of the fermata) for the new tempo. When the change is abrupt, however, you must make it on the downbeat.

These are intricate skills. In actual practice, the confidence you and your ensemble have in each other is an important factor at such moments.

MORE CONDUCTING THEORY
Pulse, Structure, and Motion

How far should ritards be prolonged? What about tenutos? How much rubato is too much? How frequently should such expressive devices be used?

We know that the listener hears what is happening at a given moment and expects it to continue indefinitely. Audience members "feel" a steady beat and anticipate that it will persist. A ritard is a surprise, then, and surprises carry emotional power with them.

Like a table spice, a tenuto conveys more impact when it is used sparingly. Rubato takes its flavor from the contrast it creates against a steady, pulsing beat. Think of the frequent ritards that occur in a romantic passage, and compare them with the effect of the one or two ritards one may find in a whole movement of Bach: Do not the tempo interruptions in the Bach work seem stronger and more important? The reason is simple. A rallentando in Baroque style interrupts a long-established, vigorous pulse (one that the listener has shared for many measures); altering that pulse is a decisive, impressive act. In some Chopin works, on the other hand, a ritard is such a frequent feature that it stirs up little emotional response.

Further, these interruptions of the pulse *postpone* events to which the listener looks forward. Like anticipated birthday gifts, delayed musical features become more desirable as they are withheld. Up to a point, the longer you postpone an expected cadence, or climax, the more your listeners anticipate it; and the more they look forward to it, the greater the ultimate impact it has.[1] One must be careful not to overdo these things, but they are very powerful factors in the interpretation of music.

Similarly, the extent of a ritard must be judged against its effect on the musical design. Every case is different, but as a general rule, the longest ritards should occur at the most important points in the structure of the work, and the shortest should decorate phrasing and special expressive moments.

We will have more specific advice for you as we look at specific passages of music in later chapters

[1]Leonard B. Meyer, *Emotion and Meaning in Music* (Chicago: University of Chicago Press, 1956).

CHAPTER 6

The Right Hand: Closure

You have already tackled the problems of the preparation beat and of the beat patterns themselves. You have studied ways of altering or interrupting the forward motion of an established pulse. Now you are ready to consider how a conductor brings the flow of the music to a stop.

MORE CONDUCTING THEORY
The Cadence Effect

Late in the last chapter, we spoke of the expectations of the listener and of the emotional effects of changing the ongoing pulse. We noted also that *delay* of an approaching, anticipated event has psychological power—that a heightened emotional involvement comes to the observer from the postponement of an expected milestone, both in Music and in Life.

This especially is the case with respect to cadences, and the more important a given cadence is within the overall structure of a musical work, the more significant this point. As music approaches a closure of some sort, those listening to it sense that moment coming, estimate how it is going to sound and exactly when it will arrive, and then look forward to its arrival. As conductor, you, with your musicians, are in control of this sequence of events.

The questions we spoke of apply here too. How much ritard, if any, should be used as the cadence is approached? How long should the next-to-last chord (with or without a fermata) last? How long should the cadential chord itself be sustained?

The answer is different for each case, but it always lies close to the principle that *emotionally powerful moments should be sustained as long as possible*—that is, until any further delay would cause the moment to begin to lose its power in the minds of the listeners. This is rather like eating a rich dessert: You revel in it until you take one bite too many, and then it begins to repel you. You must learn to judge exactly when enough is enough; to put it another way, you must develop *taste.*

How does one do that? The authors believe that good taste—good judgment about artistic matters—comes from a thorough knowledge of style. As you learn more and more music, drawing distinctions between historical periods and particular composers, you will gain more and more insight about these questions.

PREPARING FOR A CADENCE

Approaching a cadence is much like making a ritard. Once again, you signal any alteration of the pulse about a beat before you want your musicians to make the change.

Think what it is you are going to do next. Is this the end of the work? If it is, you will sustain the final chord, release it, and "freeze" for a moment (in order not to "break the spell") until the audience has time to react. Are you shifting instead to a different tempo? In that event, you should be trying to "hear" in your mind the pulse and the subdivision for the next section. Even if you are going to continue at the same pace, you should be considering the preparatory beat for the next phrase. You do not want your musicians to "sit" unthinkingly on a long note. Neither should you do so.

THE "FINAL NOTE"

In general, the longer the work, movement, or section being completed, the longer it is justifiable to hold the final chord. That is only a rule of thumb, however; there certainly are good reasons sometimes for dramatically snapping off the end of a long movement, and, conversely, there will be occasions when you want to sustain the closing sonority of a relatively short piece. The important thing is to listen, and to know what you want to hear.

Commonly, a final chord is notated with a fermata above it, indicating that you are to hold that sonority as long as you think best. Beyond the musical judgments we have already discussed, there are practical considerations here: Are your singers or wind players running out of breath? Will your string players have to change bows? Consider those issues, and be aware of them as you conduct rehearsals and performances.

In any event, to conduct this final chord, you strike its initial beat, rebound, and then move your hand slowly away from the point of the rebound until time for the release. (The direction of this motion depends on the dynamic level and on the kind of cutoff you will be using.) *Do not continue the beat pattern through this sustained note;* if all the musicians are sustaining a long note, there is no need for you to beat time, and, as we have been saying, it is the essence of good conducting to make no unnecessary (and hence confusing) gestures. Support the note with them by slowly moving your baton a short distance, parallel to the conducting plane.

If a composer has given no indication that the final chord is to be held beyond its notated value, you may prefer to count it out exactly in your mind; nevertheless, you should not beat out its duration for the ensemble. Your gesture in this case is the same slow motion away from the rebound toward the cutoff.

A REPERTOIRE OF CUTOFFS

The technique of releases, or "cutoffs," is relatively simple. The basic gesture is a small loop around the impact point of the beat on which you want the release. Often, it can be done with the wrist alone (and in quick or light releases, a tiny flick of the wrist will be quite enough). See Figure 6-1.

Cutoffs occur on every beat of the measure, not just on the downbeat. Figures 6-2, 6-3, and 6-4 illustrate other possibilities. The same procedure applies to other beats, whatever the meter.

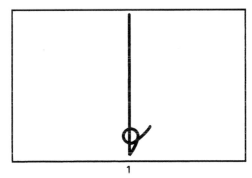

Figure 6-1 A cutoff on the downbeat

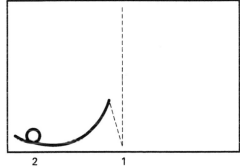

Figure 6-2 A cutoff on the second beat

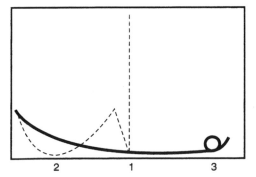

Figure 6-3 A cutoff on the third beat

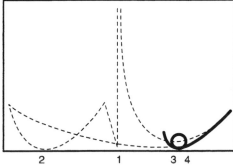

Figure 6-4 A cutoff on the fourth beat

There is a general guideline for shaping cutoffs: *The end of the cutoff motion depends on where you want the baton to be for your next gesture.* Consider what that next gesture must be. Is it a preparatory beat? On what pulse must it take place? Now you know which way your cutoff must move.

Practice Exercise 6-1   *Cutoffs on Various Beats*

Conduct the following patterns, giving a cutoff on the beat shown in each case. Then (since you must be able to show a release on any beat in any meter) follow the same regimen in $\frac{2}{4}$, $\frac{3}{4}$, $\frac{6}{8}$, $\frac{9}{8}$, $\frac{5}{4}$, and $\frac{7}{4}$. Do so daily, until your gestures seem comfortable and automatic.

$\frac{4}{4}$ ♩♩♩♩|♩♩♩♩|/ $\frac{4}{4}$ ♩♩♩♩♩|♩/

$\frac{4}{4}$ ♩♩♩♩|♩♩/ $\frac{4}{4}$ ♩♩♩♩|♩♩♩/

THE FERMATA

The "bird's-eye," or *fermata*, is an instruction to hold a sonority for a longer duration than the rhythmic notation indicates. Since the composer could stipulate exactly how long to sustain any note simply by tying it over as many times as necessary, the fermata also implies that it is up to the conductor to decide when to release it. (Sometimes, composers do provide further instruction: They may write two fermata signs side by side, or they may add the word *longa*.)

As with the final chords we have discussed, one generally does not conduct a beat pattern through a fermata. (There are rare exceptions.) Make no unnecessary gestures.

Fermatas abound in music and occur in at least three characteristic situations.

1. The fermata is placed on a final chord.
2. The music continues after the "bird's-eye," following a one-pulse release, or "breath."
3. The music continues immediately afterward, with no break after the fermata.

In every musical situation, be sure you know which type of fermata is present, and practice your baton motion accordingly. If the music terminates here, how long do you want the final note to last, and what sort of final cutoff will you use? If the music continues, does the release serve also as a preparatory beat? In such a case, your cutoff must end in such a position as to prepare the next entrance.

Work painstakingly at this technique! The fermata is a constant factor in conducting, and it occurs in circumstances dangerous enough to create real problems for the unprepared conductor.

Example 6-1　A variety of fermatas

<hr>

Practice Exercise 6-2　*Conducting the Fermata*

Conduct Example 6-1 until you are skillful at it. Note that the first fermata should be released with your baton in a convenient position to deliver a preparatory stroke on the first beat of the measure. Note also that there is to be no cutoff after the second fermata; keep your hand moving slowly through the third beat, and then show the fourth beat as a preparation.

<hr>

THE FADEOUT

Occasionally, you will have a cadence on which you want the sound to die away. This may be implied by a series of diminuendos to *p, pp, ppp,* and so on, or it may be marked "perdendo" or "perdendosi." (This effect works best when all the musicians are sustaining a final sonority.) The ideal here is to avoid making a gesture that shows the audience the music is over; no actual cutoff is used—no loop—but the baton moves in toward the body of the conductor until the sound vanishes.

Example 6-2　A fadeout, with ritard and fermata

<hr>

Practice Exercise 6-3　*Conducting a Fadeout*

Example 6-2 really is an exercise in disciplining the specific size of your beat. Try it two ways: First ignore the diminuendo marks, and go abruptly to each new dynamic level, cutting the size of your strokes as you do so. Then start again, this time reducing the size of your strokes evenly, from beat to beat, in a constant flow. And hide the final cutoff with your body!

ADDING ACCENTS

Not all notes in a melodic line should have the same value—the same importance. We need points of emphasis. One way of lending emphasis to individual sonorities is to add weight, power, or length in a process we call *accenting*.

There are at least two kinds of accents with which we need be concerned: When we add loudness to a particular note, we create a "dynamic accent," and when we increase a note's duration, we produce an "agogic accent." (We have already spoken about a form of the latter, in effect, in our discussion of the tenuto.)

We can show several kinds of dynamic emphasis in the baton; these include the sforzando *(sfz* or *Sf)*, the fortepiano *(fp)*, the wedge (ᵛ), and the accent itself (>). The gesture is much the same for all four, though the vigor and the size of the stroke vary.

1. You must signal the coming stress point one beat early, flicking the wrist sharply on that pulse. That wrist motion adds the *appearance* of weight to the beat we want to emphasize.
2. Now enlarge the rebound from the beat.
3. Next, stop the baton briefly at the peak of your rebound.
4. Finally, speed up the stroke to the next beat.

Suppose you find a *wedge* on the third pulse of a $\frac{4}{4}$ measure. To conduct that properly, you will flick the wrist at the second beat, rebound more than usual from that pulse point, stop the baton very briefly at the end of the rebound, and then throw the stick across quickly to the third beat. (See Figure 6-5.)

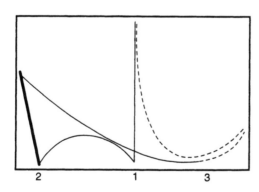

| 2 | 1 | 3 | **Figure 6-5** Conducting dynamic accents |

For the *accent*, the procedure is exactly the same, but with a bit more energy: more of a thrust at the second beat, more of a rebound, a slightly longer stop, and a longer, faster stroke to the next beat. The *fortepiano* is conducted with still more size and vigor, and the *sforzando* more yet.

Beginning conductors try to show the accent on the beat that they want to stress. By the time the accented pulse is about to sound, it is too late to signal

---

Practice Exercise 6-4 *Conducting Dynamic Accents*

Follow the same procedures as in Practice Exercise 6-1, for the same reason; you must be able to show an accent clearly on any beat in any meter. Start with $\frac{4}{4}$, run through all four beats, and then go through all the time signatures shown in Exercise 6-1.

---

the musicians. The warning you want to give them *must* come a full beat before the event.

(In both *fp* and *sfzp*, conductors may find it necessary to use the left hand to show the subsequent *p*.)

THE SUBITO COMMANDS

Just as the dynamic accents are prepared one beat early, so the *sub. p* and the *sub. f* are signaled on the pulse before the event itself. In a shift from *p* to *sub. f*, the rebound of the beat before the change is enlarged to the size of your usual *f* beat pattern. There is no "hitch" or halt in the baton's motion. In a shift from *f* to *sub. p*, the rebound is drastically shortened so that it is consistent with your *p* beat pattern; a sudden lifting of the open palm of the left hand will help to quiet the ensemble.

Example 6-3 A succession of subito commands

Practice Exercise 6-5 *Conducting the Subito Commands*

You find in Example 6-3 a succession of three subito markings. Check the circumstances of the preceding beat (where you will show the subito) in each case. When you feel confident you can do this exercise gracefully, try arbitrarily shifting the subito markings to other beats; what problems does this raise? Don't forget the final diminuendo.

MORE CONDUCTING THEORY
The Rhetoric of the Phrase

Just as we have said that some notes in a melodic line are more important than others, we may say that some cadences in a musical structure are of more significance than others. (You know that, of course, for you realize that both the cadence at the end of an exposition section and the final chord of a work are more important than the cadence at the end of the first phrase of the same work.)

Cadences have individual values, then, much like those represented by punctuation in verbal communication. When the English call a period at the end of a sentence a "full stop," they are recognizing that it symbolizes more of a termination than does a comma or a semicolon. Similarly, in music, we have cadences we can call weak, strong, and terminal.

As a conductor, you must learn to tell the difference. The kinds and amounts of emphasis you apply to certain points in a given work will depend on your view of its structure. (In choral music, the punctuation of the text can appear to give us clues to the architecture of the work, but that can be misleading; the musical design and the sentence structure of the text often have little in common.) We believe you will find it useful to think of verbal punctuation—especially the comma, the semicolon, and the period—as metaphors for the strength of cadences, the length of some fermatas, the duration of some silences within the music, and other such phenomena. We will have more to say on this subject as we undertake the analysis of specific works in later chapters.

Example 6-4   Relative importance of four cadences

Practice Exercise 6-6 *Communicating Structure by Expressing the Relative Importance of Its Cadences*

Conduct Example 6-4 several times, being careful to observe the tenutos in bars 4 and 12, the fermata in measure 8, and the ritard and *longa fermata* in the final bar. Notice how this handling of the cadences seems to make the structure of this simple form more audible.

SILENCE CAN BE MUSIC, TOO

You can use the silences that occur from time to time in music as another means of making clear the structure of the work at hand. Just as you can lend emphasis to certain cadences, using them as "punctuation" within the architecture of the music, so you can make some moments of silence more significant than others.

Practice Exercise 6-7 *Communicating Structure by Expressing the Relative Importance of Silences*

Again conduct Example 6-4 several times, this time ignoring the indicated tenutos, ritards, and fermatas. Instead, conducting with metronomic regularity, manage the cutoffs in bars 4, 8, 12, and 16 so that the structure is again made more audible. Specifically, use brief, last-minute cutoffs in measures 4 and 12, and a somewhat longer one in bar 8, and then do not drop your arms too quickly after the final cutoff, so that the silences will acquire greater or lesser relative value.

Obviously, there can be no "dynamic accents" here, for one silence cannot be louder than another, but agogic stress is possible; the pauses between phrases and sections can vary in length if you wish it so.

You also must learn to use silence for its dramatic power. Look at Example 6-5. The fermata in measure 2 comes on a dissonance; a silence after this cutoff, one longer than the listener expects, adds to the excitement of the context.

Example 6-5   A fermata on a dissonance

Practice Exercise 6-8   *Conducting Dramatic Silences*

Conduct Example 6-5 several times, making a cutoff in measure 2 and trying various
lengths of silence at the end of that bar.

Learn to *listen* to the silences in music. Some of them are boundaries, as we
have seen. Others are landmarks—dramatic towers within the scene you are
painting. Still other silences are part of the continuity. Teach your musicians to
understand that *not all breaths or changes of bow interrupt a phrase; well-timed silences—silences that are rhythmic—can be part of the flow of a phrase*, along with the
half notes and the eighths!

PREPARING A COMPLETE WORK
FOR PERFORMANCE

Although you may not be ready to undertake an extended work, you can begin
to tackle real, complete musical structures. Look carefully and thoroughly at
Example 6-6.

One must know as much as possible about a work before one performs it,
and a sure understanding of its style will suggest particular conducting approaches.[1] What follows, then, is a concise analysis intended to prepare you to attempt to conduct your first complete piece of music.[2]

The seventh movement of Bach's *St. John Passion*, "O grosse Lieb'" ("O
Great Love") is based on a melody by Johann Krüger and a text by Johann Hermann, the sixth and seventh stanzas of "Herzliebster Jesu." (The chorale returns
as No. 27 later in the work.) Note that the rhyme scheme is *aabb*. There appear to
be four phrases, with eleven syllables for each of the first three of them but only
five for the last.

The meter is $\frac{4}{4}$. The rhythmic motion is in constant quarter notes, embellished by a few decorative eighths, and interrupted only by the fermatas, of
which there are five, the first four falling on third beats.

Melodically, the soprano line covers just more than an octave, the alto part
an eleventh, the tenors (who have the highest tessitura) a ninth to a high G, and
the basses a tenth. There is one beat in bar 9 at which point the tenors cross under
the written bass part. Most of the melodic motion is stepwise and diatonic, but
there are consecutive half steps (measure 5), and other chromatic figures can surprise singers: Note the alternation of E-flats and E-naturals in the upper voices of
bars 7 and 8, for example. Most of the skips are resolved in traditional fashion.

[1]See the "spiral study" concept, and the related discussion, in Chapter 1.
[2]Note that either an entire class can sing this chorale while individual students conduct or the
chorale can be played by piano, strings, or other instruments.

The harmonies Bach has employed to set this chorale are quite chromatic; all twelve tones are used—not an unusual occurrence in Bach—in these eleven measures. The tonic is G, beginning in minor, with the first two fermatas falling on dominant triads. The second full phrase shifts to the relative major (B-flat), and the third remains there (somewhat ambiguously); the final phrase returns to G, but on a major triad.

Example 6-6 J. S. Bach: "O grosse Lieb' " (chorale from the *St. John Passion*, BWV 245), complete

What about the structure of this chorale? Perhaps the most surprising feature of the chorale lies in its proportions: The last phrase, compared with the first three, is short. The tonal organization, taken together with the rhyme scheme, suggests that the fermata in measure 6 is the most important internal cadence.

Fermatas in Bach chorales do not always imply an interruption of the meter, by the way. Bach wrote some of them simply to mark ends of phrases for congregational singing; in such cases, they merely reflected tradition. Other "bird's-eyes," however, relate importantly to textual meaning, phraseology, or both, and thus are *musically* significant; they can be used to help define the structure of a work, for example. Which are which is then a matter of interpretation, and the responsibility for those decisions is yours.

This kind of structural analysis—to which you may wish to add a textual study—is a necessary foundation for your conducting of even so brief a work. You need to do more. You should examine and compare more Bach works (and those of other Baroque composers), especially chorale settings, with this particular example. Only when you have seen many such works can you say confidently to yourself that you know how to interpret this one.

Conducting the Chorale

Building on this interpretive foundation, then, you are ready to consider the technical aspects of conducting the chorale.

It is obvious that you will use a four-beat pattern, probably legato in character. Since the first attack is a pickup on four, you will need a preparatory beat on three—a beat keyed in size to the dynamic level with which you wish to begin. Thus, the ensemble is set in motion.

How will you handle the fermatas? One choice would be to make the most important ones, structurally, longer than the others. If the formal design of the chorale is divided tonally and textually (by the rhyme scheme) at the end of bar 6, then it follows that you might make the third and fifth fermatas the longest.

Working on this premise, you could give the first fermata two full counts. (Always cut bird's-eyes off exactly on a beat, not midway between pulses.) Two beats for the second one, and three for the one in bar 6, followed by two again for the next-to-last fermata (measure 9) would maintain the plan; then the final chord could be given five or six counts.

Why is the first fermata there, so early in the music? If you have examined No. 27 in the *St. John Passion*, the other use of this chorale, you will know: Bach placed it there for the sake of the text. No such early bird's-eye occurs in the later movement.

You have studied fermata technique in this chapter, and you already know what to do in measure 1: Stop the baton as it strikes the conducting plane exactly on the third pulse; hold it there for your two-count bird's-eye, and then—with a tiny flick of the wrist to release the singers—continue the third beat-stroke, letting it rebound to the right edge of the frame. This rebound constitutes the preparatory beat for the entrance on the fourth pulse.

The process is much the same for the fermatas in bars 3, 6, and 9, save that *the baton should come to a full stop only on brief fermatas. On longer ones it should move slightly.* If it does not, there is a risk the musicians will let the intensity and forward momentum slacken. Especially on the bird's-eye in bar 6, you will want to keep the stick moving slightly, perhaps even ascending a bit, to keep the dynamic level and concentration up. On the final chord, then, you will want to move the baton very slowly, but with intensity, through to the final release.

Where should the singers breathe? In this chorale, it seems clear that the breath points are the bird's-eyes. Your musicians can use various types of breaths, by the way, depending on interpretation and text; you can see, for example, that the air intake before the last phrase is necessarily different from the one in measure 3.

We need a concept of dynamic shape, too. The first bar could be introductory—almost a preface—begun (because of the nature of the text) at a *p* or a *mp*. A gradual and modest crescendo could then follow the rising soprano line from bar 2 through the second fermata to perhaps a *f* just before the important cadence in measure 6; the end of the phrase here should taper back a bit. Now the dynamic level can recede through bars 6, 7, and 8 to the cadence in measure 9, back to the original *p* or *mp*, setting up the final phrase.

Save energy for the ending here. The starkness of the last clause of the text justifies a sudden increase in strength. You could attack the pickup to bar 10—using a larger preparatory beat—at a *mf* or so, allowing a diminuendo through the closing two measures.

This final phrase deserves more *time.* You would be justified in taking it *slightly* slower, and then adding a ritard. Start your rallentando on the second or third beat of measure 10; don't overdo it, for this is a short work and you can easily pull it out of proportion.

Throughout the chorale, **your baton must outline the dynamic contour of the music—now a larger beat for greater harmonic, melodic, or textural movement, now a smaller gesture for a quieter passage.** Yet the stick must always maintain a certain level of intensity in its motion. It describes the music.

CHAPTER 7

The Left Hand: Adding Emphasis

Now ("At last!" you may be thinking) we are ready for you to rediscover your left hand. You are going to acquire skills with it that will be of great benefit to you as a conductor. Nevertheless, always remember that *you have been able to conduct effectively without using it.*

The left hand is a bête noire, a formidable and troublesome problem for many inexperienced conductors. You might assume that is because most people are right-handed, but that really has nothing to do with the matter. Even conductors who are themselves left-handed find difficulty here, for skill with the "other hand" is not primarily a question of dexterity (or ambidexterity); rather, you must develop the independence of your left hand and a clear concept of that hand's unique function within your conducting technique.

Most beginning conductors are told, "If you don't know what to do with your left hand, put it in your pocket!" They also hear that "the worst use you can make of it is to let it mirror the motions of the right." Both those slogans are too simple. Let us forget them and start afresh.

THE LEFT HAND AT REST

In conducting, your right hand is always active. It takes the position of attention, delivers the preparatory beats, traces the beat patterns, controls alterations of the pulse, signals dynamics and cues, gives cutoffs, and manages all the other techniques we have been discussing.

Your left hand, by contrast, is not needed all the time. There are many passages in which you and your ensemble can communicate well without it. What should you do with it at such moments?

If your left hand is not in use for a time, its natural resting point is near your belt buckle, elbow bent, palm down. (See Figure 7-1.) It is perfectly acceptable, however, for your left arm to hang naturally at your side if you feel more comfortable that way.

Figure 7-1 The left hand
at rest

MORE CONDUCTING THEORY
The Uses of the Left Hand

The prime function of the left hand is to add emphasis to the directions you give with your right, not to replace it. The left hand can enlarge and clarify your wishes and worries, call special situations to the attention of the musicians, and focus on one set of nuances while the baton deals with another.

The left hand can be useful especially when you need to deliver separate instructions to two different sections of your ensemble at once. It can coordinate balance, for example, by shushing the first violins at the same time your stick is encouraging the 'cellos. It can warn of something that is about to happen. The left especially is practical for signaling

1. Cues
2. Releases

3. Dynamics
4. Crescendos and diminuendos
5. Accents
6. Sudden changes of all kinds
7. Word stresses and unstresses in texts
8. Phrase shapes

Your left hand gives you an excellent means of dealing with emergencies. At such moments, you must depend on your right hand to maintain autonomously its assigned beat pattern while you consciously direct your left into the gestures that can correct the problem. These urgent situations can be as minor as a too-loud trumpet or as severe as an early entrance by a soloist; when they occur, you must be able to "pounce" on them with whichever hand is more convenient in the circumstance.

THE "CHOREOGRAPHY" OF THE LEFT HAND

Appearance counts for something, too, whenever one stands before the public. Do not be careless about anything that can affect the joy your audience gains from your *whole* performance.

Take, for example, the way you shape your left hand. Like a serious dancer, you need to give some careful thought to making the hand without the baton look graceful.

Practice Exercise 7-1   *Finding a Comfortable Shape for Your Left Hand*

Stand in front of a mirror. Let your left arm hang straight down at your side. Notice that the middle and ring fingers almost touch each other, while the thumb and the index and fifth fingers remain somewhat separated. Next, bring the hand up to shirt-pocket height, maintaining this position. Your hand now curves gracefully.

Be conscious of your appearance in rehearsal and onstage. Watch trained dancers and imitate their gracefulness. Fine actors and singers understand these things, too, and work on their hand gestures. Learn from such people.

THE PROBLEM OF "MIRRORING"

Moving both hands at once through the beat pattern, the left hand moving backward, is called "mirroring"; one often sees amateur conductors do this. Mirroring generally should be avoided. It is a wasteful pattern, since it ties the left hand to the right in a duplicative effort; thus, it violates our rule that *good conductors make no unnecessary gestures.* Worse, it makes one look awkward and inexperienced.

Many people who mirror their hands when they conduct do so out of habit only. Don't develop that mannerism. Learn to use your left hand only when it is genuinely needed.

Once you have developed the skills you need to conduct in the most efficient ways, you will find that there are a *few* circumstances in which mirroring actually can be useful: In the conducting of a very large ensemble, for example, where the group is staged in such a wide arrangement that it is difficult for those on your far left to see some of the nuances in your baton, you may need to duplicate your beat patterns in your left hand. Similarly, mirroring can be helpful in conducting an opera or a musical comedy; in a narrow, dark orchestra pit, you may have people to your far left who, having trouble with depth perception through their stand lights, will have trouble distinguishing (in $\frac{4}{4}$) the second pulse from the fourth on the far side of your body. You also may need to mirror (very briefly) when you want to turn yourself directly toward the right side of your chorus or orchestra (toward the 'cellos, for instance); beating the pattern with your left hand (almost behind your back), in such a case, will let you "stay with" the first violins, making certain they can see your beat clearly. There are other appropriate occasions to mirror, but they are rare exceptions!

INDEPENDENCE OF THE LEFT HAND

Autonomy of the left hand is the first requirement in developing essential skills in the left hand. By now, your right hand should be working automatically much of the time. It should not need your constant conscious supervision as it shows all the gestures we have discussed already. The left hand—and all your concentration—should be freed to focus on other things.

This need for your hands to be independent of each other should not surprise you. You know that instrumentalists must have this sort of autonomy; their hands must be able to move in opposite directions or make radically different motions; at the same time, both their hands must be able to carry out quite minute, specific, and exacting operations. (Think of a 'cellist maintaining a legato bowing with the right hand while the left provides rapid, precise fingerings and the tremolo, for example.) You must develop an equivalent freedom.

Try the Practice Exercises that follow. You may find them difficult, but keep working on them. In time, you will find that you are able to do these things and that the autonomy involved applies directly to problems you face every day as a conductor.

Practice Exercise 7-2   *Left Hand Circles/Right Hand Beat Patterns*

For basic independence and control over both hands, try to maintain a clear, clean $\frac{4}{4}$ pattern with your right hand while your left moves in a large, counterclockwise circle at a pace that brings it exactly to the top of that circle just as your right strikes each downbeat.

   Now do the same exercise, reversing the direction of the left hand. Then try the same exercise in $\frac{2}{4}$, $\frac{3}{4}$, and $\frac{5}{4}$.

Practice Exercise 7-3   *Left Hand Straight Up/Right Hand Beat Patterns*

Starting with your left hand at the height of your belt, bring it straight up to eye level while beating one measure of $\frac{4}{4}$ with the right hand; next bar, take it straight back to your waistline.

Practice Exercise 7-4   *Left Hand Cueing Gestures/Right Hand Beat Patterns*

Starting with the left hand at your waist, raise it to a cueing position, straight out from the shoulder, while beating one measure of $\frac{3}{4}$ with the right hand; next bar, take it straight back to your beltline.

Practice Exercise 7-5   *Autonomy in Changing Meters*

Repeat Practice Exercise 7-4, but this time alternate measures of $\frac{4}{4}$, $\frac{3}{4}$, and $\frac{2}{4}$ (in that order) with your right hand.

   Next, try this while alternating bars of $\frac{3}{4}$, $\frac{5}{4}$, and $\frac{9}{4}$.

Practice Exercise 7-6   *Using the Left Hand to Signal Dynamic Changes*

While your right hand maintains a $\frac{4}{4}$ pattern, start your left hand at breastbone height, palm up, and move it slowly, according to the alternate dynamic patterns shown below. Then repeat this exercise, beating patterns of $\frac{2}{4}$, $\frac{3}{4}$, $\frac{5}{4}$, and a slow $\frac{6}{8}$.

1. *p* —————————— *f*   2. *mf* ——————————— *pp*

3. *mf* ——— *ff* ———— *mf*   4. *p* ——————————— *f*   *sub. p*

EFFECTIVE CUEING GESTURES

Some misunderstand the purposes of giving cues. Musicians usually know when they are to enter the ensemble fabric. Fine professionals always do. It is not just to save them from counting measures and rhythms that you signal their entrances and releases.

With cues, you tell them exactly *how* to attack, as well as when—how loudly, with what sort of articulation, with what sort of tone quality, in what balance, and more. If the entrance is a risky one, high and very soft, or otherwise dangerous, your cue can be reassuring and encouraging. Cues can clarify rhythmic features like syncopation and hemiolas and can define phrase shape. You can focus attention on almost any feature of the music at hand with this procedure if you are adept at it, and you must learn to be, for **cueing is a vital part of the whole dialogue between you and your ensemble.**

Avoid pointing at your musicians with the index finger of your left hand, for this can look graceless. "Invitations" to enter, extended with the palm up, may look more refined. If you want to point, do so with the tip of the baton, aiming either at a section or at an individual. There are eye cues, too, and your face can be marvelously expressive, conveying an enormous range of subtlety and nuance—eyebrows up for a soft entrance, or glowering for a *fortissimo* attack. And you are most efficient and expressive, of course, when you are able to combine those techniques, using the whole body as an instrument with which you can communicate.

Like all other important signals you send to your ensemble, *cues must be given one beat before the event itself.* It does no good at all to throw an index finger at a section that is already beginning a phrase, or to stress in your beat a pulse it is already too late to accent.

In the Practice Exercises that follow, imagine your cue is going to a particular section, and visualize where that section is in your supposed ensemble. Make certain those individuals see clearly the signal you are sending.

Practice Exercise 7-7   *Giving Cues with the Left Hand*

Conduct the metric patterns below. Use your left hand (palm up in an invitatory position) to cue, on the beats marked with an X, various (imaginary) sections of your ensemble. Once you have done these, invent others.

$\frac{4}{4}$ – – – – | – – – X | – – – X | – – – X | – – X –

$\frac{3}{4}$ – – – | – X – | – – X | – – – | X – – | – X – | – – X

$\frac{6}{8}$ – – | – X | – – | X – | – X | – X | – X | X – | – X | – X

$\frac{6}{4}$ – – X – – – | – X – – – – | X – – X – – | – X – X – –

$\frac{9}{8}$ – – – X – – X – – | X – – – – X – – X | – X – – X – – X –

Practice Exercise 7-8   *Cueing Hemiolas with the Left Hand*

Signal with your left hand the hemiolas indicated by each X in the metric patterns below.
Try this exercise at a variety of tempos and dynamic levels.

Andante
$\frac{3}{4}$ --- |--- |--X |-X- |--X |-X- |-

Allegro (in two)
$\frac{6}{8}$ ------ |--X-X- |--X-X- |-

Langsam
$\frac{2}{2}$ -- |-- |-- |X- |-X |-- |X

Practice Exercise 7-9   *Cutoffs with the Left Hand*

While conducting a $\frac{3}{4}$ pattern with your right hand, give cutoffs with your left hand on
the third beat of each measure. Repeat the drill, moving the cutoffs to 2, and then to 1.
    Now alternate $\frac{4}{4}$, $\frac{3}{4}$, and $\frac{2}{4}$ with your right hand while placing cutoffs with your
left hand on the second beat of each bar.

Practice Exercise 7-10   *Using the Left Hand to Cue Subito Dynamic Changes*

Against a steady beat in your right hand, signal with your left hand the expressive
markings shown.

Adagio (in four)
$\frac{4}{4}$ ---- |---- |---- |---- |
     p   *cresc.*   *f*   *sub. p*
---- |---- |---- |---- |
     sfz sfz   sfz   sfz
---- |---- |---- |---- ||
  cresc.   *mf dimin.   pp*

Allegro moderato (in two)
$\frac{6}{8}$ ------ |------ |------ |------ |
  f   *sub. p*   *sub. f*   *sfz*
------ |------ |------ |------ |
   dimin.   *pp   sfz*   *sfz*
------ |------ |------ |------ ||
   sfz   cresc.   *ff*

EMERGENCIES

Late entrances—in theory—should never happen if the musicians are watching you and you are cueing them. The most common emergencies, then, are premature attacks and faulty dynamics.

Early entrances can be stopped with the left hand raised, the palm toward the offender(s). Once you have stopped them, you must cue them again, of course, for they are disoriented at such a point—probably thoroughly lost. Overloud musicians are corrected in the same way, and timid ones are encouraged with the palm-up, invitatory gesture (wiggling the fingers, if more is still needed).

Practice Exercise 7-11   *The Ultimate Test of Left Hand Autonomy*

Once you have achieved good independence between your left and right hands, see if you can keep a $\frac{6}{4}$ pattern going in your right hand while carrying on a game of tic-tac-toe with your left hand on a blackboard. Make sure you win!

CONDUCTING A COMPLETE WORK, USING BOTH HANDS

As with the Bach chorale at the end of Chapter 6, you are to study and conduct Example 7-1; the difference in this case is that you are to use both your hands. We have a second purpose in presenting "O Beautiful for Spacious Skies" as your second complete work: Every conductor has to lead a choir or an audience in this (and "The Star-Spangled Banner") sometime. It will be good for you to think carefully about it for a few minutes.

"Materna," the hymn-tune by Samuel A. Ward, was composed as the setting of a sacred text in 1882. Ward's hymn became more famous, however, when it was coupled with this text by Katherine Lee Bates.

The soprano line has more skips than the Bach chorale "O grosse Lieb'," but these leaps invariably are triadic, which makes them easier for the singers, in general, than Bach's are. There are more repeated notes here, too. The soprano line peaks on D-natural in bars 7 and 9; the first six bars center on F-natural, bars 7 and 8 on C-natural; measures 9 and 10 fall from the D to A-natural; and 11 to 16 center on B-flat.

Example 7-1   Ward: "O Beautiful for Spacious Skies" (complete)

Metrically, we have here a standard $\frac{4}{4}$. The rhythms are simple, and much more repetitive than those of the Bach chorale. Note that the rhythm of the soprano line is exactly the same for each of the four staves; this contributes, if you wish it, to the listener's sense of four-bar phrases. None of Bach's fermatas appear here.

The tonal organization is straightforward. The first line cadences on the tonic, B-flat, and then shifts to the dominant to kick off the second line, which moves through a V/V (C^7 chord) in bar 7 to the dominant in measure 8. Another cadence on the tonic comes in bar 12 (and up to this point we have had virtually nothing but I and V chords); then the first real subdominant arrives in measure 13, and we move through four beats of unisons in bar 15 to the final cadence on the tonic. The sonorities used, and the harmonic progressions moving through them, certainly are typical of a nineteenth-century hymn.

The texture is quite homophonic. All four parts maintain the same rhythm all the time, save for the embellished cadences in bars 4, 8, and 12, which serve to keep harmonic motion from bogging down. As for tessituras, the sopranos and altos each cover a ninth, the tenors only a fifth (a dull, narrow part to sing), and the basses—with their low F-naturals—a full eleventh.

As for the text, the rhyme scheme is *ab ab cd ed* for each of the four verses, the *c* being the "refrain" words "America! America!" every time. There are fourteen syllables per line, always divided as 8 + 6. The phraseology of the four verses is strikingly different: Following the punctuation bar by bar, one finds good opportunities to vary the phrasing.

Verse 1: 2 – 2 – 4 – – – 1 1 2 – 4 – – –
Verse 2: 2 – 6 – – – – – 1 1 2 – 2 – 2 –
Verse 3: 4 – – – 2 – 2 – 1 1 2 – 2 – 2 –
Verse 4: 6 – – – – – 2 – 1 1 2 – 4 – – –

Thus, no two verses are alike, with six-bar phrases occurring in two of them; but the rhythm and the punctuation of the "refrain" in measures 9 and 10 are unchanging.

Structurally, the music is made up of four phrases, each begun by the dotted-quarter motive from measure 1. That motive, with its downward-third skip, occurs in measures 1, 5, and 13, and variants of it appear in 2, 6, 9, 10, and 14. Note, by the way, that in measures 9–11, the basses are given the *exact* soprano line from bars 1–3.

Conducting Choices

A basic aspect of your interpretation of any work is your choice of articulation. Will you perform this hymn legato, slightly marcato, or otherwise? If you are to conduct more than one verse, you may decide to vary the articulation, stanza by stanza.

A second set of primary choices relates to dynamics. We suggest that one verse could begin *p*, shift to *mp* for the pickup to bar 5, crescendo to *mf* on the pickup to bar 7, build to *f* for measures 9 and 10, and diminuendo to *mf* for the last line. Again, the dynamics could be revised for each verse; this is another way to bring some variety to the musical and textual repetitions.

A third principal concern, and another approach to adding variety to this structure, lies in its phrasing. Which commas, if any, will you choose to elide? You can make use, of course, of the textual phraseology described above. Another possibility is to bring out (in one of the stanzas) the special bass line we noticed in bars 9–11. You must decide, too, if you want (for one or more verses) releases in both bar 9 and bar 10.

All the preparatory beats come on the third pulse, since each phrase begins on the fourth.

And what about your left hand? How can you use it to focus and clarify?

1. You should use it to signal any crescendos and diminuendos, raising and lowering your arm as you have practiced. Your left hand also can correct any problems with dynamics.
2. You can use it to mark releases for the cadences. If you are going to observe the comma in bar 2 (verse 1), show the release with your left hand, as well as the baton; then, by contrast, hold it out (palm up) to ensure that there will be no break in measure 6. All the variant phrasings in the four verses can be clarified by the left hand. (Most of them are merely breath marks in duration.)
3. If you want to strengthen the attack at the pickup to bar 9, because of the peaking melodic line at that point, you might choose to mirror your right hand with your left for just that pickup and the first beat of bar 9.

Whichever stanza is the final one, you may want to indicate a ritard for the last three beats or so of measure 15. Then you could place a fermata on the final sonority, holding it for five or six counts. Do not let this last chord sag. Use your left hand to help support and sustain the energy and intensity to the end.

Have you compared this hymn with the Bach chorale in Chapter 6? Although some features are similar (the attacks on fourth beats, for example), the absence of fermatas in Ward's hymn is a major difference in motion and phrasing; each bird's-eye in the Bach slows the momentum, whereas the constant motion in the lower three parts of the Ward pushes along from phrase to phrase. Look carefully to see what other characteristics make these two styles distinct.

This may seem to you to be a surprisingly exhaustive analysis for such a simple hymn. (We have studied this work just as carefully as we did the Bach chorale.) **Everything you conduct, whether it is by a great master or by an amateur, deserves the same uncompromising and exacting consideration.** Do not mislead yourself. Nothing less will do.

CHAPTER *8*

Leadership

Conducting is Leadership. The maestro, baton in hand, is the very image of the leader. In a glance, the audience sees authority, confidence, energy, decisiveness, and related qualities radiating from the self-assured, dynamic figure on the podium. The performers recognize the same attributes, discern the conductor's wishes, and respond appropriately, willing to be guided. That is the ideal.

Can you become a leader? Are there "born leaders," as one sometimes reads, or is leadership based on techniques you can learn? Must you have a certain type of personality? Be cocksure and brash? An extrovert? A tyrant?

CHARACTERISTIC COMPONENTS OF LEADERSHIP

To be accepted as a leader by musicians, the conductor must represent *authority;* that is, he or she must be thought to be expert in the music to be performed. Whether the ensemble involved is the Vienna Philharmonic or an elementary school band, its director must seem to know more about the works at hand than any of the players involved. The conductor who appears to be less authoritative than his players is virtually forced to plead for credibility from musicians who believe they know more.

There are two basic kinds of authority: genuine and false. To really know the music, its style, and its performance practice better than anyone else present is to be in a position of true strength, able to depend on one's insights in moment-to-moment decisions as well as in the planning of an interpretation. Like the surgeon, the conductor must master the structure and style of a broad discipline, and then must bring that experience discerningly to bear on the particular work at hand.

To pretend to knowledge, on the other hand, is to risk being "unmasked" by a better musician at any second of a rehearsal or a performance. Little things trip up the poorly prepared conductor: wrong notes written in unfamiliar clefs, missing measures in one part, unnoticed transpositions, and the like. The musicians tend to trust the pretender at first; gradually, surprised as evidences of sloppiness or sheer ignorance develop, they become quizzical, then suspicious, and eventually cynical. With his or her image of authority lost, such an individual is left with no real possibility of success with that ensemble.

The conductor also represents *initiative* before the ensemble. To conduct, one must want to try out one's own ideas and to test one's skills. One does not lead by waiting for others to suggest solutions to problems.

This is not to say that ensemble performance is not a sharing of interpretations. It certainly is. (We will have more to say about this in a moment.) Nevertheless, the first conception of a work, as rehearsal begins, comes from the conductor, and the responsibility—the initiative—to accept and reject the alternatives that inevitably appear as things proceed should stay with the baton. Loss of that initiative is as destructive to the effectiveness of a conductor as loss of authority.

Command (or power to direct) arises not from the title one bears but from the *authority* and *initiative* we have been discussing. Without the image of authority, a title carries very little power; the musicians may grudgingly carry out orders, but no magic is likely to result from their efforts. And if initiative is not taken, the right to command lies unused and is without value.

The power to give orders must be employed judiciously, gracefully, and somewhat sparingly. In a good circumstance, one's musicians are colleagues and must be treated with genuine respect. Tolstoy argued that great men are borne along by the tides of history and the trends of society, and that their dictates are (when successful) merely confirmations of the public will.[1] Whether or not his somewhat extreme view is an accurate one, it is true that one's musicians bring important, valid ideas of their own to interpretation, and that those ideas may not be far from one's own.

Once those ideas have been offered, however, it is the *judgment* of the conductor—based, again, on authority and initiative—that must prevail. It is only the conductor who can "hear" the entire work in proportion and perspective. It can be difficult to maintain one's perspective all the way through a long, fragmentary rehearsal of a complicated work. One's sense of momentum through the music, one's feeling for phrase shape and for overall balance can be lost in chasing wrong notes and inaccurate rhythms. Still, it is the conductor, and *only* the conductor, whose duty it is to see that the whole work is presented as it should be, with its shape and proportions clear.

The judgment that can do this must be cool, deliberate, and intellectual. Fleeting emotionalism is not helpful. Personal motives and ego have no place here, either, nor do any other considerations that lie outside the music itself; giving a fine interpretation of a work is difficult enough without such complications.

Individual judgments must be made firmly, and must come without delay, too. *Decisiveness* is a critical quality. To appear to be unable to make up one's

---

[1]Leo Tolstoy, *War and Peace,* trans. Louise Maude and Aylmer Maude (New York: Simon & Schuster, 1942).

mind can undermine one's authority (for the musicians may think the conductor does not know enough about the music to decide the issue), and it can undercut the power to command, as well.

It is true, of course, that there are some decisions that should be postponed for a while (those that have to do with patience while one is waiting for technical growth in young musicians, for example). There are other decisions that, once made, must be reversed (perhaps because the conductor discovers problems not spotted at first). Stubbornness at such times is no virtue. The purpose of all this labor is a fine performance, not a reputation for always being right the first time.

Technical facility with the baton is absolutely necessary to leadership, of course. You as a maestro can gain esteem from ensembles for the virtuosity of your baton work. Thus, your authority and ability to command will be enhanced.

It is better (and, especially, more efficient) to let the baton do the talking. When words are necessary, however, *fluency of speech* is essential. Even those who are "naturally shy" and have little experience speaking in front of large groups must gain a certain glibness. Unexpected circumstances in a rehearsal have to be confronted and dealt with, and solutions to problems must sometimes be explained; you cannot have planned what to say at such moments; the explanation you offer must come quickly, be expressed clearly, and be effective in resolving the difficulty.

This is made easier, again, if you have a profound knowledge of the music. Almost everyone can speak at length and with spirit about favorite things.

Can Leadership, then, be learned? **All seven essential conductorial qualities—authority, initiative, command, judgment, decisiveness, technical facility with the baton, and fluency of speech—emerge from careful study and preparation of the music to be conducted,** and thus these characteristics are acquired almost automatically by those who really *learn* the works they must conduct. What is more, those who do not prepare music diligently cannot maintain the appearance of having these qualities, no matter how great their native gifts and no matter how outgoing their personalities.

You can have all these attributes. You need only to discipline your approach to the music itself.

THE PERSONALITIES OF A CONDUCTOR

Conductors find themselves in two different public situations, and that may lead them to need "split personalities."

First and foremost, they appear before audiences, of course. In this circumstance, they must always seem positive in manner, confident, serious of purpose, and pleased with the results they obtain. They must convey the impression that they are happy with the audience and delighted (if, perhaps, a little overwhelmed) with the listeners' response to their work. If the performance has not gone well, they must not show it; if one particular musician has botched something, there must be no sign that anything has gone wrong; if a disturbance happens offstage, the conductor acknowledges that something has transpired only in the most severe conditions. ("The show must go on," and it must appear to have been successful.)

All this is part of the "illusion" we in Music, Theater, and Dance are commissioned to create, and by it we move the listener out of the ordinary, routine world and into a special kingdom of Beauty.

The rehearsal hall, on the other hand, is the Realm of Reality. Here, the conductor may need to be blunt and unhappy with results—now encouraging when things are progressing slowly, now cross when sloppiness occurs. Performance is a single goal, but rehearsals are an extended evolutionary process, and so the timing and the purpose are different. Once the concert itself is over, it is finished forever, but even the final dress rehearsal is part of a transitory advance toward the performance. The conductor may end some rehearsals, then, with a statement of dissatisfaction, but public appearances aim at applause.

None of these ways of dealing with audiences and ensembles is dishonest; the listeners do not pay money for tickets to see you sulk about the stage, disappointed that *your* ideals (not necessarily theirs) were not met on this particular occasion; on the other hand, your musicians do not wish you to pretend that all is well in rehearsal when it is not. Know what you are trying to accomplish, and with whom, or you cannot lead.

ALTERNATIVE STYLES OF ENSEMBLE MANAGEMENT

In dealing with their musicians, maestros differ somewhat in personality. Some conductors act relaxed, calm, understated, and seemingly patient, and others appear fiery and energetic. Some get results by smiles of encouragement. Others curtly demand improvement. Some explode with anger.

We cannot tell you what personal styles and mannerisms are appropriate for you, but we do urge you to recognize that **every rehearsal technique you employ should be deliberate, calculated, and directed toward the results you want.** If you use a relaxed atmosphere, do so because it is the most effective way to the results you want. If you use anger, do so in cold blood, as part of your rehearsal procedure. *Avoid unplanned emotional outbursts.* (This can be difficult, for the stress of an approaching performance, and of the rehearsal itself, can cause you to lose patience; especially at such times, however, do you need to maintain control of yourself and of the circumstances.)

Should you think of yourself as "dominant" (not to say "domineering")? Should you strive for an atmosphere of collegiality? Should your musicians, whatever their ages, be your "pals"? Should you treat them as equals? As subordinates?

All of us work differently. Be yourself. Let your musicians know you as a person. If you try to "create an image"—to be a Toscanini or a Solti, or to imitate your school band or chorus director—you will convey a falseness they will sense and against which they will react.

Judge your results. Is your approach working? Is it slightly out of balance? Do you need to be more firm? More quiet in manner and tone? More patient? More precise in your requests? Do the musicians regard you as distant and unapproachable, or do they treat you with a casualness that reflects a lack of esteem?

Sometime after each rehearsal, while your memory is still fresh, take time to evaluate the results your ensemble gave you. Ask yourself what you might have done differently. Consider what you might try next. Then begin planning for your next meeting with your musicians.

Often, a less gifted individual is able to get better performances than a conductor with more native musicianship and technical ability who, nevertheless, cannot get the ensemble to work diligently and effectively. Keep working to refine your professional style.

THE IDEAL PERSONALITY

What personality features are typical of the very finest conductors? In general, we can say that they display

1. A dynamic commitment to the work at hand
2. Confidence in themselves, even under stress
3. Great energy
4. A personal style, or temperament
5. Idiosyncratic, distinctive mannerisms

Their image is not the same as it was in the nineteenth and early twentieth centuries. The arrogant, flamboyant posturer was prototypical then, and you may have heard stories about some of the haughty, overbearing maestros of that time. Even in high schools and colleges, the band programs—facsimiles of the celebrated, quasi-military organizations led by John Philip Sousa and others—often were directed by men whose manner combined the brusqueness of a cavalry officer and the lordly manner of the great European conductors.

Much of that has changed. The "dictatorial style" is now obsolete (because it belonged to another era), and the "continental manner" went out of fashion with the coming-of-age of the fine American-born-and-trained conductors: Shaw, Bernstein, Previn, and Slatkin.

Current practice suggests that you should have a personable relationship with your musicians—professional but not casual or intimate—in which they are treated with respect while you are understood to represent "expert authority."

STUDY AND PLANNING AS THE BASIS OF CONFIDENCE

No one intimidated by his or her own ignorance, frightened by unfamiliarity with the music or a lack of knowledge of its style, can be at ease, and no one who is ill at ease can conduct well. It is not just the limitations of training that will show; the uneasiness will be apparent in ill-chosen words, nervous and tight gestures, misunderstandings between you and the ensemble members, and wasted time.

Music theory, history, pedagogical methods, and conducting technique all are basic, of course. Beyond those broad perspectives, however, you must accept the responsibility to *teach yourself* before each session with your ensemble. (Because many high school and college students do very little practicing on ensemble music between rehearsals, it surprises some of them, once they become conducting students, to learn that serious conductors spend hours getting ready for a single sixty-minute rehearsal.) If you are to use the rehearsal time you have as efficiently as possible, you must plan everything so that you may respond immediately to any unforeseen situation.

What is the structure of the music? What about your interpretation, then: What tempos and phraseology do you want? Where are the difficult passages? Is there a text, with decisions to be made about diction? Is the language unfamiliar to the chorus? How much time should it require to accomplish what you want to do in a particular rehearsal?

Once you know all this, and more, you need to give thought to the rehearsal process itself. What will you do first? How will you pace the session, now pressing the musicians, now relaxing for a bit? Will you attack this work again at the very next rehearsal, or will you "put it on the shelf" for a while? *The more scores you prepare, the more often you appear in front of ensembles, and the more frequently you conduct in public, the better able you will be to undertake the next score, the next rehearsal, the next performance.*

CONSISTENCY OF TECHNIQUE AND BEHAVIOR

We have spoken already about the necessity for consistent and coherent methods of operation. Consistency is needed in physical technique, rehearsal procedures, and performance conventions, but it also is important in personality and behavior, in the maintenance of standards of discipline, and in quality expectations. This is crucial with mature professionals, for work that is inconsistent will lose you their respect, but it is just as consequential with students, for it can affect discipline.

The authors find that discipline problems rarely occur where an effective educational environment (with appropriate rehearsal procedures) is in place. It is in ensembles where quality of repertoire is low and standards of performance are lax, or where the ability of the conductor is limited, or, above all, *where excellence seems not to matter enough* that disruption and control problems are most likely to result. Where an ensemble is well trained and believes in the importance of what it does—where membership in the ensemble is sought after, in fact, by those who wish to be part of a visible and audible *image of excellence*—it is unlikely that discipline will be a problem.

In a professional group, misbehavior should not be a concern, of course, but even there—as in a school ensemble—the real issue between you and a fine performance by your ensemble may be how much *you* really care about the music, how much the musicians can see that you care, and how clearly they understand that you are right to want to do this particular work really well. **You can transfer your genuine love for a particular piece of music to your ensemble, even if they are young and shallow, or old and jaded.**

If you can show your musicians that you have given your very best efforts to study and preparation of the music, that you are a professional, with an attractive personality, and that you work for important goals, they will look hard to see whether what you are seeking is worthwhile for them, too. If they believe it is, they will respond just as you wish. (And all this is as true of the players in a great symphony orchestra as it is of the members of a grade school chorus or an amateur church choir.)

Aim for perfection! Do not just accept mistakes. No one, however young and inexperienced, *wants* to make mistakes. You need not become angry about errors. Simply require that they be eliminated, and do what you can to help solve the technical problems that create some of them. Demand that your musicians *eliminate the concentration lapses* that create most of the other mistakes. Expect their best all the time. Expectation has much to do with success!

MORE CONDUCTING THEORY
The Ensemble: A Study in Group Dynamics

Each ensemble has its own unique character. It has special attributes and peculiarities one can identify and describe: It may have a recognizable intensity about its playing or may be slow to learn new music; it may play capably in rehearsal yet flounder in front of an audience; it may have a lush, warm sound or a hard, brilliant one; it may have poor intonation. The character of the ensemble is not formed simply from individual strengths and weaknesses; the musicians interact *with each other* to produce unique results. It is their collective response to you and each other that gives the band or chorus or orchestra special attributes. In this real sense, an ensemble is more than the sum of all its members.

This collective "personality" may change. The gain or loss of one or two particular individuals may modify the corporate character of the group. Training and improvement of some members may affect the performance of the whole ensemble. In a choir, the addition of one or two voices can change the sound of your sopranos. A new violinist can have the same effect on an orchestral section. In a band, a new solo cornetist can cause the group to lose its rhythmic definition.

Members have two kinds of influence within a body of musicians: Their individual mistakes or shortcomings can be audible ones that weaken the overall effect, and their errors or unsureness can shake the confidence and clarity of the group. Similarly, the strengths of a single performer may be individually recognizable within the whole, and also can renew the assurance and precision of the team.

All of us as conductors tend to work toward the stronger members of an ensemble. We hope to encourage them to guide the others. We place them in the most responsible positions. We aim toward their particular strengths and away from their weaknesses.

Unhappy musicians—distressed by something in their own lives or by lack of progress in school or a profession—can plant the seeds of diffidence or unrest. On the other hand, confident and happy individuals can be the nuclei around which a potent, productive ensemble forms itself; they encourage their neighbors in an ensemble to be cheerful, productive people, too.

The outside world also affects the group. The day of the week can make a difference: Mondays may be down; Fridays may be up—or hampered by lack of concentration. Events outside the rehearsal room may be distracting. Friction between two or more members of the ensemble may reflect itself in rehearsal or performance.

Try to understand the circumstances that can jeopardize your work, and seek to combat them. Respect the feelings of your musicians, and seek ways to help them bring out their best. *Use humor in a natural but calculated way, just as you use anger, or indignation.* Do nothing before an ensemble that is haphazard.

Try to lend to each member of the performing group a sense of belonging. Give direction and pride to your ensemble, and then let it speak back. Let it express itself. Trust it to be what it can be.

MOTIVATION

Much of what we have said already in this chapter has to do with motivation, but it is worthwhile for us to speak about this substantial consideration more directly.

In the members of any ensemble, you will encounter a variety of levels of talent, training, and dedication. Your ability to deal with the first of these, talent, may be somewhat limited; training and dedication can be improved, however, if you and the musician involved wish it to be. Knowing what the ensemble needs, and judging accurately what is lacking in individual performers, you as conductor are the one who needs to animate the musicians to improve their training, and to increase their concentration and devotion. You can do so not just by talking but by listening, too. Hear what they do, analyze it, and then act on that knowledge.

Your musicians must have incentives. They must believe in something. They must think what they are doing has more than transient significance. You have to persuade them that it has.

In short, you must be a salesman. *Sell* the importance of the music you are doing. Sell the value of shared, disciplined work as an ensemble. Show them the future that waits for those who build on their talent.

MORE CONDUCTING THEORY
Preparing for Rehearsals

Successful rehearsals are your primary opportunities to accomplish these things. It is not in personal interviews or lectures that you motivate your musicians, but in the continuity of shared study and development that is the practice session.

The concept of rehearsal is disarmingly simple: The conductor need only lead, listen, analyze results, and fix problems. All that is true, but it is not enough. The real issue is somewhat hidden from us—hidden in our own short-comings: *We cannot fix mistakes we do not recognize.*

We have to develop our minds and "inner ears" to the point that we can hear how great a particular musical work could be! We may never have heard it performed the way we conceive it. No matter! We can "hear" it inside, and so we can lead our musicians to approach our conception of it. We can measure constantly the sounds they are producing and the rhythms they are defining against the aural images in the mind, and thus we can judge how close they are coming to our interpretation, and how to get them even nearer to it.

If, on the other hand, we are unable to imagine music in this way, we are condemned always to imitate the interpretations of others and to tolerate the casual readings of our ensemble members. To conduct without a mental matrix is like driving at night without a map through a strange countryside.

Here, again, preparation is basic, for advance study is the means by which you develop a matrix for the work. Once that "inner template" is formed, you will find that the best methods for rehearsing the work will suggest themselves rather quickly; unanticipated problems in your rehearsals will be few, and those few unexpected difficulties that do occur will prove comparatively easy to solve.

BASIC REHEARSAL METHODS

There are a number of primary rehearsal techniques. We will discuss more detailed approaches in later chapters, but for now, the basic procedures are these:

1. In the *run-through*, the most conventional method, the conductor leads the ensemble through the music from beginning to end, notes improvement from the last time this work was attempted in rehearsal, and then may put it away until the next session. Here, the ensemble members get a rather clear view (depending on how well the run-through goes) of the continuity of the work, an important consideration. Going straight through music can take a great deal of rehearsal time, however, with comparatively little spent working out specific problems.

2. In the *compartmental* approach, the conductor breaks the work up into basic components and works through portions of it once to get the rhythms right, a second time
for pitch accuracy, yet another time for the text and diction, and on through all the
facets of it until all have been practiced. Then the music is "reassembled," either a
section at a time or as a whole. This procedure's efficacy lies in the fact that the musicians are permitted to focus on one type of problem at a time. They can lose all
sense of continuity, however, until the "reassembly" occurs.

3. With the *spot-rehearsal* approach, you attack only the most difficult passages, saving
the easier parts for later. (This isolating of, say, bars 25–43, 102–146, measure 221,
and bars 309–331 can be very efficient, especially with a professional ensemble. The
technique depends, of course, on the musicians being mature enough to bring a
clear concept of the *whole* work to the spots you choose to repair. This approach is
less likely to be effective with a school ensemble.) After the problem points are repaired, one may start at the beginning and try a run-through.

4. In the *sectional* procedure, small units of musicians within your ensemble may be rehearsed by themselves. This variant of the compartmental approach can get right to
the heart of a problem, but it can be very inefficient if it leaves the rest of a large ensemble waiting and watching for long stretches of time; one good resolution of this
difficulty, if you have one or more assistants and more than one room, is to run simultaneous sectional rehearsals, each group dealing with its own worst problems.

5. In the *critical* procedure, the conductor proceeds through the work from beginning
to end, stopping at any moment for corrections of any sort, as they are required.
Here, no time is wasted working on spots that do not need to be fixed. This process
makes a direct attack on the problems. Having to work bar by bar (or note by note)
leaves the ensemble members with virtually no sense of the overall flow of the
work, however, and you yourself can lose perspective, as well.

6. With the *structural* procedure, you seek to teach the form of the work through rehearsal, in the confidence that a clear sense of design will affect their understanding
of the work, make rehearsals easier, and improve the eventual performance by helping the musicians understand how to deal with details. In this procedure, you must
take time to make certain they recognize the outline of this theme-and-variations, or
sonata form, or fugue, or whatever, and what role their own passage work plays in
the overall structure.

Which of these approaches is best? Any one of the six can be helpful in a
particular work, depending on the age and experience of the ensemble members.
Probably the best music educators and conductors are those who remember that
each offers advantages.

It may be best, for example, to use the run-through method for the first
reading of a work. This lets the musicians see all of it without interruptions (unless a complete breakdown occurs). They get a clear idea of the continuity of the
music and of the difficulties present in it. (You will find, too, that more experienced performers, making some errors in a first reading, will correct most of
their mistakes themselves the next time through.)

Now give them a sense of the structure of the work, pointing out the
basic form and noting design elements along the way. They will gain a sense
of orientation from this and may be better able to make musical judgments
for themselves.

The next step may be to isolate the weakest aspects of their work, confronting those problems before reassembling the whole fabric. If they are having trouble with harmonic intonation, for example, you may want to take one chord at a time, ignoring the rhythmic context, and then approach the same passage again, as written.

As an alternative, you might want to follow the original reading by isolating the thing your musicians do best. You can gradually add other aspects of the music, one at a time, until it is completely reassembled. (Suppose, for example, that your chorus has no difficulty with the rhythm of a movement but is facing problems elsewhere. You may want to begin by having them "dah-dah" the rhythm, adding the text after a while, and working for pitch accuracy last.)

Use the spot-rehearsal technique to deal with particularly troublesome moments. If all the difficulties are created by a few of your musicians, you may need a sectional rehearsal at this point; if possible, call a separate session at another hour for those affected. Sectional rehearsals, although they demand a great deal of your time, can be very effective; almost everything can be accomplished in them *if* you have a sharp enough image of the matrix of the work. (Some famous conductors have given *most* of their rehearsal time, on occasion, to sectional sessions, bringing their full ensemble together only at the last moment.)

Finally, it may be that once the work is pretty well in hand, and the ensemble has a clear concept of it, use of the critical approach can tighten, reinforce, and clarify that concept.

THE IMPLICATIONS OF PERFORMANCE

What if your ensemble were to have regular rehearsals but never had to face an audience—never had to perform?

It is the nature of this art of Music that ultimately a time comes when everything has to be done in one attempt, with no second tries, no tomorrows, and no excuses. That creates stress, of course. The pressure of performance can hover over each rehearsal, raising difficulties.

1. It can force you to make compromises in your plans, to alter your interpretations, and to take shortcuts to meet a performance deadline.
2. It can overstress developing student-musicians who are not yet ready to face some particular challenge in the repertoire.
3. It can lead you to make conservative choices about repertoire, tempos, structural "seams," and other risky decisions.
4. It can lead you to press too hard in your final rehearsals, adding to the tension your musicians are already feeling and causing you to make misjudgments.

But the strain of preparing for performances offers real advantages, as well.

1. Individual musicians often concentrate better and discipline themselves more effectively as a public appearance nears.

2. It follows, then, that ensembles generally improve more quickly under the pressure of the clock. Their development accelerates.
3. The very nature of performance—the reality that every work on the program must be an unbroken, communicative continuity—makes the music seem different from what it was in rehearsals.
4. The pressure of the performance forces each member of the ensemble to accept personal responsibility.
5. Most of all, **because there can be no real music without communication with an audience,** the performance validates all the work done, and all the stress experienced, to that point. It pays for the hard work and long hours.

Performances are never better than your best rehearsal, but you never know what you can attain in front of the public until you face them. Difficulties that seemed unresolved in the rehearsal hall may disappear in concert, and problems that never appeared in practice sessions may waylay your musicians in front of an audience. You cannot be certain what predicaments may arise suddenly onstage, needing your quick attention and wits.

Prepare your ensembles for public appearances as well as you possibly can. You will find it helpful from time to time, for example, to make the end of rehearsal a quasi performance, telling your musicians that you are going "to run straight through this piece, as if the crowd were listening." This will give your group an opportunity to face the real issues.

MULTIPLE PERFORMANCES

You will find, by the way, that multiple performances of a particular program are better in many ways for your ensemble than one-time, single-shot concerts. Opening night (or, for many ensembles, a career of opening nights, with never a "second performance") elicits all of the nervousness attendant on presenting a program for the first time. It is useful and satisfying to get past that.

Second nights are very different; some parts of the program can be trusted now—even developed and elaborated further—in front of the audience; other things may not have gone so well the first time, and a second performance means another chance. A conductor can take more risks in repeats of a program, too. Here, you have opportunities to improve your communication with your ensemble; they are concentrating fully in performance, and you can get them to read and follow signals from your baton that they might miss or ignore in the more relaxed atmosphere of a rehearsal. You can push them to take more risks themselves, as well; with the confidence of musicians who have already performed this program successfully, they are likely to be willing to stretch a particular phrase a bit further, to take a Presto a bit faster or a Largo even slower, and to spin out a high *pianissimo* even softer than they did on opening night.

Some conductors have no choice in these matters: Their performances happen once only, and nothing can be done about it. Others must worry about dividing their audience between two nights, thus increasing costs without gaining much income. For the musicians, nevertheless, whether they are students or professionals, there is great value in performing more than just a single time the music to which they have given such exhaustive preparation.

CHAPTER 9

Choral Fundamentals

We turn now from the basic technical aspects of conducting to the application of those skills to specific types of music. In Chapters 9–12, we will speak of the special characteristics and demands associated with vocal ensembles, examining particular choral works in that process; in Chapters 13–16, we will turn to a parallel study of instrumental ensembles.

At this stage in your life, your own experience may lead you to prefer one of these two genres—choirs on the one hand, and bands and orchestras on the other. Remember our advice that **the ideal conductor should be able to lead any ensemble.** To have the widest range of performance opportunities, you need to master the whole range of worthwhile repertoire.

THE CHORAL SCORE

Perhaps the first obvious difference between the choir, the orchestra, and the band is the appearance of the music manuscript itself. Choral scores can range from the single-staff monophony of Gregorian chant to the forty voice parts of the Thomas Tallis *Spem in alium.* Certain standard combinations, traditionally described by the voices required—SATB (soprano, alto, tenor, and bass), SSA (soprano I, soprano II, and alto), TTBB (tenor I, tenor II, baritone, and bass), and the like—without reference to the *number* of singers per part, represent for us the basic choral ensembles: the common "mixed chorus" of both women and men, the "barbershop" chorus (frequently, but not always TTBB), the "madrigal singers," the "women's chorus," the "boy choir," and others.

The size of the vocal ensemble you conduct should be determined by three factors: the repertoire, the nature of the performance circumstances, and the personnel you can recruit. If you intend to perform the Verdi Requiem in a huge auditorium with a full symphony orchestra, you probably will need to gather together an oratorio chorus of two hundred voices; if the Verdi is to be sung by a church choir with organ, on the other hand, you can get by with a vocal ensemble of only a few dozen people. A conductor may form a choir of only sixteen for a Palestrina mass. A high school chorus of sixty—a group perhaps short of altos or tenors—may not be well suited to either the Verdi or the Palestrina. In such a circumstance, you must recruit more singers or choose other repertoire.

From the notation itself we learn the usual things: how long the work is, whether it is conceived in contrapuntal or homophonic texture, the character of its melodic lines, how complex its harmonies, how insistent its rhythms, and the like. Are soloists required? What are the ranges of the parts? What about the tessituras: Does the music remain within a particular register long enough to become exhausting for some of the singers? And there is a special consideration normally present in vocal music, of course: What is the text, what is its source, and how is it woven through the music? Does it determine the shape and form of the music?

The more new music you examine, the better you will become at assessing the difficulties and merits of particular works. *The better you are at judging the difficulties and merits of new music, the more capable you will become at appraising the amount of rehearsal time and toil involved in attempting a proposed program.*

If you are a singer, perhaps you need to be looking at choral music in another way now; think no longer as a performer but as a conductor. With the baton in your hand, you face a different set of problems.

Your need to have an expanded vision is an important part of that difference. *You simply have to see more now—and hear more, too.* If you have been singing in a chorus, or playing in a band, your primary focus has been on a single part. Now you must see and hear that same part while perceiving it in perspective as only one thread in the whole fabric of the score.

And beware of the "melody"! If there *is* a single line that you can call "the melody" in a particular work, it is *not* likely to be the only important part in the texture, and although it may be the most obvious line in the ears of the audience, it may not be really the most significant. It is the complete, interwoven fabric you must present in balance.

That is not easy to do, partly because in a passage in which one line is perceived as "the melody," the performers who are responsible for "the accompaniment" have difficulty maintaining their own perspective. They may thump along on simple, repetitive figures, doing so percussively and unimaginatively, or they may understate their lines, losing concentration and even accuracy. Recognize the value of each part, and then show by your actions that it is significant; convey its importance to your musicians voice by voice, and stand by stand. Help them to esteem the purpose of the part given to each of them.

MORE CONDUCTING THEORY
The Individual and the Choir

Know your singers. In a choral group of moderate size, say forty to sixty voices, a good conductor can learn to recognize each voice and the unique contribution it makes to the overall sound of the choir as certainly as the recipient of a floral basket can tell the roses from the gladioli and the daisies from the chrysanthemums.

The authors find that the absence of a single singer from a rehearsal changes the sound and character not just of that section but of the choir as a whole (not in every single chord, perhaps, but certainly across the span of a work).

Each singer needs to hear this from you. Each needs to understand that the absence of a single person undercuts the sound and efficiency of a rehearsal (not to speak of a concert). Your choristers will not believe this, at first, for they think of themselves as lost in a group of people all singing the same notes—a section. (Given the sands of a beach, what difference can the loss of a single grain make?) This attitude is dangerous, because absences are hurtful to an ensemble in both efficiency and morale, and because the same diffidence that argues that an absence does not matter will hold that individual mistakes (inaccuracies of pitch, rhythm, or diction) have little effect on the choral whole.

You need to combat this dangerous viewpoint, and to do so in several ways.

1. First, you must prove to *yourself* that each voice is valuable and that you can identify single voices within the fabric of your choir.
2. Then, in rehearsals, treat your singers as unique contributors, not as sheep in a flock: Adjust balance in a particular passage by adding a single soprano temporarily to the alto line, or a baritone to the tenors. Compliment an individual, in front of the whole choir, on the way he or she is singing a given phrase. Let your singers know that you can hear, at any given moment, the distinctive efforts they personally are making.
3. Demand regular attendance. We are living in a peculiar era; many student singers (and instrumentalists) assume that attendance at rehearsals—and even concerts!—is optional; they come and go as they please in many elementary and high schools, most church choirs, and even some colleges. Some teacher-conductors accommodate themselves to this self-centeredness, fearing to lose membership from their ensemble; they accept random attendance as preferable to no participation at all. This is a struggle in which you cannot afford to compromise. An ensemble is much like an athletic team: A basketball coach who permits players to miss practices is a loser leading a losing team, and a conductor who accepts spotty attendance from the musicians is bound for failure, too.

   You are better served by a small choir of faithful singers than by a huge chorus of undisciplined ones. The authors have found through experience that *no* singer is so valuable as to be excused from a rule of mandatory attendance; you should dismiss even your best tenor—even your *only* tenor—if he is truant.
4. Teamwork is part of the equation here. Making a commitment to each other is basic to the process of becoming an *ensemble*. Those who violate this mutual obligation set themselves apart; and, what is more, those who stand by the commitment resent those who do not. The high morale of an ensemble whose members believe they can count on each other is worth a great deal to you.

Congratulate those singers who maintain perfect attendance, and use those occasions as opportunities to remind all of them that each voice is recognizable and valuable. Then remember to think of and use the voices as unique contributors.

TYPES OF VOICES

To operate in this way, a choral conductor has to know and recognize the various vocal classifications. The basic types are easy to remember and distinguish: soprano, mezzo soprano, contralto, tenor, baritone, and bass; more than that, however, you should learn to identify, appraise, and esteem the special qualities of at least a dozen voice categories.

Female	Coloratura soprano
	"Boy" (child) soprano
	Lyric soprano
	Dramatic soprano
	Mezzo soprano
	Contralto
Male	Countertenor
	Lyric tenor
	Dramatic tenor
	Baritone
	Bass
	Octavist ("Russian bass")

In the operatic repertoire, there are even more (that is, more finely classified) voice types than those, of course. (One often hears the term *spinto*, for example, as in "lyric spinto"; this term denotes a quality a bit darker or heavier than a standard voice of the same range.) Such specialized operatic terminology may be too detailed for your purposes, but even in a school chorus you will want to calculate the effect you get from putting a particularly large, heavy voice into a section full of lighter, more lyric sounds.

Consult the Bibliography of this volume for books on vocal technic. They will help you identify and appreciate the distinctions between the various voice types. Then, listen carefully to singers, and improve your ability to distinguish among them. Go to voice contests of all kinds to gain experience. Attend regional Metropolitan Opera Auditions, and make notes about the voices you hear. Compare recordings of professionals singing the same repertoire. *This ability to evaluate singers by range and quality is as basic to your craft as your capacity to spot wrong notes and faulty technic.*

VOCAL AUDITION PROCEDURES

Apply this newly developed ability when you choose members for your choir and assign them to sections. This is the moment you predetermine the potential quality of the chorus by deciding who has sufficient current or latent talent to strengthen the ensemble; more than that, it is the occasion when you have the best chance to locate just where each singer you select can best contribute to a balanced ensemble. In a school or church setting, you may do all this by yourself; in a college or professional situation, with assistants to help you, you may be able to assign certain parts of the process to others.

There are at least four stages in a well-organized audition procedure.

1. The auditionee should fill out an application card or sheet that provides information about her or his background and that leaves room to add your comments during the

Figure 9-1 A choral audition form for a high school or college ensemble

UNIVERSITY of ILLINOIS CHORAL AUDITION CARD	
Name:_____ Major: _____ Fr. So. Jr. Sr. Gr. U/C Address: _____ Phone, U/C: _____ SS#: _____ Parents' Name: _____ Permanent Address: _____ _____ Phone, Home: _____	**FILLED OUT BY AUDITOR** Group Assigned: _____ Voice Part: _____ Overall Rank: _____ (1= poor 15=excellent) Audition Date: 1. _____ 2. _____

Previous Choral Experience (High school, college, university, professional) _____ _____ _____	Private Vocal Study: _____ _____ _____ Instruments you play _____

To be filled out by Auditor

VOCAL SECTION: _____

Size: 1 2 3 4 5
                1=small 3=medium 5=big

Timbre: 1 2 3 4 5
                1= reedy 3= mixed 5= fluty

Intonation: 1 2 3 4 5
                1= poor 3= average 5= excellent

Sight Reading: 1 2 3 4 5

Quality: 1 2 3 4 5

Auditioned by:

1._____ 2._____ 3._____

Comments: _____
_____
_____
_____

VOCAL RANGE: General Comments: (size, quality of tone,vowels, musicianship, etc.)
_____
_____
_____
_____

audition itself. Two sample audition forms are shown (see Figures 9-1 and 9-2)—one for a high school or college choir, and the other for an adult situation. *Get as much information at this time as possible,* for it will save you time later. Addresses, telephone numbers, class standing, previous choral experience, current or former private voice study, roles sung in stage productions, experience as a soloist, other instruments studied, height (both for placement on the risers and for robe size), and such factors should be included on the audition form.

Figure 9-2   A choral audition form for an adult or professional situation

SOUTH BEND SYMPHONIC CHOIR   V   Fol

Please Print   ENR

Name: last, first, middle ((as you want it list on programs))   HOME PHONE

HOME ADDRESS: street   city   zip code   BUSINESS PHONE

PREVIOUS EXPERIENCE :
   1. About how many years have you sung in – – Symphonic Choir ? _____
                                                               – – A Church Choir ? _____

NEW MEMBERS ONLY

   2. How many years, if any ,have you taken
      voice lessons at the following stages   – – – pre-college? _____
                                              – – – college ?   _____
                                              – – – adult?   _____
   3. What other vocal or choral experience do you want us to know about ?
      _____

   4. Circle the choral part you have been singing most frequently in recent
      months:
                        Soprano I   Alto I   Tenor I   Bass I
                        Soprano II   Alto II   Tenor II   Bass II

   5. Have you served as a soloist recently ? If so, in what works (s)?
      _____
      _____

****
   Office Use Only

   SS   5   4   3   2   1   S1   S2   S3   _____
                                 A1   A2   A3   Rg
              dr   T1   T2   T3   Sp
                                 B1   B2   B3   Ag Rt
      _____   SC   V1   RS   S
      _____
      _____   Sch _____
****

2. The auditionee should be given an opportunity—should be encouraged, in fact—to warm up her or his voice beforehand.

3. A sight-reading examination should be given (even in the most rudimentary situations), for this test helps to focus attention on the importance of the reading process. The difficulty of the excerpt(s) to be read depends on the nature of the choir, but, in general, it is well to choose an example that includes at least a simple modulation. Intonation and musicality should be tested, as well as pitch and rhythmic accuracy.

4. Remember that an important aspect of sight-reading ability is tonal memory. Even those who are inexperienced as sight readers can demonstrate this capacity.

5. You must have each individual vocalize, to check range, tessitura, technic, tone quality, diction, facility in various languages, and the like. Thus, the audition form should include blanks for your written comments regarding these criteria, and for you to indicate which voice type you have recognized.

Once the auditions are completed, you will be able to use the audition forms, with all your scores and comments, to choose which applicants to include in your choir. You can keep referring to the forms as the year passes (in choosing soloists, perhaps). You may even find it useful to build the information into a computerized database.

You realize, of course, that people are nervous when auditioning. With the young and the inexperienced, deliberately plan and use light banter to relax them, giving them a little extra time to accustom themselves to you and the situation. With older professionals, on the other hand, you may want to maintain a calculated formality; their experience should show through at such times, and visible nervousness on the part of such a person may be a warning. When you hire professional singers (and well-trained graduate students), you are buying, among other things, assurance and consistency under pressure.

VOICE CLASSIFICATION

Your primary reason for having an auditionee vocalize is to classify that voice: to discover its overall range and to define its most useful and efficient tessitura. (No matter how beautifully a particular soprano can sing a high G, her voice may be of little use if she can produce only one such note per day!) Your next purpose is to observe the general timbre of the voice.

Example 9-1 shows a standard vocalise that, sung legato and at a moderate pace, is useful for determining *range*. Begun at a comfortable point, in the lower middle part of the auditionee's voice (say, the C-natural below middle C for a baritone), and moved up progressively a half step at a time, this exercise—with its perfect-fourth skip at the top—requires that the auditionee leap (eventually) to the highest notes in his or her range, while at the same time tuning accurately each note in the arpeggio (upward and downward).

The same exercise repeated staccato at a quick pace tests *agility* (including precision of intonation) rather well.

Example 9-1   A simple vocalise for use in voice-classification auditions

Mere range is not the basic consideration in classifying voices. (Frequently, both contraltos and basses are capable of a high C.) *Usable* range is more important. The *tessitura* in which a performer can sing for an extended time without strain, loss of intonation, and decreased tone quality is a primary criterion for seating an individual in a particular section.

One way of estimating this comfortable, usable range is by determining the "registration" of a given voice. Every singer has certain points in the vocal instrument at which the mechanism adjusts to a new "gear," or "register"; ascending, the voice arrives at a plateau, "shifts gears," and moves up to another such plateau. If one can identify the location of these register changes, one can estimate the *usable* range of a given voice, no matter what its overall span may be.

Example 9-2 is a standard vocalise that can be used to determine registration. Beginning in the lower middle of the voice, this exercise can be moved up a half step at a time; at the point of a register change (sometimes called a "lift"), the careful listener will hear—on the top note of the five-tone scale—a distinct *lightening* of the tone quality. This is the "gear shift" to the new register.

If this is a new concept for you, you will want to consult one or more of the books in the Bibliography that explain voice classification and registration. For our purposes, it will suffice to say that many authorities recognize three registers in the standard male voice, and four in the female instrument.

Example 9-2   A simple vocalise for checking voice registration

Using a vocalise like Example 9-2, one should be able to detect the first register change, which makes it possible to use the location of this "lift" to generalize about the type of voice at hand. Some believe that the lowest register change can be used to classify male voices according to the following list (the C-natural listed is middle C on the piano):

F   Countertenor
E   "Irish" tenor
E♭   Light lyric tenor
D   Lyric tenor

C♯   Dramatic tenor
C   "Broadway" baritone
B   Light lyric baritone
B♭   Baritone
A   Bass-baritone
A♭   Bass
G   Octavist ("Russian bass")

In the typical male voice, this shift from the low register to the middle voice will be confirmed a perfect fourth higher by another "lift" into the high voice (that is, the lyric tenor will have another register change at the G-natural above middle C).

In a similar way, the classification of female voices can be approximated by locating the lowest register change and comparing it with the following list (in which, this time, the C-natural is one octave above middle C):

F   Coloratura soprano
E   Lyric-coloratura soprano
E♭   Light lyric soprano
D   Lyric soprano
C♯   Dramatic soprano
C   "Wagnerian" soprano
B   High mezzo soprano
B♭   Mezzo soprano
A   Low mezzo/alto
A♭   Contralto
G   Low contralto

In the typical female voice, this initial "gear shift" may be confirmed by two higher additional changes, the first a major third higher, and the second a minor third above that.

It is important to emphasize that (1) *the approach to voice classification just described is only an approximation,* which may not prove wholly accurate and helpful in particular cases, and (2) there are other techniques of gauging voices that may work better with a given individual. *Any such system can only lead to what at best is an estimate, and what at worst may be completely misleading;* the foregoing lists may vary by a half step or more, or may—with a given singer—be virtually useless. This is particularly true with the well-trained voice; in general, the better disciplined the voice, the harder it is to identify the register changes, for the whole process of voice training is an effort to make vocal production even and consistent across the whole range of the instrument. With seasoned professional singers, then, your judgments regarding timbre and tessitura will be more important than such tests of registration.

More demanding exercises can be used where appropriate. Example 9-3, for instance, requires the singer to demonstrate great *control* as he or she sustains a high note through a long diminuendo. This particular vocalise can tell you a great deal about the technical assurance of potential soloists.

Example 9-3   A more difficult vocalise for testing control and assurance

FORMING YOUR CHOIR

The number of auditionees you accept—the size of your choir—depends, of course, on a compromise between the purpose for which the ensemble is formed—its setting—and the balance (section by section) of competent personnel available. How many individuals of each voice you select depends also on a combination of circumstances: You will have in mind sections of ideal proportions, but you will have to match that conception against the real strengths and weaknesses of the individuals you have auditioned.

Consider the SATB chorus: Conductors differ about the ratios of women to men, tenors to basses, and the like. Some of those differences are based on the characteristics of the repertoire involved, and some relate to personal taste. You may want an equal number on each part, you may prefer a 3:2 ratio of women to men, or you may like to add extra numbers to the lower voices (altos and basses); all these can be viable.

There are various ways to arrange your personnel. You may simply distribute your singers into the traditional SATB sections, shifting individuals one by one when a particular work calls for SSATB, SATTB, or some other texture; you lose some rehearsal time, of course, whenever special voicings must be announced.

Some conductors minimize this wasted time by dividing each of the sections, creating an SSAATTBB choir (first sopranos, second sopranos, first altos, and so on); this gives them more immediate flexibility. (In such a grouping, the second sopranos may be high mezzos and the first altos low mezzos.) This arrangement does not eliminate the need to redivide the choir whenever a work calls for something other than four or eight parts, however. A movement voiced in five parts—such as many in the Bach B Minor Mass—is not immediately suited to either an SATB or an SSAATTBB chorus.

Another possibility is to subdivide the choir even further. Although a twelve-part arrangement (SSSAAATTTBBB, with first sopranos, second sopranos, and third sopranos, and so on) looks complicated, one of the authors uses it, believing it actually saves rehearsal time. In such a distribution, your highest (coloratura) sopranos are S1s, your lyrics S2s, and your high mezzos S3s; the low mezzos are A1s, and the altos are divided between A2 and A3. This means that in works written for SSA, your women can immediately assign themselves, without discussion, to three relatively equal sections: sopranos (S1s and S2s), mezzos (S3s and A1s), and altos (A2s and A3s). In a similar way, men may be divided (with the lowest tenors and the baritones assigned, respectively, as T3s and B1s) into two, three, or four parts rather quickly. Your lowest altos (A3s) can be specially directed to double the tenor line, when you wish it, while substantial numbers of A1s and A2s remain to cover the alto part.

Whichever of these distributions you choose, bear in mind that rehearsal time is your most valuable resource. Any seating plan you choose needs to be an efficient one.

Once you have established the sections, design a seating chart. Consider that it may be well to place your best singers (especially those who sight-read well) behind the other members of that section. Some conductors like a left-to-right SATB order, some prefer all the women (or all the men) in the center of the ensemble, and some choose (for at least certain works) to "homogenize" the choir, deliberately mixing the singers so that members of a section do not stand together.

MORE CONDUCTING THEORY
Building and Encouraging Good Vocal Production

Unless you are hiring a choir of first-rank professionals, you cannot expect that your auditionees will come to you with all their technical problems solved. You will need to oversee their further vocal development in one way or another.

Many successful high school directors actually teach voice on an individual basis to some extent—before school, during school, after school—whether they call these "voice lessons" or not. Others organize and teach "class voice." Still others urge their choristers to study privately with local studio teachers, either on or off school grounds. Some such approach is necessary to build a strong pool of vocally disciplined talent at the high school level. (The great English choir schools, even though they are highly selective in their audition procedures, operate in essentially the same way, using something like class voice instruction.)

Some such training can be incorporated into your rehearsal time itself. Many excellent high school choirmasters devote, say, the first ten minutes of each rehearsal to structured work on vocal production. Most vocal problems are somewhat individual, however, so it is not likely that the individual and discrete vocal problems found in a large group of singers can be dealt with in concurrent exercises.

At the same time, it is worth pointing out that **there is no conflict between good vocal production and the kind of singing your choristers should be doing for you.** Whoever is teaching them, they should see chorus rehearsal as one of their best opportunities to *practice*. The same careful approaches to posture, breath support, and overall vocal production on which they base their singing in the studio and in the practice room should characterize their work for you. If you find yourself asking for some vocal effect that is out of step with good studio production, you should reconsider the passage in question.

BASIC POSTURE

Singing is not a function of the larynx alone. *The whole human body is the instrument.* A fine professional singer is as superior an athlete as a tennis star or a world-class swimmer.

The foundation for this is *stance.* The singer should stand fully erect, but not rigid, with shoulders relaxed (not pulled back in a quasi-military "brace"). The head should rest comfortably on this foundation, aimed forward and level (never tilted back to "reach up" for high notes, the approach some call the "necktie position"). The knees should be loose, not rigid; there should be, in fact, no real sensation of tension anywhere, save in the breath-support mechanism. The arms, if raised to hold music, should be held casually out from the sides and somewhat forward (thus giving the chest and abdomen plenty of room to expand); the score should be held high enough that the singers can see the conductor (just over the top of the music) without constantly having to shift their eyes up and down.

Some fine conductors like their singers to "stand back" rather proudly. Others prefer them to lean a bit toward the conductor (as if they were about to step forward); they believe this adds an element of intensity to both their concentration and their production. Try both approaches to see which works better.

It is necessary that singers sit during long rehearsals. (The authors find, in fact, that the alternation of standing and sitting during a practice session is an important device for "pacing" the rehearsal; always be aware how long you have had your choir up or down, and choose appropriate moments for changing positions.)

The chairs they use when they sing should be simple and straight-backed, high enough that the singers' knees are at a right angle, not bent upward, and with flat seats so that the singers do not slip back into some sort of concavity. Standard classroom armchairs-with-desks are never satisfactory. Neither is soft auditorium-style furniture. Seated, a choir member should stay forward, keeping the erect spine away from the back of the chair (sitting, that is, on the front "half" of the seat). The purpose of being seated for a while in rehearsal is to rest the legs, not to slump into bad posture. Good singing can be done in any *carefully* considered position (Desdemona's death scene in *Othello* generally is staged with her lying on her back), but when you seat your choir you will have to keep reminding them about posture, no matter how experienced they are.

Choral risers need prudent consideration, too, whether they are "built-in" levels in a rehearsal room or portable units used onstage. Avoid, if you can, extremely narrow steps (eighteen inches or more is a good tread depth) so that your singers have sufficient room to hold music in front of them. Have your last row move back as far on their step as is safe, and ask your front row to move forward on the floor, away from the risers; then the inner rows can adjust to use the extra inches well.

Never "pack" your singers onto risers. Be certain there are enough units to give them elbowroom. Each chorister should be able to stand squarely and comfortably, facing you, with elbowroom and space to hold music; each should be situated to look through the gap between the heads of the two singers in the row immediately in front. Caution your people not to "lock" their knees but to keep them loose, especially when they are on risers onstage, with hot lights overhead; this will minimize the light-headedness and fainting that sometimes occur when choristers are both tense and hot.

CONNECTING THE BREATH WITH THE VOICE

Once the posture is right, the singer is set to coordinate the release of air with the voice through the process often called breath control. In this conception, the larynx produces sounds that ride on the flow of the "breath stream" through the pharynx and the mouth, and over the tongue. The teeth and lips—the articulators—assume various shapes, thus manufacturing the vocal components (or phonemes) that make up vowels and consonants; by convention, the vowels (or all speech sounds) are said to be "enunciated" and the consonants "articulated." To put it simply, the quality of the sound produced is a result of the consistency of the breath flow, the native attractiveness of the laryngeal production, the skillful ways in which the articulators are employed to form and adjust the individual sounds produced, and the continuity in which all this is set within given words and phrases.

Working from a balanced, comfortable stance, a singer breathes naturally, rather as a baby does, aiming to fill the lungs completely. In doing so, the singer is likely to have a sensation that air enters the abdomen, not just the chest, and that the diaphragm *seems* to move down; the abdominal cavity itself *feels* as if it is filling with air (although, of course, only the lungs really can do so). With proper breathing, the singer notices that even the back muscles—low, near the belt line—move; the whole sensation is rather like filling an inner tube all around the waist.

The release of this air is carefully controlled so that an even stream, maintained under a constant level of pressure, is sent up the trachea; once the amount of air in the reservoir of the lungs falls low enough that the musculature can no longer maintain that constant level of pressure, the singer must take time to breathe. One of our standard slogans is **"Never wait to breathe until you are out of air,"** for both pitch accuracy and tonal quality deteriorate quickly when one tries to sing on an insufficient foundation of breath (that is, insufficient "breath support").

This breathing process must become routine. Management of the air for singing is conscious—not automatic, as it is in normal human respiration—but it has to be made habitual (as in swimming) so that the singer's attention can be focused on the music.

DICTION

The most distinctive feature of vocal (and hence choral) music is diction. The twin processes of enunciating vowels and articulating consonants, of which we have already spoken, are our most direct means of creating verbal meaning for our listeners. Each syllable, word, and phrase, as we have said, is composed of a series of phonemes; even the tiny word "I" has two: the vowel "ah," followed by the vowel "ee" in the combination of elided sounds we call a diphthong; similarly, the word "dot" is a continuity of three phonemes: the consonant "d," followed by the vowel "ah" and the final consonant "t." *Good vocal production is not a matter of thinking and singing individual words* but, rather, of thinking and singing *continuities of individual and separate phonemes.* The illusion of whole words, heard by the audience, is created by musical and verbal emphases, and exists only in the *minds* of the singer and the listener. We are trying to communicate ideas to each other, but we must do so *one phoneme at a time.*

The fact that our choirs must sing in more than one language complicates all this. Italian, Latin, German, French, and Spanish, as well as English—plus, from time to time, Russian, Czech, Hungarian, Polish, Swedish, Japanese, Chinese, and other tongues—are used in current repertoire. Lingual differences can be defined through use of the International Phonetic Alphabet (the IPA, found in most larger dictionaries), with which you should become familiar. It is not necessary to actually study each language sung, though that is ideal. (One of the authors sang for some years in a Washington, D.C., ensemble that annually sang in two dozen or more languages and dialects at international diplomatic occasions. These choristers were trained by use of phonetics, and then coached to greater authenticity of sound by "borrowing" consular officials from the various embassies in the city.)

The more complicated the musical texture, the greater the problem of intelligibility. Polyphony and certain musical styles with complex accompanimental patterns also can increase the difficulty of communication.

The Vowels and the Consonants

Put simply, the vowels are sounds that can be produced on a given pitch and that can be sustained indefinitely on a relatively unbroken flow of breath. We generally speak of five *written* ones, of course: *a, e, i, o,* and *u;* in speech—even just in English—there are many more, as you will remember.

The fundamental vowels we sing are shaped by the vocal mechanism in such a way that some of them feel "forward" (that is, produced particularly in the front of the mouth), whereas others are "back" vowels, and that some feel "open" (produced with relatively relaxed articulators), whereas others are "dark" or "tense." The *schwa,* or neutral "uh," tends to creep into or "modify" all the vowels as they ascend the scale in register. This happens because to maintain an efficient and attractive tone quality, we have to alter the shape of the mechanism slightly as we sing higher or lower; *thus, any single vowel sound is sung slightly differently from the same vowel produced on a different pitch.*[1]

Vowels generally are produced on a relatively free flow of air and can be pitched; most consonants are created by a substantial stoppage-and-release of the airstream, and only a few of them can be sung on a pitch. The tongue and the lips are the most common means of stopping the air flow; depending on how they are employed, different classes of consonants result (plosives, sibilants, and all).[2]

MAINTAINING PITCH

In the important skill of "staying in tune," some people place too much emphasis on native aural ability, or "having a good ear." They assume that the very *first* competence a third-grade chorus ought to exhibit is strict, stable intonation. This is rather like expecting a novice golfer to drive the ball straight for 300 yards.

Good intonation is a symptom, not a cause. Individual vocal technic, capable sight reading, physical conditioning, concentration, and other factors all contribute to the maintenance of pitch. Nervousness, bad acoustics, long periods under hot lights, weak rehearsal procedures, unwise conducting decisions, and other circumstances can lead to poor intonation. The ability of choir members to sing "in tune" should improve hand in hand with their other musical skills.

As a foundation for good intonation, it should be understood that *accuracy of pitch is impossible unless proper vowels are chosen and sung.* Good posture and breath support are fundamental, as well; pitch inevitably will sag, given a "flabby" production. Carelessness on the part of stronger singers in your sections will pull down the intonation of others. Pitch accuracy, in short, demands good production from everyone, including the very best of your choristers.

The atmosphere for good intonation is set during your warm-up period. This is the time when you get your singers *expecting* accurate pitches and *listening* to what they are producing. Thus, they establish a disciplined production for the rehearsal to come.

There are various kinds of exercises you can use during a warm-up segment to give your singers practice in tuning. One of the simplest involves having your choir sing a chord, and then asking them to tune to a new note sung by one section, as in Example 9-4. The authors have seen Robert Shaw ask his choir to sing an octave scale, with one or more sections singing quarter tones, while the balance of the group meet them at each half step; alternatively, one section may hold the tonic while the others sing a quarter-tone scale. Shaw also has a chorus raise a chord a half step by "sharping" all together over a slow eight-count—a demanding exercise.

[1]D. Ralph Appelman, *The Science of Vocal Pedagogy* (Bloomington: Indiana University Press, 1967). For a particularly clear image of these relationships, see his chart of "Stable Vowel Migrations" on p. 234.

[2]Madeleine Marshall, *The Singer's Manual of English Diction* (New York: G. Schirmer, Inc., 1953).

Example 9-4 An exercise for training a choir to listen and maintain good intonation

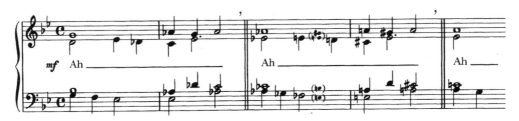

MAINTAINING RHYTHMIC CLARITY

Just as vowel accuracy is crucial to good intonation, so precise, clean, exciting rhythm is impossible in a choral setting without well-defined consonants. They are needed not just to make words intelligible; **consonants—like "rim shots" on a snare drum—are important rhythmic events.**

Initial consonants can be delivered on a beat to help emphasize it, or can be placed before (but not usually after) it. Final consonants should have an exact place in time, too, and usually should be emphatic enough to cut through the texture; sometimes, you will want their articulative power on the beat, whereas in other musical circumstances, you may think that they become too obvious and may choose to place them on a subdivision of the beat.

It is difficult to keep consonants—briefer in duration, and often forced to compete on the beat with strong rhythmic accompaniments—in dynamic balance with the vowels. Many conductors ask their choristers in a given passage to "sing the vowels *piano* and the consonants *forte.*"

This relationship of vowels and consonants must be altered, by the way, to suit the size and acoustics of varied rehearsal and performance halls. **Good vowel production and proper dynamics for those vowels should not change with the room,** for when they know how to produce their best *forte* sound, they should preserve it wherever they go; on the other hand, *the weight and duration given consonants should be adjusted to the setting.* Do not let your choristers try to "fill" a large room by shouting; they will damage their voices and pervert the tone quality. A properly produced sound with emphatic consonants will suffice in any concert hall.

Here, again, a point of view that makes handling of consonants both emphatic and rhythmic can be established during a warm-up period. Use the literature on which you are working or a drill like Example 9-5 to focus attention on this aspect, and then pursue all this consistently in rehearsals.

Example 9-5 An exercise for training a choir to place consonants accurately

etc.

BALANCE AND TIMBRE

The composite, homogeneous choral sound produced by excellent choir members (based on an even balance between sections and an impression that there are no obvious, penetrating individual voices) depends primarily on accurate vowel choices and good vocal production. Research and experience teach us that both a really efficient, powerful *ff* and a secure, beautiful *pp* are the results of unity of pitch and of vowel choice, as well as of disciplined physical effort.

Each section must be accountable for delivering a uniform, even, attractive sound, for the sake of the whole choir; to do so, every member of a given unit must take responsibility for producing a warm, even, substantial vocal output. Sopranos should not all sound alike! That is not the point; rather, it is the composite of a number of attractive, albeit different, voices that constitutes an effective section, and four or five such sections ensure one a choir that sings with power and beauty.

A very important part of your own obligation as conductor is to be certain that all the sounds that make up the musical fabric are in proportion with one another, both onstage and in the audience's hearing. The difference between the very greatest professional conductors and their commonplace competitors often is the extremely careful work the former do to achieve perfect balance within the ensemble (balance that changes from work to work and from hall to hall) so that the composer's intentions may be transparently audible. (One hears that Herbert von Karajan used the phrase "We *all* need to hear the oboe [or violas, or harp] here.") Save rehearsal time and performance energy for this vital consideration.

PHRASING

It is important that your singers strive constantly to understand and express the extended musical continuities they are facing in given works and passages. *All of us tend to focus too much on the moment at hand, in life and in music. We bog down, failing to keep the past and the future in perspective.*

Thus it happens that your choir may drag, may fail to turn pages in time to see what is coming next, may drop final consonants, and may, above all, sing shapeless passages. Teach them to read and think in phrases. Help them learn to look ahead to approaching "peaks" in the line, and to cadences. Teach them to "arch" some phrases, to build others, and to let others still subside. In short, expect them to concentrate, and insist that they sing intelligently and musically in all that they do.

We will have more to say about principles of phrasing in later chapters, within the specific contexts of choral works in various styles.

CHORAL SIGHT READING

As you may realize from your own experience, skillful sight reading is largely a matter of practice. The more of it your musicians do, the easier it will become for them to read more and more difficult passages at sight. Age has little to do with this, by the way; well-trained English boy sopranos at age 10 routinely sight-read demanding twentieth-century literature with great accuracy.

There are highly formal approaches to this discipline: *solfège* with "fixed-and movable-*do*" techniques, the Kodály system with its hand signals, Hindemith's drills, and others. Whether you use one of these (and which one) or work on a situational basis is a matter for your judgment about your musicians. Beware of "quick-cure" approaches. (The libraries of major music schools are filled with dissertations that have studied the effectiveness of training facets of this complex skill—flash cards that force instantaneous responses, drilling of intervals by memorizing famous melodies, and the like—and those research studies generally find that the impact of those narrow techniques is negligible.) It seems likely that sight reading is so complex a skill that improvement in just one component of it is not enough to have any important effect; it is necessary, instead, that the *whole* comprehensive craft be practiced at once. That is what you must help your people do.

There are some specific procedures you can employ. Teach your singers to do the following:

1. Look through a new piece of music in the last moments before they are to begin singing it.
2. Orient themselves tonally by checking to see where the initial tonic and dominant pitches (if any) lie in their voices, and finding later key changes.
3. Orient themselves rhythmically, identifying the original meter and the rhythmic subdivisions, and spotting later changes.
4. Read ahead as far as possible, not lingering over the note and word they are singing at the moment.
5. Turn the page well before they perform the last note on the previous page.
6. Watch and listen closely to the other parts in the full fabric.

Teach as much music theory as you can, tying everything you present to specific musical contexts. Help your singers to see the structure and details of works they are learning, and then expect them to apply that knowledge in future situations.

Don't let them "lean on the piano"! Read *a cappella*. If you must use a piano during reading sessions, ask your pianist to play only first beats of measures, or "the bass line alone," or brief, crucial spots. Constant leadership from the piano takes away the personal responsibility of the choristers and lets them be careless about both pitch and rhythm judgments.

Excuse no one from this responsibility and risk. Have small groups or even individuals sight-read in full view of the choir, if necessary. Some will read more expertly than others, but every one of them can get better! The important thing, again, is *practice*—daily, if possible—under your conscientious supervision. Ask more and more of them! Of those who get the notes and rhythms right, expect precise dynamics and good diction *the first time.* Of those who get the notes, rhythms, dynamics, and diction right, expect sensitive musical phrasing at first sight.

BEGINNING A CHORAL REHEARSAL

When your singers walk into the rehearsal hall to work with you, they need immediately to sense the special character this space has. Anything you can do to help them separate themselves from the concerns and interests they have "outside" will make it possible for them to achieve quickly good concentration and full commitment to the music.

Some high school conductors establish this special atmosphere by starting a familiar chorale or something similar with those already present about a minute before the class period is to commence. As more students arrive, then, they step into their places already singing; thus, their choral music rehearsal is set apart immediately from the rest of the classes they are attending. Their concept of good sound is immediately restored. They get started musically (and with good discipline) very quickly.

To get the body invigorated, ready for the athletic aspect of singing, do some simple physical exercises as part of the rehearsal warm-up. Stretching maneuvers are good: locking the hands, and pulling up on tiptoes over the head, straight out in front, or behind the back. Head rolls, shoulder rolls, shrugs, and the like help loosen up tired and tense muscles. Have your rows of singers do a "left-face" and rub the pair of shoulders in front of each of them; then have them do an "about-face" and repeat the process (or change to light "karate chops" up and down the spine).

Next, remind your choristers about posture, if necessary. Review with them the pitch and rhythm drills described earlier. Do all this quickly so that you can get into the primary work you plan for the day.

You will find that the warm-up process you use is more effective if it is a standard routine. One of the purposes of these opening procedures is to remind your singers that they function together *as an ensemble,* sharing certain rules and practices. Let the warm-up process get them "back into the groove" you have established with them at previous rehearsals.

One of the authors once spent a summer directing a college choir almost completely devoid of music majors and trained singers. All the fundamentals had to be taught. He began by teaching them a simple Buxtehude chorale, coaching *every detail* of breathing, tone production, dynamics, phrasing, diction, and the rest over a total of four or five hours. After the first week, he used this same chorale as the opening of each subsequent rehearsal to restore right habits each day. But this Buxtehude work proved even more useful: If something went wrong later in rehearsal—poor tonal quality, perhaps, or a failure to "sing through a phrase"—he would interrupt that work and have the chorus sing the chorale again so that they would reconnect their concepts with their voices. You may find yourself in a circumstance in which this device can be useful. In any event, the strategy of a routine warm-up is a good one.

MORE CONDUCTING THEORY
Rehearsal Philosophy

A full chapter later in this volume is devoted to rehearsal management, but there are some basic points you need to consider now.

Rehearsal time is extremely valuable, and always in too short supply, for **there is always something left that you and your musicians could do to improve your expression of the music at hand.** You and they need to use every moment productively.

Some have developed in American music education a shallow and insidious philosophy that "music should be `sold' as *fun*"; some teachers, anxious to build and maintain large enrollments in their programs, and fearful that "fun" is what their students really want, have yielded to this temptation. They choose only popular, simple, undemanding (and unrewarding) repertoire, and they shy away from insisting on really disciplined and precise performance.

In the long run, such a choice is deadly! The students, who may initially behave in immature ways, *will* recognize and respond to seriousness of purpose and to the glories of great music in the end, and *they know when we condescend to them*. In the authors' experience, the finest high school and college choral programs in the country are those in which the conductor daily expects of the choristers what the late coach Vince Lombardi called "a full measure of dedication to excellence," and nothing less.

That dedication must come from you, as well as from your musicians. Teach them that rehearsal time requires concentration, physical and intellectual commitment, and musical growth. Out of this effort, then, come genuine enjoyment and the great satisfaction of sharing in great performances, but rehearsals are honest, difficult work, and should be understood as such; the pleasure rests in recognizing what has been accomplished.

PLANNING AND PACING REHEARSALS

To make full use of this valuable time, both you and the chorus must know what is to be accomplished. That means you need a rehearsal plan beforehand, and the singers need to know at least the outlines of your intentions.

First, you must judge how much you can hope to achieve in a given session, and how much over a block of rehearsals. It takes practice to predict how difficult a particular passage or work will be for a given ensemble and how many minutes will be required to perfect it. As an apprentice, you should draw up a rehearsal plan calculated down to the last minute. (Of course, such a plan often will prove faulty in your early years as a conductor, and sometimes later on, but once you have gained experience, this sort of schedule will prove to be the means of getting through all the difficult passages of a major work without having to pay "overtime scale" to professional musicians.)

When you have a plan in mind, the choir needs a calendar that shows them what to expect to do on a particular day, and they need to know how each rehearsal fits into preparation for the next performance. In some very good programs, the conductor writes timings on the blackboard beforehand, perhaps showing the following:

Warm-up	10 min.
Read Britten "Concord"	5 min.
Ave verum corpus	8 min.
Brahms motet, pp. 3–6	12 min.
Fugue, pp. 8–11	14 min.
Perform the Brahms	11 min.

At least, you should have the names of the works you plan to rehearse on the blackboard before the session begins, or have the librarian prepared to issue them in the right order. Some days, you will want to take advantage of the choir's freshness by beginning rehearsal with the reading of unfamiliar music. Other times, you will prefer to review and reestablish what you accomplished in the past by starting with a piece on which you have been working. Vary these choices so that the daily pattern does not become too routine.

After the previous rehearsal, in evaluating how things went that day, you should have made specific notes about repairs and drilling you want to undertake today. Have those notes on your music stand so that you can refer to them as you proceed.

Give constant attention to how the rehearsal "feels." Are things bogging down too much? Does the choir seem tired, or bored, or frustrated? Have you managed this session so that you have been able to give them enough real encouragement? *Pacing is one of your basic duties.*

1. Judge when to push them hard for details.
2. Judge when, on the other hand, to let them have the satisfaction of singing through a longer passage.
3. Judge when to have them accompanied by the pianist and when to expect them to sing *a cappella.*
4. Judge when to have them stand and when to have them sit, depending on the nature of the music and of the rehearsal. Don't forget, thus leaving them standing or seated too long.
5. Judge when to relax the atmosphere with a bit of humor or a recollection.

In short, working from your rehearsal plan, manage and balance the session sensitively and efficiently. **Always lend your rehearsals a sense of urgency.** As you work, make quick decisions, based on comparisons between what you expected of the choir and what you actually hear them doing. Work for variety, as well; be careful not to be too predictable, doing always the same things, in the same style, or tempo, or order; balance here is important, too.

In choral music, one constantly is deciding when to use the piano. It is very good for the choir to work *a cappella*, of course, for it forces them to depend on themselves; nevertheless, working without piano can be expensive in time spent. Use your accompanist when you have to, or when you can afford to, but demand as much personal responsibility as you can from your singers.

When you must stop for repairs, try to speak *in tempo*; you do not want to lose momentum. Issue instructions as quickly as possible, and give the next prep and downbeat in same tempo. Refer quickly to measure numbers, or to rehearsal numbers you have had your librarian enter in the parts; if neither of these is present, have a standard routine—page, staff, and bar number, for example—always spoken in the same order.

SECTIONAL REHEARSALS

Rehearsing one section at a time, either in separate sessions or (briefly) during a full-ensemble meeting, is an important technique, one of several basic rehearsal procedures outlined in Chapter 8. Sectionals give you the opportunity to isolate problems and deal with them one at a time.

If *you* are good enough, and ready enough, you can accomplish more in sectional rehearsals than in a full-ensemble session. (The authors recall that the great Robert Shaw, preparing his Chorale for its last United States tour some years ago, a tour on which the entire program was twentieth-century music, depended almost entirely on sectional rehearsals for preparation of his ensemble. Faced with high pay scales for the singers, and limited thereby in the number of hours of rehearsal he could have per day [beyond which overtime would have to be paid], Shaw assigned several days to sectional rehearsals. He brought the whole ensemble together for a single tutti dress rehearsal before their opening performance.) If you can do this sort of thing, it will give you an ideal chance to shape and refine the utterance of your choral sections so that each will contribute its very best to the composite result.

When the whole ensemble is present, you want to keep everyone involved and working productively all the time, if you can. When there are difficulties somewhere, especially on material that everyone sings sooner or later, one technique you can use is to have the entire choir sing a single voice part. It can also be helpful to have a section that is having trouble rehearse with another group that is doing all right. This reinforces and encourages the problem section.

CLOSING A REHEARSAL

Even though much may remain to be done on the work at hand, the last minutes of a rehearsal are a good time to validate the work you already have done with a "performance" of sorts. Having labored over details, stopping and starting often, perhaps, your choristers will benefit from a chance to synthesize these bits and pieces into a more-or-less coherent (albeit still flawed) whole. This will establish in them a clearer memory image of what they have done, too, which will help you with your next rehearsal.

Call them back once to good posture, disciplined breath support, and all, and try a run-through, working for the best performance possible at this stage. Make this a summation for the day and an audible step of progress toward concert readiness for the choir and the work.

End the rehearsal with encouragement for them, if it is deserved. Then give them an idea of what you plan to do in your next session.

You probably will want to tape at least some of your rehearsals (and not just so that you can play passages back to your choir): A rehearsal tape gives you a chance to evaluate *your* management of the session. How much time do you spend conducting? Talking? How interesting and useful do your comments sound the next day? Are you making the best use of your rehearsal time, or do you need to eliminate wasted remarks and extra motions?

Evaluate your rehearsal *immediately* afterward; even though your singers leave, *your* rehearsal is not over until you have "debriefed" yourself. If you wait until the next day, you will forget many details, and still will spend much time at it. If you take time to do it right away, fifteen minutes may be enough, and everything will be fresh.

MORE CONDUCTING THEORY
Building the "Choral Instrument"

Like a floral basket, the most interesting choir is not a cloning of a single voice type in every section but a *bouquet* of voices, each singing its best.

It follows, then, that there is no shortcut to getting excellent singing from each of your choristers. There is no substitute for private study in a good voice studio. Only in the finest circumstances will you have a choir made up entirely of such people, however; as an alternative, you must give your choir what instruction you can—in warm-up sessions and during rehearsals—according to the principles of good vocal production explained in the standard literature.

One often hears the word *blend* applied to choral sound, by the way; we doubt that this is a very useful concept. What you want, we believe, is not so much a choir of audible "photocopies," in which each particular voice imitates the quality of the others; you need a balanced ensemble of compatible, though distinctive, tonal qualities. Let each of your singers be herself or himself; honor individual differences, but refine them into a rich mixture.

Reinforce your ensemble psychologically, too. Give them a proud sense of how special their choral talents are, whatever their ages. **The vocal music program can be the most stable element in any school, for example; no matter how great disciplinary problems may be elsewhere in the building, the sense of teamwork, risks and goals of public performance, and the beauty of the music that emerges from this communal effort can make the choir an island of real harmony.** School administrators, who seek the same outcome from interschool athletics (in which fewer students can be direct participants), will reward the music program wherever it can lend such an atmosphere to the entire institution.

TYPES OF CHORAL ORGANIZATIONS

So far, we have spoken generically about choirs, without identifying the varieties of choral ensembles and distinguishing between the literature they sing. The standard *concert choir*, which performs a fairly broad spectrum of repertoire (generally leaning toward the central classic works), is the basic ensemble. It often ranges from 40 to 80 SATB voices, and the music it performs can demand a skilled pianist. The *symphonic or oratorio choir* specializes in large masterworks, sung usually with orchestra, and may be staffed by a roster of 100 to 250 voices; sometimes, two or more choirs may be combined for blocks of rehearsals to provide the large body of singers needed for this literature.

Show choirs devoted to popular, Broadway, and folk music are very common these days in high schools and colleges. They can be very complex organizations; since their members generally are expected to do at least some dancing as part of the entertainment programs they perform, choreography is needed, and a small instrumental group frequently accompanies many of them. In an ideal situation, particularly in a college or university, the conductor of a show choir is likely to oversee a staff including a choreographer, an assistant director for the instrumental group, one or more arrangers, a costumer, lighting and sound technicians, and a stage crew. In auditioning prospective members for such an ensemble, one considers vocal ability, dancing and movement, appearance, stagecraft, ease of manner in front of an audience, and related aspects.

The *madrigal group* (sometimes known as the *chamber singers*) is a small select ensemble for the performance of sixteenth- and seventeenth-century madrigal literature or other demanding small-chorus works, including some twentieth-century compositions; much of what this organization does may be sung *a cappella*. The *vocal jazz ensemble*, more closely related to the madrigal group than to the show choir, is also a highly specialized organization committed to more-or-less demanding jazz arrangements and compositions, each presented in its historically accurate jazz style. This virtuosic group often features singers who are capable of improvising "choruses" (à la Ella Fitzgerald), just as jazz instrumentalists do; here, again, instrumentalists may be added to the ensemble, either as soloists or for "backup work."

There is much music written for either *all-male* or *all-female choirs*, of course, generally in three or four parts. The English-style all-male choir typically is made up of 14 to 18 boy sopranos (from seven or eight years old up to the ages at which their voices change) who sing the first and second soprano parts; these are joined by about 4 male altos (countertenors), 4 tenors, and 4 to 6 basses. The standard repertoire for this ensemble is the music of the Anglican church. Other *organizations based on ethnic or cultural heritages*—the American *"gospel choir,"* for example, or *"barbershop" quartets and choruses*—perform traditional repertoire in their historic styles.

A comprehensive university choral department is likely to include most or all of these variants. First-rank high school choral programs will offer at least a concert choir, a madrigal or chamber group, and a show choir, and perhaps also a vocal jazz ensemble. Such variety may reach and serve a broad spectrum of the community, as well as creating fresh performance opportunities. Alternative ensembles can draw new members to all of them, too, including singers who would not have auditioned at first for a standard concert choir.

There certainly are risks, however, especially the danger that the intellectual and artistic legitimacy of the choral program will be diluted by values that have to do primarily with entertainment and relatively narrow cultural identifications. The authors believe that **the standard concert choir must be the central focus of any choral department,** and that no peripheral organization can be permitted to detract from that primacy. In such a setting, further, we believe that *standard vocal production of the kind we have been describing should remain the basis of all these choirs.* Although stylistic variants in jazz or ethnic groups may call for singing in other than the classical *bel canto* tradition, such special sounds should emerge from an already-trained, well-disciplined, legitimate utterance.

Your program will not be well served if it becomes a narrow one centered on an idiosyncratic vocal style, outside the standard repertoire. Once a basic vocal technique is set, however, one can recognize that balance is needed in almost all choral programs, and that all sorts of music may be appropriate for certain levels of age and experience.

FURTHER STUDY RESOURCES

The whole field of vocal pedagogy and its applications to choral singing obviously is too broad for this or any other single book. We urge you to read widely in this field, then, beginning perhaps with the works on vocal production, diction, languages, sight reading, and related technical components that are listed in the Bibliography.

In this chapter, we have introduced a substantial list of technical terminology, words like *phoneme, tessitura, spinto,* and *coloratura.* You need to be familiar with this special language, for it is both the basis for understanding concepts within your own thinking and the means of communication between yourself and other professionals. Make regular use of it, now and as your conducting career begins, until all this language is familiar to you. (When we move into our study of instrumental ensembles, we will encounter another special vocabulary used by band and orchestra personnel.)

PLANNING FOR CHORAL DEVELOPMENT

Most conductors—evaluating their choirs at the end of a season of work, and noting weakness—probably should draw up a year-long plan for vocal and musical development for the following season, a plan that includes methods for dealing with those weaknesses in sequential steps, with regular reinforcement of their demands. Important progress in music theory, choral diction, voice production, sight reading, and other technical aspects can be achieved if a conscious effort is made over a long span of time, and discipline in these areas is the true foundation of a strong choral tradition.

CHAPTER 10

Style and Performance: Medieval and Renaissance Vocal Works

Now, after several chapters of discipline and detail, the music begins! You have invested much time and energy in building technical skills and gaining understanding of the philosophy and process of conducting. You even have conducted a couple of brief chorales. Real masterworks—the creative efforts of towering geniuses—await your insights, and you are ready now to address them.

MORE CONDUCTING THEORY
Technique versus Interpretation

Some young trumpet pupils constantly ask their band director, "What is the right fingering for D-flat? How do I play G-sharp below middle C?" Trumpet fingerings are a matter of personal drill, and the band director cannot really help with such problems. All he or she can properly reply is, "Practice! Our job in this rehearsal is to learn to make the music before us beautiful, not to drill elementary skills."

Similarly, some students of conducting ask, "Am I doing this right? Are my hand gestures clear?" The professor can properly reply, "I don't teach conducting. *I teach interpretation of music.*"

That is no evasion. Conductors must learn to refine the physical aspect so that they can arrive at an artistic interpretation of a given work; that means that

1. You have already established in your mind, through prior study of the work, a clear, complete image of how you want it to sound.
2. As you stand now on the podium, seeing again the notes that represent the rhythms

and harmonies of that work, you hold in your "mind's ear" your intended interpretation, knowing what you want the musicians before you to do.

3. You can trust your eyes, as they see those notes, to signal (through your brain and nervous system) your hands, arms, face, eyes—indeed, your whole body—to make the exact gestures that will indicate to your musicians how you wish the music interpreted.

That is the basic problem: getting your ideas about a work across to the ensemble. Any refinement of your conducting technique helps you communicate those ideas more directly, more clearly. Any shortcoming in technique makes that communication more difficult, less clear. Here is the point, then: **As a conductor, you must try to get out of the way of the music, by minimizing clumsiness, flamboyance, and confusing, unnecessary gestures. This means your body must learn to move habitually,** employing movements that result from your technical practice and experience; thus is your mind freed to concentrate its best attention on the nature of the music itself and on the shaping of the performance at hand. The process of conducting leaves you no time for thinking about which direction your baton should move in next, or for telling your left hand to cue the saxophones now.

The best conductors are those who can get every member of an ensemble to work toward a single conception in a concentrated effort that matches the composer's wishes, as they are expressed in the score. Seeing Solti work, you realize that he is spending no more conscious thought on his baton's movements than Adolph Herseth (Solti's principal trumpet in the Chicago Symphony Orchestra) spends telling his fingers which valves to push. Each of them is playing his instrument (for the conductor, the ensemble in front of him) with his mind fully concentrated on *expressing his interpretation of the music.* Great conductors generally work with great musicians, professionals who already understand so much about Brahms or Stravinsky or Josquin that their leader may hardly need to conduct a beat pattern or throw cues. Her or his gestures, such as they are, can serve to reassure and balance more than to direct; they are not so much shapings of the phrase as they are merely *temperings* of it.[1] The conductor seems to be experiencing the music *with* the other performers, who are as much involved in the interpretation as is their leader.

So it must be with you. Build a strong, dependable, habit-engrained technique. Then concentrate on the music. You will find, now, that **your best rehearsals will be those in which you actually do very little because your whole ensemble already have come to understand what musical ideal, what shape it is toward which you and they are working.** The technique you use will be so

---

[1]One of the authors once had the pleasure of watching the Berlin Philharmonic play the complete Brahms Symphony No. 4, in E Minor, Op. 98, under von Karajan, in which that maestro appeared not to conduct a complete beat pattern during the entire performance. His gestures only assured, reminded, and balanced his musicians as they delivered the interpretation he and they already shared.

consonant with what you want the musicians to produce that it will merely reinforce what they already can see as the goal.

Your technical skills are developing, and you already have a foundation for work as a conductor, but that actual work lies in interpretation of music—the music of each of the great eras in the West, both choral and instrumental in character. Hence, we shall approach, in turn, representative works (great works, each of them) of the Medieval world, of the Renaissance, Baroque, Viennese Classical, and Romantic eras, and of our contemporary age. Every musical style is the product of the society around it; electronic music today reflects the nature of our world and its attributes, and each of the idioms you are going to study is just as legitimately a mirror of the values and qualities of its own period.

From each work you should gain an understanding of the style features of that period, of the interpretive choices open to you, and of the techniques necessary to convey those choices to an audience. With that background established, you will be ready to tackle any repertoire in your professional life.

A NEW BEGINNING: GREGORIAN CHANT

We challenge you first with Gregorian chant. That may seem a strange choice to you, since chant comes from a world so long gone, now foreign to us—the Medieval realm of priests and monks in long processions through great stone cathedrals, the time of castles, Crusades, knights, and pilgrimages. Yet one of the duties of a conductor—indeed, of any musician—is to bring to life for the people of today the worlds of the past by presenting the musics of those eras. The character of chant is as different in style from the music of our own time as are those cathedrals from today's skyscrapers.

And there are good practical, professorial reasons for confronting Gregorian chant.

1. The monophonic character of chant permits us to begin our conducting with a texture in which there are no conflicting, fugal entrances. We need not concern ourselves, yet, with multiple voices and chords.
2. The rhythmic nature of chant requires the conductor to *modify the beat pattern constantly*, a prerequisite that gives you the chance to build a flexible, dependable baton technique through routine practice.
3. Chant melodies are the basis for a large share of the choral music written between the dawn of polyphony and at least the seventeenth century, as we shall see. Studying it can teach us to understand aspects of the "cantus firmus" compositional procedures.
4. Beginning with chant means we approach all the choral music in this book chronologically.

There are other benefits; conducting chant teaches us a different, earlier notational system: the four-line staff, which is still in use for liturgical music. This study is one more step on our road to thorough preparation as conductors who have no limitations of style or medium.

Notational and Structural Characteristics of Chant

Although to a considerable extent Gregorian chant was shared among the priests and monks who most frequently sang it through the oral tradition (that is, by rote learning), various systems of notation for chant were in development by the year 1000. The one that the Roman church finally made universal, and still uses, employs a *four*-line staff on which *do* is designated by the symbol ⌶ placed around one or another of the lines, as in Figure 10-1.

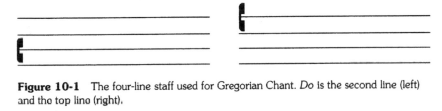

Figure 10-1 The four-line staff used for Gregorian Chant. *Do* is the second line (left) and the top line (right).

Similarly, a particular chant may be notated with *fa* (indicated by the symbol ⌶) as the clef designation, instead of *do*. See Figure 10-2.

Figure 10-2 On this four-line staff, *fa* is the bottom line (left) and the third line (right).

The pitches arranged on these four lines can be classified into some eight scales, the "church modes" you have studied in music theory. In general, each mode is organized tonally around a *final* (the pitch that literally is to be the last note sung) and a *reciting tone,* on and around which much of the melodic activity occurs (especially the repetition of several text syllables on a single written note). There are no key signatures, and only one pitch mutation (accidental) is permitted; the syllable *ti* is marked to be flatted in certain modal situations. All Gregorian chant is, in short, *diatonic.* Chromaticism does not occur.

In general, the notation assumes one syllable per note, and these individual notes (called *neumes* in this music) are square in shape (■). Neumes are joined together (┱ and ┱ are examples) whenever more than one pitch is sung on a single syllable. A large number of these two-note, three-note, and longer neumes, in various shapes, are used in chant.[2]

---

[2]It is not our purpose that you learn them all now. Only those necessary to the chant passages studied in this book will be introduced.

The most important quality of Gregorian rhythm is flow. This essential forward motion takes its impetus from the text being chanted, pausing or stopping at significant punctuation points. It is the careful shaping of these graceful melodic and textual curves that is at the heart of the expression of this music.

The rhythmic notation itself is not complicated. A dot after a neume (■·) doubles its length. A dash under a neume (an *episema*, ●) merely lengthens it somewhat. Vertical lines (much like modern bar lines) indicate breathing points and pauses. The briefest of these are indicated by a quarter-stop and a half-stop, which are not intended to interrupt the motion; a full bar line terminates a complete phrase of the text, and a break in the flow is appropriate there; the double bar marks the end of a whole chant passage. See Figure 10-3.

Figure 10-3 Punctuation marks in chant: the quarter, half, full, and double bar lines

Gregorian chant is nonmetric, of course. The syllable accent structure of the text means, however, that both duple and triple beat-groupings occur, and the conductor must signal these changes with the baton (as we shall see in the passages that follow). Other expressive patterns (concepts of *arsis* and *thesis*, for example) are matters of interpretive choice and have to be heard and seen in context.

Finally, *singing* Gregorian chant does not require a highly disciplined vocal technique, but it does demand thought and care. As one of our best contemporary sources says:

> The singing of chant must be characterized by the three virtues of sobriety, simplicity and restraint. . . . But this does by no means imply that the chant is to be sung heavily or slowly. There must never be a sensation of dragging in the rendition of the chant. It must be sung *lightly* and it must *move*. The rhythm, the melody and the text all contribute to this lightness and movement which make the chant by nature so capable of lifting our minds and hearts to God in liturgical prayer.[3]

[3]*Chants of the Church* (Toledo, Ohio: Gregorian Institute of America, 1962), p. xi. This thin volume contains sixty selected Gregorian chants, together with Ordinary and Proper chants for the Mass itself, buttressed by very useful explanations of chant notation and interpretation, all in keeping with the stylistic practices of the Benedictine monks at Solesmes (which we have chosen as our standard for this book). There is also a brief Latin pronunciation guide, according to Roman usage. See also Dom Eugène Cardine, *Gregorian Semiology* (Solesmes: Abbaye Saint-Pierre de Solesmes, 1983); Joseph Gajard, *The Rhythm of Plainsong According to the Solesmes School*, trans. Dom Aldhelm Dean (New York: Fischer & Brothers, 1945); and Willi Apel, *Gregorian Chant* (Bloomington: Indiana University Press, 1958).

Background and Perspectives

A few words about the history of this music: "Gregorian" chant takes its name, of course, from Gregory the Great, pope from 590 to 604, who may or may not have played a significant role in the collection and standardization of the various musical and liturgical practices employed during the early Middle Ages. There were, and are, other bodies of chant in use both in the West and in the East, but it is the Gregorian repertory that has had the most influence on Western music, from at least the ninth century to the present. There were in earlier times hundreds of chant melodies in that repertory. Malpractice and theological considerations led to reforms, especially those of the Council of Trent in the sixteenth century. Later "reformers" went too far, however, and Gregorian chant itself declined. The nineteenth century saw fresh efforts to return to Gregorian roots, among these the widely accepted work of the Benedictines at Solesmes.

The Chant *Pange lingua*

The Text of **Pange lingua**

In the beginning of choral music came the Text, and so it is with all chant, for the tradition of singing scriptural and liturgical passages probably arose from twin desires to amplify (acoustically) and beautify the presentation of the words. Ideally, then, chanting should make the text more accessible to the listener (through clear diction and syllable stress), as well as more lovely.

Let us begin work on one of the most famous of all the Gregorian chants, *Pange lingua* (Example 10-1).[4] Get a good Latin pronunciation guide, if you need one,[5] and read the Latin text several times aloud and not too fast, with the proper syllables accented, until your reading develops an easy, natural rhythmic flow. *Herein you hear the underlying music.* As to verbal meaning, Example 10-1 provides a word-by-word interlinear translation, with accents shown.

[4]*Chants of the Church*, pp. 125–126. Used by permission of Gregorian Institute of America. This also may be found, as may all such chants, in the *Liber usualis*.

[5]Recommended pronunciation guides for the languages used in this book are listed in the Bibliography.

Example 10-1   The Gregorian chant *Pange lingua* (complete)

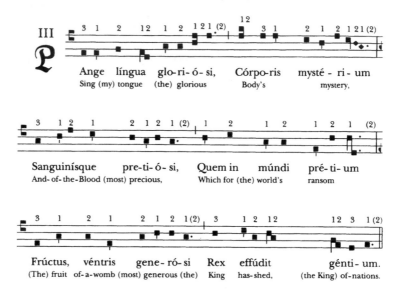

III

Ange língua glo-ri-ó-si,   Córpo-ris mysté-ri-um
Sing (my) tongue (the) glorious   Body's   mystery,

Sanguinísque   pre-ti-ó-si,   Quem in   múndi   pré-ti-um
And-of-the-Blood (most) precious,   Which for (the) world's   ransom

Frúctus,   véntris   gene-ró-si   Rex   effúdit   génti-um.
(The) fruit of-a-womb (most) generous (the)   King   has-shed,   (the King) of-nations.

2.

Nóbis dátus, nóbis nátus
To-us given, for-us born

Ex in-tá-cta Vírgine,
Of a spotless Virgin,

Et in mún-do conversátus,
And in the-world dwelling,

Spár-so vér-bi sémine,
Scattering the-word's seed,

Súi móras in-co-lá-tus
His course of-life-on-earth

Mí-ro cláu-sit ór-di-ne.
Wondrously He-closed in-its-order.

3.

In suprémae nó-cte coé-nae
On the night of His Last Supper

Recúmbens cum frá-tri-bus,
Reclining with (His) brethren,

Observáta lé-ge plene
Observing (the) Law fully

Cí-bis in le-gá-li-bus,
With-food in law-prescribed,

Cí-bum túr-bae du-o-dé-nae
(As) food to-the-company of-twelve

Se dat sú-is má-ni-bus.
Himself He-gives by-His-own-hands.

4.

Vér-bum cá-ro, pá-nem vérum
(The) Word made-flesh, bread truly

Vér-bo cár-nem éf-fi-cit:
By-his-word to-His-flesh He-changes:

Fít-que sán-guis Chrísti mérum,
And-turned to-blood of-Christ (is) wine,

Et si sén-sus dé-fi-cit,
And if (our) sense fails (us)

Ad firmándum cor sincérum
To confirm (the) heart sincere,

Sóla fídes súfficit.
Alone, faith suffices.

5.

Tántum er-go Sa-cra-mén-tum
So-great, therefore, (this) Sacrament,

Venerémur cér-nu-i:
Let-us-adore (it) bending-low:

Et an-tí-quum documéntum
And (the) ancient covenant

Nó-vo cé-dat rí-tu-i:
To-the-New shall-yield, to-this-rite:

Praé-stet fí-des suppleméntum
Provide-may faith (a) supplement

Sén-su-um deféctui.
For-our-senses' deficiency.

6.

Ge-ni-tó-ri, Ge-ni-tó-que
To (the) Father and to (the) Son

Laus et jubilátio,
Praise and jubilation,

Sá-lus, hónor, vírtus quoque
Salvation, honor, virtue also

Sit et benedíctio,
Be, and benediction:

Pro-ce-dén-ti ab utróque
To-Him-proceeding from both

Cómpar sit lau-dá-ti-o. Amen.
Equal be (our) praising. Amen.

Analysis of Pange lingua

Example 10-1 is written on a four-line staff. The top line is designated as *do;* assuming, then, that *do* equals C-natural in this case (although it could be any other comfortable pitch), the first note shown is what we would call an E-natural, the third neume an F-natural, and so on. Each neume is intended to provide music—one pitch or more—for one syllable; thus, there is one pitch for each of the first three syllables, and a pair of notes (the fourth neume) for the second syllable of "lin*gua*." Double- or triple-pitch neumes are sung from left to right, and from bottom to top, so the fourth neume (a *clivis*) is an E followed by a D, and the *podatus* on "gloriosi" is an A followed by a C. The first syllable of "*Corporis*" (another podatus) is a C followed by a high D, and the three-note succession on "mysteri*um*" (a *climacus*) indicates B–A–G. The final syllable of "pretium" (a *pressus*) is a skip from A (note that the A in this neume comes first) down to D. The neumes on "effu*dit*" and "*gentium*" are handled just like the clivis on "lin*gua*."

Unless they are dotted or underscored (with a horizontal episema), treat both the square-shaped neume (the *punctum*) and the diamond (the *rhombus*) mentally as eighth notes; each of them, in other words, is a pulse in this music. The C at the end of "gloriosi," being dotted, is doubled in length, but the quarter bar line (which permits a quick breath just after the C) must be subtracted from its value; think of the C as a dotted eighth, followed by a sixteenth rest. The final G of "mysterium," on the other hand, ends with a full bar line; regard that G as a full-length quarter note, and add an eighth rest for the full bar line. The rest of the bar lines in this chant function in exactly the same ways. (There are no horizontal episemas here; if there were, each would lengthen its neume slightly.)

If we were to transcribe this chant into modern notation, it could look like Example 10-2.[6]

Example 10-2   *Pange lingua* as it might be scored in modern notation

[6]We show you this transcription only to clarify the explanation we have given you of this notational system. Learn to read the four-line scoring; it is not difficult, and conductors should be comfortable with all clefs, of which this is merely one type. You should *not* "transpose" this music into modern five-line scoring, for the notation itself gives insight into the style and character of these melodies, and gives us some sense of how Renaissance and later composers viewed these melodies when they were adopting them as canti firmi.

Conducting Pange lingua

Now to conduct this beautiful, evocative chant. You are learning the Solesmes approach, the method developed by the Benedictines in their monastery near Le Mans, France. Their edition has come to be regarded as orthodox (although there are musicological controversies about their work, as there are about any restorations of ancient music).[7] We have chosen to use it partly because their conducting techniques will be easier for you to handle now, as well.

Although we have been speaking of a *pulse* in this music—a pulse *that should be kept constant*—we need to suspend our modern sense of *meter* in chant, in favor of a feeling of phrases made up of varied numbers of pulses, all in a flowing continuity built of word stress and melodic shape.

The monks at Solesmes mark certain neumes (on both stressed and unstressed syllables) with apostrophe-like "vertical episemas," calling each of the two- or three-note units ( ) thus demarcated an *ictus*. They do not mean that these notes should be either accented or lengthened, however; these are, most simply, points at which the neumes can be divided into groups of two or three, as a means of keeping the singers together and as part of the overall shaping of the phrase.

In Example 10-1, these episemas are shown, and the neumes they affect are divided for you (into groups of twos and threes) by the arabic numerals we have added underneath. Each ictus (each unit marked off by vertical episemas) will get a beat, but these beats will vary in length between two and three pulses. (The "guide note," the partial neume at the end of each line, merely warns the singer what the first note of the following line will be. It is not performed.)

We will use a form of our one-beat to conduct chant. That probably comes closest to the feeling we want to convey. The ultimate goal, however, is to "soften" the impact of the beat. Avoid any sense of the "downbeat"! The episema is not a point of stress, remember; it has more the quality of a springboard, giving a forward impulse. The one-beat pattern appropriate here should be a bit more rounded than usual. (See Figure 10-4.)

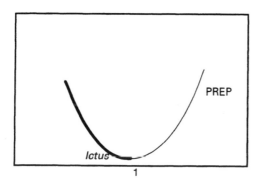

Figure 10-4 A modified one-beat pattern for use in conducting Gregorian chant

---

[7]See the detailed discussion under "Plainchant" in the *New Grove Dictionary of Music and Musicians*, ed. Stanley Sadie (New York: Macmillan, 1980).

Practice Exercise 10-1 *Singing Chant, Using Ictus Groupings of Two and Three*

Sing Example 10-1 several times, using the arabic numerals shown, instead of the words (3 1 2 12 1 2 12 1 (2), 12 3 1 2 1 2 1 2 1 (2) rest, and so on), until you can do so with accurate pitch and rhythm.

Then, try placing a one-beat on each vertical episema—that is, on each ictus. Make the beats that must cover three neumes a bit longer and slower than the ones that signal just two pulses. Repeat this until you become fluent at it. Once you are comfortable with the basic beat pattern, add cutoffs at the quarter and full bars, and at the end.

Here are a few more suggestions about performing Gregorian chant.

1. Keep the line flowing, lyric, and liquid in character. Work for continuity and flexibility.
2. Ask your singers to avoid audible breaths.
3. Remember that the text is the most important element here; express it, giving it proper word stress. No final syllables are stressed. Don't emphasize or accent the episemas. Almost understress them!
4. Study the overall melodic shape of the line. It rises and falls in waves, like those of the sea; do not let it become humdrum and square. Take advantage to shape beautifully any upward and downward sweeps between the full bars. Consider, too, the relationships of the bar lines, which define the priorities of the overall form; remember that it is the kinds of bar lines employed that help indicate to you the relative lengths of the pauses within and between phrases.[8]

Familiarity with the *Pange lingua* chant will be especially useful to you in the future, for great composers used it as a *cantus firmus* (a melodic compositional foundation) in longer works. The *Missa Pange lingua* by Josquin des Prez is a famous and lovely instance of this, and we shall meet it again later in this chapter.

The Chant *Ave Maria*

Analysis of Ave Maria

Example 10-3 presents another notable chant used often by later composers for their works: *Ave Maria.*[9] (Josquin's four-part *Ave Maria* motet is surely one of the most beautiful of all Renaissance choral works.)

---

[8]For a detailed discussion of expression in Gregorian chant, see *Chants of the Church*, pp. vii–xii. As a convenience for your later use, the authors include in Appendix B a summary of style and performance practice in Gregorian chant.

[9]*Chants of the Church*, p. 86. Used by permission of Gregorian Institute of America.

Example 10-3 The chant *Ave Maria*, but with no beat-pattern numerals present[10]

A - ve   Mar- i - a, *grá- ti- a pléna,   Dóminus   técum,
Hail   Mary,   with - grace replete,   (the) Lord (is) with - Thee

benedícta   tu   in   mu- li - é- ribus,   et   benedíctus   frúctus
blessed (art) thou among   women,   and   blessed   (is - the) fruit

véntris   tú - i,   Jésus.   Sáncta   Ma- rí- a,   Máter   Dé- i,   óra
of - the - womb of - thee, Jesus.   Holy   Mary,   Mother of God,   pray

pro nóbis   pecca- tó- ribus,   nunc et in   hó - ra   mórtis nó -
for   us   sinners,   now and in (the) hour of - the - death of -

stræ.   Amen.
us.   Amen.

This time, we want you to do the necessary analysis, but we will lead you step by step through an order of priority.

1. Read the text several times, getting a feeling for the "music of the words," the vowels and the consonants, the word accents, the length and shapes of the phrases.
2. What does the clef sign indicate?
3. Are there any accidentals? (There is one in this chant; on what pitch is it? Notice that the flat sign is on the space, not on either of the lines.)

[10]We have not included the beat-pattern numerals in this chant because we want you to compute them for yourself. Once you have done so, you can check them against our calculations (the commas, semicolons, and periods represent bar lines of the various kinds):

3 1 2 3 1 2 12, 1 2 3 1 2 12, 1 2 1 2 12; 1 2 1 2 12,
1 2 3 1 2 3 1 2 12; 1 2 1 2 1 2 1 2 1 2 1 2 1 2 12.
3 1 2 1 2 12 1 2 1 2 12; 3 1 2 1 2 1 2 1 2 1 2 3 12;
1 2 1 2 3 1 2 3 1 2 1 2 1 2 12.

4. What bar lines are present? (The half bars indicate a formal priority, a stratum above that of the quarter bars and below that of the full bars. Note the double bar that divides this chant into two major units. What expressive opportunities do these structural divisions offer? Where does the flow of the chant push forward? Where are the relative points of rest? Here you begin your interpretation.)

5. Are there any unfamiliar neumes? (No, although the fourth one looks a bit complicated: You know already that the D is sung before the A, and the B-flat comes last.)

6. Are there any other unfamiliar signs? (There is a single horizontal episema on the first syllable of "plena," so the singers should lengthen the first note of that neume slightly. Notice also the asterisk after "Maria" in the text: This indicates a change of voices; in this case, it means that the priest should sing the words "Ave Maria" (as an *incipit*) and the others present sing everything after the asterisk; in other instances, this sign can indicate an alternation of antiphonal voices.)

7. Trace the rhythmic organization of this chant.

8. Where will the singers breathe, and how will these breaths affect the rhythm?

9. What does the text mean? From what source (book and passage) does it come?

Practice Exercise 10-2 *Practicing to Conduct the Chant* Ave Maria

Devise now your own practice routine as your physical preparation for conducting *Ave Maria*. This is the sort of disciplined assignment you will have to give yourself each time you study a work you are going to conduct. (This time, if you need help designing a routine, look back to Practice Exercise 10-1.)

Conducting Ave Maria

You will want to use the same modified one-beat pattern we employed for the chant *Pange lingua*. Since the alternations of duple- and triple-note groups are more frequent in this chant, you will find it more complicated to conduct than was *Pange lingua*, but as you practice, it should become easier within minutes. Here are some specific suggestions:

1. Give a great deal of thought to the overall rise and fall of the melody. Keep the line interesting.

2. How do you "help" make the form clear for the listener? A diminuendo at the end of each section is a cliché in chant. A *slight* ritard at the end of each major section is permissible, too. These expressive choices will make the structure more audible, as will the rise and fall in the melodic line.

MORE CONDUCTING THEORY
Unity versus Variety in Music

Every composer faces the question "What note do I write next?" Each must avoid creating a shapeless muddle, and so each seeks some concept, device, or other influence to use as a thread of continuity that can serve to unify each composition.

In the twentieth century, Igor Stravinsky deliberately imitated (and modified) the forms and media that had been used by earlier composers. Béla Bartók borrowed the essential character of Eastern European and North African folk melodies (without actually using the melodies themselves); Charles Ives, Aaron Copland, and others applied some of the same techniques to American tunes. Arnold Schoenberg (with his serial procedures) and Paul Hindemith (in *The Craft of Musical Composition*) invented compositional formulas to get them across what Stravinsky called "the Abyss of Freedom."[11]

For Renaissance composers (as for their predecessors, who had written polyphony in the Medieval era), the principal means of assuring an element of unity was the use of the cantus firmus, a previously composed melody employed as a basis for a new composition. Both "liturgical" and "profane" melodies were employed (with or without the texts that were the primary means of classifying them as one or the other), and each type was used in both sacred and secular Renaissance compositions.

The principal bodies of melodic materials available for cantus firmus use by a fifteenth- or sixteenth-century composer were Gregorian chant and early varieties of the *chanson*. It will not surprise you, therefore, that much of the sacred polyphony of the Renaissance has as a compositional basis a cantus firmus from the vast repertory of Gregorian chant. Sometimes, the composer's usage is such that the chant melody itself is obvious to the listener (in the soprano part, perhaps, and unaltered); sometimes, on the other hand, the cantus firmus is hidden from the ears of the audience (in long or highly ornamented notes, perhaps in the bass part). Either way, it has served his purposes.

A RENAISSANCE MASTERWORK

One such cantus firmus, employed by Josquin des Prez in his masterwork *Missa Pange lingua (The "Pange lingua" Mass)*,[12] is our old friend, the chant *Pange lingua*. (See Example 10-1 or Example 10-2.) Here, Josquin's use of this cantus firmus is both easy to see and easy to hear.

Look at the melody. It begins with what is called a Phrygian second, a half step up from E (which will prove to be the *final*) to F; that interval is distinctive and will tend to be audible in any new tune that uses it. Many features of Gregorian chant melodies are easy to recognize when they reappear in a polyphonic work.

---

[11]Igor Stravinsky, *Poetics of Music* (from the Charles Eliot Norton Lectures at Harvard University, 1939–1940; New York: Vintage Books, 1956), pp. 66–69.

[12]Josquin des Prez, Kyrie from *Missa Pange Lingua*, ed. Albert Smijers (G. Alspach, 1952). We can be reasonably confident of the accuracy of *Missa Pange lingua* scholarship, for over a dozen complete sixteenth-century sources of the work still exist, in both manuscript and printed form. (Your professor may choose to assign the entire work or only the opening Kyrie section at this time.)

Example 10-4 Josquin des Prez: *Missa Pange lingua,* Kyrie

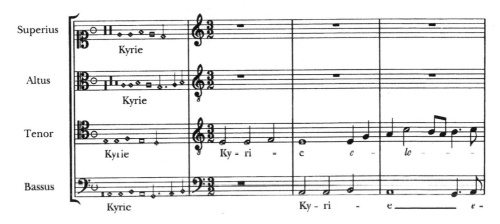

Example 10-4 *(cont.)*

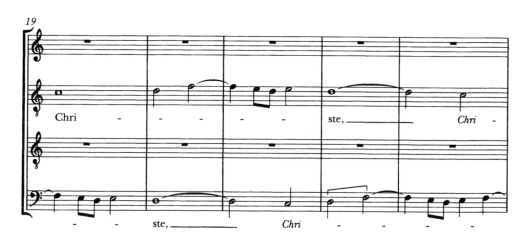

Example 10-4 *(cont.)*

Used by permission of Vereniging Voor Nederlandse Muziekgeschiedenis (VNM), postbox 1514, 3500 BM Utrecht, Holland.

Background and Perspective: The Music of Josquin des Prez

There is good evidence that there should be a J among the three B's. Josquin des Prez was the equal in his own time of Bach, Beethoven, and Brahms in theirs. No less a world figure than Martin Luther is said to have called him "the Master of the Notes." Born in the middle of the fifteenth century (we do not know the exact year), he was trained within the mainstream of the Flemish tradition, the peak of European musical culture in that era. His service at papal and ducal courts across Western Europe helped to make him the ranking composer of his time; we know he served two popes, the d'Este family in Ferrara, and others in Milan, Florence, Italy, and France: Some of his music found its way into the Habsburg imperial collection in Vienna. The master had the luck to become well known in Italy in the early sixteenth century, just as the printing of music began, and Petrucci himself issued three volumes of his masses. Josquin is thought to have died in Burgundy in August 1521.

Many of his works (especially some of his instrumental pieces) are homophonic in texture, but he became one of the most skilled contrapuntalists of all time.[13] His choral settings of sacred texts (sometimes characterized as *musica reservata*) have for many a mystical, prayerful beauty unmatched by the other Renaissance masters.

Certainly, his sensitivity to the haunting power of the texts he used is manifest in his motets and masses, and in no case more than in the *Missa Pange lingua*. Here, the words are set to long, arching lines that, for all their restraint and dignity, still have great rhythmic interest and vitality.

One consistent feature of his counterpoint is his "pairing of voices." In this procedure, he binds two parts together (his tenors and basses, say) in effective counterpoint; shortly, two more voices (in this case the sopranos and altos) enter, singing the same counterpoint, while their predecessors continue their own evolving lines. In Josquin's most intricate writing, based on mensural values, the complexity of his contrapuntal relationships can rival those of Bach himself.

Study of Analytic Procedures and Rehearsal Techniques

Many of the tools you need to analyze this Kyrie are already your own; what you now know about music theory and history will serve you well in studying this movement. You can examine its melodic, harmonic, textural, and temporal characteristics, and make judgments about how you want it to sound. You can make guesses at what your musicians will find difficult (the features that will take the most rehearsal time) and easy.

We have some suggestions for you about that process of analysis—some guidance for you as you approach not just this Kyrie but also any future repertoire. Some of these recommendations relate to topics as broad as structural analysis, and some are as specific as choosing tempos and dynamics. This is not the moment in this book to launch into an organized study of "analysis and interpretation," however. That will come after you have acquired a more routine approach to conducting.[14]

---

[13]Some have wished that Fux had chosen the more rhythmically sophisticated counterpoint of Josquin, instead of that of sixteenth-century Palestrina, as the stylistic prototype for his text *Gradus ad Parnassum*, which had such great influence on the teaching of counterpoint in the West.

[14]See Chapter 18. If you wish (or if your professor wishes it), you may undertake that study now.

Both rehearsal procedures and performance considerations demand the same sort of comprehensive examination that we have said score analysis deserves, and this theoretical overview should be kept separate, we believe, from the (more limited) study of a particular work. In this book, as a consequence, we will discuss rehearsal techniques in Chapter 19 and performance matters in Chapter 20.[15]

Analysis of Josquin's Kyrie[16]

As you will discover from a thorough study of the complete work, the *Missa Pange lingua* is a profoundly crafted setting of the complete Ordinary of the Mass, using the plainchant *Pange lingua* as its principal unifying factor. We cannot be certain exactly when it was written, but it displays the maturity of technique and style of a composer at the peak of his powers. Although (we are sorry to note) it is rarely sung as service music now, but rather in concert, in Josquin's lifetime these movements would have been part of a eucharistic liturgy. The Kyrie and the Gloria would have been sung consecutively, and his other segments would have been performed later in the ritual. The remaining parts of the Mass (the Proper) would have been chanted (that is, would have been monophonic). A motet and a few responses would have been the only other responsibilities of the choir.

A glance at the score shows you the clefs and the time signature from the original source; Smijers, the editor, has shown you the first half-dozen notes in each part so that you can see how Josquin notated this movement, and then he has gone on to present the work in modern calligraphy. Note that there were no bar lines in the original (just as there were none in the *Pange lingua* chant, on which the movement is based).

A Kyrie is the first element of the Ordinary of the Mass; the (classical Greek) text in full is:

Kyrie eleison	(Lord, have mercy upon us)
Christe eleison	(Christ, have mercy upon us)
Kyrie eleison	(Lord, have mercy upon us)

This would suggest to our modern minds—full of analyses of Beethoven and Brahms—an *ABA* form; the reprise of the first two words would recommend to us a repetition of the initial section of music, too, but it was not so in the Renaissance. Josquin's approach (like that of his contemporaries) is to set the second Kyrie section to different music from that of the first one.

---

[15]Once again, if you wish it (or if your professor wishes you to do so), you may study either chapter now.

[16]Here, the authors provide the beginning outline of the sort of analysis you should prepare for each work you conduct. Your own work should be more detailed, of course, including complete examinations of textual, melodic, harmonic, tonal, textural, metric, rhythmic, and unique aspects.

That music is based on what is sometimes called "point of imitation" writing, in which a melodic line is introduced in one voice and then repeated (starting on the same or different pitches) in fugal entrances in the other voices. One sees in the Kyrie I, the Christe (beginning in bar 17), and the Kyrie II (which starts in measure 53) that the entrances *are* fugal and imitative, and that in each section they evolve to a cadence in which all four parts are present (measures 16, 50–52, and 68–70). One sees also that the "pairing of voices" of which we have spoken is present; the tenors and basses enter one bar apart at the beginning, and then the sopranos and altos (four measures later and an octave higher) replicate the lower voices exactly. This technique—fugal`entrances of paired voices—is used throughout the movement, first with the lower voices leading, then with the basses and altos introducing the Christe, and finally with the upper voices presenting the Kyrie II motif.

Let us look more carefully at the first subject. In Example 10-5, we see the opening bars of the tenor part. Compare this pitch order (ignoring the rhythm) with the melody of the chant *Pange lingua* (see Examples 10-1 and 10-2). Josquin has indeed used the chant as a cantus firmus, beginning the Kyrie I with the exact pitch order of the plainsong, while inventing in the process an effective rhythm for it. (Then he has imitated that new subject in the other three parts, as they enter.) The Phrygian second we noted earlier is the first feature of that subject, and the prominent skips from D up to G and from A up to C (both obvious in the original chant itself) help make this melody easy to remember.

Example 10-5   Josquin des Prez: *Pange lingua*, Kyrie, opening measures of the tenor part

Josquin's melodic lines are reasonably conservative, with the motion primarily stepwise. Consecutive skips in the same direction are rare (there are none in the Kyrie), but he does permit (as Palestrina would not) skips in the same direction in which an otherwise-conjunct line is moving (see the D–G–A–C succession in measures 2 and 3 of Example 10-5). Octaves are common, and sixths (especially upward sixths) occur frequently; in this movement, there is even an ascending seventh in the tenor line; such large skips tend to be "resolved" by stepwise motion in the opposite direction (as would be the case in Palestrina). Repeated notes occur often.

Be certain you study these voice parts carefully. **Never ask your choir to sing lines you do not know.**

Practice Exercise 10-3 *Learning Voice Parts in the Kyrie*

Sing each of the four voice parts in the Kyrie movement of Josquin's *Missa Pange lingua* until you are confident you can "hear" each of them well *in your mind*. Find the difficult passages, and learn what problems to expect from your choir members. This process will also give you a good sense of the shape of each phrase.

The first harmonic interval (measure 2) is a perfect fifth, as we might expect. Renaissance composers began and ended especially their sacred works on perfect intervals (for reasons both of theology and of practice). Of the three principal cadences, the second (bars 49–52) is plagal, ending on a D minor triad. The first and last (bars 15–16 and 67–70) use what we would now call a dominant–tonic relationship, and end in open octave and open fifth sonorities; note, however, a salient stylistic characteristic of Josquin's time: In the last of these, the third (the G) of what would be a cadential E minor triad is present at first but dissolves in the moving vocal lines over the final two measures. This "disappearing third" was used partly for political reasons, an earlier pope having forbidden (on the basis of theology) the use in terminal cadences of such "imperfect consonances" as the major and minor thirds. Josquin's procedure in the last three bars of his Kyrie is an evasion of that church canon and is typical of his (and his Flemish contemporaries') cadences.

Otherwise, triads are basic to this style. Passing dissonances abound, and suspensions occur (see measure 4), as in Palestrina, but Josquin does somewhat more radical things, too: The skip of a seventh in the tenor (bar 63), for example, is a leap away from a dissonance, an unusual feature later in the sixteenth century.

Note again the rhythmic values of the original manuscript (shown at the very beginning of Example 10-4). You will remember that routine modern bar lines were not in use in the era of Josquin des Prez, and musicians gained from the time signatures not so much a sense of meter (in a nineteenth-century manner) as an understanding of how longer note values were to be divided by smaller ones (that is, broken into subdivisions of two or three). Thus, the full circle just after the original clef signs indicates that in Kyrie I, the primary "beats" (in the modern edition, the half notes) are grouped in threes, and that each can be divided into a pair of quarters. The Christe, on the other hand, employs pairs of half notes, each divided duply. The Kyrie II again is triple, with a duple subdivision.[17]

---

[17] It is very important for modern conductors to be able to see what the original notation of these works looked like, and to understand the implications of those symbols. If aspects of Renaissance mensuration—including terms like *prolation* and *semibreve*—are unfamiliar to you, you should research the matter in major reference works and texts on music history, especially beginning with the fourteenth century.

Josquin uses a wide variety of rhythmic values in the Kyrie, ranging from modern whole notes and dotted whole notes to eighth notes. He frequently skips a rhythmic level (see the tenor part in bar 2, in which he moves directly from whole note to quarter, without a half note in between; also in the next bar from half to eighth, without an intervening quarter note), a rhythmic flexibility less common later in the sixteenth century.

Each section begins with longer note values (especially the Christe), and he returns to long values for the three important cadences. The rapidity of rhythmic activity in the overall texture appears to increase as he approaches each of these terminal points. There is a kind of built-in acceleration; in each case, there are at least three or four consecutive measures in which every quarter note is articulated somewhere in the texture (a phenomenon the authors call the "constant quarter.") We should note also that—unlike earlier polyphonic writing (in the Ars Nova, for example, when slower note values generally were assigned to the lower voices)—Josquin's fugal imitation involves all the singers in all the rhythmic values and features of his style.

Tempo Decisions in Renaissance Choral Music

One of your most important leadership decisions is the choice of tempo. There are three different sections within the Kyrie, and three different time signatures; each represents a tempo determination you have to make.

The basis for motion in the music of the Renaissance was the *tactus*, a kind of standard pulse based (in this era long before wristwatches and metronomes) on the human heartbeat and the pace of normal walking—that is, on common physical rhythms of life. This tactus apparently was permitted to vary slightly to fit the character of particular pieces and to avoid monotony. Various authorities place the tactus at a range of speeds from 60 to 70 or 72, or even 80, beats per minute (our MM = 60 to 80, that is).

Admitting, then, that tempo in the Renaissance is based on this tactus, it is necessary to *connect the notation of the piece at hand with that concept.*

1. Looking at ancient manuscripts, one can make that connection by evaluating the original mensural signatures and deciding which rhythmic value is intended to represent the beat in each case.
2. When one is working with a modern manuscript, however, one cannot tell what the composer's intentions were unless the edition shows the opening passage (as does this one), one consults another edition, or the modern editor has indicated which modern value is to be made the beat.

In this case, the early manuscripts indicate a full circle for the Kyrie I and a semicircle for the Christe; the circle appears again for the Kyrie II, but at least one of the existing sources has a slash through that last circle, apparently to counsel a brighter tempo for the Kyrie II than for the opening.[18] The authors believe that since the motion in Josquin's Kyrie seems to be dominated by the semibreve, *the tactus here is represented by the semibreve (and thus, in the modern edition given you, by the half note)*.

We therefore suggest that you try the following tempos for this movement:

1. For the Kyrie I (originally a full circle), the modern half note at MM = 60 to 64
2. For the Christe (originally a semicircle), the half note at MM = 60 to 66
3. For the Kyrie II (originally a full circle, with a vertical slash edited in by a contemporary), the half note at MM = 66 to 72

Whether you choose to use these tempos or not, you should understand now the basis for tempo decisions in this period.

The Choir in Josquin's Time

We gather from the tessituras of the four voices here that Josquin probably intended the top part to be sung by boys, and the three lower ones by men (countertenors, tenors, and basses). We can only guess at the numbers he would have used. Since we know from one of the manuscripts that the *Missa Pange lingua* was probably sung at the papal court, and that Leo X had about two dozen singers in his choir (which, as the papal choir, likely was the most sumptuous of its time), we can generalize that at least a dozen singers, and perhaps as many as twice that figure, would have sung the work in Josquin's lifetime.

As is often the case in Renaissance music, the alto part was written for countertenors instead of females and, therefore, lies very low[19]—too low for most women; the other parts are reasonably comfortable. How can you fit this work to a modern choir?

1. One alternative is to have the altos and the tenors trade parts at such times; they could do so for the entire Christe, for example, with the tenors making the alto entrance in bar 19 at their usual pitch and the altos entering in bar 25 (reading the tenor part an octave lower); returning to their own parts for the Kyrie II, they could manage nicely to the end (with a tenor or two helping the altos out on the low E's in bars 68–69).
2. Another alternative is to have some altos and some tenors share these spots throughout.

---

[18]The great music theorist Glareanus (a contemporary of Josquin, writing just a few years after that towering master's death) said, ". . . but whenever musicians wish to accelerate the tactus, which they consider should be done when they believe the hearing is fatiguing, namely in order to remove weariness, they draw a line downwards through the circle and they call this quality 'diminutio,' not because either the value or the number of the note is lessened, but because the tactus becomes faster." Glareanus, *Dodecachordon, Book II*, p. 2:232.

[19]Note that the alto part in Example 10-4 is indicated by the clef sign to be sounded an octave *below* the treble clef.

3. It also is possible to transpose this music to accommodate these tessituras.[20] Some Josquin works might be shifted by as much as a major third. Experiment, and see what seems to work.

A Culminative Examination of the Text

In general, it is best to look at the music and the *articulation* of the text first—matters of diction, translation, and the use of certain textual effects—thoroughly analyzing the work as a piece of *music;* then, with the musical shapes clearly in mind, we delve into the meanings that underlie the text. We do this so that sentimentality about the words cannot have undue influence on our understanding of the musical structure.

In this case, the overt meaning of the brief text is straightforward enough, as is its place in the liturgy. Glancing back at the *Pange lingua* text, however, we find added meanings to consider: The first two verses of the plainchant text clearly refer to the Crucifixion and to Christ's Body and Blood; verses three through five relate those elements directly to the Last Supper; the final verse is a doxology. The whole content implies use of this chant during Holy Week, which seems to have been the practice during Josquin's lifetime.

Since the cantus firmus is audible throughout the Kyrie, it follows that listeners in the sixteenth century would have known, and would have been thinking of, the words of the original plainsong. Those words would have influenced their attitude toward the *Missa Pange lingua,* and would have affected their own worship on that particular day. These words certainly affected Josquin des Prez as he set the chant melody to his polyphony, and they should influence our interpretation of that work.

Conducting Josquin's Kyrie

It follows, then, that if you were to perform the entire *Missa Pange lingua* (or even just the Kyrie) you might do well to have your choir or a soloist sing several verses of the original plainchant first, letting the audience gain some familiarity with this melody the sixteenth-century worshipers would have known so well.

As you prepare to conduct the Kyrie, note the literal but decorated quotations of the six phrases of the plainsong: The first is in the tenor part in bars 1–5, and the second in the bass starting in measure 9; the third phrase (the one after the initial full bar in the chant itself) appears in the bass (transposed) starting in bar 17 (and on the original pitch in the tenor from bar 25), and the fourth phrase begins in the alto in measure 35; the fifth (after the chant's second full bar) com-

---

[20]Although transposing this music has been considered controversial in the past, current research appears to warrant doing so in at least some situations. Among the justifications for transposition are these: Pitch was not fixed to A-440, as it is now, and the high pitch of much of Josquin's music suggests the organ available to him may have been pitched low.

mences in the top part (the "cantus") in measure 53, and the last phrase begins first in the same part in bar 60. You will see that Josquin fills in many of the original chant's skips with stepwise motion, but the contours of the plainsong melody are still both visible and audible.[21] Each phrase accelerates, as we have seen, growing more florid as it builds toward one of the principal cadences, at each of which the basses sing the final note of the corresponding phrase of the chant *Pange lingua.*

In this detailed analysis of the Kyrie you have noted each of the vocal entrances, and you have sung all the parts. You understand the role of the text in the movement and the purpose for which the work was written. What more is necessary to prepare you to conduct it?

1. Look at the ways the entrances and voice parts interrelate. Where do the pairings (coupled parts) occur? How does the rhythmic activity in the various voices combine at various times—halves against quarters, quarters against quarters, and so forth—and how does this change as a section progresses?
2. Choose your tempo for each of the sections.
3. Decide on the basic beat pattern(s) to be used.
4. What sort of articulation do you want from your singers in each section? How does the kind of articulative definition you choose relate to the feeling you believe Josquin wants in each line?
5. What are the phrase lengths you want, and where may your singers breathe? Where may they *not?*
6. What about dynamic levels? Do you want the three basic sections to contrast in loudness? Will you have each line build (naturally) as it ascends, and recede as it descends? How will you relate the three major cadences in this respect? How do you want the parts balanced?
7. Are there dissonances, or other momentary effects, to which you want to call attention in your performance?
8. Where do you expect difficulties to occur during your rehearsal? How can you prepare to resolve them?
9. Where might ritards be properly employed, and why?
10. Is there—the most intimidating question for all conductors—*anything* else you need to know about this work?

As preparation, try playing one part at the piano while singing another, to help build your sense of the counterpoint. If you can, play all four parts together, or start with two parts, add the third, and finally try to include the fourth. Speed is not important in this practice, but accuracy and a consistent tempo are crucial if this preparation is to be of help to you. It is even more important that your eyes become accustomed to reading all the parts at the same time.

---

[21]You see that Josquin apparently uses more accidentals than did the original *Pange lingua* chant. Some of these, in any modern edition, are likely to be editorial recommendations. For the moment, we suggest that you accept the ones shown in Example 10-4. In Chapter 18, we will have advice regarding the whole problem of judging which accidentals to believe and which to delete.

Last points:

1. Make certain your preparation beat is a good one, and in tempo.
2. Cue each entering voice section with your baton one beat ahead of their entrance. In bars 5 and 6, for example, cue the sopranos on the third beat of bar 4, and signal the altos on the third beat of measure 5. At the same time, remind the tenors and basses they are ending a phrase; taper them down with your left hand. This same process happens again and again.
3. Manage the overall dynamic level you want with your right hand, as you have learned, but control balance and individual problems with your left.
4. Be certain to warn of any ritards.
5. Plan exactly what sorts of cutoffs you will use, and expressly where.
6. Remember to give a clear "prep" beat after each cutoff.
7. Pace the closing bars precisely, sensing carefully the temporal proportions by which you want to relate the final ritard (if any), the last note, the cutoff, the silence afterward, and the release of tension.
8. On a more sophisticated level, look at the rhythm of each part, remembering that there were no bar lines in this era; this means that the C in the tenor part in measure 3 (for example) is *not* a syncopation, nor is the one in bar 4. Work instead to group the notes in your mind as you did with Gregorian chant. Notice that this means the figures in two parts will conflict rhythmically with each other at times. Deal with the flow of the tactus, and try to avoid binding these lines to a modern meter!
9. In this flowing style, word stress produces important agogic accents. Add dynamic accents to the first note of each phrase if you like, but avoid crudity and obviousness.
10. It is characteristic of this style to taper down the ends both of phrases and of sections. (Josquin's music inherited this approach from Gregorian chant, of course.)
11. Listen for other opportunities to make it clear that this Kyrie is a descendant of the chant *Pange lingua*.

Now you should be ready. This is a wonderful work, and the movement you are attempting is a splendid one. Enjoy it. Once you have conducted it, you can be confident that you have in your repertoire a solid example of Renaissance choral style,[22] and you will be ready to approach other works from that period.[23]

---

[22]As a supplement (and a somewhat easier Renaissance choral work than this Josquin movement), we include a conductor's analysis of the Morley madrigal *April Is in My Mistress' Face* as Appendix A.

[23]As a convenience for your later use, the authors include in Appendix B a summary of style and performance practice in Renaissance choral music.

CHAPTER *11*

Style and Performance: Baroque and Classical Vocal Works

We turn now from the art of a distant world—that of the Medieval musician and his Renaissance successors—to the more familiar landscapes of Baroque Europe and Classical Vienna. You may have found the preceding chapter a difficult one, with much to learn. This one should encourage you as you rediscover how much you already know.

BACKGROUND AND PERSPECTIVES: THE BAROQUE REVOLUTION

The Renaissance had developed an extremely sophisticated language, with the intricate and precisely engineered counterpoint of Josquin des Prez, Cristóbal de Morales, Giovanni Pierluigi da Palestrina, Orlando di Lasso, and Tomás Luis de Victoria as perhaps its highest achievement. For an era that had begun with its primary focus on its vocal tradition (especially its sacred vocal tradition), it had shown surprising innovative vitality in the burst of genuinely instrumental music that flowered, notably in Venice, during the sixteenth century (as we shall see in Chapter 14), a development that would have great significance in the years to follow. Drained of its vigor by decades of energetic growth, Renaissance musical evolution ended (gradually, not suddenly, in a period of change that lasted from about 1575 to about 1625). That proved to be the turning of one of the great hinges of music history, and what we now call the Baroque era began.

The new style was half-formed at first. Elements of Renaissance practice remained—old wine in new vessels, and vice versa—but differences were obvious right from the beginning. A principal complaint registered by the new composers was that the disciplined and complex counterpoint of the sixteenth century had been too cool, tranquil, and dispassionate. "Music," they said, "should be more directly expressive. It should portray real human emotions."

Early opera was a product of that attitude: Mythical and legendary figures confronted tragic situations onstage and attempted to display to audiences specific emotions their characters were experiencing; a gradual result was the working-out of the so-called doctrine of affections *(Affektenlehre),* a theory in which certain kinds of music were said to represent certain precise emotions. According to this theory, the passionate content of music could be manifest only if one emotion were presented at a time; conflicting sentiments would confuse the communication process, as Renaissance counterpoint was thought to have done.

Perhaps the most striking innovation of the period lay in the parameter of texture. Composers designed Italian monody, an extremely lean, economical texture, as a vehicle for this new conception of communicating moods. Monody superimposed (1) a single expressive vocal line on top of (2) an instrumental bass line and (3) a keyboard mechanism assigned to fill in notes between the voice and the bass. Obviously, this use of keyboard-and-bass (the combination that came to be called the *basso continuo)* reflected a growing tendency to identify and reuse certain vertical sonorities heretofore understood only as acceptable outcomes of melodic activity in counterpoint; musicians were approaching the point where they would begin to think in "chords," and, seen in that light, the new basso continuo was a device in which one instrument played a "fundamental bass line" (made up primarily of what we would now call the "roots" of chords) while a keyboard instrument provided the other members of each harmony. *This potent functional structure, the basso continuo, was to constitute the indispensable foundation of virtually every musical work of the Baroque era* (and would continue to influence the character of compositions even beyond the Haydn concerts in London during the 1790s).

Other stylistic developments were outgrowths of these two primary features. Baroque melody became more jagged, with more skips (including frequent consecutive skips in one direction as the singer "outlined" the chords the continuo was[1] playing). Dissonance had a new potency, too. No longer a rigidly controlled phenomenon relegated primarily to weak temporal situations, sharp dissonance could be placed on strong beats (leapt to or leapt away from) as a means of expressing tragic agonies.

Consciousness of meter and tonality was emerging, too. The few bar lines that Renaissance composers had employed had been used almost exclusively in lute and keyboard music; now the clavier instruments employed in the basso continuo brought this notational device with them to the new monodic texture. Bar lines, combined with evolving time signatures, began to imply a matrix of metric accents. Rhythmic values began to be understood as events "riding" on a

---

[1]By convention, *continuo* is treated as a singular noun, even if more than one performer is involved.

flow of meter; in this context, syncopation becomes a practical possibility (as do metric conflicts of more complicated kinds).

As a theoretical concept, tonality also developed slowly across the century and a half of the Baroque. Its effect as an organizational factor became increasingly evident as the seventeenth century unfolded.

Our contemporary use of the word *movements* comes from this era. Once one determines to create a passage of music that expresses a single "affect," or emotion, one is led philosophically to the view that only a certain, unique musical fabric—a synthesis of text, melody, harmony, *meter, and tempo*—can represent that passion really efficiently. That combination of parameters has about it a particular "motion" derived from its feeling in time—that is, a "movement." Thus arises the term we use to designate separate units within a large work.

Counterpoint was out of favor, but only for a time. The new monodic texture was distinctly melody-with-accompaniment, and that technique was basic to the newest structures in use: the recitative, the aria, the developing solo sonata, the solo concerto, and the like. As the Baroque period evolved, the native ingenuity of innovative composers led naturally to a reemergence of counterpoint and, eventually, to the peak of highly sophisticated fugal writing the works of Bach and Handel. Composers discovered that two, three, or more contrapuntally related voices could be superimposed on the basso continuo; the results were the so-called trio sonata (actually two soloists plus, generally, two continuo players), choral works with several voice parts, and the concerto grosso (two or more soloists above an "orchestra," part of whose function was to amplify the work of the basso continuo).

Instruments (led into the Baroque texture by this continuo role) came into their own in this era. No longer conceived just as alternatives, substitutes, and supports for voices, they became timbral ends in themselves. At first, there was a pragmatic willingness to accept surrogates, so a violin sonata might have been played by a flute or an oboe, or a concerto for two violins might have been shared by a violin and a flute; composers were distinguishing between vocal and instrumental writing but not yet giving each kind of instrument its due. As time passed, however, they began to recognize the idiomatic strengths and weaknesses of these various media and wrote specific passages appropriate only to the bassoon, or to the viola da gamba. *The essential timbre of the Baroque, as a consequence of this new idiomatic consciousness and of the pervasive use of the basso continuo, is a homogenized voices-and-instruments sound in which neither color dominates.*

From the radical experiments of early Monteverdi to the summits of the Handelian oratorios and the Bach passions, it is an exciting age, and one with an invigorating repertoire for conductors.[2]

---

[2]For a detailed discussion of Baroque performance practice in practical terms, including selection of instruments, realization of keyboard parts, concertino/tutti relationships, tempos, ornamentation, recitatives, and related matters, see Don V Moses, Robert W. Demaree, Jr., and Allen F. Ohmes, *Face to Face with an Orchestra* (Princeton, N.J.: Prestige Publications, 1987), beginning at Chapter 6.

Henry Purcell: *Come, Ye Sons of Art*, Opening Chorus

One of the greatest figures of the Middle Baroque was the English composer Henry Purcell, chorister, organist, and composer at Westminster Abbey and in the royal court during the reigns of Charles II, James II, and William of Orange. Purcell wrote much sacred music for Anglican services, but also did an impressive amount of scoring for the theater. His opera *Dido and Aeneas* is one of the masterworks of his time.

One of his responsibilities as composer to Their Majesties William and Mary was the creation of celebratory works: pieces to mark special occasions, birthdays, and anniversaries; "Welcome Songs" to be sung when a royal patron returned to court from a long journey; and music for other such festivities. For each of Queen Mary's six celebrations from 1689 through 1694 (the year of her death, at which time Purcell himself had but a year of his brief, Mozartean span to live), he wrote her a "Birthday Ode," the last (and perhaps the best) of which bears the title *Come, Ye Sons of Art*. When Purcell died the next year, he had earned a tomb near the kings in Westminster Abbey, bearing the felicitous epitaph "Here lyes Henry Purcell, Esq.; who left this life, and is gone to that blessed place where only his harmony can be exceeded."

Rather like a choral cantata, *Come, Ye Sons of Art* opens with an orchestral overture, following which comes a sequence of solos, duets, and choruses, scored for 2 oboes, 2 trumpets, percussion, strings (2 violins, viola, bass) and continuo, plus 2 recorders for the fifth movement, one of the arias. The first of the vocal movements (No. 2 in the complete work) is our Example 11-1.[3]

Made up of three 28-bar repetitions (A–A^1–A^2), this movement is binary in design, though not in key structure (for it remains in D major throughout). One of the 28-measure units is shown in Figure 11-1.

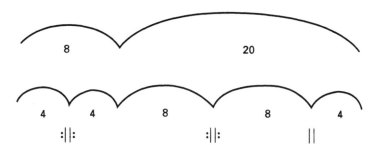

Figure 11-1 A 28-bar section of the opening chorus of Purcell's *Come, Ye Sons of Art*

[3]Henry Purcell, *Come, Ye Sons of Art*, ed. William Herrmann (New York: G. Schirmer, Inc., 1974), pp. 7–11.

Example 11-1 Purcell: *Come, Ye Sons of Art*, opening chorus

Example 11-1 *(cont.)*

(a) Or Countertenor Solo

(Chorus)

Example 11-1 *(cont.)*

* The Duet should follow after only a brief pause.

A glance at the alto solo (originally for countertenor), bars 29–44, gives you a good idea of the melodic and harmonic style here. This music rests on standard I–IV–V–I.harmonic progressions, and the tune outlines and embellishes those basic chords; skips move between chord members, and such dissonances as can be found occur in stepwise passages between chordal tones. The use of D major is no surprise; when seventeenth- and eighteenth-century composers wanted a bright, positive orchestral sound, they most often chose this key.[4]

The $\frac{3}{4}$ meter is unbroken in this movement, and the phrases are consistently four bars in length. The texture through all three sections is melody-with-accompaniment. The editor has suggested a tempo of ♩ = 126 for the orchestral section, and this should be continued through the solo and the chorus.

The text is not profound; written by one of the court poets, whose first duty was to flatter the royal patron, it has the virtue, at least, of leaving most of the interest to the music. In this movement, the alto soloist and the chorus share the same lines, which are made even more naive by their rhyme scheme of *aaa* and by the repetitions of the word "come."

Baroque Ornamentation

At first glance, this movement appears so repetitious as to be boring. We might say that the design offers far too little variety: It consists of sixteen measures that are direct repeats of the other twelve, and is recapitulated twice, with only the orchestration changed; the simple rhyme scheme and the repetitions of words and phrases add redundancy. How can one make the audience *really* listen to *three* "verses" of this song, especially when the text does not change?

If you are to conduct Baroque music—if you are really to interpret that music in its own style—you must understand the viewpoint of Baroque musicians and the common performance approach they took with this music. They did not slavishly reproduce exactly the notes on the score; instead, like jazz players, they improvised extemporaneous variations of the written matrix they were given by the composer, and he expected that they would do so!

They did this primarily by adding "ornaments." Taking *advantage* of the direct repetition in the music, which otherwise would become intolerable after a while, they freshened each repeat with embellishments—somewhat showy interpolations that had the added benefit of making the performer look even more virtuosic. These ornaments were especially useful as enrichments at the most important structural points (cadences at the ends of major sections, for instance), but they also were used to garnish internal elements of phrases.

What ornaments were used? You know most of them already.[5] There are at

---

[4]See, as typical examples, the "Gloria" and the "Et resurrexit" of Bach's Mass in B Minor, "The trumpet shall sound" in Handel's *Messiah*, the "Gloria" in Haydn's *Nelsonmesse*, and the Vivaldi movement we will study next (all of which include trumpets in the orchestra).

[5]For further information on this topic, see the standard reference sources, or Sally Allis Sanford, *Seventeenth and Eighteenth Century Vocal Style and Technique* (Ann Arbor, Mich.: University Microfilms, 1979), beginning on p. 149.

least three basic types: ornaments used to add excitement to a note by decorating it floridly (the *effetti*, and so on); ornaments that filled in melodic gaps, changing skips into stepwise motion (scalar additions); and alterations in duration (ritards, tempo rubato, and the like). Two or more of these types could be combined in one embellishment, as well.

Among the first category are trills, mordents, turns, appoggiaturas, and (in keyboard playing) arpeggios; among other procedures that can intensify a note are the dynamic decorations: the *esclamazione* (a quick decrescendo–crescendo within the duration of a note) and its complement, the *messa di voce* (not the same as *mezzo voce*), a crescendo–decrescendo.

The second class includes the filling in of skips with the *tirata* and similar stepwise figures, but it also encompasses the *intonatione* (a slide or "scoop" up to a written note, usually from a diatonic third below) and related devices of parallel purpose and effect.

The third type embraces simple changes in rhythm and also treats the ritard and other *temporary* alterations of the pulse as ornamental in character. Perhaps the most important of these is the *cadenza*, an interruption of the structural flow of the work for a florid, virtuosic passage made up of an extended set of supposedly improvised figures of all sorts. Traditionally, the cadenza occurred on a I_4^6 chord just before a very important cadence; because of its ostentation, it should be used sparingly, and then only at structural points that deserve special emphasis. (In the classical concerto, for example, it generally was reserved for the final passage played by the soloist.) Its use is appropriate in most arias.

Some ornaments lend themselves more idiomatically to one instrument than to another (the arpeggio is such a case, as we have said), but the basic figures were common to all Baroque singers and players.

Unless you are working with very experienced soloists, it takes time, of course, to plan which ornaments to use; in any case, the assignment these days of embellishments to ensemble musicians—whether singers or players—requires marking the parts in advance or using up valuable rehearsal time to announce your choices. (*Do not assume that even professional orchestral players know very much about this subject*, for they spend most of their time playing music from the nineteenth and twentieth centuries, and an understanding of the intricacies of Baroque ornamentation is not required for that repertoire.) The time you give to this editing is worth it, however, for its effect on the music, and it is essential if your interpretations are to be legitimate ones.

Application of Baroque Ornaments to the Purcell Movement

In the opening section, several factors make it easy to add Baroque ornaments: This is the first presentation of this music, so it needs less enrichment than it would if it came later; Purcell has lent variety to the successive phrases by changing from the oboes to the strings, and back again; and his 28-bar design, with its 4-, 8-, and 4-bar repeats has at least the initial advantage of being asymmetrical. We suggest that you accept the trills that editor Herrmann has marked, invite your keyboard player to add some arpeggios, and leave this segment otherwise unchanged.

The solo section, however, needs more attention, especially since all these ideas have now been heard by the audience. You might edit it as follows:

1. Measures 29–32 can be sung as is the first time. In the repeat, the soloist could use an intonatione on beat three of bar 29, sliding from a D up to the F-sharp; the eighth notes in bars 30 and 32 could then be changed to dotted-eighth-and-sixteenth figures.

2. Again, measures 33–40 could be sung unaltered the first time, *mf*, as marked by the editor. The repeat could be sung *p* and embellished with passing G's added to the first beats of bars 33 and 34, with the eighths in measure 35 changed to sixteenth–eighth figures. A crescendo on the third beat of bar 36 could bring the singer back to the earlier *mf*. Intonationi on the first beats of measures 37, 38, and 39 could follow.

3. Finally, the dotted rhythms suggested by the editor could be observed in bars 41 and 42, as well as his trill in bar 43. Start the trill from F-sharp, of course, and double-dot the E (double-dotting is always permissible in the Baroque, if effective), which makes the last note in bar 43 a sixteenth.

4. Be certain to make all the same changes in the instrumental parts.

The result (eliminating the first presentation of each phrase) would look like Example 11-2.

Example 11-2   An ornamented version of the solo section of the first choral movement of *Come, Ye Sons of Art*

The choral section, as the third round of this material, certainly will need decoration. Consider these possibilities:

1. Leave bars 45–48 unaltered, sung *f*, as marked.

2. For the repeat, change the dynamic to *p* at bar 49. Dot the eighth notes in the sopra-no and alto parts in measure 50, and double-dot the first note in each of the tenor and bass voices in the same bar. In bar 52 add an esclamazione ($\Longrightarrow$ $\Longleftarrow$).

3. Keep measures 53–60 as written (returning to *f* at measure 53).

4. In measures 61 and 62, change each pair of eighths to a sixteenth-and-dotted-eighth figure. Employ the marked decrescendo in bar 64, returning subito to *f* on the third beat in 68, and take the poco ritard indicated.

5. Remember to make the orchestral parts consistent with this.

Conducting Purcell's Opening Chorus

The music begins in the silence before the first note commences. If you are a singer, you (unfortunately) may regard any passages that occur before the first vocal entrance as "an introduction." There really is no such thing! Even the very dramatic and effective snare-drum roll "before" the National Anthem is part of the music. Whether the opening passage is a statement of the *A* material, as it is here, or some sort of preface, treat it all in your conducting of it as important.

Notice that Purcell has voiced the chorus with the melody in the alto at measure 45. (To do otherwise would mean either a change of key or a very high tessitura for the sopranos.) Give that voice and the all-important bass part prima-cy. Balance the sopranos and tenors against these lines.

All three sections are in three, and there are no fermatas or other serious complications; there is only one ritard to consider. You should not find this diffi-cult to conduct. We would like you to *let your baton do the work automatically,* fo-cusing your real attention on interpretation.

Here are a few specific suggestions:

1. This is not the same line as Josquin's. A nonlegato (string players would say *détaché*) is probably the right articulation here, although you may want to vary one or two individual phrases. *The standard nineteenth-century legato is not appropriate in this style.* Research shows that a distinct separation would have been maintained between every pair of notes not specifically marked with a slur.

2. Remember to cue the alto soloist before bar 29, and the choir before measure 44, giv-ing clear "prep" beats each time.

3. Show the subito attacks at bars 29 and 45 in the size of your beat, and reinforce all dynamic changes with your left hand.

4. Be certain you direct your cutoffs to the right individual(s), choosing, in each case, the right gesture for the beat involved.

5. Enlarge your beat for the poco ritard in bar 71, and add a modest fermata to the final chord.

It may be best to rehearse the movement straight through the first time *without ornaments* to check any basic problems; then add the embellishments, and revise any that do not work well. Experiment with the placement of your soloist, too; try her in front of your orchestra (or piano), between the orchestra and cho-rus, and in the choir itself. See what works best for this movement in the hall in which you are performing.

Antonio Vivaldi: *Gloria,* "Cum sancto spiritu"

The chorus "Cum sancto spiritu," which ends Vivaldi's famous *Gloria,* is our next project. This will be a good chance for you to practice your skills in cueing entrances, and this movement also is a good exercise in balancing voices, working with fugal subjects and countersubjects, and handling word stresses.

Antonio Vivaldi was one of the greatest Italian composers of the Baroque period and the creator of an enormous catalog of vocal and instrumental works of all kinds. Trained as a cleric, he was known in his lifetime as "il prete rosso" ("the red priest") because of the color of his tonsured hair. Vivaldi spent the bulk of his career in Venice. At nearly 50 years of age, he moved to Vienna in the hope that the Emperor Carl (father of Maria Theresa) would take an interest in his music. Apparently, little such enthusiasm was shown him, for Vivaldi seems (we have almost no documentation on his life) to have died destitute; his funeral was at St. Stephen's Cathedral (and Haydn, as a choirboy, may have sung for it), but it was a very modest one.

His music deserved better. His counterpoint lacks the intricacy, and his structures the scope, of Bach's, but the fresh, vital, sunny brilliance of the sounds of his *Gloria,* like so many of his works, reminds one immediately of Vivaldi's Venice and of the Italian operas he wrote in his early days.

Of the history of the *Gloria* itself we know virtually nothing. Since at 25 he became a teacher at the Ospedale della Pietà in Venice, it is generally assumed that he wrote the *Gloria* for service music there. We know he was proud of the "Cum sancto spiritu" movement: Not only did he make it the finale of the *Gloria,* he used it (with slight alterations) in his *Chamber Mass,* as well. (We do not know which of these works came first.) It is easy to see why he did so.

Analysis of "Cum sancto spiritu"

This finale can be classed as a fugue, of course, but that is a problematic term. There is no question that the writing is "fugal," but so was the Josquin Kyrie; you remember that each new subject there was treated with contrapuntal entrances in each voice. The difference in Example 11-3 is that Vivaldi does not write a new subject for each new phrase of a lengthy text. If there were a standard form for the "fugue," it would resemble what students traditionally are taught: a structure made up of "fugal expositions," in each of which the same melodic subject (with, perhaps, one or more countersubjects) is stated first by one voice, and then imitated by each of the other voices in turn, in entrances generally spaced at a perfect fourth or fifth (or octave) away from the first statement; contrapuntal "episodes" (in which, by definition, the subject is *not* present) separate the expositions.[6]

[6]There is no rigid standard for fugal form. See Willi Apel's quip, just after he has written a full page about fugal structure, that such prototypes hardly exist: Willi Apel, *Harvard Dictionary of Music,* 2nd ed. (Cambridge: Harvard University Press, 1969), p. 336.

The subject itself (as well as the countersubjects) may be developed in various ways—compressed, elongated, turned upside down, truncated, stated against itself (in *stretto*), and so forth. The invention of the subject is therefore a crucial process, for the melody created must be suitable (must have characteristics that make it malleable for such development). Countersubjects should be compatible with it, complementary in rhythm and shape; both subject and countersubject must be recognizable and memorable.

Vivaldi's "Cum sancto spiritu" fugue, shown as Example 11-3,[7] is built of four choral expositions separated by orchestral passages. (Only the first is an "episode"; all three instrumental interludes are dominated by entrances of the subject and countersubjects.) The first three of these expositions begin on the tonic D major, and each modulates (the first to the dominant, the second to the relative minor, and the third to the mediant) as a means of providing tonal variety; the last one begins (with the countersubject) on the dominant so that Vivaldi can bring us "home" to D major at the end.

Why D major? (You should know the answer this time.) Just as Purcell preferred this key for a brilliant use of the Baroque trumpet in his *Come, Ye Sons of Art*, so Vivaldi apparently has tuned his entire *Gloria* to the appearances of the trumpet in the opening chorus (which is repeated just before this fugue) and the finale. Every other vocal, instrumental, and melodic consideration in the work ultimately is subordinated to this element of orchestration.

"Cum sancto spiritu" is planned dramatically. It begins with only choir and continuo. The strings and oboe cap the first exposition, entering in measure 12, and continue into the first instrumental episode, which commences in bar 16, building up to the entrance of the trumpet on a high A in bar 18.

The "Subject" is the line sung by the basses (and doubled by the continuo) in measures 1–6. Against this, the sopranos deliver Countersubject I in bars 2–6. After a legato line in measures 7 and 8, the sopranos also introduce a syncopated figure that becomes Countersubject II; see its use in the tenor part in bars 12–16. These three themes are shown in isolation in Example 11-4.

Vivaldi's melodies—throughout the *Gloria*, but especially in Countersubject I—use many repeated notes (certainly more than we would expect to find in the refined lines of Renaissance composers like Palestrina). This may reflect the Baroque device (which dates from Monteverdi, at least) called "agitated style" (*stile concitato*), a use of repeated notes to add excitement and intensity. Certainly, it is easier for singers to enunciate clearly on repeated notes, so good diction should be easy here. The tessituras are moderate, for Vivaldi leaves the high A's to the instruments.

[7]Antonio Vivaldi, *Gloria*, ed. Clayton Westerman (New York: Edwin F. Kalmus, 1967), pp. 72–87. The authors recommend you consult also the 1961 edition by Mason Martens. The well-known Alfredo Casella rendering is often regarded now as faulty. See our discussion of *Gloria* editions in Moses, Demaree, and Ohmes, *Face to Face with an Orchestra*, p. 100, as well as the list of alternatives in the bibliography, p. 115. (Space considerations limit us to the use of the twenty-seven measures shown here. Please see your library for the complete score.)

Example 11-3 Vivaldi: *Gloria,* Finale, "Cum sancto spiritu," mm. 1–27, full score

Example 11-3 (*cont.*)

Example 11-3 *(cont.)*

(Keyboard only)

Example 11-3 *(cont.)*

Example 11-3 *(cont.)*

(Keyboard)

Example 11-4   Thematic materials in Vivaldi's "Cum sancto spiritu," with some suggested ornaments added

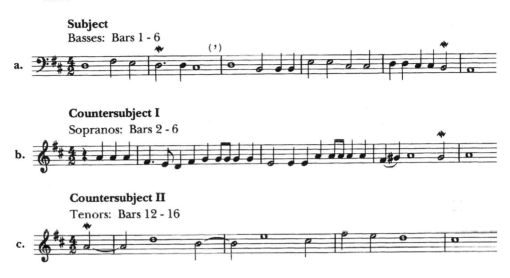

Subject
Basses: Bars 1 - 6

Countersubject I
Sopranos: Bars 2 - 6

Countersubject II
Tenors: Bars 12 - 16

Note that the meter is $\frac{4}{2}$, *alla breve*, and that a full five rhythmic levels are used. The harmonies are traditional, and Vivaldi's use of dissonance is rather conservative.

The text is limited to the last eight words of the standard Gloria in the Ordinary of the Mass. Vivaldi assigns the full eight words to both the Subject and Countersubject I. (Note that he sets the word "spiritu" to a dotted figure in each case.) Countersubject II consists of only the word "Amen." With the exception of the "Amens" (which we will discuss later), he is careful to respect word stress in his metric placement of syllables.

Just as in *Come, Ye Sons of Art*, it is important to edit in appropriate Baroque ornamentation. Not so much will be needed in "Cum sancto spiritu" as in the Purcell chorus: This is for use in church, not in a secular setting, so it was not intended to be flashy; it has considerable complexity and interest already built into its fugal texture; it has more variety of rhythmic values present; it involves less direct repetition than Purcell's phrases; and it has no solo passages requiring the high-powered decoration characteristic of such sections in the era.

Nevertheless, you should not underestimate the usefulness of Baroque embellishments here. Vivaldi's audiences were accustomed to them, and his fabric deserves both the impromptu feeling and the enrichment that these decorations provide. We recommend that you *not* alter the rhythms or fill in the skips within the Subject and Countersubjects (since that would tend to make them less recognizable, a serious fault in fugal counterpoint). A mordent on the dotted half in the Subject would certainly be practical, and another on the first note of each new

"Amen" would help emphasize the word stress.[8] Modest trills could be assigned to the sopranos, the violins, or both, on the next-to-last note of each major section; a somewhat longer one, complete with a *nachschlag* (or final turn), could be given to the trumpet. Ask your keyboard player for arpeggios and other embellishments in appropriate places. Finally, since this is the finale of a major work, you likely will want a substantial ritard at the end.

Forces Needed for "Cum sancto spiritu"

Our guess is that Vivaldi never heard more than two dozen singers perform the *Gloria*, and for a choir of this size a string body of 3-3-2-2-1 (violins I through bass viol) is probably sufficient. In a performance of the whole work, you might use a harpsichord for the solo movements, adding a Baroque organ for the choruses (thus, both keyboard instruments would be played in the "Cum sancto spiritu"); complete the continuo with a 'cello (or a *very good* contrabass), and add a bassoon, if possible, for the choral movements. The trumpet part is, as always, an exposed one, and the musicality of the oboe player is consequential (especially in the beautiful sixth movement, "Domine Deus"), so at least those instrumentalists should be chosen with the greatest care.

It may be necessary for you to compromise on these choices. A choir of sixty may be compulsory in your circumstances, and surely is acceptable; in that event, a string body of 6-6-4-4-3 should be about right. Certainly a piano can be used, if that is all that is available, but your pianist should play lightly, *without pedal*, in that case. In determining balance, remember that the *a cappella* chorus is not the paradigm of the Baroque; the idiomatic sound is a homogenization of (in this case) oboe, trumpet, harpsichord, organ, strings, and singers; the singers probably used less vibrato than do modern-day professionals, too. Work for that sort of balance and timbre.[9]

MORE CONDUCTING THEORY
Tempo Choices in the Baroque Era

What about tempo here? We have good sources for this decision, for there are treatises written by some of the greatest working musicians of the eighteenth century to guide Vivaldi's contemporaries (and us). Carl Philipp Emanuel Bach (son of Johann Sebastian and a major influence on Haydn), Johann Joachim Quantz (flutist and court composer to Frederick the Great), Leopold Mozart (father of the genius Wolfgang, and himself the finest violinist of his time), the

---

[8]Many Americans accent the second syllable (ah-MEN), but Europeans stress the first syllable. (Note that these mordents have been edited into Example 11-4.)

[9]Again, for further practical counsel on these matters, see the authors' *Face to Face with an Orchestra*, especially page 25, all of Chapter 6, and all of Chapter 9.

philosopher Jean-Jacques Rousseau, and others who performed music during the Baroque and Classical eras have left for you precise suggestions, based on their first-hand experience.[10]

Mistrust second-hand advice on performance practice. The professional conductor should go directly to good *primary sources* (data from the time itself), whatever the period involved. This is the sort of background you need to buttress your judgments.

When you have learned everything you can from musicians of that era, turn to solid secondary sources: later (perhaps modern) scholarship by reputable researchers who themselves have gone to primary sources and the music itself.[11] Build a reference library you can trust, and keep it handy.

Choosing a Tempo for "Cum sancto spiritu"

You have seen that Vivaldi has marked this movement $\frac{4}{2}$, *alla breve*. Quantz wrote that he used the "pulse beat of a healthy person" as a basis for his standard tempo. Simple $\frac{4}{4}$ at Allegretto, then, he took to be a quarter note per pulse; an Allegro assai matched the half note with the pulse, and an eighth note became the pulse of an Adagio cantabile. With an *alla breve* marking, says Quantz, everything shifts one notch: The quarter note represents one pulse at Adagio cantabile; at an *alla breve* Allegretto, he gives each half note one pulse, and at Allegro each whole note. On such arithmetic he *began* his calculations.[12]

Thinking this way at least has the advantage of emphasizing to beginning conductors a mathematical relationship between tempos. It is not enough, of course. Quantz goes on to emphasize that the raw, pulse-based tempos just described must be modified sensitively to allow for the fastest note values involved, the key and mode, the meter, the level of dissonance, the circumstances of performance, and the mood of the movement, among other factors; a movement with thirty-second notes, that is, tends to be paced slower than one in which the quickest value is the eighth. Similarly, we are told, works in a minor key, pieces set in $\frac{4}{4}$ rather than $\frac{2}{4}$, movements with complex harmonic rhythms and involved dissonances, works for the church, and pieces with an obviously melancholy or reflective quality would be assigned slightly slower tempos. As Kirnberger put it (in a perfect example of the influence of the Baroque doctrine of *Affektenlehre*): "In fact, every passion and every sentiment—in its intrinsic effect as well as in the words by which it is expressed—has its faster or slower, more violent or more passive

---

[10]Each of these primary sources—along with less renowned Baroque musicians like Daniel Gottlieb Türk, Friedrich Wilhelm Marpurg, and Johann Mattheson—is listed in the Bibliography, and an English translation is shown for most of them.

[11]For Baroque performance practice, for example, note the work of people like Carse, Dolmetsch, Donington, Dürr, Ehmann, Neumann, and Veilhan.

[12]Johann Joachim Quantz, *On Playing the Flute*, trans. Edward R. Reilly (London: Faber & Faber, 1958), pp. 285–286.

tempo."[13] Today, we would add that the size and acoustics of the hall are very important factors. So is the ensemble size you choose.

Can we now apply all this to "Cum sancto spiritu"? In $\frac{4}{2}$ we would regard the half note as the basic beat, of course. If we take the average pulse rate to be something between MM = 60 and MM = 70—say 65—we would establish the half note at MM = 65. But Vivaldi has marked this "alla breve" with his ¢ symbol, so we are entitled to double the pace to MM = 130!

What about the other factors? The major key, the absence of involved dissonances, and the general spirit of the music suggest a slightly brighter tempo—perhaps even MM = 136. Recalling that this is liturgical music, on the other hand, and that eighth notes are present (the equivalents of sixteenths in $\frac{4}{4}$), and allowing extra time for the listener to appreciate the fugal process—all *big* factors—the authors finally would recommend holding the tempo to something near MM = 104. Having considered all the evidence, you may arrive at a different decision and be perfectly justified, given especially the circumstances of your ensemble and physical setting. The important thing is to give enough thought to the evidence.

Conducting "Cum sancto spiritu"

In fugal writing, it generally is best to assign one type of articulation to the subject, and a different type to the countersubject. Here, we have three thematic ideas. For the Subject itself (a six-bar theme, divided into two- and four-bar segments), we could use almost a legato—connected, but with just a little extra definition on each half (or longer) note; try adding a little more articulation for the second "Dei patris," and be certain your singers stress the "Ah" of "Amen."

Give this Subject a sturdy feeling. It should have audible strength. Have the entire choir sing in unison the bass line for bars 1–6, while you give them a quasi-legato beat. Then get it to sound the way you hear it in your study.

Countersubject I must have a different character if it is to be heard clearly by the listeners, and *so you must show a different character in your baton when you cue it.* More sharply etched gestures, more detached ones, are needed here. The repeated words (measure 4: "in gloria . . . ") can be given slightly more emphasis. Once more have the whole choir sing the soprano line through bar 6 until they give you the articulation and overall phrase you want.

Countersubject II (since it is always syncopated) could be assigned a marcato articulation. This would help to define rhythmically the weaker beats (in contrast to the natural accents on the first and third beats in the other two themes). Try this, too, with the choir.

[13]Johann Philipp Kirnberger, *The Art of Strict Musical Composition*, trans. David Beach and Jurgen Thym (New Haven: Yale University Press, 1983), p. 376.

The separations provided by nonlegato, marcato, and staccato we call articulatory silences. They are important, for—as we keep saying—silence is music, too. Honor those silences. Make certain they are "audible" and clean.

Watch syllable stress! Diction is a rhythmic factor, remember, as well as a source of intelligibility. Be certain the singers are stressing the right syllables. What your orchestra members play must match the articulation types you have assigned to the choir. Emphasize to all that it is not enough to stress the accented syllables; it is just as important *to unstress the weak syllables*. Figure 11-2 displays the stress/unstress (´/˘) symbols for the "Cum sancto spiritu" text, as we would like it sung.

Cŭm sānc – tŏ spī - rĭ - tŭ, ĭn glō – rĭ - ă

Dē – ĭ pa – trĭs. Ā – mĕn.

Figure 11-2 Text of "Cum sancto spiritu" with syllable stresses and unstresses marked

Check the entrances. In the first exposition, both the Subject and Countersubject I appear three times; in the first instrumental interlude, each occurs once. (And note the reappearance of the soprano's legato figure from bar 7 in the violins II, measures 19–20.) In the second exposition, there are two Subject entrances in the men's voices, Countersubject I appears twice in the women's, and so forth. Some of these statements are modified; you should take note of that, for it may affect the accuracy of your singers.

Specific points:

1. Be certain that at the end of the first exposition you give just as much energy and attention to the orchestral passage that begins in bar 16 (even if you are working only with piano) as you did to the full ensemble before. Conductors must always decide how to treat materials, whoever performs them. Here, the string entrances in bars 16–17 lead up to a crowning trumpet-and-violins-I attack in measure 18, followed by an energetic viola entrance with Countersubject I in bar 20, and all this must be balanced and shaped.
2. Give clear baton cues to each section, as it enters.
3. Keep the character of the three thematic ideas distinct, both in your baton and in your ensemble.
4. Maintain good balance, with relatively unimportant materials understated.
5. In this same regard, note that the final Subject statement in the sopranos and violins II (beginning at measure 72) occurs rather low in their voices, while the other parts are doubling the Countersubject I. (Perhaps Vivaldi meant to let Countersubject I dominate the Subject at the end.) Decide how you want to handle this problem.
6. This movement is the finale of the *Gloria*. It is likely, therefore, that Vivaldi expected a ritard at the end. How much do you want, and where will you begin it?
7. Plan exactly how long you want to hold the final fermata. Gauge this by the wind instruments; the singers and the string players can "stagger" their breathing and

bowing, of course, if you ask them to, but the oboeist and the trumpet player cannot. (Remember, your harpsichord sound will fade quickly.)

You should be ready now to undertake Vivaldi's splendid "Cum sancto spiritu."[14]

BACKGROUND AND PERSPECTIVES: THE VIENNESE CLASSICAL PATTERN

The extent to which the Viennese Classical style of Haydn, Mozart, Beethoven, and Schubert represented a disjunction, a divorce, from the musical features of the Baroque is sometimes overstated. Joseph Haydn, who established most of the structural and conceptual characteristics of the Viennese idiom, was a revolutionary but no radical. Although he was almost self-taught, his long years of singing as a choirboy at the village church in Hainburg and at St. Stephen's Cathedral in Vienna gave him a thorough familiarity with many great Renaissance and Baroque works. It followed, then, that the music he wrote was composed by a mind and ears filled with good counterpoint.

Others followed Haydn's lead. By 1775 a consensus had defined the standard instrumentation of the orchestra, and the string quartet had become both a form and an ensemble. Riding Gluck's reforms and Mozart's genius, opera was turning away from excesses of ostentation toward balance and cohesive integrity. Haydn's great masses were exhibiting an astute synthesis of liturgical materials and symphonic structure.

The principles of sonata-allegro design were penetrating, moreover, virtually all the forms of the period; Haydn's invention of development procedures in his Opus 33 string quartets and his crafting of developmental and variational techniques showed the way to Beethoven, so that organic unity became a central feature of the overall Viennese Classical style. Slow movements, finales, and eventually even the scherzos began to be shaped by this process.

Within virtually all Haydn's structural designs resides an impelling momentum. With the unbroken rhythmic continuity of the Baroque in his ears, he makes *motion* dominate most of his forms; typically, he starts a movement with limping rhythmic values, focusing first on melodic contours; then he turns to the impetus of constant eighths or quarters, adding unbroken sixteenths as he presses toward an important cadence (after which this accelerative procedure begins again). At emotional peaks in movements, he often ruthlessly interrupts this rhythmic drive, leaving his audience hanging for a moment (just as Beethoven will do a generation later).

The other point of focus in Haydn's structures is his management of tonali-

---

[14]As a convenience for your later use, the authors include in Appendix B a summary of style and performance practice in Baroque choral music. There also you will find a list of additional Baroque choral music suitable for young conductors.

ty. His increasingly sophisticated technique involves an early departure from the home base, development of materials in distant tonal regions, enticing feints and hints about a return to tonic, and an eventual restoration of that original key. His overall designs generally are constructed of joists of impelling forward motion that span and connect pillars made of tonally related cadences.

Melodic originality was less important to Haydn than to Mozart, and it would become the focus of Schubert's style. In the music of Mozart and Schubert, regular phrase lengths and "closed tonality" (beginning and ending on the same tonic) are basic features. Even when Mozart writes an initial *five*-bar unit, he tends to maintain that phrase length. (This is not true of Haydn, who manipulates phrase length alternately as a means of variety and unity.) The well-known "four-bar phrase" becomes standard, not in Haydn, but in the music of Mozart, and continues so in Schubert.

Chromaticism is present in the Viennese Classical style (no more so than in Bach, but differently employed). Haydn generally prefers to use chromaticism harmonically; secondary dominants and other such mutated chords occur commonly and serve both to decorate simple melodies and to smooth out modulations. Mozart's use of chromatics is more frequently melodic: Consecutive half steps appear often in his lines (as we will see in *Ave verum corpus*). With respect to the harmonies employed, this is the "era of common practice," in which functional chordal progressions, archetypical use of deceptive cadences, and the like are primary harmonic procedures.

Even though Baroque musical features can be observed, this was a new age. The long-term impact of the Reformation, with its emphasis on individual human judgment as a basis for finding truth (as opposed to the *dicta* of the older order), had produced the era of the Enlightenment, in which truth was uncovered by dialogue between reasonable people. The string quartet—a balanced conversation between four relatively equal partners is the musical metaphor of the period. Passion is present in these exchanges, but a courtly grace is characteristic.

Thus, it is easy to underestimate the power here. There *is* a courtly grace about this music; like polite conversation in a salon, Viennese Classical style begins with a certain reserve, a reluctance to display homely, naive emotions. Deep feelings lie just below the surface, nevertheless, and from time to time the composers parade them in bright sunlight. For you, the greatest risk is "cuteness," a shallow, adolescent obviousness that misses the passionate sophistication and philosophical depth behind the grace.

Wolfgang Amadeus Mozart: *Ave verum corpus*, K. 618

What need we say to you of Mozart? Perhaps it is most useful to speak of the influences on his life. He had, in a sense, *two* fathers. Leopold Mozart was his biological sire and his first musical guide; probably the finest violinist of his time, Leopold was author of that era's definitive textbook on violin pedagogy and performance practice;[15] his prestige carried young Wolfgang through important doorways. So it was that the boy's first symphony appears to have been written under the direct supervision of no less than Johann Christoph Bach in London in the 1760s. So it was that Wolfgang heard the Mannheim Orchestra, the best at the time, during his travels. So it was that the name Mozart was an advantage to him, even before he made it timeless.

Wolfgang did not meet Franz Joseph Haydn until the early 1780s, but he knew the older master's music well before that, and used the dedication of his own six "Haydn Quartets" as a means of opening personal communication between them. To Haydn, young Mozart was both son and brother. The classical sonata-allegro principles Haydn was conceiving and amplifying influenced Mozart directly; on the other hand, the younger master's richer use of chromatics affected the writing of the older composer; so it went, from parameter to parameter across the spectrum of style features. Mozart had the advantage of this exchange for just a decade. His early death left Haydn to build on their shared ideas for an additional fifteen years. (Beethoven during those years was learning from them both.)

Of course, not all these "shared ideas" are to be found in *Ave verum corpus* (Example 11-5).[16] (No sonata-allegro process is present either in this little motet or in the Schubert Kyrie, which comes next, for example.) In other respects, these two works are typical of Viennese Classical style.

Mozart had but six months to live (though no one would have thought his life was to end at 35) when he wrote his *Ave verum corpus*. It is short, and not difficult, but it is not "simple." Mastery is manifest in the working-out of every measure.

It had been a decade since Wolfgang had abandoned Leopold's Salzburg, and—having left behind the Archbishop, with whom he had quarreled, as well—he had avoided the writing of sacred music during that period. Now, for his friend Josef Stoll, a schoolmaster-choirmaster at the nearby spa of Baden, he created this little motet for the Feast of Corpus Christi. It was to be his last complete sacred work, for he died before he finished his Requiem.

Mozart scored the *Ave verum corpus* (a text proper to the Corpus Christi feast) for four-part choir, standard string orchestra, and organ. Its forty-six measures of Adagio follow the tonal design of a binary form: A modulation away from the opening D major, beginning in bar 12, establishes A major (the original dominant); a tonally ambiguous passage from measure 22 to measure 28 returns to A major, and then the key shifts back to D major for the final seventeen bars. The principal cadences all fall on A (bars 10, 21, 29) until the deceptive resolution at 37 and the end.

[15]Leopold Mozart, *A Treatise on the Fundamental Principles of Violin Playing,* trans. Editha Knocker (London: Oxford University Press, 1951).

[16]Wolfgang Amadeus Mozart, *Ave verum corpus,* ed. Dr. Ernst Tittel (Vienna: Musikverlag Styria, 1952).

Example 11-5 Mozart: *Ave verum corpus*

Example 11-5 *(cont.)*

Example 11-5 *(cont.)*

Example 11-5 *(cont.)*

Example 11-5 *(cont.)*

The phrase structure is just as we would expect. All the choral units are four bars in length, save the very last one. (Mozart extends this phrase to six measures to give the motet a feeling of finality.) The melodic chromaticism that we have said is characteristic of him is immediately obvious: The opening soprano line descends from A through G-sharp and G-natural to F-sharp. (See also, in this respect, such passages as the bass line in bars 13 and 14 and the soprano in bars 39 and 40; note the mutation in the tenor in bar 23, as well.) Most of his voice leading is stepwise. Skips tend to outline the harmonies. Step progressions are used to control the shape of longer lines.

Note the *alla breve* marking. (Remember the recommendation from Quantz that an *alla breve* should be taken twice as fast as a movement in $\frac{4}{4}$?[17]) Note also the harmonic rhythm: Mozart tends to change chords here on the half note, not on the quarter. The authors believe the ¢ symbol indicates that Mozart intended that the musicians *think* in two. On the other hand, the constant quarter notes here—unbroken, save at the bar 30 reprise (a break that helps define the structure), at measure 36, and at measure 42—constitute an audible and important level of motion. The Adagio marking advises a slow tempo, of course; taken all together, it appears best for the motet to be heard (and conducted) in a rather slow, subdivided *two*. To put it another way, any Adagio can be an Adagio in two, or an Adagio in four; look for the composer's signals to decide which, and then temper your choice, if necessary, with subdivisions.

Mozart writes a deceptively simple harmonic counterpoint here, supported by arpeggios and other moving figures in the strings. For variety at bar 30 he couples the voices in pairs, getting a rich harmonic effect from the transient seventh chords that result. The orchestra establishes the rhythm in the very beginning, doubles the choral lines, provides a climax and maintains impetus from bar 18 to bar 22, and finally closes the motet with a brief coda.

Here is the text, translated approximately word by word:

Hail true body, born of Mary the Virgin,
Truly suffering, sacrificed on the Cross for man.

(From) whose side, pierced, water flowed and blood,
Be to us a foretaste [a reassurance] in death's agony, in death's agony.

Note that the pace and the intensity of harmonic change increase on the words that refer to Christ's suffering; Mozart employs dissonance to emphasize (in tone-painting) such words as "cruce" and "sanguine," and the final phrase "in mortis examine." He also stresses "sanguine" and "examine" with decorative

---

[17]There is reason to think that Padre Martini's teaching influenced Mozart's use of *alla breve*. Whether the term is a metric or a tempo indication in a given composer is a controversy; in addition to Quantz, see the two extreme positions argued under "Alla Breve" in Erich Leinsdorf, *The Composer's Advocate: A Radical Orthodoxy for Conductors* (New Haven: Yale University Press, 1981), and Apel, *Harvard Dictionary of Music*. The authors' view is that Mozart intends ¢ to be taken in two in faster tempos, but that in an Adagio, or at an even slower pace, he would think it reasonable to subdivide that two.

turns. The only ornament he indicates, however, is the trill in the violins in measure 45. (The "grace note" in bar 20 is really a convention: It is a C-sharp eighth note, followed by a B-natural quarter.) The overall effect is passionate but within the bounds of Classical refinement. One is left wishing that Mozart's Requiem, rushed through in part and then left to be finished by other hands, had been so organic a conception and its proportions so carefully and clearly balanced as this lovely motet.

Conducting Ave verum corpus

We have recommended a subdivided two-beat pattern for this motet. *You may subdivide your beat wherever you think it useful either for clarity (that is, safety) or for emphasis and intensity.* We suggest full-length beat-strokes on the first and third quarter notes, with shorter gestures on the second and fourth, in each measure.

Why not simply use a four-beat pattern? The advantage to a subdivided two is this: In four, the baton actually changes direction on each quarter note; in two, the stick marks the moment of each quarter, but the rebound continues the same line. Establish this subdivided-two pattern clearly with the orchestra in the first two bars. (A pattern like that shown in Figure 11-3 would be useful.) The choir begins with a half note, and you can help them "think in two" by minimizing the size of your subdivisions in measures 3 and 4. Throughout the motet, avoid unnecessarily large emphases on the second and fourth quarter notes; then when you *want* an offbeat stress (perhaps on the second quarter of bar 23, for example, or the fourth quarter of bar 36), the effect will be a pronounced one.

Further suggestions:

1. For a chorus of sixty, an ideal string body would be 7 or 8 firsts, 5 or 6 seconds, 4 violas, 4 'cellos, and 3 basses. The organ registration should be modest, not Romantic, in character.
2. We agree with the editor of Example 11-5 that ♩ = 66–72 is an appropriate tempo.

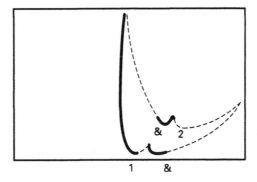

Figure 11-3   A subdivided two-beat appropriate for use in *Ave verum corpus*

3. The unbroken four-bar choral phrases can become burdensome here. *Look for opportunities to break up their regularity.* An eighth-rest release after the first "Ave" disguises the problem, for instance, and the passage from bar 11 through bar 21 should build without a break to the high F-sharp (in the violins) in bar 19. Measures 22–29 can be treated as a single unit, and so can 30–37.

4. Notice that we regard neither the orchestral momentum nor the overall design as reaching an important cadence in bar 18 (or in 43, for that matter). Be careful not to treat the orchestral passages (in measures 19–21 and 43–46) as of secondary importance to the choral music. The choral-orchestral fabric is an integrated whole.

5. This analysis, which seeks to elide four-bar units into longer phrases, suggests that both singers and players need to be thinking of continuous flow—of "line." At the same time, the singers' consonants and the players' articulations must be clearly defined. Although this movement is cantabile in manner, be careful not to let the legato here become lugubrious and sentimental. Keep it clean, with some separation where the line permits it.

6. Plan carefully where the releases are to be placed, from the rest after the first word (which must be an eighth, since the lower three voices must wait to release at the same time as the sopranos) to the final cutoff. Decide how you want measure 37 to work (perhaps the only spot where Mozart's intentions are unclear). Should (a) the sopranos release their first G on the second quarter while the other voices carry to the third, (b) all release together on the second quarter, or (c) the sopranos carry through bar 37 without a break? The choice is interpretive, and it is yours.

7. Consider the very end. Here, your subdivisions really help the intense passage from bar 40 on. *Maintain your tempo,* however, until measure 42; a *slight* ritard there could be followed by a more substantial slowing in bar 45. Add a fermata to the last chord, and judge sensitively the duration of that sonority.

8. The building and easing of impetus is the important element of these phrase connections.

9. Although you may regard this motet as perfect, note for note, as it stands, it still is your right to consider adding a limited and judiciously chosen number of ornaments in genuinely important places.

Ave verum corpus can be done very well with keyboard alone, of course, if no orchestra is available, but the intensity the strings can provide as they "press through" notes (which quickly decay on the piano) adds to the effectiveness of this beautiful little jewel.

Franz (Peter) Schubert: Mass in G Major, D167, Kyrie

Although almost exactly a quarter-century lies between Mozart's *Ave verum corpus* and Schubert's Mass in G Major, the differences in style between these works are far less important than the similarities.

Franz Schubert was born six years after Mozart died. At age 11, he became a chorister at the Habsburg court chapel in Vienna, where he sang the standard sacred choral literature of the time. In October 1814, when he was not yet 18 years old, his first mass (D105, in F Major) brought him his first popular recognition as a composer. (That same month, he wrote his song "Gretchen am Spinnrade.") He had just thirteen years of his brief life left when he wrote his G major mass the next March. Scored for SATB choir, STB soloists, strings, and organ, it was not to be published until 1846, eighteen years after he died, but its popularity since then has been unbroken.

Schubert's gift for lyricism and his predilection for the simpler structural designs are already obvious here. His Kyrie is an *ABA'* design, as you see in Example 11-6:[18] A "Kyrie eleison" choral section begins in G major and then modulates (starting in bar 24) to A minor; the contrasting "Christe eleison" soprano solo that follows moves from that key through a fragmental choral passage, and then back to G major for the Kyrie reprise (which itself is altered only by a brief coda).

Schubert establishes an interesting pattern of phraseology here. Two four-bar units in G major (measures 1–8) are followed by a five-bar phrase that cadences on the dominant in bar 13. After a two-measure orchestral extension comes a reprise of those three phrases in the same order—4 + 4 + 5—modulating this time to A minor.

In the Christe section, a similar asymmetrical measure (the "added bar") occurs in measure 38, just before the material is repeated; the solo passage ends in E minor in measure 46. At that point, the modulatory choral entrances (centering for a few bars on C major) carry us eventually, at bar 60, to the dominant seventh chord of the original key; a three-bar orchestral transition follows, and the Kyrie returns in G major. Here, the same pattern—two four-bar phrases, plus a closing unit of five measures—recurs in bars 68–80; then the three phrases repeat one last time (ending differently, this time, with an elision in the tenor line that drives the codetta).

Melody is a focal element in the movement, as we would expect of Schubert. The opening soprano line is attractive, and the soprano solo is well shaped; note that it is not just the *top* voice that matters, however, for the tenors (with their arching peak in bar 2) and the basses (with their ascent through bars 1–3) are just as melodically important to the opening phrase as the sopranos. It is the tenors in measure 90 who provide the melodic interest in the coda, as you have already seen.

The rhythmic organization of the movement is effective. The singers ride the triple meter generally at the level of the quarter-note beat. The orchestra, on the other hand, establishes the eighth note as its rhythmic level from measure 1, and maintains that subdivision throughout; only three times—the last two beats of bar 29, measures 66–67, and the two final bars—is that constant eighth interrupted. Why at those spots? Because measure 29 is the end of the first A section, and measures 66–67 are the terminus of the B unit. *Schubert, just as Haydn would do, is breaking off a constant rhythm as a means of making the structure audible. Rhythmic motion is defining form here, as it does throughout the Viennese Classical era.*

[18]Franz Schubert, Mass in G Major, in *Neue Ausgabe Sämtliche Werke*, ed. W. Dürr, A. Feil, and C. Landon (Kassel, 1964).

Example 11-6   Schubert, Mass in G Major, Kyrie

Example 11-6 *(cont.)*

Example 11-6 *(cont.)*

Example 11-6 *(cont.)*

Example 11-6 *(cont.)*

Example 11-6 *(cont.)*

Example 11-6 *(cont.)*

Example 11-6 *(cont.)*

Example 11-6 *(cont.)*

Example 11-6 *(cont.)*

There is nothing remarkable about the use of harmony in the Kyrie—nothing far removed from what we have just seen of Mozart's practice. Seventh chords occur prominently, and there are augmented triads (reached by skip, in the case of bar 50). Schubert's little coda is a "plagal extension"; settled in G major in the A' section, the music pivots in measure 90 (with the tenor F-natural) toward the subdominant C major chord (maintaining G-natural as the bass in both choir and orchestra), and returns to the tonic chord in bar 94.

Conducting Schubert's Kyrie

Having studied the Josquin movement in the previous chapter, you already are familiar with the succinct Kyrie text and its translation. The problem with a Kyrie is that a composer has so few words to set in what must be a movement of at least reasonable length. Schubert uses a great deal of repetition, with his reiterations of separate "Christes" and "eleisons," for example, in measures 47–64.

Compare the two settings: How does Schubert's approach differ from Josquin's? *Do consonants play a more expressive or dramatic role in this Kyrie?* Are there other differences?

Here are some detailed points to consider as you prepare to conduct this Kyrie:

1. Schubert has given you a practical problem at the very beginning. The singers must begin on the downbeat, without any instrumental "introduction." How do they "get the pitch"? You could have the concertmaster (or the pianist, if you have no orchestra) give them a G-natural; a better approach would be to *teach them to find their notes from the A to which the orchestra tunes.* No one gives each player his or her pitch! Why should the singers need special help?

2. You will want to conduct this in three, using a legato beat pattern. We suggest that you try tempos between ♩ = 72 and ♩ = 80.

3. You could use about the same forces here as for the Mozart: say, strings of 8-6-5-5-3, plus organ.

4. This is harmonic counterpoint. Various voices (including orchestral parts) become more or less important, bar by bar. In the first four measures, the tenor and bass lines need to be heard clearly, as we have observed already. Your job is to keep all these shifting focal points in balance. Remember that this, like the Mozart, is out of the Viennese tradition, and keep the lines articulate. Do not allow a sticky legato to obscure the contrapuntal fabric.

5. What need you do to make the *structure* "audible"? You may decide you want very modest ritards in measures 29 and 67 (with an *a tempo* in the next bar, in each case). And at measure 30, the repeated notes in the orchestra suggest a different articulation—more separation (détaché, perhaps)—for measures 30–45, with a return to the original legato at measure 46.

6. We have seen that Schubert has placed unbroken eighth-note motion in the orchestra. Choose places where you think you need to show this subdivision in your (triple) beat pattern. Ritards are such spots. Another place is bar 30, where you can

change to a more detached articulation if that is your choice; you can make the separations cleaner, and the rhythm clearer, by subdividing a couple of measures.

7. This movement can be good exercise for your left hand. Use it to help your baton shape the phrases. (If you conceive of bars 1–4 as an arch, for example, show the crescendo to bar 3 and the diminuendo to bar 5 in your left hand, as well as with your baton.)

8. Schubert lends drama to his otherwise-lyric Kyrie primarily through dynamics. A *sfz* is an accent, whereas a *fp* is only a dynamic change. Examine the *fp*s here. The first one occurs in measure 8; since you always show everything one beat early, your baton must signal this *fp* to the orchestra (or piano) on the third beat of bar 7. (The baton actually stops for a moment, as with a staccato beat.) As the *forte* is being performed, one count later, you must be cueing—again one beat ahead—the choral entry on the second pulse of bar 8. Schubert gives you ample opportunity to practice *fp* preparations here.

9. Tied to these *fp* markings are the stresses produced by the recurrent "k's" of the frequent Kyrie attacks. You may want the ones that occur on second beats (bars 8 and 10 are instances) to be more emphatic than those that begin the more lyric phrases; similarly, the "k's" of the isolated "Christe" attacks in bars 47–61 may be treated more dramatically. This is a matter of using diction not just for intelligibility but also for expression. Give careful thought to how you want "Kyrie" and "Christe" and "eleison" enunciated in this long succession of occurrences. (The repeated "Kyrie" attacks may encourage the chorus to get louder. Keep your ears alive to this risk.)

10. Some editions show wedges, not staccatos, in bar 29. There is controversy about this marking, but we believe that *in the Viennese Classical style*, the wedge requires a detached, slightly more emphasized note than the dot. Use an accented beat.

11. The most troublesome entrances often are those which follow a long tacet passage. Make certain to give your singers good solid preparatory beats and cues in bars 46–48.

12. Know exactly how you want the transitional passage in bars 46–67 shaped (in intensity, direction, peak, and so on).

13. Be careful not to impose too great a ritard in bars 66–67, for Schubert has already slowed the motion from eighths to quarters here.

14. Show the crescendo-and-diminuendo in measures 94–95 with your left hand, as well as with your baton.

15. Don't let the chorus relax during the final four *pp* bars. Keep their concentration, even though they have stopped singing. Surprise them about this in rehearsal, abruptly asking them to "Freeze!" here.

16. We have reached the threshold of the Romantic era, in which embellishments traditionally are written, not improvised. Nevertheless, even in this late Classical work, the soprano soloist, at least, could be given some liberty with respect to ornamentation, if that is in keeping with your interpretation.

With respect to the soloist, expect to spend coaching time with her (to help with finding her entrance pitch, breathing spots, tone quality, diction, phrase shape, ritards, and all). In rehearsal, watch balance between the soprano and the orchestra, and be consistent in cueing her. She needs to feel she can rely on you when she is nervous.

One final point: Since scholars generally agree now that Schubert was essentially a "Classicist," and not a "Romantic," it follows that his music deserves some restraint (but not coldness) in expression. You may want a slight broadening in spots like bar 15 (only the second and third beats, at most), measure 38, and bar 82, but be careful not to overdo these rubato effects, for the sake of the most important structural points in this Kyrie, measures 29–30, 67–68, and 98–99; these three sites should get more obvious and audible ritards than any other spots in this charming, lyric work.[19]

[19]As a convenience for your later use, the authors include in Appendix B a summary of style and performance practice in Classical choral music.

CHAPTER 12

Style and Performance: Romantic and Twentieth-Century Vocal Works

In many respects, what has come since the death of Beethoven (and Schubert, the following year) has been a continuity; almost all the great Romantic composers sought to "free themselves" from the "common practice" that had arisen during the eighteenth century, and sought to test the limits of meter, tonality, harmony, melody, and structure. We do not yet have a descriptive name (or a set of names) like Baroque, Classical, or Romantic for the music of the twentieth century, but we can recognize today the same expansive experimentalism in the works of Debussy, Ives, Schoenberg, Webern, Hindemith, Stravinsky, and more recent figures.

That is not to say that there has been no formalism in our time: Several major figures of the twentieth century (notably, Schoenberg, with his serial procedures, and Hindemith, with his theories of tonality and harmony) have constructed artificial "systems" or processes, seeking unifying methods to supplant the architectural designs (sonata-allegro, fugue, and so on) of the Baroque and Viennese Classical periods. When the next great epoch will begin—if it has not already done so—is not yet clear at this writing.

BACKGROUND AND PERSPECTIVES: ROMANTIC STYLE

The attitudes and social outlooks of the Romantic composers were formed in the backwash of the American and French revolutions in the last quarter of the eighteenth century, and were affected by the resumption of European political turmoil, which came to a head in the civil conflicts of 1848. Enthusiasm for "freedom" (often indistinguishable from "license") was trendy, especially in those who already had it. (The most vocal of all the Romantic rebels, Wagner—who himself occupied the barricades in 1849—certainly did.) As has been the case in the twentieth century, artists in the Romantic era felt a sometimes-egoistic need to demonstrate a full commitment to social progress. They sought a "relevance" in their music and reflected that search in personal political pronouncements. Their broad commitment to a general revolution of sorts can be seen in their new approaches to harmony, meter, and the other parameters.

The illusion that such changes in musical style had in themselves real sociopolitical significance—that they were "progressive" (a viewpoint manifest in phrases like "the emancipation of dissonance")—was a pervasive piece of wishful thinking.[1] Music is a realm separate from politics.

The horrors of global warfare and mass extermination in the twentieth century disillusioned those who, like Wordsworth earlier, had thought to see a new dawn in revolutionary movements worldwide. (Some artists and composers were led thereby to speak of "the unparalleled stress of working under the constant threat of nuclear destruction." The truth is that each human age has its clarifying terrors and that no generations have faced greater risk of annihilation in this century than did the artists of the fourteenth century, confronted with the Black Death). **It is difficult in one's own time to keep passing popular slogans separate from issues of genuine artistic merit; yet, it remains one of your most important responsibilities as a conductor to ignore extramusical irrelevancies so that you can make clear-headed judgments about the lasting worth of each work you study.**

The style changes adopted by composers during the last three-quarters of the nineteenth century were substantial, whether or not they had social relevance. Perhaps the most obvious outgrowths of the search for extramusical significance were the attempts to link music directly to other aspects of human life: to figures of legend, from Wagner's *Ring* heroes to Sibelius's Lemminkäinen and beyond; to biographical scenarios like Strauss's orchestral tone poems *Tod und Verklärung* and *Ein Heldenleben*; to new emphasis on "hybrid arts," like opera and ballet; to poetry, to visual art (we will study Mussorgsky's *Pictures at an Exhibition* in Chapter 16), and to other sources of "program music." Like paintings, some of these are giant works and some are "miniatures."

Another influence on music of the nineteenth century and beyond has been the force of nationalism. After the French Revolution, the ideal of patriotic loyalty became the prevalent substitute for the faded ideal of a unified Western Christendom. Inevitably, composers sought ways to weave evidences of this new devotion into their works; Russian, Spanish, French, English, and eventually American folk songs began to appear in serious works. Openly chauvinistic

---

[1]As Leonard Meyer has demonstrated, novelty in musical style from one period to the next represents change but not progress or evolution. See Leonard Meyer, *Music, the Arts, and Ideas* (Chicago: University of Chicago Press, 1967), especially beginning on p. 87.

pieces like Tchaikovsky's *1812 Overture* became widely popular, and politicians (Hitler in the 1930s and many others before and since) learned to use music to rally the masses to often-shameful purposes.

Some Romantic works continued to use (with modified characteristics) the Classical forms, or at least to use them as a point of departure. Increasingly, however, structures implicit in extramusical "programs" became the real organizing matrix within a composition; thus, a nineteenth-century tone poem might exhibit a traditional sonata-allegro design but be driven really by events in the life story of its hero. A listener would have to know and be interested in the details of the "program" (the story of Hamlet, perhaps) to find any coherence in the sequence of musical events. Of the traditional forms, the simplest, being the most flexible, were the most frequently used; ternary *(ABA)* designs grew pervasive, from songs to symphonies.

As composers sought freshness and variety, an enormous expansion of media took place. Instruments of all kinds joined the orchestras: the "secondary woodwinds" (piccolo, English horn, alto and bass clarinets, contrabassoon), the tuba (and the whole battery of "Wagner tubas"), the harp, the celeste, the saxophone, and a range of percussion instruments far beyond what Haydn's timpanist could have dreamed. In the nineteenth century, the trend was not toward new ensembles but toward larger ones; orchestras grew toward the 100-member milestone as the century progressed, and "festival choruses" sang in their thousands.

Heard by ears familiar now with Bartók and Boulez, the tonal and harmonic innovations of the Romantic composers (which caused public furors, even riots, in their time) seem tame. Chromatic usages in melody (half-step passing tones and the like) became so common as to be classifiable as (for example) French sixth and diminished-seventh "chords." In the Viennese Classical style, the tension of tonic, dominant, and other clearly related keys—polarized against each other—is central to the aural perception of form. By the later years of the nineteenth century, the variety and subtlety of tonalities had weakened that polarity so much that the sense of "coming home" to tonic was no longer so audible, and thus the influence of the whole parameter of tonality on structural designs became minimal in many works. Dissonance had not yet become random, but its frequency of use had increased so much that its impact on the listener began to lessen.[2]

The metric clarity of the eighteenth century was traded for complexity and flexibility in the Romantic world. The "tyranny of the bar line" was attacked, and so one finds—especially from Schumann on—changing meters and direct conflicts between implied downbeats in different voices within a texture, conflicts obvious long before composers actually began to notate successions of metric changes bar-to-bar. Hemiolas and sophisticated syncopations occur frequently

---

[2]It is no longer possible for us to really hear a dominant seventh chord as "dissonant," for example, although it still was so perceived when the opening measures of Beethoven's Symphony No. 1, Op. 21, in C major first were heard.

(see the opening of Schumann's Symphony No. 3, Op. 97, in E-flat major, the *Rhenish* Symphony). Rhythmic complications abound, especially intricate patterns of two-against-three and three-against-four.

Dynamic markings were another area of development during the Romantic era. Composers (no longer, like Haydn, working daily with the same musicians) of necessity notated specific dynamic instructions in much greater detail, but they also asked for what appears to be a wider range; by the end of the nineteenth century, markings from *fffff* to *ppppp* were in use. This can be misleading, however, for, after all, dynamics are relative. "Very soft" is very soft, whether it is marked *pp* or *ppppp*. Romantic composers are not "freeing" us to play louder or softer, for *ff* in a Beethoven piano sonata is probably just as "loud" in real terms as *fffff* is in Debussy; they are asking for more and subtler levels of dynamic shading within the absolute range of "very loud" to "very soft." In this aspect, and in general, *the Romantic outcomes—disregarding the chatter about "ideals"—are added complexity and more restrictive instructions from composer to performers (through notation), not radical change.*

Johannes Brahms: Motet *Schaffe in mir, Gott, ein rein Herz*, Op. 29, No. 2

Within the full catalog of Brahms's compositions, choral music is a major component, and *a cappella* sacred choral works are significant both in numbers and in importance. Just as we can examine Haydn's stylistic development by studying his string quartets alone, it is possible to survey and assess Brahms's evolving idiom simply through his choral literature. There are three sets of works specifically called motets: The earliest is the pair of works in Op. 29 (1860), one of which we are about to study; the second is the pair in Op. 74 (finished in 1877); and the last is the three in Op. 110 (1889). Brahms was just 27 when the first set appeared, in the same year he and Joachim signed their celebrated manifesto against Wagner's *Das Kunstwerk der Zukunft* ("Music of the Future").

Still in Germany at the time (for he would not make a professional visit to Vienna until 1862, and would not move there until 1878), Brahms was concentrating primarily on chamber music, lieder, and other choral works. His first piano concerto and the two orchestral serenades are the important items in his symphonic writing up to that point.

Among his later choral creations, the great *Ein deutsches Requiem*, Op. 45, with its powerful fugues, would prove to be the towering masterpiece. Brahms was always interested in older forms and studied imitative counterpoint (including canons and fugues) with care; these techniques are apparent throughout his writing, so the features of style we see in *Schaffe in mir, Gott, ein rein Herz* are consistent with those of *Ein deutsches Requiem* itself.

The first motet in the Op. 29 pair, *Es ist das Heil uns kommen her*, is a setting of a five-line religious poem. This Brahms begins with an SATBB chorale-style section, some 14 measures long; then he uses the same text for a sophisticated, 69-bar five-voice fugue in which four of the parts operate contrapuntally at the rhythmic level of the quarter note, while the baritones enter periodically to intone the original chorale melody in half notes. The motet is in E major, with the opening chorale written in $\frac{4}{4}$ and the fugue in $\frac{4}{2}$.

Schaffe in mir, Gott, ein rein Herz, which you see in Example 12-1,[3] is Op. 29, No. 2.[4] After the mixed vocal-and-instrumental fabrics of the Baroque works in Chapter 11, we find ourselves back in an *a cappella* texture.

Example 12-1   Brahms: *Schaffe in mir, Gott, ein rein Herz, Op. 29, No. 2*

Piano for rehearsal only

[3]Johannes Brahms, *Schaffe in mir, Gott, ein rein Herz*, Op. 29, No. 2 (Leipzig: Breitkopf & Härtel Musikverlag, 1980), pp. 11–19.

[4]You should be ready by now for the complexities (after the comparatively simple opening) of the second and third movements of *Schaffe in mir, Gott, ein rein Herz*. Your professor may choose to assign only the first movement or to divide up the whole work between members of the class.

Example 12-1 *(cont.)*

Example 12-1 *(cont.)*

Example 12-1 *(cont.)*

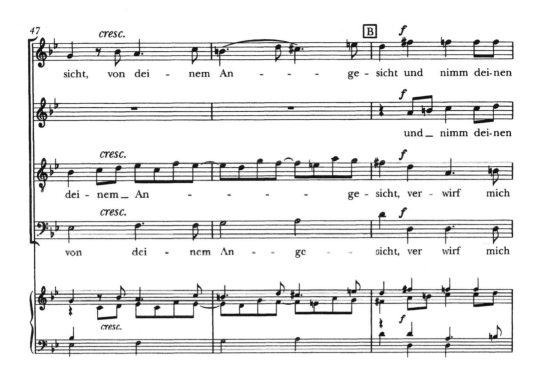

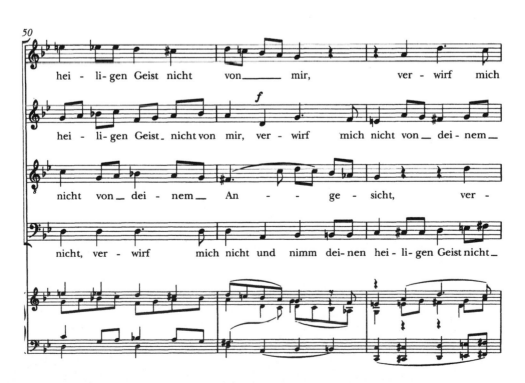

Example 12-1 *(cont.)*

Example 12-1 *(cont.)*

Example 12-1 *(cont.)*

Example 12-1 *(cont.)*

Example 12-1 *(cont.)*

Example 12-1 *(cont.)*

There is no chorale-style writing here: Brahms avoids pure homophony (save for the final cadence of the motet). The brief (25-bar) first movement, cast in G major, is constructed of imitative lines in the context of two sections of harmonic counterpoint. The second movement is a 55-measure fugue; based on a subject that begins in a tonally ambiguous way, it proves to be set, for contrast, in the parallel G minor. The finale returns to G major; here, an Andante section featuring antiphonal use of the men's and women's voices is followed by another fugue (itself ended by a spirited coda).

We suggest you study this work at your desk first. Try to hear the counterpoint in your "inner ear" before you take the score to the piano; then, check your mental images at the keyboard. Keep working to build up these aural skills. (You should become able to study a score in a library or a plane, or almost anywhere.)

The harmonic language here is richer than that of the Viennese Classical works, of course. Chromatic resolutions within harmonic progressions are a common phenomenon; see measures 34–40 for examples of this: In bar 34, the second-beat D major triad moves (across an alto passing-tone B) to an F major triad, for instance; seventh chords are another feature of this passage, and of Brahms's style in general. Suspensions, anticipations, and other linear dissonances of all sorts contribute to the intensity of his writing.

One of his favorite devices is the "pedal point," the sustaining of a long pitch against changing harmonies. A traditional "tonic pedal in the bass" occurs at the final cadence of the first movement (measures 22–25). On the other hand, Brahms uses an "inverted pedal on the tonic" in the soprano through bars 127–133, while the lower parts continue with harmonic elaboration. He employs several other pedal points in this motet.

His vocal writing is enriched by this chromaticism and this dissonance. A glance at the counterpoint in the tenor and alto voices in bars 26–34 demonstrates this: All twelve pitches of the chromatic scale occur, and consecutive half steps are present in long strings. Much of Brahms's melodic work is still stepwise; where skips occur, they generally outline the underlying chords, but those chords commonly are more complex than would have been standard in the previous century.

The master apparently began this motet in 1857, left it unfinished, and returned to complete it in 1860, the year he turned 27. He took the its text from Psalm 51; for the first movement he used the tenth verse. In English translation, it reads:

> Create in me, God, a clean heart
> And give me a new, steadfast spirit.

The second movement sets verse 11:

> Cast me not away from thy countenance
> And take not thy holy spirit from me.

And the finale continues with the twelfth verse:

> Rejuvenate me with thy support,
> And uphold me with thy revivifying spirit.

Brahms is very interested in the impact of the text—its sound, flow, and meaning—on the overall work. This is not instrumental style, as Bach's vocal lines sometimes are; here, the sensitive setting of individual words and syllables is often obvious.

Make certain of your facility with this text. (This is the first choral work in German studied in this volume.) Go over it carefully with a pronouncing dictionary, but be certain also to try out your diction on a fluent speaker of the language. There are dialects of German, by the way, just as we have English in "BBC," New York, Texas, "Plantation Southern," and other "accents." The standard "High German" you want to use as the basis for your diction is usually said to be that spoken in the area around the city of Hannover. Try to find someone who speaks that variety.

Conducting the Brahms Motet, Movement by Movement

As the importance of the individual word differs here from Baroque choral music, so that the process of text setting is different, so too is the singing style different. As we said in Chapter 11, the instrumental style of the Baroque implies articulation in which the notes are more-or-less separated (unless a slur is present); much of this rhythmic definition continues through the Viennese Classical style,[5] but the character of Romantic melody is different. In Brahms and his contemporaries, *smooth connection* of all the notes is the ideal (unless staccato dots or other notated or implied contraindications are present). Legato singing means, literally, that one is joining the *vowels* together as closely as possible; that means that the consonants will have less time to be enunciated and that—if you want clear diction—your singers must work extra to emphasize those consonants within the flow of the legato vowels.

Another stylistic difference lies in the size of the choral force employed. By Brahms's time, large choirs were common in Europe and the British Isles. For this motet (as for *Ein deutsches Requiem*, for that matter), anything between 30 and 200 singers is probably acceptable, though with very large choirs (more than 100, say) you will have some difficulty keeping the fugal counterpoint quick and clean.

---

[5]See the discussions of vocal performance practice in Chapter 11.

Movement 1

The Andante moderato is marked "espressivo," and the time signature is *alla breve*. The harmonic rhythm generally moves at a half-note pace. For the upper four parts, the movement divides into two segments at bar 13, arriving there at a cadence on C major; we could view bars 1–6 as an antecedent phrase, and 7–13 as its consequent; similarly, within the second half of the movement, we can recognize phrases in bars 13–17 and 17–25. Note, however, that the basses II sing the text only *once*—not twice, as do the other parts—and their part is, in many ways, continuous from measure 1 to measure 25. We can view this movement as *A–A'*, but with the reservation that the bass line elides the two sections by its text and melodic impetus.

Brahms scored this for SATBB voices (and the other two movements for other combinations). You will have to redistribute your singers to do this motet. Unless you have twice as many basses as you have tenors, a simple split of the whole bass section is likely to cause balance problems, for the tenors (singing in a higher tessitura and outnumbering the baritones and the second basses) will overpower the lower sections; we recommend, instead, that you divide your entire male force three ways, putting your baritones and some of your second tenors on the bass I part.

What about tempo? You have learned already that *alla breve* implies that the half note is the beat; try this at about ♩ = 56, and make your musicians responsible for feeling the quarter-note subdivision; do not try to "show them" the quarters they sing. They need to "feel" this *movement* in two, and comprehend for themselves the hierarchy of whole notes, half notes, and quarter notes.

It is much harder to conduct slow tempos than fast ones. Preserving a metronomic pulse, sustaining intensity, and still encouraging good tonal production—avoiding choppiness and colorless sound—is more difficult than managing thirty-second notes. Your beat pattern can tend to become too large, for one thing, and you can find yourself needing to show a crescendo when your motion is already encouraging a *fortissimo*! This first movement will be good exercise for you in this regard. Keep your baton moving in proportion to the dynamics, showing energy and intensity within its flow, and still signal the crescendos in the size of your beat.

Observe these other details for this movement:

1. Since there is no instrumental introduction, your singers will have to find their pitches beforehand. You can (a) give them the G-natural (or all their notes, if you must) from the piano, (b) have one of them give the G (unobtrusively) from a pitch pipe, (c) have someone with "perfect pitch" hum the note, or (d) expect the choir to find their pitches by remembering the tonic chord of the last work they sang.
2. Brahms asks you to focus on individual parts at certain moments. Notice, for example, that he has given the tenors a new start on the text, and a pair of "hairpins" (crescendo and decrescendo marks), in bar 3, apparently to spotlight their ascent to the high G in measure 4, and their subsequent descent. Use your left hand and your eyes to shape this special moment.

3. You see that all the parts, in fact, have different texts and different dynamic patterns. Recalling that tenor highlight in bars 3–4, look for other points of focus in individual lines.

4. The general diminuendo in bars 11–12 (note the special "hairpins" in the basses II in measure 12, a characteristic expression for Brahms) is an important aspect of the cadencing process in measure 13. (Show this in the baton, of course.) You may want to "stretch" the first beat of bar 13 a bit, before the releases (the altos and the tenors— and perhaps the second basses, who could elide over this cadence—on the second quarter of bar 13, the sopranos and the first bases on the third).

5. After the text begins again at this point, maintaining balance between the parts remains important. Note the focal soprano and baritone lines in bars 13–16 and the tenors in bars 13–20 (especially 17–20). Particularly oversee the unfolding succession of ascending crescendo lines in measures 20–23, which (against the tonic pedal in the basses II) constitutes the climax of the movement. Use a sufficiently small beat pattern in bars 13–20, saving "room" for the expansion in 20–22.

6. Manage carefully the "decay" in bars 24–25 from the peak in 22–23, controlling precisely your ritard through the quarters in bar 24 into the fermata in 25.

7. An emphatic "st" at the cutoff of "Geist" is needed here, but it must be precise. Sibilant and plosive consonants are especially dangerous at release points.

8. *Keep your baton up* after the cutoff of that fermata to forestall applause between movements. If you drop your hands, the audience may begin to clap.

Movement 2

Brahms has written the second movement, with its rather sensuous fugue, in $\frac{4}{4}$, again with the marking "espressivo." Rhythmic motion is primarily in quarters and eighths.

The *subject* (see the tenor line in bars 26–28) is entirely stepwise, save for two distinguishing downward-fourth skips; constructed on an embellished D–C–B♭–A–G step-progression, it makes use of both B-natural and B-flat. The chromatic *countersubject* that follows (in the tenor: "und . . ." in bar 28 to ". . . mir" in bar 34) is made up entirely at first of descending half steps, reminding one somewhat of a Hassler line from the turn of the seventeenth century. (Brahms repeats this countersubject immediately in the tenor, starting on the high F-sharp in bar 34, under the soprano entrance, and uses it again several times.) The second and fourth entrances of the subject (altos in bar 29 and basses in measure 37) are "tonal answers" (that is, altered intervallically), not "real."

The tonic is unclear until the tenors reach bar 28, and this tonal vagueness (often an advantage in a subject, as you can see from any analysis of Bach fugues) will allow Brahms harmonic and modulatory opportunities. The B-flat at measure 27 is the first signal we get that the previous movement's G major may be superseded by the parallel minor. The initial fugal exposition—in which the alto, soprano, and bass voices enter at three- to five-bar intervals—is extended in bars 40–46 by a stretto of entrances just one measure apart (with the sopranos in bar 42 and the tenors in 45 using inverted forms of the subject). This harmonically complex passage reaches a climax in bars 49–51.

A new exposition devoted entirely to the *inverted* shape of the subject begins with the alto entrance in measure 51; the distinctive skips of a fourth are upward now, and stretto is the rule: Starting with that alto statement, five subject entrances occur in bars 51–55, and three more in 59–61 (the tenor one in bar 59 in *augmentation*). There are, besides, bass and alto entrances in measures 61 and 62 that maintain the rhythm of the opening of the subject. Here, the bass establishes a pedal point on F, which—taken together with the upper voices—implies a shift to the relative major, B-flat. The counterpoint is more complicated than that, however, and elements of E-flat major and F itself obtrude, so that the cadence at measure 65 is ambiguous.

Simultaneous original (though tonal) and inverted statements of the subject occur at bar 65, and stretto entrances (in the original form at bars 69–70, and inverted at 74–75) guide us back to the home key of G minor. The countersubject continues to play a part in all of this, appearing (inverted, like the subject itself) for the last time in the tenor line, beginning at bar 74. The final climax is reached in measures 69–73, and the codetta in 74–80 recedes quietly *mezza voce* into a low octave resolution, which—since it includes neither a B-flat nor a B-natural—allows Brahms a graceful shift back to G major for the last movement.

The concept of the "episode"—a fugal passage in which the subject is not present—plays almost no role in this design. Recurrent statements of the subject are separated by contrapuntal elaborations of the principal motif itself; development, not an alternative melody, is the governing principle here.

Although the tempo decision depends to some extent on the size of your choir, we suggest you consider something close to ♩ = 84 for this fugue. The pulse must be even and consistent throughout, for there are enough harmonic complexities already. The first attack is anacrustic; Brahms makes the meter at the beginning as vague as the tonality, and this lends extra power to the *forte* passages at bars 34 and 49, especially, for they seem clarifying.

We are back in four parts for this movement, so you need not worry about distribution of voices, save for any adjustments you may want to make in high or low spots. Play the subject through several times, in each of its variant forms, until you know it well. Feel how it fits itself to the flow of the text. Notice how Brahms voices the vowels in the various tessituras. See where the strongest consonants fall.

In rehearsal:

1. Your first beat (the quarter rest in the tenor part) must start high and *come straight down.* You must not show the choir any trace of an upward motion, for that would be a "fourth beat"—a "preparation" of your "prep beat." Be clear!
2. A poco legato beat, with extra intensity added as a preparation for the stressed syllables, is what is needed here. Have all the choir sing the tenor line in bars 26–34, until they fully understand the shape of the subject and its text.
3. Use your whole repertory of cues to encourage these fugal entrances—baton, left hand, eyes, elbows, whatever.

4. Keep the subject clearly audible through the counterpoint. Watch balances throughout. Show them *p* at the beginning, and a clear crescendo in bar 33 to the *f* in 34. Drop back to a smaller gesture by bar 40, resuming the *p* level—and so on through the movement.

5. Make your singers aware of the controlling power of the step-progressions Brahms has written: Show them how the tenor line in measures 46–48 is organized around the ascent from C through D–E♭–F–G to A, for example. Again and again, the master uses this device.

6. At the very end, the sopranos are tacet. Make certain they understand the drama of this quiet ending, and caution them not to move or do anything that will distract the audience at the terminal moment of the movement.

7. Again remember to keep your baton up after the cutoff, lest the audience applaud before you begin the finale.

Movement 3

The basic harmonic motion of the opening section of this Andante is at the dotted-half level but is a bit ambiguous: The quarter-note motion, much of which is only neighbor-tones and the like, often can be construed as progressive harmony, so the metric issue of six versus two must be considered.

The opening, which begins in G major, divides into three units; the first two (each ten measures long) contrast the men with the women antiphonally in a setting of the first clause of the text; the third (twelve bars in length) completes the text and employs only the men. Each unit is elided into the next; counterpoint within each unit elides each pair of phrases, too, so that the overall result is unbroken flow from bar 81 to the Allegro fugue at 110. The connecting purpose of these graceful elisions should be understood by your singers.

The fugue that follows at bar 110 continues in G major. Its subject is much less complicated than the one in the previous movement: It outlines the tonic octave in both its "real" and its "tonal" forms, and avoids any tonal or metric ambiguity. Beginning in four parts, it becomes five at measure 122. The second (descending) half of the subject becomes the basis of the continuous eighth-note motion that leads into the Animato coda. The sopranos' inverted pedal in bars 127–133 governs this coda. A "Handelian" cadential interruption in measure 133, followed by a dramatic pause, sets up the majestic closure on G major in measure 137. The entire closing Allegro/Animato restricts itself to the last clause of the text, and Brahms hammers home the words "erhalte mich" with the final chords.

Once again you must divide your men three ways, probably contributing both tenors and baritones to the middle part; similarly, your women must form three sections, with your mezzos covering the alto I assignment. At the Allegro, all return to their SATB distribution, but the men must resume the three-part split at the tenor entrance in bar 121, just before the basses divide in 122; this five-part voicing continues to the end.

Most groups probably should do the Andante in two, rather than six, although this decision could go either way. We believe less experienced singers will maintain the flow better—will achieve more continuity of "line"—in two. A mature ensemble could take this more slowly (and beautifully) in six; this option depends largely on the ability of the musicians to "sing through" the phrases at that tempo, in spite of the tessituras, the length of some phrases, and the rest. A well-chosen tempo for the Andante will stand, then, as the basis for the Allegro/Animato; specifically:

1. Try the Andante at about ♩. = 52. Use a modified two-beat pattern (one, that is, with subdivisions added where needed to give emphasis to important quarters).[6] Add a ritard in bar 109 to break this tempo, setting up the soprano entrance in 110 (an entrance Brahms in a sense owed to and has been saving for the sopranos, since he left them out of the last measures of the previous movement). Then return to the same Andante tempo, still in two for the fugue (or push it up no higher than about ♩. = 56 if you have a very good choir). The fact that the motion of the Allegro is in quarters and eighths is enough to make the fugue feel much faster than the Andante, without an increase in tempo. The Animato can be bumped up a bit, then (perhaps as high as ♩. = 64), starting at the pickups to measure 126.

2. Make full use of the espressivo character of the opening Andante. The "hairpins" in bars 82 and 83 establish this quality right away. Play with overlapping "hairpins" and the elisions wherever you find them, and make use of the poco crescendo beginning in measure 102 and the diminuendo in measures 108–109 (together with your ritard) to dramatize the Allegro attack. Show the crescendo in the baton, but *be sure* to bring the size of your beat back down; if you do not, your choir will continue singing at the higher dynamic level.

3. It is probably best to subdivide measure 109, to control the ritard precisely. Then go back to a two-beat for measure 110. (If your choir must do the Allegro slower than we have suggested, you can use this ritard to camouflage that reality.)

4. The Allegro *must* be in two. To take it in six would make it too choppy. (If you have *mastered* the modified two-beat described in Chapter 11, you could emphasize occasional quarter notes to gain musicality, while maintaining absolute control.)

5. After two-and-a-half movements of legato singing, you could change to a more marcato articulation for the fugue, thus lending added excitement to the finale.

6. In the fugue, Brahms tosses eighth notes from part to part, setting up antiphonal pairs of voices in thirds against the bass II pedal beginning in bar 123. Make certain these descending scales stay metronomic. Do not let them slow down.[7]

7. Press this energy home through the Animato, underneath the soprano pedal point.

8. If you choose to take a ritard in measure 132, maintain it through the next bars into the cadence. The duplet notes in the tenor part in bar 135 can be conducted (with a subdivision), if you must lead them through this rhythm; make them feel and sing it themselves, if you can.

---

[6]Review the modified two-beat pattern recommended for the Mozart motet in Chapter 11, Figure 11-3. The subdivision here is triple, not duple (as in the Mozart), but the concept is the same: In the Brahms Andante you will need to articulate in your beat no more than three or four of the quarters per measure.

[7]Many times, singers with some training can be told to "think of ascending scales" in spots like this. By imagining they are singing upward, they keep the support and energy needed to pursue descending lines evenly.

Here you have prepared a complete multimovement work, the first such we have presented to you. Be certain that you conceive all three movements in relation to each other when you conduct it.[8]

MORE CONDUCTING THEORY
Proportional Tempo Choices

We recommended that the first movement of the Brahms motet be paced at ♩ = 56, the second at ♩ = 84, and the opening of the finale at ♩. = 52 to 56. Are you wondering how you find those tempos onstage? You could check a metronome offstage for the opening, of course, but how can you be certain about that second tempo?

Many tempo relationships between movements in major works are *proportional*; that is, they constitute a simple mathematical ratio. We know this by looking at metronome markings indicated by composers, and we know it also because conductors have found that certain masterpieces demonstrate this quality.

Why would that be the case? It seems likely that composers sometimes want to "hear" relationships between consecutive movements in their music; if they write in that way, they make a temporal continuity out of a whole work. (There is no fault in their doing so, unless the rhythms they choose for two movements sound too much alike.)

What about the Brahms tempos? If we set the first movement at ♩ = 56, as we have planned to do, the second movement is almost exactly half again as fast: 56 divided by 2 × 3 = 84; in other words, 84/56 = 3/2. If you can find in your mind that 3/2 ratio, you can set a tempo of 84 from a previous pace of 56. Example 12-2 shows you how to do that.

Example 12-2   Finding a 2:3 tempo relationship, from ♩ = 56 to ♩ = 84

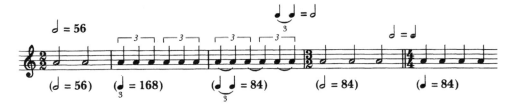

To find the starting Andante for the finale, we simply reverse the process: 84 divided by 3 = 28 × 2 = 56 (or 84/56 = 3/2). (Temper this back to ♩. = 52, if you must.) This process is shown in Example 12-3.

---

[8]As a convenience for your later use, the authors include in Appendix B a summary of style and performance practice in choral music from the Romantic era. There also you will find a list of additional Romantic choral music suitable for beginning conductors.

Example 12-3   Finding a 3:2 tempo relationship, from ♩ = 84 to ♩ = 56

What we are doing is using groupings of rhythmic values to arrive at tempos that are closely related by ratio. The easiest such shift would be from, say, ♩ = 60 to ♩ = 120 or 180, but you can build all sorts of mathematical relationships to help you find new tempos onstage. (One hopes that one knows a work so well that the tempo will come firmly to mind as one "hears" the opening notes in one's mind. The stress of performance affects one's judgment, however, and it is well to have a double-check like this as an extra protection.)

Practice Exercise 12-1   *Finding Proportional Tempo Relationships by Grouping Rhythmic Values*

Using metric relationships like those in Examples 12-2 and 12-3, it is easy to go from MM = 50 to MM = 75 (if half notes = MM 50, then triplet quarters = MM 150; if the triplet quarters are tied in pairs, they equal MM 75). Now find your way from MM = 144 to MM = 36, from MM = 72 to MM = 48, from MM = 112 to MM = 84, and from MM = 84 to MM = 126.

BACKGROUND AND PERSPECTIVES: TWENTIETH-CENTURY STYLE

Most of the *philosophical* predilections of nineteenth-century music continued into the twentieth. The search for "aesthetic freedom" (which both centuries have regarded as absolute) and the belief that "experimentation by its very nature is good" were two such continuities; far from worrying about the preferences of noble patrons, as Haydn had to do, artists of more recent times have insisted on complete privilege in these regards.

The preference for deriving formal designs from extramusical sources instead of designing abstract internal structures also has persisted. So has the Romantic tendency toward extremes of scale—huge works on the one hand, and tiny ones on the other.

And parallel continuities carried the *musical* processes of the 1800s far into the following century. Wagner's tonal freedom in *Tristan und Isolde* led to Schoenberg's ideas of atonality. Schumann's assault on "the tyranny of the bar line" evolved into Carter's metric and rhythmic convolutions. The complicated harmonies of the later Romantics ("incomplete 11th chords," and the like) became the quartal sonorities and tone clusters of Hindemith and Cowell. In short, the strategies remained the same while the tactics were modified, and the pride in innovation that most composers of the 1900–1950 era felt—the assurance that they were "breaking new trails"—proved largely misplaced; the melodic, harmonic, tonal, timbral, and structural procedures they used were in general merely extensions of the revolutionary choices made by Schumann, Berlioz, Chopin, Wagner, and their immediate successors. It had become fashionable to claim novelty for the music of the early twentieth century (surrounded as that music was by newsworthy scientific developments and technological inventions), but by the last quarter of that same century it was clear that the much-hailed novelty had been more apparent than it had been substantial. The "new ideas" were mostly old ideas given new names.

That is not to say the tactics were not radical. One can take any old process to (or past) its reasonable limits, and to do so is an extreme, a radical act. It is in this light that many of the most famous "innovations" of twentieth-century music probably should be viewed. Schoenberg's once-controversial "twelve-tone technique"—his serial procedure—was a new *compositional* procedure, but the *musical* results he and his disciples gained from it proved to be more-or-less logical extensions of the expanding tonal and harmonic palette of the previous century.

The jaggedness and chromaticism characteristic of many melodies of the period also continued a trend well developed in the Romantic era. Even the most important feature (probably the one most heralded by musicians themselves)— the focus on the parameter of timbre—unquestionably was a prolongation of the search for a richer vocabulary of sounds in the huge nineteenth-century orchestra, with its Wagner tubas, its secondary woodwinds, its *divisi* violin sections, its "thunder machines," and all. The new electronic instruments of the last half of the twentieth century only added means to carry timbral emphasis as far as those devices could go. In this milieu, the phrase "new sounds" became both an overriding purpose and a cliché.

Caught in the middle of a century that honored as a primary virtue the reality or pretense of innovation were composers whose aesthetic preferences were not radical, but who—like Bach in his time—suffered from the criticism that they were not "modern enough." Gaudy gimmicks were proving financially rewarding in all the arts, and musicians observed that some of the most extreme painters, for example, were becoming the wealthiest. Some composers went too far, trying to satisfy pressures to "be experimental"; others, some of whom appear in retrospect to be the most effective in communicating with audiences (Britten, for example, and—among the immediate members of the "Schoenberg School"—Berg), consistently made choices that, if relatively conservative, honestly reflected their own *aesthetic* (as opposed to sociopolitical) insights. Thus they produced bodies of music exceptional for their integrity and coherence.

Samuel Barber: "Sure on this shining night" and "Anthony O Daly"

One of these moderates was the American Samuel Barber, born in Pennsylvania in 1910. His style could be called eclectic (as is the case with many composers of the twentieth century); one finds that he wrote frankly tertian harmonies in one circumstance and quartal chords in another; similarly, his metric and rhythmic operations may be complex in one case and simple elsewhere. Traditionally schooled, he was skilled at contrapuntal techniques.

One aspect of that musical training can be seen especially often: Barber studied voice (as well as composition and piano) at the Curtis Institute, and his enthusiasm for lyric melody is that of a singer; it permeates many of his works—his catalog is filled with opera, oratorio, choruses, and songs—but not just the vocal and choral ones; perhaps his most famous composition, the Adagio for Orchestra, brings this same lyricism to the strings.

"Sure on this shining night," shown as Example 12-4,[9] is a conservative example of Barber's work. In the years 1939–1942, he had returned to Curtis as a faculty member; one of his responsibilities was conducting a choir there, and that encouraged him to write choral music. Like the Adagio for Orchestra, taken from a string quartet movement that Barber scored for string orchestra, this chorus is a transcription of an earlier composition, the Op. 13, No. 3, song of the same name. The text is a poem by the American writer James Agee, a passage from one of whose novels Barber later used for his work *Knoxville: Summer of 1915*.

Agee uses the title phrase twice: at the beginning, and again (see measures 21–22) two-thirds through his poem. Barber uses this repetition as reason for recapitulation; he creates an *ABA'* design to set the Agee text, with the middle unit building to the overall climax in bars 13–16. Elisions at bars 10 and 21 smooth the transitions between sections.

The B-flat major tonality is clear and is established by the one-bar introduction. The end of the *A* section pivots to D minor for the middle unit, which itself returns to B-flat in measure 17, as a relaxation of tension after the peak; then the original tonic continues through the short codetta.

Barber establishes B-flat major for the singers and the audience with a very practical first bar; what follows, then, in the SATB texture, is a deceptively simple harmonic counterpoint. From the beginning, the sopranos and tenors are in canon (at the third) to the elided cadence at measures 9 and 10. Imitative entrances echo each other through the middle section, and then the tenors and sopranos reverse their relationship at bars 21 and 22. This time, however, the altos replace the tenors in bar 24 as the voices flow on to the measure 28 cadence. The codetta in bars 30–34 is homophonic.

[9]Samuel Barber, "Sure on this shining night" (New York: G. Schirmer, Inc., 1961).

Example 12-4   Barber, "Sure on this shining night," G. Schirmer 10864, 1961

Example 12-4 *(cont.)*

Example 12-4 *(cont.)*

Once Barber establishes the eighth-note motion in measure 1, he carries it unbroken all the way through his *ABA'* design. There are *no* interruptions (just as we would expect to be the case in Bach) until the "loud" silence on the first beat of bar 32; the eighth notes resume there, and their momentum ceases only in the final measure. Barber enriches his triple meter with phrase entrances on the first and third beats in the *A* sections, contrasting them with a series of second-beat attacks during measures 13–16 of the *B* section and with some syncopated entrances in bars 17 and 19 (in the alto and tenor parts). The $\frac{3}{4}$ itself is kept fresh by brief escapes into $\frac{2}{4}$ and $\frac{4}{4}$ at the first transition (bar 9) and after the climax (bars 17–19); in view of the rhythm of the sopranos there, you might want to think of measures 8 and 9 as a single $\frac{5}{4}$ bar; measure 19 is really a type of written-out ritard.

The lines here are very lyric in character, very singable. Largely conjunct, they are relatively easy to read. Ranges and tessituras are modest. Barber is considerate in setting open vowels on high notes, too; see the sopranos' high G on "All" (bar 13) and the F on "High" (bar 17). The harmonies are tertian and function quite progressively (that is, traditionally). The counterpoint creates many lovely dissonances in passing, a number of which are left by *skip*; in this regard, as in so many other respects, Barber's writing here is quite Romantic.

Conducting Barber's "Sure on this shining night"

The composer has given you a metronome marking for his Andante and has indicated both "molto legato" and "espressivo." You will want to use a legato three-beat. Insist that the musicians be responsible for the eighth-note level. The singers should give you the same legato production you asked for in the first movement of the Brahms motet earlier in this chapter. Everything should be connected and should flow smoothly.

At the same time, the value of this beautiful text is great, and Barber means the words to be understood. Make use of the repeated initial "s" sounds in the first line—"sure, shining, star-made, shadows," for example; have your singers emphasize these slightly, but keep them short, and don't overdo it. Lengthen the "l" sounds in the middle section a bit. (Barber gives you a wonderful chance to do this on the sopranos' high F on the first beat of bar 11.) And there is more of this useful, evocative alliteration in the final passage: The composer has even marked dashes over the "w" sounds in "weep" and "wonder" (measures 22–24); here you want the singers to lengthen somewhat the "oo" at the beginning of the "w" diphthong.

Some details:

1. In the overlapping, wavelike action of the contrapuntal entrances, balance between voices is everything. If this texture loses its transparency, much of the loveliness of the work is gone. Barber has marked dynamics meticulously, bar by bar in places; follow those instructions just as carefully.
2. The vowel in "sure" is dangerous, especially sung high. Have your singers open it a bit (toward "uh") wherever necessary. Do not let it become too tight or throaty.

3. In focusing on the canonic voices, don't miss the other beautiful lines here: See the splendid, lyric, well-shaped alto contours in measures 2–11, for example.

4. To define the rhythm of the attacks in measures 13–19 (especially the second-beat and syncopated entrances), each of them needs some extra emphasis. This can be done in one of two ways: by a glottal attack on "All" or by making certain you get a rhythmic, clean, articulate release of the "th" of "north" and "health," and the "d" of "healed," on either the previous quarter or the previous eighth, in each case. (The authors prefer the latter—the more legato—choice.)

5. At the peak, after bar 16, comes that gorgeous *subito piano* in measure 17. Be careful not to give away the surprise. Don't "telegraph your punch," as boxers say. Have the lower three voices drop suddenly, and then let the sopranos float their line over the rest of the choir.

6. Note especially the contradictory "hairpins" in bar 20; the women fade and the men crescendo (probably without a breath in the tenors) into the bar 21 phrases.

7. Make certain the choir members hold their concentration through the important transition in bars 30–32.

8. The tessituras are low in measures 32–34, and the dynamic level is *pp*. Inexperienced singers will not give enough breath support in such a spot. Remind them.

9. A clean "t" release at the end is essential.

Conducting Barber's "Anthony O Daly"

"Anthony O Daly" (Example 12-5[10]) is a more acerbic example of Barber's choral writing, composed during the time that he was conducting the choir at the Curtis Institute. As in "Sure on this shining night," rather sophisticated counterpoint is a foundation of the form, and again a fine English poem is the text. "Anthony O Daly" is part of Barber's *Reincarnations,* three movements of a whole, setting poems by James Stephens: The first of these, "Mary Hynes," is a delightful whirlwind of young love; the second, "Anthony O Daly," is a bitter dirge; the third, "The Coolin," is a now-languid, now-passionate seduction. Each of the three is substantially more demanding for the musicians than was "Sure on this shining night," and, moreover, the set is *a cappella*.

Perhaps the first feature one spots in this SATB fabric is the metric conflict. The opening soprano line, the primary "subject" for the fugal entrances that follow, is set, plainly enough, in $\frac{3}{4}$; the abbreviated version of this subject that the tenors begin at bar 6 on different words is note-for-note the same (an octave lower). Other voices contradict this simple triple meter, however.

1. The basses have been singing from measure 1 a five-beat ostinato that forcefully establishes a $\frac{5}{4}$ meter in the ears of the listeners. The downbeats of the sopranos' $\frac{3}{4}$ and the basses' $\frac{5}{4}$ conflict already in bar 2, and that conflict becomes more obvious; the two downbeats coincide only every fifth measure, as in bar 6.

2. When the altos enter in measure 7, singing the subject, they commence on the first pulse of the bar, in a one-beat stretto against the tenors, so that we hear from them *an implied downbeat* on the second pulse of measure 7. (That makes three "downbeats" in bar 7: the sopranos and tenors on the first beat, the altos on the second, and the basses on the third!)

[10]Samuel Barber, "Anthony O Daly," from *Reincarnations* (New York: G. Schirmer, Inc., 1942).

3. The version of the subject that the altos sing (to new words) from bars 13–18 begins on the downbeat with what originally were the "pickup notes."

4. At bars 18 and 19, the sopranos, altos, and tenors engage in a three-voice stretto at one-beat intervals. Again the implied downbeats fill each measure (effectively neutralizing any metric sense, so that *one hears pulse but not meter*). This metric ambivalence continues to the beginning of the final section at measure 74.

Note that the rhythms remain simple through all this temporal complexity. The excitement comes from metric conflict and not from rhythmic intricacy.

The ostinato, the fugal stretti, and all the overlapping meters have a powerful effect on the overall design. *Any fugal process tends to promote continuity within a structure, for expositions and stretti make everything sound elided.* The result here is that we probably hear one big section from bar 1 to bar 73, followed by a final section (perhaps even perceived as a coda) from 74 to the end. Within the fugal unit itself, certainly one hears—prompted by important entrances (as in any traditional fugue)—subsections starting at measures 13, 18 and 19, and 40 and 41, at least; at a lower level of the architecture, the parallel attacks at bars 6 and 7 and 47 and 48 are distinguishable. A real "development section" on the "For O Daly is dead" motif makes an elaborate ascension (beginning at bars 22 and 23) to a first climax at bars 33–36; the intensity subsides only a bit, then, before a second development passage (commencing at bar 58 on those words) passes through a three-beat modification of the ostinato (measures 63–67) to the ultimate peak at measures 68–74.

The ostinato firmly establishes E-natural as the tonic, and sustains it throughout (with the help of the subject, which itself is a step-progression from E down an octave to E). The fugal entrances, spaced at octaves, fifths, and fourths (see the tritone interval between altos and tenors at bar 19), taken together with many parallel fourths (see especially the men in bars 60–63), help to define the harmony from bar 1 to bar 68 as essentially made up of the same intervals. There is an important augmented triad, too, used at bars 13, 33, and 54 with that variant of the subject.

These harmonies turn fully tertian suddenly at bar 68, where a C♯ minor$_6$ chord shifts to a climactic C major triad. After that, the "coda" assembles entrances based on a tritone E–A♯ within an implied diminished-seventh chord (E–C♯–A♯–G), and resolves this into a final sonority of open fifths and octaves still based on the tonic E-natural. Again in this final section, everything overlaps, everything is elided.

The Stephens text is "after the Irish of Raftery," and a Gaelic lament is the obvious basis for it. Powerful intensity drives through both the text and the music; the first climax (bars 31–36), with its wordless soprano passage (bars 33–36), is a stylized wail. We can see that Barber is concerned with syllable stress: The most important words and syllables get the longest rhythmic values in the subject, and thereafter; even at the ultimate peak (the three emphatic chords in measures 68–73), the rhythm he sets for the ostinato—"An-tho-ny" as half note, quarter note, half note—is retained in augmented durations. Barber is using words like weapons, both for their inherent verbal meanings and for their sheer sounds.

Example 12-5   Barber: "Anthony O Daly," from *Reincarnations*

Example 12-5 *(cont.)*

Example 12-5 *(cont.)*

Example 12-5 *(cont.)*

The composer has marked ♩ = 76 as the tempo. This movement could be taken slightly slower than that, however, if your choir is capable of sustaining the all-important intensity at a more deliberate pace. Get the feel of the work with your singers, and a moderate tempo choice accommodating both your wishes and their capabilities will begin to emerge.

This is not difficult melodically. The opening subject is conjunct, cast in an easy tessitura, and essentially a natural minor scale (with a chromatic F-natural immediately mutating the earlier F-sharp). You can view this as a descending Aeolian mode (with a passing F-natural) or as Phrygian (with a passing F-sharp), as you think best. This F-sharp against F-natural cross-relation serves Barber very well in his harmonic activity through the rest of the movement.

Harmonically, however, this is more difficult; tuning the sonorities, with all the perfect intervals and the tritones, is demanding in this *a cappella* texture, and you will find that pitch inaccuracies begin to snowball after a while. If your singers miss a given note, or even mistune it a bit, other notes in other parts will begin to "come unglued." **In choral work (and, to a lesser extent, in instrumental music), one pitch error tends to prompt another one.** In the dangerous passages, try isolating each sonority—singing them in sequence but out of rhythm—by sustaining each one, so that your singers can hear the exact tunings; then reassemble the results in proper rhythm.

Here are some suggestions for working through the movement in detail:

1. Since the text is such an effective, moving one, it is doubly important that diction be clear and efficient. Barber has marked the subject "espressivo" at the beginning and in the entrances at bars 6 and 7, suggesting a lyric production; try to walk a fine line, then, between connecting these notes smoothly and defining the consonants cleanly: Something like an instrumentalist's nonlegato (rather than either marcato or legato) should work here.

2. Note the dashes over the syllable "An-" in each repetition of the ostinato. This is Barber's signal that the dash is the "downbeat" in this voice; have the basses (and later the other voices) stress this syllable, but tastefully. See also the alto part from bar 7 through bar 22; the dashes here have the same purpose and should be handled similarly. (Notice that Barber has *not* placed dashes in the tenor and soprano lines in measures 1–18, because the downbeat placement in these parts makes the dashes unnecessary, but that he adds dashes to the tenor voice in 19–22, once it is "offbeat.")

3. The accents, which begin to appear in bar 23, are simply a more emphatic version of these dashes.

4. Be very precise about balance in this movement. Do not let the ostinato be lost against the higher voices, but do not let it overpower them, either. In spots like bars 18 and 19, be sure the three upper parts are in balance. Work especially to let your audience hear the "tossing" of dashes and accents from voice to voice.

5. Keep the incidental perfect intervals in tune: We mean that you need to help your singers hear the relationship between notes like the F-sharp and the C-sharp in measure 10, and the F-natural and the C-natural in measures 10 and 11. If these pairs stay on pitch, the other notes around them should be in tune, too.

6. Pace the dynamic growth patiently from the opening *mf* through the *più f* at measures 18 and 19 and the *crescendo poco a poco* in measures 24–32, so that the *f* at measure 33 is not too loud.

7. Make sure it is not only the tenor and soprano parts at bars 32–36 that are heard.

8. Since Barber has marked *f* already at measures 40 and 41, and permits a *ff* only at measure 68, his "with increasing intensity" notation at 48 is ambiguous. How does one do this? One answer might be to let the articulation become more emphatic—that is, more and more marcato—from bar 48 to the climax at bar 68. (If you do so, the "stylized wail" in the tenors at measures 54–57, slurred as marked, will cut through the octave ostinato even more effectively.)

9. One of the most difficult techniques in conducting is the gradual acceleration or deceleration. The secret to the *stringendo* and *molto stringendo* in measures 58–67 is to make the beat smaller (and progressively faster) to pull the tempo up, while increasing the intensity of the stroke to encourage the crescendo. (You also can move your *left* hand slowly toward the choir, asking them for more and more strength.) Keep your singers on the tip of your baton. Do not let them lead you, and do not let them drag. Keep the beat clear, and don't let the sound grow too big too soon. (For the conductor, this is an important skill, if a demanding one; the same sort of process is of critical consequence, for example, at the "final trumpet" passage in the sixth movement of Brahms's *Ein deutsches Requiem*.)

10. The trading of accents between voices is particularly important again at measures 63–67.

11. On the word "Anthony" at measures 68–73, you can employ a modified one-beat, just "touching" the second and third pulses in each bar. (If the tempo is bright enough, you can use a standard one-beat.)

12. Ask for a very bright, "forward," focused "ee" vowel in measure 71, preceded by a good, nasal "n." The cue for the attack at bar 74 is the same gesture as the cutoff for the three lower voices, but it must be properly prepared for the accented entrance of the sopranos.

13. Insist that each of the attacks in measures 74–83 maintain the same accent structure, energy, and dynamic level.

14. The technique for the *allargando molto* in measures 83–85 is the mirror image of that employed for the earlier *stringendo*. The baton stroke should gradually *increase* in size in a very well controlled scenario. (The last seven measures of the movement are a chance for you to demonstrate real technical mastery, as you signal in sequence the *f*, the accents, the dim., the *mf*, more accents, the *sfp*, and the fade to *pp*, all during the overall *molto allargando*.)

15. Get a good, sharp "b" on each "but" in measures 84 and 85, and an emphatic "gr" at the start of "grief" at the *sfp*. (You may want to increase the drama by taking a cutoff before this last word—that is, at the end of measure 85.) As your singers fade down (with the final hairpin) to *pp*, try having them lengthen the final "f" of "grief" just a bit, for the painful hiss this consonant produces.

In short, try to get every bit of the power, music, and meaning out of this imaginative and dramatic work. You will find that a good choral ensemble will be excited by it, once they begin to sense its potential.

Here we conclude, for the moment, our survey of choral styles from Gregorian chant to the twentieth century, turning now to instrumental music.[11] In Chapter 21, you will find a major, multimovement choral work to study.

---

[11]As a convenience for your later use, the authors include in Appendix B a summary of style and performance practice in choral music of the twentieth century. There also you will find a list of additional twentieth-century choral works suitable for beginning conductors.

CHAPTER *13*

Instrumental Fundamentals

There are *two* cardinal instrumental species to be considered. These days in America we somewhat arbitrarily classify players by consigning them to one of two basic ensemble types: the "orchestra," which does include a central body of strings, and the "band," which does not. It may surprise you to learn that this distinction is rather recent and that the difference between the two types is sometimes more semantic than real.[1] The English have tended to use the noun *band* as the more generic category, and they often have referred to their greatest orchestras by the names of their conductors ("Richter's band," for example).[2]

Sometimes we speak of an organization made up entirely of winds as a "military band"; it is probably true, in fact, that most laypeople think of a "band" as a musical organization that *can* march (whether it does or not) and of an "orchestra" as one that cannot! Whether this confused differentiation has real musical significance or not, it has been embedded in our society by bureaucratic and economic circumstances (for conductors are hired to direct one ensemble or the other, and, unfortunately, fine players are classified in this way). The semantic distinction exists in America but not in Europe; in Germany, "der Dirigent" is someone equipped to conduct any combination of voices, instruments, or both. This last is the view of the authors also (as you have read already). Be careful not to let any previous musical experiences cause you unwisely to limit yourself and your career. Try to minimize in your mind the differences between the two species, focusing instead on the effective interpretation and performance of all the repertoire you program, no matter what personnel happen to be required for a given work.

---

[1]As with, for example, the middle-ground term *symphonic wind ensemble*, which is applied both to (1) the body of woodwinds and brass (perhaps with percussion) of an existing symphony orchestra, extracted from that full ensemble for the *ad hoc* purpose of playing a particular work (the Strauss Serenade for winds, as an instance), and to (2) a standard but more-or-less elite band that considers itself to be concerned primarily with fine wind-and-percussion repertoire for any size organization.

[2]Lully's historic "Twenty-Four Violins of the King" was known also in the seventeenth century as "Le Grande Bande."

THE ORCHESTRA

The Orchestral Score

The string body generally is the primal force in orchestra literature. The strings, by convention, are notated at or near the bottom of the score in the order (top to bottom) violins I, violins II, violas, violoncellos, and contrabasses. (If the work in question is for strings only, there will be nothing else on the page. Still, the work will be said to be "for orchestra.")

At the very top of the score are placed the woodwinds, arranged (like the strings) in order of tessitura, usually in pairs, with the flutes above the oboes, clarinets, and bassoons. If any of the so-called secondary woodwinds are employed, they are notated adjacent to their closest relatives. Just above or below the flute(s), for example, appears the piccolo, if it is in use; just under the oboe(s) comes the English horn; immediately below the clarinet(s) appear the alto and bass clarinets, and under the bassoon(s) the contrabassoon.

Next down the page are the brass. The French horns come first (four are standard, arranged on two staves), located above the trumpets not because they play a higher tessitura (for they do not, of course) but because they often have been voiced with the woodwinds (as they are in the traditional woodwind quintet). One to three trumpets and one to three trombones follow in the basic orchestra, supported by the tuba.

The "battery" (that is, the percussion section) is next. The most frequently used of these, the timpani, are listed first. Below them, either on separate staves or combined in pairs (perhaps because one player is expected to cover two instruments), come the triangle, snare drum, marimba, castanets—whatever the composer has employed—with the bass drum and the gong generally placed at the bottom. The harp(s) may follow.

If there are soloists, as would be the case for a piano concerto, for example, or an oratorio, they appear next. If the work includes a chorus, it follows in SATB order. Then come the strings. Keyboard instruments are usually placed at the bottom of the page, below the strings, save in the case of a continuo instrument; a harpsichord, for example, would occupy the space just below the violas and above the "continuo bass" (whether 'cello/contrabass or gamba).

Orchestral Seating

One principle on which this set of notational conventions is based is this: Those instruments that most often sound together should be closest to each other (though in a particular work this may not prove to be the case). It follows logically, then, that instruments that most frequently play together should be seated near each other (as in the case of the first flute and the first oboe, for example). This serves the needs both of the players, who are concerned that their phrasing and intonation match perfectly, and of the conductor, who can see and cue them more conveniently.

Acoustical balance is the prime consideration in seating. Placement of instruments ultimately must be based on the effect that seating has on the audience's aural perspective. Here again there are historical conventions that guide the conductor (but should not restrict her or him from flexible seating choices).

The first violins traditionally belong at the front of the orchestra, immediately on the conductor's left. As is the case with all the strings, they are arranged two to a stand, which allows the lower-ranked (the upstage) player to turn pages quickly while the downstage violinist continues to play. The remainder of the string body is arranged in a semicircle around the conductor—moving clockwise from the first violins, typically with the second violins next and the violas, the violoncellos, and (placed in a row just behind the 'cellos) the contrabasses following in order. In each of these sections, the principal player (the leader of the first stand, or "desk") is seated on the downstage side.[3]

This standard arrangement (shown in Figure 13-1) is not without disadvantages. Whereas the two violin sections are turned with the F-holes (the sound openings on top of their instruments) toward the audience, the 'cellos are facing sideways, an acoustical hindrance. Some conductors, therefore, prefer to seat the strings as in Figure 13-2, which allows the 'cellos to play face-on toward the listeners. This arrangement produces an attractive effect whenever the two violin sections, seated on each side of the conductor, play antiphonal passages, but it turns the F-holes of the seconds upstage, weakening that section's sound. A third alternative (Figure 13-3) lays on the violas the same disadvantage; this design returns the seconds to their place just upstage from the firsts, and trades the violas for the 'cellos.

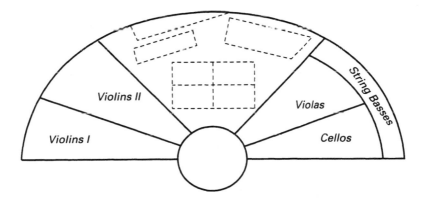

Figure 13-1   A traditional design for seating the strings

---

[3]The principal of the first violins is styled, of course, "concertmaster." The other player on the same stand may be known as the "assistant concertmaster."

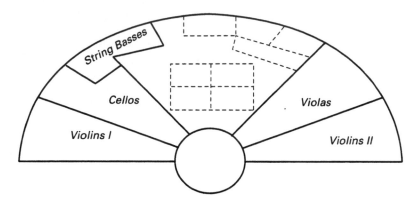

Figure 13-2   One possible alternative for seating the strings

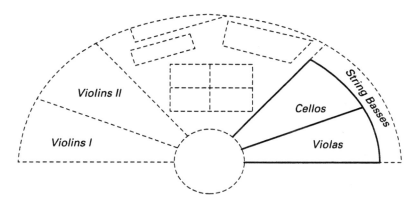

Figure 13-3   Another possible alternative for seating the strings

If you are the "permanent conductor" of your orchestra, the choice between these seating arrangements is yours. You can vary it from time to time for the sake of a given work, of course, but since the players get used to hearing each other in a certain way, it is probably best for you to stick to one consistent plan most of the time.

In general, the winds and the percussion are placed to the rear of the strings, seated one to a stand, with the woodwinds in front and the brass behind. The percussion battery on one side can be a counterpoise for the contrabasses on the other, as in Figure 13-4.

Soloists traditionally stand between the conductor and the string principals (an enlarged space there having been created). For a violin concerto, for example, the artist usually is placed just downstage of an imaginary line from the conductor to the concertmaster. For vocal soloists, chairs may be added either downstage of this string semicircle or inside it.

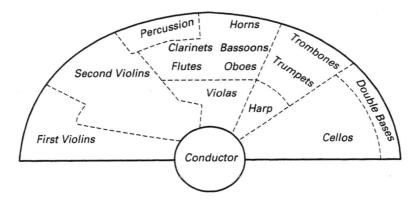

Figure 13-4 A traditional design for seating the full orchestra

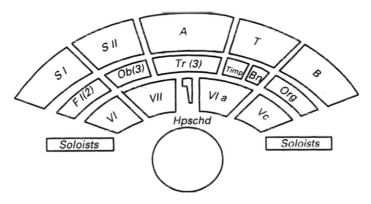

Figure 13-5 Seating arrangement for complex Bach cantata forces, including soloists, chorus, strings, winds, timpani, harpsichord, and organ

Whenever a large keyboard instrument is used, more adjustments must be made. For a piano concerto, the norm is to site the piano—keyboard toward stage right, of course—at center stage directly downstage of the conductor. (The conductor, standing on a podium, will be visible above even the raised piano lid.) If a piano (or an organ) is needed as part of the ensemble itself, it generally is best to insert it into the back row of the orchestra, somewhere between the brass and the percussion or between the brass and the contrabasses. For a Baroque work, however, where the harpsichordist needs to be near the continuo bass player (and the soloists, if any), the keyboard instrument needs to be as far downstage-center as is feasible. Figure 13-5 illustrates a possible arrangement for the performance of a Bach cantata, one involving soloists, chorus, strings, winds, timpani, harpsichord (for the recitatives and arias), and organ (for the choral movements).

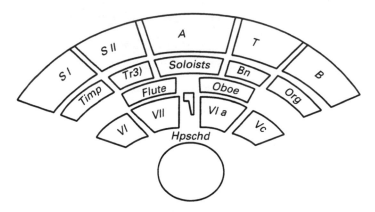

Figure 13-6 An alternative arrangement that places vocal soloists behind the orchestra

Vocal soloists in front of the orchestra are standing behind the conductor and are difficult to cue; they also may overbalance the other components. Figure 13-6 offers an alternative in which they are placed in front of the chorus but behind the orchestra.

THE BAND

The Band (Wind Ensemble) Score

The score layout of works for winds and percussion may vary more than the standard orchestral page. The overriding principle of keeping like instruments close together remains the same, however. Many band and wind ensemble scores are arranged essentially in the same order as is the orchestral score, with the exceptions that the strings are missing[4] and certain instruments not used (or employed more rarely) in orchestras are present. (Standard orchestral and wind ensemble score pages may be compared in Examples 13-1 and 13-2.) Thus, the piccolo and the flutes appear at the very top of the page, with the other woodwinds laid out below them in tessitural order. The B-flat clarinets (in the band, a large choir of three sections, in function replacing the orchestra's strings) are given three staves, one for each section; below the bassoons may be placed the saxophones, occupying perhaps several staves.

The French horns and the other brass come next, with space usually reserved between the trombones and the tuba for the latter's relatives, the euphoniums (or "baritone horns"). The percussion are found just below the brass (or sometimes between the woodwinds and the brass). Keyboard instruments and other special cases generally follow at the very bottom of the page. (In some school music scores, a piano reduction may be provided, as well.)

---

[4]Note, however, that one or more string basses *are* often used in "wind ensembles."

Example 13-1 One page from the score of Gustav Mahler's Symphony No. 5, in C-sharp Minor

Example 13-2 One page from the score of Symphony in B-flat for Band by Paul Hindemith

As is the case with most orchestral scores, a good copyist seeks to make the instrumental groupings more immediately recognizable on the page by carrying bar lines across whole sections; the woodwind staves may be interconnected, that is, by continuous bar lines, and the brass similarly conjoined. The eye tends to "find itself" more quickly that way, as it scans large scores.

Seating the Band or Wind Ensemble

Again, the related principles of physical nearness and acoustical balance are the basis for seating the band. Since the clarinet choir (which may include the high E-flat clarinet and the alto and bass cousins, as well as the three sections of B-flat instruments) serves many of the functions of the orchestra's violin sections, the clarinets generally are seated two to a stand just to the left of the conductor, in three or more rows, with the "solo clarinet" (the counterpart of the orchestra's concertmaster) in front and downstage. Oboes and flutes fill out the rest of the first and second rows. Behind the flutes, to the conductor's right, may be placed the saxophones, with the first alto sax downstage. To their right, between the saxes and the clarinets in the center of the band, may sit the French horns (or the alto horns, if any, or both).

Behind all these, in one or more long rows, may be seated (from stage right to left) the cornets (with the solo cornet downstage, of course), the trumpets, the tuba, the euphoniums, and the trombones. The timpani and the rest of the percussion battery can occupy the upstage corners, behind the brass (as may such taller instruments as harp and contrabass). In general, wind ensembles use a wider variety of percussion instruments than do orchestras; the amount of space required for the battery, then, can be significantly greater. With other special instruments, the considerations of physical arrangement for a band are usually the same as those for the orchestra. Figure 13-7 illustrates one standard seating arrangement for a concert band.

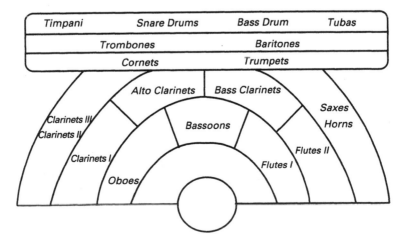

Figure 13-7 A standard seating arrangement for a large band or wind ensemble

UNDERSTANDING THE INSTRUMENTS

You need to know as much as you can learn about the strengths, weaknesses, tone qualities, articulatory attributes, and other idiosyncratic traits of the instruments in your ensemble(s). Make this study a continuing interest in your professional life from now on. There are at least three ways to achieve the familiarity you need.

1. Read everything you can in the technical sources.[5]
2. Although it would be best if each of us could play well each of the instruments we conduct, that is too much to ask of anyone. (We can try, however: Collegiate "instrumental techniques courses" offer future school music teachers opportunities to do some rudimentary playing of each of the primary instruments in each family.) More practical is to observe expert performers. Try to find among your acquaintances a superior player of each orchestral instrument, and ask if you can watch that individual practice. Ask questions: "What is hard about this spot?" or "Is that passage easier to play legato or nonlegato?" or "Can you take that whole phrase without a breath?" Learn what is difficult and what is not from direct contact with those who understand best the problems involved.
3. Study intensively the music written for each of the instruments by the great masters, especially those composers who are regarded as the most skillful at orchestration. See what they asked the players of a particular instrument to do. Think, then, what they did *not* ask—what they assigned to some other medium instead.

This sort of comprehension becomes an important aspect of your research into comparative musical styles. What is asked of specific voices or instruments in a given era is both a cause and a symptom of the artistic purposes and values of that time.

THE INSTRUMENTAL FAMILIES

The Strings

It is natural to begin with the strings. As the media that make up the central element of the traditional symphonic organization, the string (that is, "stringed") instruments have been given a central role in almost all the post-Renaissance music of the West. In the Viennese Classical style, for example, virtually all new melodic ideas are introduced first in the strings (usually in the first violins). In a sense, the string body continues to serve as the basic timbral element of the orchestra through at least the nineteenth century, with the woodwinds, brass, and percussion reserved for coloristic "seasoning" and for increasing the power of tutti pas-

---

[5]Only brief references to each of the instrumental families is possible in this space. An enormous amount of detailed information about the instruments, their characteristics, and their limitations is available to you in the standard literature, and can be of immense value. Begin by consulting Don V Moses, Robert W. Demaree, Jr., and Allen F. Ohmes, *Face to Face with an Orchestra* (Princeton, N.J.: Prestige Publications, 1987), pp. 5–17, a good orchestration text, or both. Consult the Bibliography.

sages. It is for this reason (more than the factor of sheer numbers) that the concertmaster is, by custom, the chief member of the orchestra.

By "string family" we mean, in this context, not such instruments as the guitar, the lute, the piano, the harpsichord, or others in which the sound is produced primarily by plucking or striking the strings; we are referring, instead, to the "bowed" instruments, and, more particularly, to the violin, the viola, the violoncello (or 'cello), and the contrabass (also known as the double bass, bass viol, or string bass). Each of these primary orchestral instruments has a hollow body, inside which a *sound post* (carefully and individually placed) improves the tone and resonance heard through the pair of openings called *F-holes.* The four strings pass from the bottom of the body over the *bridge,* and then are attached by adjustable tuning pegs to the top of the *fingerboard.* The fingers of the left hand *stop* the strings, pressing them down against the fingerboard at the point that produces the desired pitch. (There are no frets [ridges] on these fingerboards, as there are on a guitar or a ukulele.) By thus reducing the length of the string with a finger, the player causes that shortened length of gut or wire to emit a higher pitch than would the *open string.*

Sound is produced in one of two basic ways: (1) Normally, the player pulls a bow (of special wood curved to stretch long horsehairs) across one or more strings at a time, maintaining a steady and calculated pressure in an alternation of *upbows* and *downbows* (so named from the direction in which the bow is traveling); (2) in specially marked circumstances, the player plucks the string with the right index finger in the technique known as *pizzicato.* In either case, it is standard for the player to move the finger stopping the string rapidly from side to side in the technique known as *vibrato,* which (like the vibrato used in singing) is intended to give additional warmth and beauty to the tone; without vibrato, the sound can be strident and colorless.

It is for this reason that players generally prefer to produce a pitch on a stopped string rather than to use an *open* (unstopped) one. The violin's low G-natural can be generated only on its open G string, of course; when this note is called for, as in the bars immediately after the slow introduction to the first movement of Beethoven's Symphony No. 1, in C major, it must be played "open" (and we must assume that in this case Beethoven wanted that rather brazen quality); if he had written his symphony a fifth higher, the same note would have been a D-natural, and players probably would choose to produce it from a stopped G string, rather than from an open D string.[6] In general, good players will use vibrato except where a fingering problem or another special situation leads them to choose an open string.

As you may gather from this, all but the lowest notes on any of these instruments may be produced on two or more strings; in a given case, which fingering

---

[6]This important detail tells us something about the interpretation of this Beethovian passage: If Beethoven was willing to have the entire first violin section emit with raw power these open G-naturals, then he must have wanted an emphatic, unpolished, somewhat coarse energy for this violin phrase. This insight gives us, in turn, the beginning of a concept of sound and shape for the entire movement. In analysis of a work, the tiniest feature can signal the composer's intention.

should the player choose? In most cases, she or he will use the highest string possible (that is, the highest string for which the notes written are not too low). If the passage is stepwise, it may be easiest to take all the pitches on one string (moving the left hand up and down the fingerboard, as necessary, in the procedure called "shifting positions"). If, on the other hand, there are skips present, the player may try to avoid shifting the left hand by "crossing" (with the bow) over to another string for one of the notes of the skip.[7]

The quality of sound produced by these instruments depends on several factors, including the acoustical nature of the hall, the physical attributes of each individual instrument, the merits of the bow used, the way the bow *attacks* the string (the type of "bowing" employed), the *speed* at which it is pulled across the string, and the size and speed of the vibrato. Since the bowings chosen have such effect on the sound of a given phrase, it is standard practice for all members of a section to use the same bowing at the same time; these choices are marked in the parts, as necessary. In this way, the tone quality and the articulation of that section, thus unified in pitch, rhythm, and bowing, are made consistent.

The fundamental alternation of downbow ⊓ and upbow ⋁ strokes is rather like breathing out and breathing in: A certain amount of the one demands, in most cases, an equivalent amount of the other. String players need to keep the two in balance; for example, a long down-stroke, followed by a short up-stroke, followed by another long down-stroke causes one to "run out of bow."

Ideally, the conductor marks her or his own bowings. (This may be done without, but preferably with, the help of the concertmaster and the other string principals.) This editing process relates phrasing (keeping "the downbow on the strong or accented beat") and the connection or separation of notes (in legato or staccato passages, for example) to the players' practical need to balance out the up- and down-strokes. Thus bowings are not simple successions; two or three consecutive short up-strokes may follow a single downbow, or vice versa, and a number of notes may be grouped within one bow-stroke.

Fine string players learn to execute a whole repertoire of bow-strokes. These can be classified into two fundamental types: on the string and off the string; the former is a stroke that begins with the bow already in contact with the string; the latter has the bow strike the string as part of the continuing motion of its stroke. Playing off the string demands greater technical assurance from an orchestral section, for these strokes are more likely to result in ragged attacks; as a consequence, then, most ensemble playing is done on the string. Soloists make much more use of the off-string strokes.

Good tone quality is easiest to achieve for most string players when they are producing "full bows" (long, continuous up- and down-strokes, with quick, almost-inaudible changes of bow direction); this is essentially a legato bowing. It can sound wonderful, but you should avoid overuse of it, for the result can be to

[7]That is, with violin strings tuned a fifth apart, a skip up of a sixth can be negotiated either by reaching up six steps on one string or by crossing to the next higher string and reaching up only one step.

romanticize your interpretation. *The basis for standard orchestral playing, especially in the seventeenth, eighteenth, and twentieth centuries, is the détaché stroke.*[8]

Just as singers in a choir can "stagger their breathing" in such a way that there is no interruption in the sound of a choral part, so a string section—faced with a particularly long note (at the end of a work, for instance)—deliberately can suspend their practice of bowing together, using *staggered bowing*. This allows them to sustain a pitch for as long as the conductor wishes.

Mutes (small clips that slide over the bridge) can be used to reduce the extent of string vibrations. (The standard markings are *con sordino* to add mutes and *senza sordino* to remove them.) Remember, however, that *mutes are intended to change timbre, not to solve balance problems* by stifling the string sections!

Divisi is an arbitrary assignment of certain players in a section to alternate notes of a sonority or to alternate lines in counterpoint. To carry out this effect, a conductor may assign all the downstage players on string desks to take the upper note while all the upstage people play the lower one(s), or certain stands may be designated to cover certain pitches. In unusual cases, a composer (an Impressionist, perhaps) may delegate to a single section the production of several simultaneous notes.[9]

The Woodwinds and the Brasses

There is an excitement to the sound of the woodwinds: The flute (especially in its fife form) has long been used for military music, and the double reeds have a skirling brilliance that arouses the ear. There is great beauty, too, in the warmth of the clarinet's *chalumeau* register and the mellowness of the saxophone timbre. To hear an endless Bach melody spun out (apparently without breathing) by an artful oboe player is a wonderful experience.

On each of these instruments, tone is produced by causing a column of otherwise-static air to vibrate in certain precise ways; pitch is controlled by lengthening or shortening that column, pressing keys in certain combinations (*fingerings*) that open or close openings along its length. The air is set in motion (and replenished) by blowing into the "pipe" within which the column is enclosed. That vibratory process is begun and ended by the tongue, which moves away to permit the airstream to flow (thus initiating a note), and stops it again (to end that note); this process is called *tonguing*, of course.

The power and the glory of the brass winds extend back to the age of Giovanni Gabrieli in the Duomo San Marco, and beyond. "Horns" (the word itself shows us its animal origin) and trumpets were used in the orchestras of the Baroque era; the trombones and the tuba joined that ensemble during the nineteenth century.

---

[8]For a thorough discussion of these matters by one of the greatest violin teachers, see Ivan Galamian, *The Principles of Violin Playing and Teaching*, 2nd ed. (Englewood Cliffs, N.J.: Prentice-Hall, 1985).

[9]You should familiarize yourself with many more special string effects (natural and artificial harmonics, multiple stops, *sul tasto* and *sul ponticello* playing, and even *col legno, scordatura*, "Bartók pizz," and so on).

Here, again, sound is produced by causing a column of air within either a cylindrical or a conical pipe to vibrate. Brass players do this by blowing through a metal mouthpiece, "buzzing" their lips inside it in such a way as to activate the air column. The open pipe resonates at each of the pitches of its overtone series; new pitch possibilities are created by adding—in half-step increments—short lengths of tubing; this is done by pushing down a piston called a *valve*. (The longer the pipe, the lower the pitch.) These valves can be used in combination, too, so that finally the whole chromatic spectrum becomes available to the player—each note within some overtone series.

Thus, a valveless tuba might produce an ultralow B-flat, the B-flat an octave higher, the F and the B-flat in the next octave up, the D, the F, an out-of-tune A-flat, and the B-flat in the next octave, and so on; pushing down the second valve (only) would lower this whole system a half step, so that A, A, E and A, C-sharp, E, an out-of-tune G, and A would be made available, and so forth.[10] Although the modern trombone has no such valves, the principle remains the same; in moving the slide out to first, second, third, and further positions, the trombonist is adding more tubing in exactly the same sense that valves do so.

Articulation is as complicated a matter, and deftness as critical, in the winds as in the strings. Tonguing must be as subtle and skillful as must bowing, and must be as rapid at times as an artful vocal melisma. Lightness, evenness, and precision are the ideals. There are traditional articulation patterns for the winds that deserve your consideration: Fatigue is always a potential problem with long stretches of fast tonguing; thus, as one example of these patterns, the "slur two, tongue two" technique makes it easier to play swift scalar passages evenly than if the same phrase were to be taken with everything tongued.

Double- and triple-tonguing techniques allow wind musicians to increase their agility. Single-tonguing is something of a "tuh-tuh-tuh" movement of the tongue's tip. Rapid passages can be played more efficiently if the middle top of the tongue can be employed as an alternate articulator, as well; hence, double-tonguing is a "tuh-kuh, tuh-kuh, tuh-kuh" operation, and triple-tonguing a "tuh-tee-kuh, tuh-tee-kuh, tuh-tee-kuh" use of three articulatory sites. Fast triplets can be played with great facility by professionals, including the tubists.

Flutter-tonguing is a somewhat theatrical effect that has become expected of wind players (especially flutists and trumpeters) over the past century or so. The physical technique is that of tonguing with a rolled-R motion.

Mutes are employed to change the timbre of brass instruments, from the horns and the trumpets to the tuba. The most common variety is the straight mute, which is used with all the brass, but other types—the cup mute, the wa-wa, and so on—are available and are especially prevalent in jazz work.

---

[10]Some notes in each series are badly out of tune. This can be compensated for in two primary ways: (1) Many notes appear in more than one series, and the player is responsible for knowing which alternative is most trustworthy in each case; and (2) the *embouchure* (the shaping of the lips) can be used to make slight pitch adjustments.

Glissandos are possible in the winds (recall the evocative clarinet "gliss" in the opening bar of Gershwin's *Rhapsody in Blue*, for example). They are easiest for the trombone, of course, which can manage certain passages as smoothly with its slide as can the strings. For the other brasses, a "half-valving technique," in which one or more valves are partially lowered and then (while playing) slowly released, permits some glissandos.

Among the other effects possible are *directional maneuvers of the bells of the winds*. Composers and conductors sometimes direct wind players to turn their bells up, hide them behind their music racks, or even stand up, thus aiming them directly at the audience, for the acoustical impact these postures have. Having an entire trumpet or trombone section stand has been a routine mode in "big bands" since the 1920s.

The Percussion Battery

The military-sounding term *battery* is used to encompass the vast spectrum of percussion instruments. Everything may be used in this family at one time or another: tuned steel drums, auto wheels, sheets of steel or tin (for "thunder"), wind machines, exploding "guns" and real artillery (for firing during the *1812 Overture* and similar works), bells of all kinds, and on and on. Only the most commonly used members of this huge group can be considered here.

Some percussion instruments produce precise pitch. Perhaps the most important of these are the *timpani* (the singular form of the name is *tympanum*), large, tunable membranophones often known from their shape as "kettledrums." (You may judge wrongly that a good sense of intonation in your string or wind players is more critical than in your percussionists. The reality is that retuning a tympanum while the ensemble is playing is very demanding. Judge timpanists not just by their mallet technique but by their aural skills, as well.)

The quality of the instrument is not the only physical variable with timpani or other percussion media: Just as important are the point at which the drumhead is struck and the type of mallet used. There is an optimum contact point on any percussion instrument for the specific dynamic, timbre, and articulation you seek, and the percussionist should know where that point is. The striking implements are, by convention, usually called *mallets* with pitched instruments, and *beaters* with unpitched media; *sticks* is the generic term. They run from small to large, and soft to hard, and are made from a variety of materials. The sticks are part of the artistic responsibility of the player. He or she should make sensitive choices in this regard, too. The ultimate decision, nevertheless, belongs to the conductor. Take an interest in this matter, as you would in a choice of bowing, for the kind of articulation you will get depends on it.

Parts for individual, unpitched percussion instruments can be written on single lines; often, however, the snare or tenor drum is written on an upper space—and the bass drum on the lower space—of a standard five-line staff.

Miscellaneous Instruments

The most important of the other media used in major ensembles are the keyboard instruments and the harp. The *portative and regal types of early organ* are appropriate for many works from the Renaissance; *harpsichords* and *Baroque organs* are standard equipment for seventeenth- and eighteenth-century works; larger concert-hall organs are needed for some nineteenth-century compositions, and the piano is incorporated (rather as a percussion instrument) into a number of works composed in the twentieth century; the electronic keyboard media (synthesizers) also are gaining an increasing role in contemporary ensemble music.

The acoustic *guitar* and the *lute* are among other instruments that sometimes join the instrumental ensembles for specific works. Both are soft-voiced, and—like the harpsichord—in modern-day concert halls, they usually present the conductor with a balance problem.

AUDITIONS AND SEATING[11]

As in Chapter 9, the all-important audition process operates in at least four stages: Information is obtained, including personal data, experience in music, and practical details, such as potential conflicts (a sample instrumental audition form is shown here as Figure 13-8); a warm-up opportunity is provided; sight-reading skills are examined; and technique and musicianship are determined by the playing of a prepared piece, exercises, or both.[12] It is important in auditions to take candidates to—or just past, without humiliating them—the limits of their technical abilities.

If you are hearing students, see how efficiently they assemble the instrument itself; note also the condition in which they keep it. See how much they know about their instrument, too. Then include a tuning problem in each audition.

You must fit the music you choose to the instruments you are hearing, of course. In the ideal audition, you will form judgments about range, agility (in regard to both rapidity and control during skips), intonation, rhythmic accuracy, stamina at higher tessituras, tone quality (in each register), musical taste, experience, and sight-reading ability. Carefully select music that will allow you—within the limited time you can give to the hearing of each individual—quickly to calculate how that person stands against all these criteria.

Make certain that you get a good sense of how to rank individuals auditioning on the same instrument. This hierarchy of seating within the section is a major difference between the instrumental ensemble and the choir, of course. Here, in a sense (especially in the minds of the players), every seat counts! In

[11]There is no need to duplicate in this chapter all the tactical and procedural suggestions presented elsewhere in this volume. Chapter 9 includes many passages dealing with handling choral ensembles that apply in parallel ways to bands and orchestras. Chapters 17–20 will cover in great detail matters of planning, organization and management, programming, rehearsal procedures, and performance considerations.

[12]See the earlier discussion of audition procedures in Chapter 9.

```
BROADWOOD CITY BAND
Membership and Audition Application

Applicant: Please provide the following information.  Print clearly.

_____       _____
Last Name    First Name    MI          Principal Instrument

_____
Complete Address                                 (Zip)

_____       _____
Instrument (s) You Double              Daytime Telephone No.

_____
Title and Composer of Prepared Solo
========================================================
               BELOW THIS LINE FOR STAFF USE ONLY

Audition Date_____ (Basis:  4 excellent to 0 poor, per item)

        Prepared Solo    (DNA), if need be)   Sight Reading

        _____           Tuning Accuracy         _____

        _____           Pitch Maintenance       _____

        _____           Rhythmic Accuracy       _____

        _____           Range/Stamina           _____

        _____           Agility/Technic         _____

        _____           Tone Quality            _____

        _____           Musicianship (times 3)  _____

        _____           TOTALS                  _____


Disposition: Seats _____ // Hold for Opening ____ // Rehear _____

Date notified of decision _____ First Rehearsal _____
```

Figure 13-8 An information form for use in instrumental ensemble auditions

the professional situation, these rankings may be established by an "audition committee" of principals, players, and others. In such a case, the conductor is likely to have at least the power of the veto, to ensure that her or his criteria are met, too.

Some ensembles, especially leading orchestras, use systems of "chair rotation," particularly in the string sections. The front desk or two, including the principals, may remain unchanged week after week, whereas the players further back trade seats on some sort of schedule.

Most student organizations permit members to "challenge"—that is, to ask during the season for special auditions in which a player attempts to defeat in competition someone seated "above" her or him. The conductor (or a committee headed by the conductor) usually takes responsibility for judging them.

FORMING YOUR ENSEMBLE

You will have in mind before the auditions an image of the ensemble you are building, of course, and a list of the open seats. As you listen, you likely will begin to recognize individuals who can fill gaps in your band or orchestra. Other seats will remain vacant in your mind until you have heard everyone; then compromises probably must be accepted and adjustments made.

In the abstract, one should hear in one's mind the instrumentation and numbers the composer would have chosen, had he been wealthy; in the world of the practical, ensemble size is never that artificial. If every performance were *ad hoc*, and new players were obtained for every work, then a Bach ensemble really could have a perfect roster of personnel, and so could a Wagner orchestra. In reality, most ensembles are *established*; they continue from concert to concert with a reasonably stable roster of musicians, and some ways must be found for that fixed organization to adapt itself to the specific instrumentations appropriate to varied repertoire. How that is done (and the extent to which it can be done with ruthless precision) depends on the situation; with paid professionals there are likely to be budgets and union rules. With student organizations some humane adjustments usually prove suitable.

If no compromises are necessary, if no limitations of budget or personnel availability impinge, what would constitute a reasonable (not to say extreme) roster for a concert band?

Here is a model ensemble:

1   E-flat clarinet
5   1st clarinets (including the solo clarinet)
5   2nd clarinets
5   3rd clarinets
2   alto clarinets
2   bass clarinets

6   flutes (1 doubling piccolo)

3   oboes (1 doubling English horn)

2   alto saxophones (1 doubling bass saxophone)
1   tenor saxophone
1   baritone saxophone
3   bassoons (1 doubling contrabassoon)

2   1st horns
2   2nd horns
2   3rd horns
2   4th horns

3	1st cornets (including the solo cornet)
3	2nd cornets
3	3rd cornets
2	1st trumpets
2	2nd trumpets

3	1st trombones
3	2nd trombones
3	3rd trombones (at least 1 bass trombone)

3	euphoniums
5	tubas
1	(string) contrabass

1	timpanist
2	mallet players (xylophone, glockenspiel, etc.)
3	other percussionists
81	**TOTAL PLAYERS**

Among these musicians should be some who could double the less frequently used winds—the alto flute, the contrabass clarinet, and the like. Additional winds and percussion still will be necessary for some works (particularly, for example, whenever large antiphonal forces are needed).

For the symphony orchestra, a roster like the following is ideal:

16	1st violins
14	2nd violins
12	violas
12	violoncelli
8	contrabasses

3	flutes (1 doubling piccolo)
3	oboes (1 doubling English horn)
3	clarinets (1 doubling bass clarinet)
3	bassoons (1 doubling contrabassoon)

5	horns (including an assistant 1st)
3	trumpets
3	trombones (the third a bass trombone)
1	tuba

1	timpanist
1	mallet player (marimba, bells, etc.)
2	other percussionists

2	harps
1	pianist
1	harpsichordist
1	organist
95	**TOTAL PLAYERS**

Again, additional winds would be necessary for some nineteenth- and twentieth-century works.

Most school and community-based bands and orchestras probably are half to two-thirds the size of these recommended prototypes. That is not necessarily a shortcoming; in artistic endeavors, quality is always more important than quantity. If a conductor makes carefully considered judgments about repertoire, such smaller organizations can produce very successful musical results.

Sight reading is of special significance in these ensembles in which many members have *sole* responsibility for some lines. Some players will take their skills for granted. The finest professionals are not so cavalier, for sight-reading ability is of prime importance to a first-rank'career. (Great recording-studio musicians receive wages at rates so high that rehearsal time becomes almost prohibitive; they prepare carefully, and they sight-read extremely well. The best of them may actually read more than one staff below the notes they are playing at any given moment, which gives them time to study and comprehend any peculiar or unfamiliar notation. As a result, they are able to play "perfectly" the first time through a passage, and rehearsal becomes largely a matter of communicating the planned interpretation. This is the ideal for all of us.)

Intonation is even more an issue with instrumentalists than with singers, for here the potential difficulties do not arise just from the aural misjudgments of the musicians; they reflect acoustical characteristics and limitations of the instruments themselves. Be certain that you know enough about them to know what the risks are (which notes on a trumpet are likely to be flat, for example). Be prepared to respond to problems in rehearsals, and take plenty of time to deal with this matter.

One good opportunity to do so, if you are working with a student or community ensemble, is in the warm-up period. Do not minimize this; it is not just an inconvenient postponement of real rehearsal. It is a moment in which you can get your musicians listening again—to themselves and to others.

One of the principal sources of faulty intonation and poor tone quality in the winds is the combination of embouchure and reed or mouthpiece. Learn to know what a bad reed or a badly chosen mouthpiece sounds like. (In a school situation, you may have to learn to cut oboe and bassoon reeds to get good ones.)

Stamina is an important consideration, especially with the brasses. Young string players may become tired quickly, but mature ones can play for long stretches of time, and woodwind players generally do not fatigue easily. Even experienced brass players wear down under the pressure of a long passage at a high tessitura. (It is for this reason that "assistant firsts" are used in many horn and trumpet sections.) Be calculating in this regard, especially as you choose programs and plan rehearsals. Be sensitive to it during sessions, too, and give your players time to recover, if need be.

OTHER ASPECTS OF THE INSTRUMENTAL PROGRAM

Smaller ensembles are important components of any balanced instrumental organization, from the high school band to the major symphony orchestra. You gain from these the chance to try out a wider spectrum of the works of the composers you are performing and to deal with your musicians in other contexts. Smaller media offer the players opportunities to encounter more fine repertoire, and to do so in another framework, using "different ears" to judge matters of balance, timbre, and phrasing. These groups bring to the audience fresh literature, too, and the interest of hearing different forces in action.

Many smaller combinations of instruments are reflected in the literature. Among the most consequential is the *string orchestra*, made up essentially of the string body of the symphonic organization; a great deal of older and recent literature exists for this ensemble. The *chamber orchestra*, a symphonic body of reduced size—anything from fifteen players or so to fifty—can play the standard symphonic works of the seventeenth and eighteenth centuries and music written specifically for this ensemble (Wagner's *Siegfried Idyll*, for example, or Schoenberg's *Kammersymphonie*, Op. 9). The chamber orchestra can be your premier performance group, either because you have only limited numbers available or because you want to create a special force for your very best musicians.

The *wind ensemble* can fill this same role within a band program, if you make it a select group. Here again a body ranging in size from a dozen or so up to about forty can perform with real finesse both standard band repertoire and works written for special combinations of instruments by some of the greatest masters. A fine, forty-piece wind ensemble can be a pleasure to conduct, particularly in performances of the best English and American band literature.

The *brass choir* heads another class of smaller media. Whether specially created or drawn from the brass section of a band or an orchestra, this ensemble sounds magnificent and plays music of great power and beauty—a catalog of literature spanning the centuries from the glorious days of the Gabrielis in Venice to compositions and special transcriptions of the present day. (Many works written for brass also require percussion—or timpani, at least—so your "brass choir" may include an auxiliary battery.) Brass tonal production resembles singing in most important ways; considerations of breath, range, tessitura, and such factors parallel vocal practices, and the feeling of "line" is therefore virtually the same; it follows, then, that conducting techniques with brass are in some respects much like those with choirs.

An analogous organization is the *woodwind choir*. Generally, this is made up of the entire woodwind component of a band, from the piccolo and the E-flat clarinet to the contrabassoon. French horns and percussion may be added for some works, if you wish. Until recent years, composers have not written as frequently for this body as for the brass choir, but the available repertoire is increasing.

There is a substantial catalog of literature for the *percussion ensemble*. Works composed for percussion ensemble call forth a vast array of drums, mallet instruments, traps, experimental media, and other percussion devices. Rhythm is the focus here, but the mallet instruments offer melodic and harmonic resources, and some very imaginative percussion ensemble music exists.

A well-balanced instrumental program will encourage the formation of string quartets, brass quintets, woodwind quintets, and other chamber music units, too. In professional ensembles, the players will tend automatically to group themselves for the playing of chamber literature. In school situations, it is much to your advantage to supervise this area.[13]

JAZZ AND POPULAR MUSIC ENSEMBLES AND APPLICATIONS

The *jazz ensemble* may be made up of players drawn from a larger instrumental organization, or it may stand alone. The name itself is generic, for whether the repertoire one is playing is "jazz," as such, depends on the biases, taste, and sophistication of the musicians and the listeners. (Most "popular music" is not "jazz," and much "jazz" draws so select an audience it can hardly be called "popular.") For our immediate purposes, we will regard any organization of thirty or fewer that plays what is or once was called jazz or popular music, and that includes in its performances improvisation as a significant, integral ingredient, as a "jazz ensemble." From its earliest days, jazz has incorporated improvisation as a primal element, and that can give us a means of identifying this medium.

Two tradition-laden ensembles can be easily identified. The *Dixieland band* has its roots in music of the New Orleans waterfront brothels in the early years of the twentieth century; this group typically included a cornet (or trumpet), a clarinet, a trombone, and a tuba (or one of its relatives), but beyond those instruments one cannot be specific, for the usages of that time were fluid and depended on available personnel. Sometimes a banjo or a piano was included, and sometimes other instruments; on occasion (an important funeral, for example), the "band" could become quite large. Performance consisted of "theme-and-variation" interpretations of certain standard tunes from the "blues" and other period styles. Written parts were almost unknown, for many of the players could not have used them anyway.[14]

If this music is to be recognizable, today's performances must be "stylized"; that is, they must reflect the standard instrumentation, procedures, and musical

---

[13]The *marching band* is not discussed here. Parade and stadium show procedures and applications are a field of study too specialized for the purposes of this text. The reader should refer to the existing literature addressed specifically to this topic.

[14]Legend has it that one of the greatest of the New Orleans players, asked why he did not enhance his powers by learning to read music, asked, "What would I do when the lights go out?"

attitudes of their time (just as good presentations of Renaissance music must be true to the ideals of that era). *In jazz, as in every genre, study of the historical style and performance practices is the basis for honest and accurate interpretation. Perhaps the most exciting aspect of jazz performance now is the emphasis finally being given to treating this music as "classical"—as worthy of this disciplined approach.*

The second of these traditional jazz ensembles is known variously as the *big band*, the *dance band*, or—the term we will use here—the *stage band*. This ensemble was firmly defined by the 1920s as the American social replacement for the older, European-style dance orchestra; in the '30s and '40s, it experienced a golden age in the era of bands headed by Glenn Miller, Woody Herman, Benny Goodman, and others; the Stan Kenton groups of the 1950s were a sophisticated extension of the style. Instrumentation for a later edition of these bands was likely to include five saxophones (perhaps two altos, two tenors, and a baritone), whose players might "double" clarinet, flute, and other instruments; five trumpets, five trombones (including one or more basses); a "rhythm section" of piano, string bass, drums, and, sometimes, guitar; and one or more vocalists, sometimes with a "back-up vocal group" of three to five. Each "leader" sought a unique "sound" or timbre. (The Glenn Miller orchestra, for example, had its first alto sax player use a B-flat clarinet to introduce melodies.)

Smaller jazz ensembles (amounting to chamber units) have ranged over a whole panorama of genres. Typical prototypes include Louis Armstrong's neo-Dixieland "combos" (the "Hot Five" of the 1920s, for example) and the Dave Brubeck Trio of the 1950s and later (which aimed at a "cool jazz").

Rapidly changing styles in jazz and popular music have been influenced heavily by the impact of electronic technology, more than by experimental additions of traditional instruments like the violin or the horn.

An important figure in the jazz field is the "arranger"—so called by convention, though the role played really is that of composer—whose task is to create wholly new works or to use an existing jazz or popular *cantus firmus* in a new version called an "arrangement." This individual must have a clear image of the style of the ensemble for which the music is being written, and—in the case of stylized works—of the essential features of the idiom at hand.

If the personnel you are using are not professionals, they must be taught to improvise. Personal inhibitions are as much an obstacle here as are limitations of technic, and good aural skills must be developed or enhanced. You cannot teach this discipline unless you can do it yourself (and you should be able to, if you are to lead a jazz ensemble).

"ANCIENT" INSTRUMENTS

As the twentieth century neared its end, an important movement brought many serious musicians back to the forms of instruments on which the music at hand originally had been performed. Wooden flutes, Baroque violin bows, sackbuts, and other Renaissance instruments reappeared in the concert halls of Europe and America. This development was partly the result of, and partly an encouragement for, the formation of *early-music ensembles* of various kinds. Such groups now are common in university settings, and some professional organizations (the New York Pro Musica and London's Academy of Ancient Music, to name just two) have been markedly successful. You may need to consider including an ensemble of this type in your instrumental program. Certainly you will want to find opportunities to perform some of this important literature. Although this field is too complex, and the forces used too varied, to be comprehensively addressed here, the next chapter will bring us face-to-face with instrumental possibilities and performance practices of this kind.

CHAPTER 14

Style and Performance: Late Renaissance and Early Baroque Instrumental Works

Now we revert to our stylistic analysis–interpretation–preparation matrix. We return first to the Renaissance, pondering again the nature and performance features we saw in Chapter 10.[1]

BACKGROUND AND PERSPECTIVES: THE GLORIES OF SAN MARCO

If a musician could climb into a time machine for a journey back to the last years of the sixteenth century, he or she surely would choose to travel to Venice. There were artful composers elsewhere, as well, but here, beside the famed lagoon, the combining of voices and instruments in precise, new ways was the basis for a fresh, exciting music as rich as the golden mosaics covering the vaulted interior of St. Mark's Cathedral.

Adrian Willaert, who had studied with Jean Mouton, an adherent of the contrapuntal style of Josquin des Prez, had come down to Italy from his native Flanders to Ferrara and Milan in the 1520s. He became *maestro di cappella* at San Marco in the Advent season of 1527 and remained there until his death in 1562, composing, leading the musicians in rehearsals and services, and teaching; among his brightest pupils were Cipriano de Rore, the theorist Gioseffo Zarlino, and Andrea Gabrieli.

---

[1]It is unnecessary for the authors to duplicate here the historical and theoretical background presented in Chapter 10, for the reader can glance back at any time to those discussions and can consult the general summary of Renaissance style and performance practice in Appendix B.

San Marco, with its celebrated balconies at the ends of its transepts, was fitted with *two* organs; antiphonal polyphony—already in limited use elsewhere—would reinforce the spectacular visual beauties of the great basilica. Willaert accordingly began writing polychoral works (two four-voice choirs singing alternately, and then together in eight parts), and that practice evolved in the music of those who followed him.

His two most important heirs proved to be the Gabrielis—Andrea and Giovanni (uncle and nephew)—who became "first and second organists" at San Marco during the closing third of the century. Andrea continued the tradition of antiphony, writing for two and three choirs at times and playing duo-organ recitals with Claudio Merulo (Giovanni's predecessor); he taught well, too: His nephew and Hans Leo Hassler were among his pupils. After Andrea's death in 1586, Giovanni continued at San Marco through the early years of the seventeenth century, playing, composing, and teaching. Maintaining in works like his magnificent motet *In ecclesiis* (for solo voices, double chorus, strings, brass, and organ) his inheritance of antiphonal music, he added to it a new concern for specific instrumental timbres. His uncle had written five-part motets "suitable to be performed, sometimes, by the living voice, sometimes by all kinds of instruments";[2] for Giovanni that was no longer enough, for his wish was to specify exactly who would play and sing what, and how they would do so. *Here begins, in a real sense, the discipline of orchestration.* A distinguished teacher in his own right (Heinrich Schütz was his student), Giovanni sent forth from Venice to Europe and the world both the polychoral tradition and this newborn concept of orchestration.

Giovanni Gabrieli: *Sonata pian e forte*

A prototype of Giovanni Gabrieli's innovative and sophisticated style is the famous *Sonata pian* (or pian') *e forte*, one of his *Sacrae symphoniae*, said to date from 1597. Here, Gabrieli writes a sonata for two choirs of instruments. (In this context, "sonata" means only that it is to be "sounded"—as opposed to "cantare," sung.) He identifies exactly which instruments are to play, and where: A "cornetto" (not the modern instrument but, rather, a more delicate ancient wind) and three trombones (Renaissance sackbuts) make up his "Coro I," and "Coro II" comprises a "violino" (more like our viola, for the instrument that became our violin was then called "violino piccolo") and three more of his small-bored trombones.

[2]Gustave Reese, *Music in the Renaissance* (New York: W. W. Norton & Co., Inc., 1954, rev. 1959), p. 496. When Reese argues, however, that with the compositions of Giovanni Gabrieli "we have definitely crossed the border into the domain of Baroque music," he goes further than the authors can support on the basis of Gabrieli's style.

Gabrieli goes on to stipulate that certain passages are to be played "pian" and others "forte," the *first such notation of contrasting dynamic levels*. (What is really happening here is that the composer is taking control in manuscript of a parameter that until this time had been left unmarked.) The two quartets are employed antiphonally and tutti in a series of passages that at times include echo effects.

Let us look at the work in detail in Example 14-1.[3] In this version, the instruments used are modern ones; Choir I has two B-flat trumpet parts (shown in German as "Tromba in B") and two horns in F; Choir II is voiced for trombones, with the bass model doubled by tuba.[4]

In *Sonata pian e forte*, a string of melodically unrelated phrases, generally elided (frequently by antiphonal entrances), form a flowing continuity. In this regard, the design resembles the point-of-imitation structure of the Renaissance—in which one finds a succession of new musical motifs—except that here there is only incidental fugal imitation. The focus seems, instead, to be on sonority, as well as antiphony.

Practice Exercise 14-1   *Reading Instrumental Transpositions and Tenor Clef in Open Score*

As you see, Example 14-1 is written in open score. Play through Choirs I and II separately at the piano. For Choir I, make the appropriate transpositions for B-flat trumpet and horn in F. For Choir II, gain familiarity with the tenor clef.

Next, try to read both choirs. Take it as slowly as you must, but keep the beat steady. Keep working at it until you can do this successfully.

The opening statements by each of the two choirs are relatively lengthy ones: Choir I plays three phrases, totaling fourteen bars, and then Choir II (entering with an elision) adds twelve more; the first tutti phrase (also elided) lasts six measures. From this point on, the succession of antiphonal entrances is more rapid. Three-bar, one-bar, and even half-bar alternations occur. The longest tutti is the final one, occupying the last ten measures. Only a couple of cadences are not elided.

---

[3]Giovanni Gabrieli, *Sonata pian e forte*, from *Sacrae symphoniae*, ed. Fritz Stein (New York: C. F. Peters Corporation, 1960). (At our publication date, permission to reprint is restricted to these forty-four measures. Please see your library for the complete score.)

[4]Gabrieli's original manuscript is transcribed into modern notation in Archibald T. Davison and Willi Apel, *Historical Anthology of Music* (Cambridge: Harvard University Press, 1962), I, 198–200. The edition reproduced as Example 14-1 is edited by Fritz Stein (C. F. Peters 10964) for modern brass; other instrumentation possibilities are discussed later in this chapter.

Example 14-1   Giovanni Gabrieli: *Sonata pian e forte*, mm. 1– 44

Example 14-1 *(cont.)*

Example 14-1 *(cont.)*

Example 14-1 (cont.)

Example 14-1 *(cont.)*

Complete major and minor triads are the characteristic harmonic units. Where open sonorities (fifths and octaves) occur in one quartet—as in the cadence at bar 14 of Choir I—the "missing third" shows up in the other unit (in this case, in Choir II's second trombone). Standard Renaissance dissonances abound: Suspensions, passing seconds, and neighbor-tones are present everywhere, but they function and are resolved in conformity to sixteenth-century practice. The next-to-last bar sets up a plagal cadence typical of the Renaissance era. The sonata opens on G and closes on G; overall, this tonal center predominates, but mutations (including alternations of B-flat and B-natural) and passing cells keep obscuring that centrality.

Melodic motion here is largely stepwise—as much so as if this were vocal writing—and there are many repeated notes, a result primarily of the increased focus on vertical sonorities. Where skips occur, they tend to move between what in a later period would be called "chord tones." The mutations follow standard concepts (B-flat is preferred for descending lines, and B-natural for rising ones, and so on).

Although our modern edition uses bar lines, Gabrieli did not, and we can be confident that he did not think in such terms. In rehearsal, you may need to use language like "watch the F-sharp on the 'first beat' of measure 8," but you should caution your players not to give "downbeat" notes any metric stress. Their approach should be more linear, and their concern should be for phrase shape rather than metric rigidity. Ask them to stress the important notes in the lines (and show them which pitches you mean, if necessary). A fairly wide variety of rhythmic ideas appears here, from the straightforward half-and-quarter motion of the opening bars to the crisp figures of measures 60–62 and the involved stack of imitative entrances in the closing tutti. Rhythmic clarity is critically important here: Hand in hand with articulation, it must keep the recurrent half–quarter patterns from a plodding sameness.

The "Pian" and "Forte" markings—written out as full-length words, the antecedents of our *p* and *f*—are Gabrieli's own, as we have said. Remember that their combined effect really is that of *four* dynamic levels: (1) one choir alone at *f*, (2) one choir alone at *f*, (3) both choirs, briefly, at *p*, and (4) the tuttis at *f*. Keep the "two dynamics" clear in your players' minds, but listen for all four yourself.

There is substantial contemporary evidence that ornamentation was improvised as part of the performance routine at San Marco; Merulo, in fact, is described as having been expert at this in keyboard work.[5] Some embellishment could add excitement to this sonorous music, providing it highlights the focus on sonority, emphasizes important structural spots, and does not obscure rhythmic figuration with too much floridity. You may choose, for example, to add trills just before cadential chords. That would fit the style and would tend to freshen predictable resolutions. Look through the sonata for points where ornamentation would be effective, and edit it accordingly.

---

[5]Reese, *Music in the Renaissance*, pp. 544–545. See also Willi Apel, *Harvard Dictionary of Music*, 2nd ed. (Cambridge: Harvard University Press, 1969), p. 629. You may review, as well, our discussion of ornamentation in Chapter 11.

Conducting Choices in Gabrieli's Sonata

There are many possibilities for orchestration of the *Sonata pian e forte*. Taking Gabrieli's own dispositions as guidelines, decide on the instrumentation.

1. The first and most legitimate alternative (but one that may be impractical, given the players and instruments available to you) is to use precisely the "cornetto, violino, and tromboni" Gabrieli stipulated in his own manuscript—eight musicians.

2. Diametrically opposite this use of ancient instruments is the option of the modern brass choir. Example 14-1 is scored in eight parts; the number of players per part is up to the conductor, however, and the choice is not so simple as it may appear: It is an old rule of thumb among orchestrators that two horns equal one trumpet or trombone. It follows, then, that you may want twice as many horns as trumpets in Choir I. Here are three possibilities:

   a. At a minimum, use two trumpets and four horns in Choir I, with three tenor trombones and a tuba covering Choir II—ten musicians.

   b. Given a full brass choir, use four trumpets and eight horns in Choir I, with six tenor trombones covering the upper three parts of Choir II and a bass trombone and a tuba playing the bottom part—twenty musicians.

   c. With two brass choirs, assign eight trumpets and sixteen horns to Choir I, and have twelve tenor trombones, two bass trombones, euphonium, and tuba cover Choir II—forty musicians.

3. It is also possible to employ a mixed body of strings, woodwinds, and brass here.

   a. Other Renaissance instruments could be used: For example, a family of krummhorns covering one choir could be contrasted against a family of recorders (each part doubled, for balance). In this case, as with other instrumentations, some adjustment of octaves might be necessary.

   b. In the preface to this edition, editor Stein suggests that Choir I might comprise two English horns (doubling the first part), two alto trombones, and a tenor trombone, with Choir II made up of four or five violas on the top voice, two tenor trombones, and a bass trombone below—twelve or thirteen musicians.

   c. With a small orchestra at one's disposal, one could assign the Choir I parts to the first violins, second violins, violas, and 'cellos, in turn, and could voice Choir II with two horns on top, two bassoons, tenor trombone, and bass trombone or tuba (the trombone or tuba doubled by the contrabasses)—perhaps twenty-five players.

   d. One could contrast woodwinds with brass, too; pairs of oboes, clarinets, English horns, and bassoons could cover Choir I, with Choir II made up of two horns on the top voice, two tenor trombones, and tuba—thirteen musicians.

   e. One could use an entirely heterogeneous blend of available instruments, watching to be certain the tessituras are feasible and the numbers are in balance.

With any of these choices, in fact, the numbers are up to you. The only real issue is to weigh balance, timbre, and historicity against practicality.[6]

---

[6]An elegant approach for your audience would be to give *Sonata pian e forte* two consecutive performances in a concert, the first with Renaissance instruments (perhaps with the two choirs on opposite sides of the stage but clearly visible) and the second with modern brass (one choir in the balcony).

Geographic placement of the two choirs is an important consideration here, whatever instrumentation you choose. Separating the forces helps clarify the opposing textures, of course, and it can either help or hurt balance. We know that Gabrieli himself had the sounds of one choir coming from a gallery many yards from the other unit in the opposite balcony. Look for ways to emulate him, recognizing that the surprising power of antiphonal music—although perhaps not as shocking as it must have been the first time the Venetians heard it centuries ago—is still great.

The edition used for Example 14-1 suggests a tempo of $\downarrow$ = 66–72. A pace as slow as $\downarrow$ = 60 is possible, but be careful not to let the motion drag.

It is likely that sixteenth-century players would have played these lines with some separation. (The natural effect is greater separation between the notes of a skip, and less within stepwise successions; this is probably the style you should strive to reproduce.) Even if you employ modern instruments, the connections should not be as smoothly legato as Wagner brass passages can be.[7] It follows, then, that you will want to use your nonlegato four-beat pattern.

Sonata pian e forte offers the beginning conductor wonderful opportunities to gain assurance in cueing entrances. Here one has two separate units, each entering now *p*, now *f*, and doing so on various beats of the "measure."

Choir I plays first, commencing softly. Your preparation beat must show the tempo, the *p* dynamic level, and the articulation you want. Three phrases—four bars, plus five, plus five more, each connected smoothly with the next—make up this initial passage, which ends with an elided entrance of Choir II. Guide your players toward the climax of each phrase, and then taper back their sound enough to achieve a refined dovetailing into the next phrase. Consider bars 11–13 the peak of this unit.

At measure 14, the tapering process happens in macrocosm: Here the upper choir must fade down a bit, both for the sake of the shape of their own phrase and for a polished transition to the lower choir (also marked *p*). The conductor turns her or his body slightly toward the incoming unit, cueing their entrance, while using the left hand to control the diminuendo in Choir I.

The next segment (bars 14–26) proceeds in the same way. At measure 26, then, comes the *f* (elided by the third trombone) joining the two choirs together for the first time. *Watch the pace of the eighths here;* some players have a tendency to underplay short notes, or to start them late. Watch the balance, too; with eight parts going, listen to the weaker instruments. Keep the bass line clear in your mind, especially, and then relate the other voices to it. Should the articulation change here in any way? (You might ask for more separation, for instance, in *f* passages.)

Let us look now at particular spots.

1. At measure 31, decide whether to taper back Choir I (in keeping with the Choir II marking) or to have them make a subito shift down to "Pian."

---

[7]Editor Stein's use of dashes-under-slurs (measure 2, Tromba II and Corno I, for example) appears to be his way of warning that this style of nonlegato seperation is needed.

2. Here your cueing becomes more complex: There are three-bar alternations of the choirs first, then one-bar exchanges (measures 38–41), and finally two-beat trades (50–52). Make your gestures quick and clear but not hurried, each "prep" beat reflecting *one beat early* the articulation and dynamic level.

3. The breath marks in Example 14-1 are editorial, of course, and you may have your players follow them or not, as you prefer. The editor has placed them after cadences, and not at the start of eighth-note motifs. (Any change in the breath marks implies a change of phrasing, of course.)

4. Bar 55 can be a really strong cadence. You might choose *not* to taper it back, asking Choir I to enter *subito p* in measure 56. Note the breath marks in the upper choir's parts at the end of bar 55 (there are none shown here for the lower choir), and be certain both groups know what to do. Do you want them to release together, or do you prefer that Choir II carry over to Choir I's attack?

5. At measure 60, give the musicians clear beats and make them do the work! **Never overconduct syncopations or other rhythmically complex spots.** If your pattern is sharp, it is their responsibility to maintain good ensemble; should you try to beat shorter values, you are likely to slow them down. Note the hierarchy of articulatory separations in bar 60, by the way: Every note here has a silence of a different length after it.

6. At bar 64, watch the balance against the first trombone. At 68, be sure the upper choir tapers and releases cleanly so that the tutti attack at the "Forte" is not ragged. Taper back in bars 71–72 to give the eighth notes a chance to be heard.

7. The passage from measure 72 to the end is wonderful and offers you more good cueing practice. Study the interlocking of parts here, working out the phrasing clearly so that this does not become a blur of sound. Whether or not you decide to honor the editor's view that a somewhat broader tempo and a slow crescendo are warranted, *keep direction and momentum in all the parts.* Point out who has the important part at any given moment.

8. Gabrieli wrote no fermata at the end. The beginning of a ritard might occur in measure 80, but the real slowing takes place in only the third trombone in bar 81; if you observe a fermata, then, it is essential that you keep the baton moving to the final half note. Don't just stop the stick. Use both the left hand and the baton to keep the sound up and vibrant.

"Manage the silence" at the cutoff. If you are in a concert hall (or a church) with a great deal of reverberation, you want to keep the players and the audience quiet so that they can hear the echoes fade slowly away. In a cathedral, this can take six, seven, or even eight seconds![8]

BACKGROUND AND PERSPECTIVES: MONTEVERDI AND THE NUOVE MUSICHE

In the year 1607, Claudio Monteverdi, *maestro di cappella* to the Duke of Mantua (and already the composer of five books of madrigals), presented for the ducal court his initial opera, *Orfeo*. The first of the new musical dramas to be crafted by a genuine genius, *Orfeo* was immediately successful and became the foundation of the towering tradition that is Italian opera.

---

[8]A list of additional Renaissance instrumental works for student conductors can be found in Appendix B.

Monteverdi had been a boy chorister at the cathedral in Mantua and would move to San Marco in 1613, a year after Gabrieli's death, to have charge of the service music there for the remainder of his life. In February 1607, at the premiere of *Orfeo*, he was just short of his fortieth birthday.

The newborn Baroque style—the *nuove musiche* was barely postpartum at the time. Many of what would be its mature features (characteristics we have cataloged already[9]) were not yet fully formed. Monody had been introduced by the Florentines, however, and the musical tactics intended to achieve the much-sought expression of the emotions (the *Affektenlehre*) were the subjects of experimentation.

Monteverdi took part in this "radical experimentation." He was more than just a revolutionary, however; he was a man of musical judgment. In composing *Orfeo*, he demonstrated a comprehension that this heavy-handed Florentine monody—with its austere, endless, almost shapeless recitative—was too limiting to be a basis for a lasting artistic tradition. With clear-headed, sensible craftsmanship, he balanced the plot elements of the monodic recitative with reflective arias, duets, and ensembles; he also added dance and committed to the production a substantial body of instruments (the forerunner of all the "pit orchestras" in the centuries since).

Some of his compositional choices were genuinely radical. In his fourth book of madrigals, published four years before the *Orfeo* premiere (and not yet a decade after the death of Palestrina), he was writing unprepared dissonances, long stretches of repeated notes, tritones "resolved" by skip, jagged melodic lines, and other departures from the rigorous procedures of Palestrina and his contemporaries. He may have begun the use both of the string tremolo and of pizzicato. His management of vertical sonorities suggests a "chordal" point of view in many circumstances, and the manner in which certain of his harmonies relate to each other heralds functional harmony. One can regret that today, Monteverdi may be the least-performed of all the first-rank composers.

Claudio Monteverdi: Overture to *Orfeo*

For his opera *Orfeo*, Monteverdi composed an instrumental "toccata" as an introduction to the prologue of the opera. (See Example 14-2.[10])

The overture comprises an opening Allegro, followed by a "Ritornello," which is also marked Allegro. (The original notation showed four half notes per measure; Example 14-2 treats each of these macromeasures as "compound bars"—using dotted bar lines to convert the original nine bars of the opening Allegro to eighteen, and the four bars of the Ritornello to eight.) Brief as are these

---

[9]See the historical and theoretical discussion of Baroque style presented in Chapter 11, and consult as needed the general summary of Renaissance style and performance practice in Appendix B.

[10]G. F. Malipiero, Overture to *Orfeo*, in *Tutti le Opera di Claudio Monteverdi*, vol. 11 (Vienna: Universal Edition, 1926).

opening instrumental passages, they still foreshadow the multisectional opera overtures that evolved in Italy and France over the next century. (We will see such an overture in mature form in the initial movement of *Messiah* in the next chapter.) The first section is an elaboration of a C major triad—no harmonic changes occur—with passing and neighbor-tones decorating the chord members. The second section begins on D minor (the tonic of the impending prologue), passes through A minor and F major cells (one bar each), and cadences on D major.

Example 14-2   The opening pages of Monteverdi's *Orfeo,* including the overture

TOCCATA CHE SI SUONA AVANTI IL LEVAR DE LA TELA TRE VOLTE CON TUTTI LI STROMENTI, E SI FA UN TUONO PIÙ ALTO VOLENDO SONAR LE TROMBE CON LE SORDINE.

RITORNELLO

"Toccata" from Monteverdi L'Orfeo, edited by Malipiero. Used by kind permission of European American Music Distributors Corporation, sole U.S. and Canadian agent for Universal Edition.

There is no harmonic motion, then, in the opening Allegro. The ritornello is triadic, each bar ending in a dominant–tonic progression. More than that, however, each of these cadential patterns includes a straitlaced, legitimately prepared 4-3 suspension right out of conservative Renaissance practice. The bass line moves stepwise, in contrary motion to the conjunct descent of the top parts; all this bespeaks traditional training in counterpoint.

With respect to melodic style, the opening Allegro is made up of two drone parts on the bottom, a florid top voice largely conjunct, and two inner voices that arpeggiate tones of the C major triad. (The repeated notes here remind one of the Early Baroque idiom known as *stile agitato*, in which quick repetitions and tremolo are supposed to express excitement.) In the ritornello, with its harmonic motion, conjunct melodic lines are the rule, but measures 3 and 4 of the vulgano part include a succession of skips (A–D–G–E–B) one would not expect to see in a Renaissance movement. There is a surehandedness in Monteverdi's positioning of the one high B-flat (there were high G's, topped by one high A, in the first Allegro, and then A's in the top voices of the ritornello, surpassed by this single B-flat); his overall melodic curves are evocative.

The bar lines here (both the original and the dotted ones) can be taken to represent a metric feeling. The rhythmic relationships are complex, with all the values from whole note to sixteenth note in constant use throughout the opening Allegro. Quarter-note motion is unbroken from the entrance of the upper voices to the double bar.

The rhythms of the ritornello are more homogeneous. Here the range of values is limited: halves, quarters, and eighths. Again the constant-quarter motion is uninterrupted.

The initial section superimposes a flamboyant, imposing melodic line on an animated accompaniment. The absence of harmonic motion, taken together with the character of the top voice, gives this Allegro the complexion of an opening fanfare. The rhythmic stratification of the four lower parts, with the lowest two condemned to reiterate long notes, reminds one of Machaut and his contemporaries, but this is the seventeenth century.

The ritornello engages the upper two parts in a doubling of the same melodic idea at the third or the sixth. (In the original notation, by the way, the quinta crosses above the clarino from the high A-natural at the end of measure 2 until the clarino steps back on top of the texture for the high A at the end of measure 6. You could trade these voices in your ensemble, if you wish.) The lower three parts offer repetitions of a four-quarter, two-half rhythmic pattern as a four-bar sequence. In this tiny ritornello, with its two lyric, crossing voices riding above a stolid accompaniment, one already can see the misty image of the exquisite duet in the second movement of Bach's Concerto in D Minor for Two Violins, BWV 1043, over a century further along the path of Baroque style.

Conducting Choices
in the Monteverdi Overture

Monteverdi's original score includes a long roster of instruments, a kind of "pool" from which—at any moment in the opera—specific media can be chosen. There is no implication that all of these are simultaneously to play together as an orchestra (just as there is no requirement that all the doubled reeds in a jazz ensemble must be employed at once). One purpose for this large list of choices was to give Monteverdi coloristic opportunities, on a scene-by-scene basis, throughout the opera; the Underworld could be painted in dark shades, for example, and the flowering fields above could have brighter hues.

If you can use period instruments, you should consider doing so; on the other hand, it certainly is permissible to employ the media you have available (as did Monteverdi in his own time). Try at least to maintain the spirit of his orchestration—dark and bright sounds, loud and soft instruments, and the like.

1. The "clarino" was an early form of trumpet on which (without valves) Baroque virtuosi played melodic parts by using the upper harmonics of the overtone system. In a modern context, a trumpet or an oboe would reproduce this stirring line well.
2. For the "quinta" part, a second trumpet could be used, or—with either a trumpet or an oboe above it—an oboe or an English horn. If your choice is the oboe, the player must be good enough to handle the low C's gracefully (for they tend to be stentorian). If you choose instead the English horn, you will need to switch to oboe for the ritornello (for the high A-naturals are at the extreme upper limit of the English horn's range).
3. Viola, English horn, bassoon, French horn, or tenor trombone (the trombone perhaps muted) would be appropriate for the alto e basso voice in the opening section, but the tessitura of the ritornello would lie high for either bassoon or trombone.
4. The "vulgano" part probably was strummed. It could be bowed nicely by viola or

'cello, of course, or you could assign it to a guitarist. (To maintain balance, you may need to use two or more players, or double this with a low wind of some sort.)

5. The lowest voice could be bowed on 'cello or contrabass (the latter at the written octave) or played by bassoon or tuba. (Watch the balance here, too.)
6. Some sort of continuo keyboard is necessary, even though none is stipulated in the score; probably harpsichord would be best. The player should fill out all chords but also can take up in certain passages some of the thematic motifs.

An ideal modern orchestration of this overture might be (top to bottom) trumpet, oboe, English horn, tenor trombone, and tuba. As an alternative, one could employ for the opening section all brass—two trumpets, two horns (doubled on the alto e basso part), tenor trombone, and tuba—and shift to woodwinds—two oboes (or oboe and clarinet) on the two top parts, English horn, and two bassoons—for the ritornello section.

Here is another possibility: Since the sections may be repeated at will here, you could designate one body of instruments for the first playing of the opening section, and another for the repetition (returning to the original instrumentation for a third time, if you so desire). An unchanged orchestration of the second Allegro would be appropriate, given the element of stability inherent in the concept of the ritornello.

Using period instruments, on the other hand, one could assign a zink or a cornetto (or even an oboe da caccia) to the top voice for the opening Allegro, covering the lower parts with doubled krummhorns and strings; the ritornello, for contrast, could be assigned to doubled recorders and strings. (With some of these choices, octave adjustments would be necessary.)

The original notation indicated eight quarter notes per measure; this suggests treating the half note as the beat (since playing this music in eight probably would make it sound stodgy). If the original concept, then, was $\frac{4}{2}$, consider taking Malipiero's half-length bars in $\frac{2}{2}$ at $\downarrow$ = 60–64. Much of the motion is at the quarter-note level, nevertheless, so maintain a clear subdivision in your beat where necessary (especially at entrances).

Within this section:

1. Give thought to the phrasing of the clarino lines. Releases occur on the rests, of course, and on the tied notes (which can be treated as eighths) in measures 8 and 11. See this phrase structure as "blocks" of music, riding on top of continuous motion in the lower parts.
2. The quinta and alto e basso voices, then, are clearly accompanimental, acting as a kind of motor underneath the dominant clarino.
3. The two lowest voices need to be sustained evenly across each duration, with clean separations between notes (whether strummed, bowed, or blown).
4. Mark articulation for everyone here.
   a. Repeated sixteenths and eighths should be staccato.
   b. Other sixteenths should be played almost full-length, with some slight separation.
   c. Other eighths should be well separated.

    d. Repeated quarters should have dashes.

    e. Notes followed by rests should be played full-length.

    f. All other notes should be played with some separation.

  5. A quick cutoff just before the last chord, to permit a fresh, clean attack, could be helpful. Beware of a routine ritard here.

The ritornello can be taken in the same $\frac{2}{2}$ meter, at the same tempo, if you wish, or either a bit faster or a bit slower, as you prefer. Avoid conducting these quarter notes; **using a longer metric value as the pulse allows your musicians to reach for a longer, more expressive line,** instead of binding them to a choppy beat.

Otherwise:

1. Separation is still important here, but the connections can be closer, for contrast against the opening section. Avoid a soupy legato. Keep the articulation full of life.

2. A ritard at the end of this section, especially the last time through it, is appropriate. Time the resolution of the suspension in the quinta as part of the flow of the descending eighths in the clarino (that is, treat these quarters as tied eighths).

3. Keep in your mind, as part of your guiding conception, the sense that this ritornello was intended to prepare the initial D minor attack of the *Prologo* that follows; this overture was never an isolated whole. Be sure that your players share this perspective.

The whole range of Early Baroque ornamentation is available to you for this overture, of course. For repeats of each section, different embellishments can lend new vitality to the music, as we have seen in Chapter 11. For important repeated notes (the first quarter-note G in the clarino in measure 4, for example, or the clarino's first quarter-note E in bar 8), a mordent could be inserted. For the clarino's half note in bar 8, or for the quinta suspension in bar 13, a trill (with a nachschlag to the C-sharp in the latter case) would be effective; appoggiaturas, intonatione, and esclamazione can be used. The harpsichord can emphasize trills and arpeggios.

Consider that the rhythmic values in the opening section of the overture, at least, already are complex. Avoid cluttering the piece with ornaments, but bear in mind that unembellished Baroque music can sound naive, and—in any case— is uncharacteristic of the performance practice of what we know to have been an exciting master composer.[11]

---

[11]A list of additional Baroque instrumental works for student conductors can be found in Appendix B.

CHAPTER *15*

Style and Performance: Late Baroque and Classical Instrumental Works

In the early years of the eighteenth century, the musical evolution that had started with the innovative works of Monteverdi and his contemporaries was reaching a level of sophistication about to culminate in the creative output of Bach and Handel. The tonal organization we hear had enlarged to include concepts of near- and distant-key relationships, modulations, and deliberate tonal ambiguity. Chord-progression patterns had developed into the framework later to be called functional harmony. The new Baroque counterpoint set atop this foundation of tonality and chord progressions was to become, in the fugues of Bach and Handel, as elaborate as the most intricate designs of Josquin and Palestrina. Complex metric and rhythmic relationships were woven through these fabrics.[1]

Inventive technological improvements had made the musical instruments of the era much superior to their predecessors. The finest stringed instruments ever constructed were coming out of the Stradivari workshop in Cremona in the first quarter of the eighteenth century. The oboe as we know it had first appeared about fifty years earlier, and a flurry of experimentation prompted by the importance of the basso continuo in Baroque textures was producing a wide range of keyboard media. This new wealth of timbral possibilities was leading composers to be more and more specific about instrumentation.

Multimovement forms—structures responsive to the ideal of the *Affektenlehre* in Baroque aesthetics—pervaded both vocal and instrumental music. The suite, the sonata (especially in its solo and trio forms), the solo concerto, the concerto grosso, the cantata, the oratorio, the opera, and more represented a new commitment to large-scale designs.

[1]It is unnecessary for the authors to duplicate here the historical and theoretical background presented in Chapters 11 and 14, for the reader can glance back at any time to those discussions and can consult the general summary of Baroque style and performance practice in Appendix B.

BACKGROUND AND PERSPECTIVES: GEORGE FRIDERIC HANDEL AND MESSIAH

The story of the composition of *Messiah*[2] has assumed the aura of myth. Handel had been writing oratoriolike works for a third of a century (partly to generate new career opportunities during the season of Lent, when his operas—like all theatrical productions—were temporarily banned from the stage); *Israel in Egypt* preceded *Messiah* by two years. We are told that he wrote the latter in a three-week whirlwind of creative energy—hardly eating, hardly sleeping—at the end of the summer of 1741. The result struck Western audiences like lightning.

The oratorio form was a familiar one to Handel, for it differed little in structure or content from the operatic designs to which he had devoted most of his life. The overture, the recitatives, the arias, the duets, and the choruses were all components of both these macroforms. The primal difference was that of subject: The choice of a Biblical theme meant a libretto taken from scripture and implied a concert-style production, but (as with Bach's great Passions) still allowed the casting of "roles" and the dramatic shaping of a theatrical "plot."

Messiah itself, in fact, reflects that ambivalence about the sacred and the profane, for it includes movements Handel borrowed from earlier, secular works of his; some of the most famous choruses in *Messiah* are former Italian duets, musically revised and set to the Biblical libretto submitted to him by Charles Jennens. The quasi-operatic image is less sharp in *Messiah* than in most of Handel's oratorios, however, for there is no plot, as such, and thus no "characters." Part the First (as Handel named it) is concerned with the prophets' heralding of Jesus Christ, and with His birth; Part the Second recalls His suffering and death, and the evangelists' response to those events; Part the Third examines the significance for the individual of His incarnation and resurrection.

Once the public successes began, Handel himself performed *Messiah* again and again, both in England and in Ireland, modifying the manuscript substantially over the years, changing solo assignments, adding or deleting sections of movements, revising key relationships, and the like. One of the problems one faces in undertaking a performance of the work is to decide which of these variant constituents are to be fitted into the mosaic this time.[3]

George Frideric Handel: *Messiah*, Sinfony

The word *sinfonia* (or "Sinfony," to use Handel's term here) had various meanings in the Baroque era, but its primary application was to instrumental introduc-

---

[2]The correct title is *Messiah*, not (as one often hears and reads) "The Messiah."

[3]For a detailed analysis of conducting choices of various kinds in the Sinfonia, and indeed all of *Messiah*, see Don V Moses, Robert W. Demaree, Jr., and Allen F. Ohmes, *Face to Face with an Orchestra* (Princeton, N.J.: Prestige Publications, 1987), beginning on p. 45.

tions for operas, oratorios, cantatas, and similar works; thus is it employed in this case. Handel, for all his German birth and Italian training, has written a "French overture" for *Messiah*, following Lully's standard design of a two-part structure: the first section a Grave dominated by stately dotted rhythms, and the second an Allegro moderato driven by rhythmically infectious fugal counterpoint. See Example 15-1.[4]

The Grave is cast in E minor and, like the first half of a Baroque binary form, modulates (through a somewhat ambiguous tonal cell on the relative G major) to the dominant at the first ending. It repeats, returning to the dominant at the second ending to set up the E minor beginning of the Allegro moderato. (This E minor tonality employed for the Sinfony prepares the listener for the E major settings of "Comfort Ye/Every Valley," and for the succession to follow through Part the First of G major, D minor, G minor, D major, and so on, as Handel moves on to nearby keys.)

The Allegro moderato begins with a five-bar subject, introduced by the first violins and oboe I. Fugal entrances by the second violins and oboe II (measure 17) and the basso continuo (bar 21) follow, and the movement unfolds through a series of episodes (the first coming in the second violins in bar 25) and statements—often in truncated variants—of the subject. From the initial E minor, the music passes through G major, B minor, A minor, and other temporary cells, negotiating long transitional passages along the way. The final statement of the subject begins in the violins I in measure 86 (in E minor again) and leads to an emphatic cadence in that key.

The Grave is in $\frac{4}{4}$ and is saturated with the dotted figures already noted; almost every rhythm in the section involves a dotting either of the quarter or of the eighth. The Allegro moderato, on the other hand, although it is also duple, avoids dotted patterns in favor of straight successions of quarters, eighths, and halves—most beginning off the beat. Long passages of "spinning" (*fortspinnung*) propel the violin lines toward tessitural peaks, at which points the rhythms of the subject resume.

Handel's melodic work helps keep the Grave and the Allegro moderato distinct from each other. The former is the more jagged in its lines (with almost half the intervals in the violin I part disjunct, for example); the latter is rather more conjunct, partly as an effect of the *fortspinnung* passages. Long step-progressions control the direction of melodic motion (see, as an instance of this, the stepwise ascent of the first violins from the E-naturals in measure 37 to the high D's in bar 43); this step-progression is concurrent with others in the second violins in measures 39–42 and in the bass in bars 39–45.

[4]George Frideric Handel, *Messiah, an Oratorio*, ed. Alfred Mann; 3 vols. (New York: ABI/Alexander Broude, Inc., and Rutgers University Press, 1983), pp. 1–4.

Example 15-1   Handel: *Messiah*, Sinfony

Example 15-1 *(cont.)*

Example 15-1 *(cont.)*

Example 15-1 (cont.)

Example 15-1 *(cont.)*

Example 15-1 *(cont.)*

The harmonies here are progressive and triadic, of course, resting on a figured-bass conception. Dissonances tend to be melodic in character: See measure 1, where the first eighth note in each of the violin parts constitutes a dissonance leapt to and resolved by step; observe also the on-the-beat passing F-sharp in the bass line of bar 2; note the 7-6 (rearticulated) suspension in the first violins in bar 3. These examples are typical of Handel's enrichment of his sonorities through transient melodic clashes. He depends on his performers to provide further enrichment through ornamentation, as we shall see.

Conducting Handel's "Sinfony"

The size of the string ensemble to be used for this movement is conditioned by at least four factors. First, one should recall that Handel's experience of this work (at least until very late in his life) was of choruses of twenty-five or thirty singers, supported by orchestras of equivalent size; the huge forces sometimes employed since his death are destructive of this music, taking away what Robert Shaw has called "its light, bright, chamber" character. Second, it is important that the special timbre of the harpsichord not be lost to the power of the strings; and, third, the oboes, too, must be clearly present in the balance—must "season" the overall sound into that blend of strings, keyboard, and winds that is characteristic of the

Baroque orchestra. Finally, the nature of your own ensemble and the hall in which it performs should influence your judgment.

We know that Handel used a pair of oboes for *Messiah* and that his continuo unit included bassoon. Considering the rosters of players available to him, and calling to mind the performance practices of the period, we might define an ideal force for the sinfonia as 6-5-4-4-3 strings,[5] plus two oboes, harpsichord, and bassoon.

This view is conditioned by scholarship and performance experience since 1970. In that time, much attention has been given to antique instruments (and copies thereof) and to their influence on performance possibilities. In general, some of the older instruments lacked the sustaining power, efficiency, and resonance of some modern ones; this limitation would imply more separation between notes—longer articulatory silences—and, therefore, more lucidity, more "transparency" of texture than, say, a romanticized performance played on today's instruments.

You properly may focus a part of your planning, then, on an effort to recover the "Baroque sound ideal" when you perform this music. Don't approach the sinfonia with a rich, sustained legato in mind. Find the "Baroque skeleton" in the texture—the melody on top and the bass line in the continuo—by playing these voices through at the piano; then reconstruct the harmony in the inner voices and the keyboard. This process will teach you the textural values inherent in the music, should give you a clear sense of the balance needed, and should lead you to strive for a much lighter, more vivid timbre than that produced in many performances of *Messiah* over much of the nineteenth and twentieth centuries.

You already understand how important fresh, historically legitimate ornamentation is to this concept of a "Baroque sound ideal."[6] Many embellishments in *Messiah* are indicated in Handel's own hand. Others are implied by indigenous factors, and still more can be inferred and confidently improvised by well-prepared, imaginative musicians. A basic principle is that **ornaments commonly are used in Baroque style to emphasize dissonances.** It follows, then, that the D-sharp in the first violins in measure 2 is a logical site for a trill. Ornaments also can add impetus to a melodic motif; thus the D-sharp two measures later can be heard to be driven forward by a trill toward the F-sharp-and-G resolution, and the G-sharp in bar 14 can help thrust the subject upward to the A-natural in the next measure. The cliché in this matter is the trill on the penultimate chord, of course (in this case, on the F-sharp in bar 96). To the extent that you encourage improvised ornaments, as well as written ones, be certain you make clear who has responsibility—the harpsichordist, the concertmaster, the whole violin I section, the oboe I, and so on—for embellishing a given passage.

Proportional tempo relationships can be very useful throughout *Messiah*. If you decide, for example, on a rather slow pace for the Grave, say ♩ = 50, you

---

[5]Conventionally, string bodies are described by counting the players in the violins I, violins II, violas, violoncellos, and contrabasses, in that order.

[6]See the discussion of Baroque ornamentation in Chapter 11.

could simply double (actually quadruple) that marking (to $\downarrow$ = 100) for the Allegro moderato. The authors take the Grave in four and prefer a tempo of $\downarrow$ = 56–60; this allows one to use a 2:3 relationship for the Allegro moderato, setting it at approximately $\downarrow$ = 88–92.[7]

In the Baroque style, think of conducting and shaping the continuo part as much as or more than the melody. Like the "rhythm section" of a jazz group, the Baroque continuo sets the temporal context for a "movement"; those performing the melodic line tend to get their own sense of how to give contour to their lines from that foundation.

With respect to the details of the Grave, note the following:

1. In this era, performers were free to double-dot simple dotted figures, as a matter of personal taste. Both approaches to this Sinfony have been used by great conductors, and you may choose either the stateliness of the written version or the excitement of the double dots, as seems best to you. Be certain your players know which way you want the Grave played, and make them responsible for either rhythm.[8]
2. "Listen" to the music to find its "peaks and valleys." Where is the high point of the phrase? Where does it have (or need) strength to push toward that peak? Where does it need to relax away from a climax, and how long? Decide, in short, how to get from bar 1 to bar 6, beyond that to bar 8, and on to the first ending.
3. Measure 8 is crucial, for if it is not shaped properly the Grave becomes directionless. Note the descending bass line in the last half of measure 8: Handel is adding tension (through that D-natural) right where you need it.[9]
4. Another Baroque principle, as you know by now, is to vary repeated passages. At the end of the first ending, there are several choices to be made.
   a. Many conductors, having taken the first twelve bars at *f*, add a decrescendo to the first two beats of the first ending, and mark everything after the third beat *p*.
   b. One also can change instrumentation here. Two possibilities: Drop the double reeds for the repeat; reduce the strings to one desk per part (leaving them at *f*, perhaps).
   c. Change ornamentation. If you have used only a few embellishments up to the first ending, add more for the repeat.

For the Allegro moderato, note these details:

1. In fugal counterpoint, make your beats—which cannot be all of the same size and character—show the shape and direction of the subject to your musicians. Give them a clear image of the contours and momentum. If necessary, talk and play through this central melody until its articulation, harmonic underpinnings, and other characteristics are clear. Example 15-2 illustrates one such interpretation; in

---

[7]Dividing each Grave quarter note (at MM = 60) into triplet eighth notes, and then tying those eighths in pairs, produces in the tied pairs of eighths "new" half notes at MM = 90. For an overall discussion of proportional tempo relationships, see Chapter 12.

[8]See Moses, Demaree, and Ohmes, *Face to Face with an Orchestra*, pp. 47–48, and Robert Donington, *A Performer's Guide to Baroque Music* (New York: Scribner's, 1973), p. 4.

[9]Handel changed the E-natural on the third beat of measure 8 from a dotted quarter, making the D-natural a full quarter, to strengthen this progression. See Handel, *Messiah*, ed. Alfred Mann, p. 85.

Example 15-2 One interpretation of the fugal subject of the *Messiah* Sinfony

studying it, however, remember that no two consecutive notes (even though marked in the same way) have the same duration and function in this music. (The two eighths in bar 13 are different in length, as are the quarters in measure 15.)

2. Make certain the other voices enter with the same strength and interpretive identity provided by the first violins and oboe I.

3. The entrance by the second violins and oboe II at measure 25 is very important, since it introduces the first episode. So is the continuo attack at bar 29.

4. The lower voices deserve emphasis, too; they support the long ascent by the first violins and oboe II from bar 39 to the cadence in 46. The pattern of three eighth notes to a quarter note must be rhythmically clean; if this motif starts late, it creates severe problems for the first violins and oboe I.

5. The D-natural in the bass at bars 46–50, like all such pedal points, should *aim* somewhere—should have momentum and direction of its own—while the other voices pursue their one-measure entrances above it.

6. The continuo entrance at 73 begins an important dialogue between the bass voice and the top line.

7. The last four measures deserve a ritard.

Once you have in your ears a concept of this movement, it is important that you not *overconduct* it. Stick with the size of beat pattern appropriate to the dynamic marking and articulation you want. Make the orchestra listen.

Two final points about this sinfonia: You may need to mark specific dynamic changes in the Allegro moderato section, both for the sake of balance and to make clear your interpretation. And remember that modern orchestral concerts have made us more accustomed to a dominating string sound than Handel's ears are likely to have been; keep striving toward a real Baroque timbre.[10]

BACKGROUND AND PERSPECTIVES: FRANZ JOSEPH HAYDN IN 1787

Joseph Haydn, Kapellmeister to His Serene Princely Highness, Herr Nicolaus Esterházy, was nearing the apex of his career when he wrote two more symphonies, Nos. 88 and 89 (not the "Paris Symphonies," Nos. 82–87), for the Parisians. Fifty-five years old, and writing in a style honed by almost four decades of experience, Haydn was at that moment the most famous living musi-

[10]You will find a list of additional Baroque instrumental music suitable for student conductors in Appendix B.

cian in the Western world, for the 1780s had seen wide distribution of his music around Europe to France, to Spain, to the British Isles, and to other parts of the German states.

The attributes of Haydn's style, admired by Mozart and Beethoven, combined elements of the Baroque idiom (especially a tendency toward monothematicism and an adaptation of *fortspinnung*) with self-taught developmental and variational techniques, metric and tonal procedures, manipulations of phrase length, and other features. The whole of his compositional approach forms a working definition of what we now call the Viennese Classical style.[11]

In a sense, Haydn never was Viennese, although his last great successes (*The Creation*, for example) were to be celebrated in the imperial city. Born in a dirt-floored farmhouse (but not, strictly speaking, of peasant stock, for his father and grandfather both were craftsmen), he always felt close to the common people; he once remarked that his lifelong proximity to the rich and powerful never had led him to prefer their company. He is known also to have liked the food, wine, and music of the commoners. During his years in Eisenstadt (on what is now the Hungarian border but was at that time a part of the prince's Hungarian estates), Haydn went often to a nearby village of people of Croatian descent, where he enjoyed their folk dances and their music. That affection shows up in the master's own work: Speaking of the minuet we are about to examine, the Haydn scholar Robbins Landon calls it

> a scene out of Breugel: stamping peasants dancing round kegs of wine and tables groaning with harvest feast. If one seeks the difference in a single minuet between Haydn and Mozart, one may compare this rich, earthy peasant scene with the fantastic sophistication and fastidious elegance of the "Jupiter" Symphony's Minuet, both composed within a year of each other.[12]

In his string quartets (after Op. 2), his minuets were placed alternately as second and third movements—late in his career generally third. (The last time a minuet falls second in a Haydn orchestral work is in the Symphony No. 68, in B-flat major, written over a decade before No. 88.)

Long before 1787, Haydn had noticed a problem with this form. The minuet offered him "both confidence in a stable, established design and concern for a uniformity that could become static."[13] He is said to have hoped "someone would compose a really new minuet,"[14] and kept reworking the form himself.

[11]Historical and theoretical background on the Classical period can be found in Chapter 11, and the reader can consult the general summary of Classical style and performance practice in Appendix B.

[12]H. C. Robbins Landon, *Haydn: Chronicle and Works* (Bloomington: Indiana University Press, 1976–1980), II, 630.

[13]Robert W. Demaree, Jr., *The Structural Proportions of the Haydn Quartets* (Ph.D. diss., Indiana University, 1973), 141.

[14]H. C. Robbins Landon, *The Symphonies of Joseph Haydn* (London: Universal Edition and Rockliff Publishing, 1955), p. 216.

Franz Joseph Haydn: Symphony No. 88, in G Major, Minuet

Haydn's Symphony No. 88 (Example 15-3[15]) is scored for flute, two oboes, two bassoons, two horns, two trumpets, timpani, and strings. After an Adagio introduction, the opening movement (in which the trumpets and timpani are not used, an unusual feature) proves to be a splendid, artful Allegro. The Largo that follows is one of the greatest sets of orchestral variations in the symphonic literature, a powerful work both majestic in stature and brilliant in orchestration. After the peasant-dance minuet with which we now concern ourselves, the symphony closes with a vivacious, contrapuntal finale.

There is nothing really surprising about the structure of this minuet. The full orchestra is used. The "Menuetto" section, a compound binary form, begins in G major, modulates to the dominant at the first repeat sign, and then continues through a tonally fluid passage to a reprise of the opening; the passage closes in G major at another repeat sign. The first section is about half the length of the second.

The "Trio" moves to the dominant at the first double bar, repeats, and then proceeds through an A minor tonal cell to another G major cadence, and another repeat. A *da capo* indication reprises once again the original Menuetto. By convention, the repeat signs are ignored the second time. Again, the *B* section of the Menuetto is substantially longer than the *A* section. There are none of the devices Haydn sometimes uses at the end of his Trios to obscure the reprise or otherwise camouflage the minuet form.

Although Haydn had already applied the term *scherzi* to the minuet movements of his Op. 33 string quartets, written six years before this symphony—and although the *spirit* of the scherzo is clearly present in the humor of this minuet—the traditional $\frac{3}{4}$ meter is still obligatory here. See the rhythmic twists and turns; look, for example, at bars 1 and 2—three quarters leading to a half, with the downbeats metrically accented—and compare them with measures 7 and 8, where the stepwise patterns in the melody (E to D, and G to F-sharp) form an off-beat $\frac{3}{2}$ effect, a *hemiola*.

One compositional procedure that usually has structural significance in Haydn's music is the "rhythmic constant," a rhythmic value unbroken over long stretches, as a type of motor. Here, quarter-note articulations happen somewhere in the texture on every beat from the opening pickup to bar 9, and again from measure 21 through measure 42. The interruptions in this pulselike continuity feel "clumsy," like a stumbling dance, and may be part of the reason Landon hears a rustic, peasant-village atmosphere in this music.

---

[15]Franz Joseph Haydn, Symphony No. 88, in G Major, ed. H. C. Robbins Landon (Philharmonia Universal Edition, 1964).

Example 15-3   Haydn: Symphony No. 88, in G Major, Minuet

Example 15-3 *(cont.)*

* Sources:

Example 15-3 *(cont.)*

* *f* In some old sources

Example 15-3 *(cont.)*

Example 15-3 *(cont.)*

Example 15-3 *(cont.)*

Example 15-3 *(cont.)*

Example 15-3 *(cont.)*

Menuetto da capo

Now compare these constant quarter-note passages with the Trio, in which the quarter-note level is unbroken from beginning to end. But that is not all: In the Trio, the *eighth note* is constant over bars 49–54 and 57–70; there were no such streams of eighths in the Menuetto, but most of the Trio is *driven* by the momentum of these eighths. *Haydn is using contrasting rhythmic levels to help the listener hear structure*—to hear that the Trio is different from the Menuetto. This is typical of his skill at making form audible.

He clarifies form in other ways, too. One has to do with phrase length: The opening Menuetto is constructed of a four-bar unit (the pickup note through the first two beats of measure 4), followed by a two-bar fragment; another four-bar phrase (beginning with the pickup to measure 7) is followed by a pair of two-bar fragments. All repeats. After the double bar come three more of the two-bar units and a pair of four-measure phrases (or a single eight-bar unit, if you hear it that way). Another four-measure phrase carries us back to the original dominant, and a pair of four-bar phrases reprises the original melody. (Notice, however, that the "hemiola" effect is avoided this time by a simpler line.) Another pair of two-bar units closes the Menuetto, *the melodic basis of which has been the four-bar phrase.*

Compare that with the Trio. Here, a pair of two-measure fragments occupies measures 45–48; next, however, a *six* bar phrase carries to the double bar. (Note that Haydn inserts *fz* markings in measure 52, emphatically denying that a four-bar phrase could end there.) Another two-measure fragment follows the repeat signs, and then *two seven-bar units*, elided at the cadence on the first beat of bar 64 (or an unbroken fourteen-bar unit, if you hear it that way). At that point, Haydn returns to his Menuetto, with its four-measure phrases.

The master is using phrase length, just as he employs rhythmic constants, to make the Trio audibly distinct from the Menuetto. His concern for clarity of design—clarity his audience *can* hear—is manifest in this movement, and this minuet is typical of most of his work.

The sort of "interruptive" technique we see so often in Beethoven is present, too, not just in Haydn's breaking off his rhythmic constants, but in his management of texture and orchestration, as well. He is working with homophonic textures here; the Menuetto is chordal, and the Trio offers an accompanied eighth-note line, but note again the two-bar fragments in bars 11–14, the antiphonal *f* and *p* alternations in measures 15–20, and the jocular *p* violin/bassoon/timpani effect in bars 41–42.

Typically, Haydn's harmonies are triadic. Such chromaticism as he employs tends to be harmonic in function, rather than melodic. The jarring shift to flats at measure 19 is part of the broad, rustic humor of the movement; so too is the "bagpipe" effect, the "drone fifth" in the bassoons and violas at bars 55–68.

It is difficult for us, who have heard all sorts of cute, complicated orchestrations written for huge ensembles by imaginative composers over the past couple of centuries, to understand the extent to which Haydn is using his instruments in fresh, experimental ways in this symphony. Look again at the timpani at measure 11 and at the horns in bar 13: These instruments were used in this period primarily as sound reinforcement for *f* passages; here, however, they are employed for mysterious, coloristic *p* effects. Do not let this whimsical minuet sound old-fashioned, and (above all) do not let it sound naive; this kind of writing was revolutionary in its time, and with intelligent interpretation and deft playing, it still can be made to sound vital and exciting today.

Conducting Haydn's Minuet

A part of your "intelligent interpretation" must be a decision about the overall character of the work. A minuet, for example, can be made to sound very elegant—very *gallant*—and some minuets should be performed in that mode; but this Haydn movement appears not to be of that flavor. It was written to be performed for sophisticated, cosmopolitan nobles in a lavish court. It is *not* crude, or vulgar, and was *not* intended as entertainment for peasants, but it is boisterous and rollicking in the manner of a Burgenland winefest.

On that decision about the essential character of the work hangs at least a subtle shading of your tempo choice. For this Menuetto, something close to ♩ = 120 seems appropriate. (It must be taken in three, not in one, for the nature of each note in these lines is different. **Your baton must show the character you want each note to have.**) In the melody, the opening pickup is strong, the downbeat of bar 1 is left by slur, and the second-beat note is weak. (You will want to hold the Trio to virtually the same tempo.)

With respect to other details in the Menuetto section of this movement, note the following:

1. Do not let the players rush these detached pickup notes. They will tend to hurry through the silences.
2. The three-note turns that ornament many of the melody notes should come on the beat and must be played as rapidly as possible, with much energy.
3. The articulation is diverse here. In measure 1, for example, the flute and the violins have slurs, the bassoons and the low strings are staccato, and the other instruments are unmarked. The authors believe Haydn intended this variety; the unmarked parts should be played with separation (but not staccato) so that a transparent relationship of instrumental families is heard.
4. With respect to this matter of separation (here very similar to the approach we suggested for the Handel sinfonia), no two notes of the same notated value are likely to deserve the same duration. In measure 3, as one instance, each quarter in the unmarked parts probably should be given a different length; varied silences should follow each note. This could be articulated in more than one way. "Listen" to this line, and make an interpretive choice.
5. Similarly, what sort of stroke do you want from the timpani in measure 11? (What sort of sticks should the timpanist use?) And in bar 13, what articulation do you prefer from the horns? (The authors recommend moderate separation—not too staccato.) How about the comparative length of the *f* staccatos in some bars and the *p* ones elsewhere?
6. The mordents that appear late in the Menuetto should (like the turns) be played on the beat.

We turn now from the Menuetto to the rather more delicate Trio section.

1. Note the unusual *forte assai* for the bassoons in measure 45. (The parallel case in bar 55 is editorial.) Here, Haydn rather encourages these winds to emphasize their double drone pedal against the *p* dynamic in the other voices.
2. The duplet articulation should be clearly contrasted with the even patterns (compare the oboe markings in bars 47 and 49, for example), as well as with the staccato passages (as in measure 57).
3. Throughout the Trio, keep the strings in balance against the oboe, which adds real spice to the line.

Take time. Let the music breathe. Do not hurry the structural points. (When you repeat the Menuetto, allow more space before the reprise in bar 32.)

Why *do* the bassoons have that *forte assai* at measure 45, and why are the *fz* markings spattered all over bars 66–68? How do those *sforzandos* compare with the ones in measure 52? Take note of the sudden *forte* at bar 22, which *should* have come on the pickup to measure 21, should it not? And what about measures 15–18, and that abrupt tonal shift at 19?

There *is* a great deal of humor in this movement. Allow it to happen. *Use the silences!* Haydn is setting up expectations before many of these spots, and then confounding them unexpectedly, for the sake of freshness and wit. Give your audience every opportunity to be misled by his preparations. Don't give the secrets away by "telegraphing" the surprises. Make your listeners laugh out loud with delight at this music.[16]

---

[16]You will find a list of additional Classical instrumental music suitable for student conductors in Appendix B.

CHAPTER 16

Style and Performance: Romantic and Twentieth-Century Instrumental Works

We come now to an era of vigorous development for instrumental ensembles and their literature. The eighteenth century had seen the birth of some fine orchestras; the Elector at Mannheim had one, and Haydn had another (the so-called band of professors). The great, established ensembles we know today began to appear at Leipzig and Paris just before the turn of the nineteenth century, and what would become the Vienna Philharmonic made its first concert appearances in the 1840s. By the middle of the twentieth century, the bureaucratic rigidities of labor-management relations and fixed rehearsal-performance schedules were both stabilizing and smothering these great institutions in Europe and the Americas.

The concert band—born of two parents, the military band and the wind–percussion section of the orchestra—is not widely established so far. Outside the armed forces, there have been fewer standing professional bands than orchestras (although amateur and school wind groups have proliferated across Europe and America over the past century or so). That is one reason for the slower evolution of an indigenous repertoire composed for the concert band; many marches have been written over the years, but orchestras have elicited the bulk of the new major instrumental literature. There is, nevertheless, a body of fine music available for this ensemble, some of it created expressly for the band (including some recent works especially commissioned by band conductors), and some of it transcribed from orchestral repertoire. We are about to look at an excellent example of the latter type.

BACKGROUND AND PERSPECTIVES: MUSSORGSKY, RAVEL, AND LEIDZÈN

The freedom taken by nineteenth-century composers to base works on extramusical foundations led to the creation of much "program music." A large share of this literature sought to express its composers' nationalism, sometimes with folk melodies and rhythms, sometimes through attempts to "tell" heroic tales, and sometimes in efforts aimed at the tone-painting of visual images.[1] These ventures were written in an idiom in various ways more complex than had been the Viennese Classical style, a music of complicated metric and rhythmic relationships, weakened ("broadened") tonality, rampant dissonance, extremely detailed dynamics, and increasing emphasis on timbre.

Such a composer was the Russian Modest Mussorgsky, and such a work was his *Pictures at an Exhibition*, written in 1874. Half-trained as a musician and bound to a government job, Mussorgsky depended on great natural gifts and the advice of friends like Rimsky-Korsakov to produce a roster of Russian-idiom compositions, headed by the opera masterpiece *Boris Godunov*. Modal melodies and harmonies in asymmetrical, changing meters poured forth from his pen. Those who attempted to "help" him—both during his life and after his death—by "refining" his manuscripts (as Rimsky-Korsakov did when he reorchestrated *Boris*) generally were unable to tell the difference between unschooled vulgarities and unorthodox flashes of genius. Not until the middle of the twentieth century did it become generally accepted that his work was masterful.

In writing *Pictures at an Exhibition* for solo piano, Mussorgsky created an aural art gallery, basing it on a showing of drawings at the St. Petersburg Academy of Fine Arts by architect Victor Hartmann. Ten movements frame "pictures"; a "Promenade" theme, which represents the viewer walking through the gallery, is used first as an introduction and then recurrently in variations between several of the movements.

Half a century later, Maurice Ravel was asked by Maestro Serge Koussevitsky to transcribe Mussorgsky's powerful piano work for a large symphony orchestra. If there had been questions about Mussorgsky's skill as an orchestrator, about Ravel there could be none. Artful, subtle, and imaginative, the Frenchman translated the monochromatic original into a vibrant, glowing tapestry of timbres. Koussevitsky premiered the transcription with his Paris orchestra in 1922, Ravel's forty-eighth year.

Two decades further into the twentieth century, the band arranger Erik W. G. Leidzèn produced for the Goldman Band (a professional concert ensemble conducted by Edwin Franko Goldman) a further transcription of *Pictures at an*

---

[1]It is unnecessary for the authors to duplicate here the historical and theoretical background presented in Chapter 12, for the reader can glance back at any time to those discussions and can consult the general summary of Romantic style and performance practice in Appendix B.

Exhibition. Goldman, a cornet and trumpet player as well as a conductor, was founder and president of the American Bandmasters' Association, and was committed to broadening the repertory of the concert band by the commissioning of major works for his ensemble. (Again a conductor was securing an arrangement of Mussorgsky's masterwork.) Thus, we can view *Pictures at an Exhibition* in three different versions.

Mussorgsky/Ravel: *Pictures at an Exhibition,* "Promenade" and "Bydlo"

Ravel has faithfully transcribed Mussorgsky's twenty-four measures of piano "Promenade" into twenty-four bars for an orchestra of woodwinds-in-threes (including, that is, the secondary instruments: piccolo, bass clarinet, and contrabassoon), four horns, three trumpets, three trombones, tuba, and strings. (Additional forces are used in his later movements.)

Example 16-1 illustrates Mussorgsky's original "Promenade,"[2] and Example 16-2 presents an excerpt from Ravel's transcription of it.[3] There are no classical forms here. Pairs of phrases gradually are extended and elaborated; one of these variants (beginning at measure 9 in the orchestral score) provides additional rhythmic impetus as the movement builds toward a climax. (Ravel, with an entire orchestra at his command, emphasizes that growth by an expansion toward full orchestra at bar 13; when all the trombones enter at bar 21, the peak has been reached.)

The governing tonal center is B-flat, but temporary cells appear (F and A-flat flash past early in the movement), and modal ambiguity (the relative minor at measure 3, for example) obscures other spots. The final cadence is a clear-cut B-flat.

The modal character of this music governs its melodic and harmonic character. The tritone plays a smaller part here than in much of the literature of the nineteenth century. Major and minor chords, flavored by many chromatic mutations, are the basic sonorities, and the melody flows over those harmonies in chord tones and conjunct passing tones. There is comparatively little dissonance. Its harmonic interest comes from its modal nature.

Mussorgsky permits himself phrases any number of quarter notes in length; as a result, meter is variable here, shifting back and forth between $\frac{5}{4}$ and $\frac{6}{4}$, as the melodic shapes require. There is a constant quarter note, unbroken through the movement; the two-eighths-to-a-quarter pattern is the mortar that glues the phrases together.

[2]Modest Mussorgsky, *Complete Works,* ed. Paul Lamm (New York: Edwin F. Kalmus, 1930), 17, 5–6.

[3]Mussorgsky-Ravel, *Pictures at an Exhibition,* opening "Promenade," mm. 20–24 (New York: Boosey & Hawkes, Inc., 1929), pp. 1–5.

Example 16-1   Mussorgsky: *Pictures at an Exhibition,* "Promenade," complete

Allegro giusto, nel modo russico, senza allegrezza, ma poco sostenuto

Example 16-1 *(cont.)*

attacca

Example 16-2 Mussorgsky-Ravel: *Pictures at an Exhibition,* "Promenade," mm. 20–24

It must have surprised Mussorgsky's listeners to hear a major piano work begin with a monophonic line. (Ravel saw an opportunity in this, however, and assigned the "strolling" motif to the first trumpet.)

For the "Bydlo" (sixty-four measures both in the original and in the orchestral arrangement), Ravel retains the woodwinds-in-threes, the four horns, the tuba, and the strings (dropping the trumpets and the trombones), and adds harp, timpani, and tenor and bass drums. He also divides both the 'cellos and the contrabasses.

The "Bydlo" drawing was of a huge oxcart. In this aural structure (the complete Mussorgsky original is shown in Example 16-3,[4] and an excerpt from the Ravel movement in Example 16-4,[5] the oxcart approaches the listener, passes, and gradually disappears in the distance. In musical terms, the form resembles an arch. Only the lower voices are used at first; more are added as the cart "comes closer," so that a sempre crescendo, starting at measure 21, controls the design. (Ravel has the full orchestra reach *fff* at bar 38; the retreat begins at bar 44, and turns into a sempre diminuendo at bar 47; instruments are withdrawn again, as the low tessitura is regained.)

Modal ambiguity is an aspect of this movement, also: The "motor" rhythm in the low voices begins with alternating G-sharp minor and B major chords; again, the relative major and minor both are present, and B-natural is actually the final pitch at the end, although the metric positioning of the G-sharp minor sonorities gives that tonal center the advantage. A second idea, beginning at bar 21, offers variety; the initial melody returns, then (in Ravel with full orchestra), at measure 38 and continues to the end, so that an overall *ABA'* design can be heard (although the *B* section is a weak one).

Again the emphasis is on modal melody and harmony. Triadic sonorities are the basis, although somewhat more dissonance can be found here than in the "Promenade." The first theme is more extended than any in the previous movement; units of nine and ten bars carry the movement over to the *B* idea at measure 21. Again chromatic mutations permit Mussorgsky to have either a major or a minor chord at any given moment.

The driving force here is the motor. It clarifies in its duple pulsing (in a way that nothing did in the "Promenade") the metric shape of this movement. The "Promenade" had a constant quarter; in "Bydlo" it is the eighth that is unbroken, all the way from measure 1 to the last two bars. The most distinctive rhythmic factor, outside of the motor, is the tied-eighth-and-two-sixteenths pattern (as in measure 2).

The opening section of this movement sets up a melody-with-accompaniment fabric (in the orchestral version, the tuba against the bassoons, contrabassoon, and low strings), and this set of relationships is replicated in the texture from bar 38 to the end. The middle passage, from bar 21 to bar 38, is homophonic, and thus this textural contrast helps to convey the structure.

[4]Mussorgsky, *Complete Works*, ed. Paul Lamm, pp. 17–19
[5]Mussorgsky-Ravel, *Pictures at an Exhibition*, "Bydlo," mm. 21–27 (New York: Boosey & Hawkes, Inc., 1929).

Example 16-3   Mussorgsky: *Pictures at an Exhibition,* "Bydlo," complete

Example 16-3 *(cont.)*

Example 16-4 Mussorgsky-Ravel: *Pictures at an Exhibition,* "Bydlo," mm. 21–27

Conducting Two Movements from Pictures at an Exhibition

Ravel's big orchestral score offers an increased challenge to student conductors. As many as twenty-six instruments occupy as many as twenty-one staves. On some pages, two systems of staves appear, and on others, only one; the eyes must adjust quickly, finding now the second clarinet, now the harp, now the tuba.

The "Promenade" Movement

1. Study the long, idiosyncratic tempo marking. We suggest that you consider taking this at about ♩ = 92.
2. Note the articulation marks. You will need to use a tenuto-style beat pattern.
3. The $\frac{5}{4}$ measures divide both ways: Some are 2 + 3, and some 3 + 2. Examine these bars carefully, and decide which is which in your interpretation.
4. In spots like measure 6, where the entrance is not on the first beat, the strength of your cue must be greater.
5. Show the crescendos and diminuendos in measures 12, 16, and 17, as well as the *p* in bar 15.
6. The $\frac{3}{2}$ bar is a subdivided three, not a six. Show a clear cue for the strings (on the fourth beat).
7. Distinguish in your beat motion between the tenuto markings and the accents at bar 18 and elsewhere.

The "Bydlo" Movement

1. The word *pesante* in the tempo marking is probably the most important indication. Taken in two (not four), this could go well at about ♩ = 50. At certain points, you may need to shift briefly to four, depending on the experience your musicians have.
2. The principal difficulty here is controlling the crescendo that begins at bar 21, given the large instrumentation. It is not easy to maintain balance across this large force while still allowing the flexibility each important voice requires. Conserve room yourself—keep the size of your baton motion moderate until you enlarge it to the *fff*. Do not allow your musicians to reach the summit too early.
3. Even at the peak of that buildup, you still must have the physical freedom to show the accents that are present.
4. The decrescendo (from bar 44 on) is the same problem in reverse. Don't cut back too far too soon, and don't let your players do so, either.
5. "Invite" the tuba to continue its solo at measure 47.
6. Your cue to the muted first horn at measure 57 is very important. Horn entrances are fragile; encourage the player, but do not *demand* anything with a sharp gesture.
7. If this is your first experience working with harp, be especially conscious of balance. Take care that enough of the harp sound is present.

Conducting the Leidzèn Transcription

This arrangement for concert band presents the same sorts of conducting problems as the orchestral transcription. The instrumentation changes, but the musical shapes and structures remain the same. Again, a principal difficulty for the student conductor is remembering how to find each instrument on these complex score formats; just as experienced conductors know where to look for the horns and the violas on the orchestral page and do not have to hunt for them each time, the complete conductor knows where the saxes and the euphoniums are in a band manuscript and does not have to search.

Comparative glances at the orchestra and band scores suggest that Leidzèn was well aware of Ravel's version. Leidzèn did not simply return to the Mussorgsky original and transcribe it for band. Many coincidences of voicing imply that the band arrangement is a third step (not a second) in this evolution. Like Ravel, Leidzèn has been faithful to the exact notes and rhythms Mussorgsky wrote (although he has added a conjunction to the original tempo marking of "Bydlo," which now is headed "Sempre moderato *e* pesante").

Let us look specifically at some of the revoicings used here (see Example 16-5[6]). Note that Leidzèn assigns the opening line of the "Promenade" not to the trumpet but to the principal solo instrument of the *band's* brass section, the first cornet (although the trumpet is available to him in the band, just as it was to Ravel in the orchestra). His band trumpets, instead, take over some of the pitches Ravel's horns played. At measure 9, the lines (beginning on concert A-flat, E-flat, and A-flat) that Ravel had allocated to the first violins, violas, and second violins are given by Leidzèn to the first, second, and third clarinet sections. *These substitutions reflect the fundamental functions of ensemble sections: The same role normally played by the violins and violas of the orchestra tends to go to the three clarinet sections of the band, and the responsibilities of the orchestral trumpets are met in the band texture by the cornets (not the trumpets).* So it goes, section by section.

Looking, in turn, at the "Bydlo" movement (Example 16-6[7]), we find that *even with more than one tuba present,* Leidzèn assigns the solo line at measure 1 not to a tuba but to the euphonium (doubled by the tenor saxophone); this is because in the absence of whole orchestral sections of 'cellos and contrabasses, he must save his brass basses, bassoons, and bass clarinet for the low-tessitura "motor" sonorities. At measure 38, when the first theme returns, we find the clarinets I assuming the responsibilities not of Ravel's violins I but, rather, of his violas; here, the ability of the band's *best* clarinetists to play sonorously and musically in their low *chalumeau* register makes the firsts a good choice for this voicing. Leidzèn's employment of harp in a band is a bit unusual, but it would be difficult to produce this plucked-string effect any other way. (If you have no harpist available, one alternative would be to use a piano with a damping cloth or strip laid over the strings.)

---

[6]Mussorgsky-Leidzèn, *Pictures at an Exhibition* (New York: Carl Fischer, 1941), pp. 5–9.
[7]Mussorgsky-Leidzèn, *Pictures at an Exhibition*, pp. 31–39.

Example 16-5   Mussorgsky-Leidzèn: *Pictures at an Exhibition,* "Promenade," complete

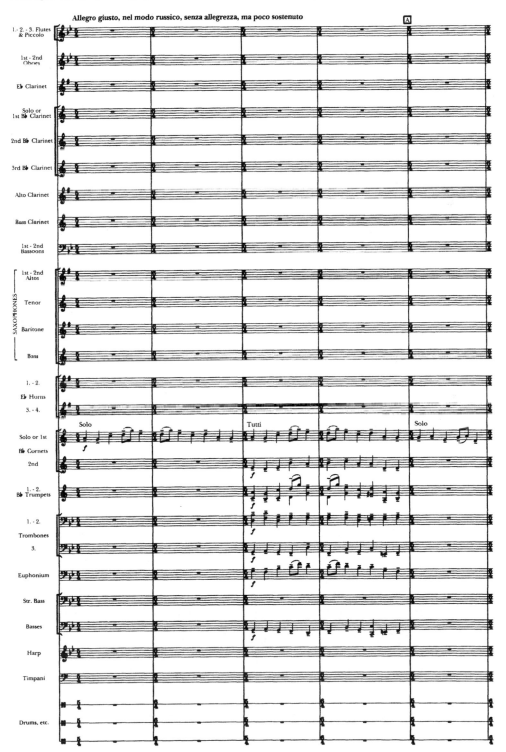

Example 16-5 *(cont.)*

Example 16-5 (*cont.*)

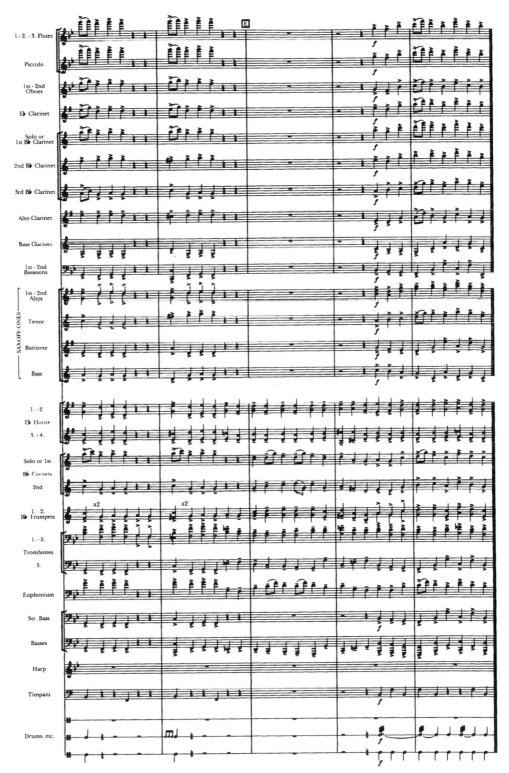

Example 16-6   Mussorgsky-Leidzèn: *Pictures at an Exhibition*, "Bydlo," complete

Example 16-6 *(cont.)*

Example 16-6 *(cont.)*

Example 16-6 *(cont.)*

Example 16-6 *(cont.)*

Choices of tempos for the Leidzèn transcription are essentially the same as those for the Ravel. The other conducting problems—the beat patterns, the crescendos and diminuendos, the accent and tenuto markings, and the rest—will differ little from your interpretation of the orchestral version.[8]

BACKGROUND AND PERSPECTIVES: HINDEMITH AND HIS CRAFT

As twentieth-century composers moved further away from traditional structures and practices, each major figure found he needed some sort of more-or-less arbitrary foundation for his designs, a matrix, a "system" that would guide him through the myriad of pitch and rhythm alternatives open at any given movement.[9] The "serial" approach taken by Schoenberg and his disciples, the ethnomusicological ideas of Bartók, and the American nationalism of Copland, Gershwin, and Harris are examples of the systems various composers developed; another was the comprehensive theory of tonal relationships developed by Paul Hindemith and described most fully in his two-volume *Unterweisung im Tonsatz* (translated as *The Craft of Musical Composition*). This treatise was not completed until 1939, but the theories on which it was based were forming in Hindemith's mind, and being tested in his practices, years earlier.

If it is true that many of the premises of twentieth-century music were neo-Romantic, it is also true that there were classical viewpoints put forth by some; one composer who exhibited such attitudes was Hindemith. His use of traditional forms like the sonata and theme-and-variations, his facility with fugal counterpoint, and his postures on aesthetics were illustrative of the influence of neoclassicism on his music.

In 1927, the same year Hindemith was appointed to the composition faculty of the Berlin Hochschule für Musik, he wrote the *Spielmusik*, for Strings, Flutes, and Oboes, Op. 43, No. 1 (Example 16-7).[10] Intended for a relatively small orchestra, it is a specimen of his commitment to writing *Gebrauchsmusik* (i.e., music that can easily be programmed in as many circumstances as possible). His reputation eventually would rest on such works as *Mathis der Maler, Symphonic Metamorphosis,* the contrapuntal *Ludus Tonalis,* the *Requiem: When Lilacs Last in the Dooryard Bloom'd,* the *Mass,* and his catalog of solo sonatas (at least one for each of the orchestral instruments), and, especially, on his influential teaching. To complement that teaching, he wrote a set of widely used textbooks.

---

[8]You will find a list of additional Romantic instrumental music suitable for student conductors in Appendix B.

[9]Review as necessary the historical and theoretical background on twentieth-century music presented in Chapter 12, and consult the general summary of twentieth-century style and performance practice in Appendix B.

[10]Paul Hindemith, *Spielmusik*, Op. 43, No. 1 (Mainz: B. Schott's Söhne, 1927), pp. 11–12. (At our publication date, permission to reprint is restricted to partial movements; hence, we provide here measures 1–12 only. Please see your library for the complete score.)

Example 16-7   Hindemith: *Spielmusik,* Op. 43, No. 1, second movement, mm. 1–12

Example 16-7 *(cont.)*

Hindemith, Spielmusik, Op. 43. Copyright 1927 by B. Schott's Soehne, Mainz. Copyright Renewed. All Rights Reserved. Used by permission of European American Music Distributors Corporation, sole U.S. and Canadian agent for B. Schott's Soehne.

Paul Hindemith: *Spielmusik*, Op. 43, No. 1, Second Movement

The "Mäβig bewegte Halbe" that opens the *Spielmusik* is a spirited mix of staccatos and slurs moving through a bright two; the finale, also in two, is quick and rather heavily accented. Both use the full instrumentation.

Hindemith cast the second movement in four and omitted one oboe and both flutes, assigning solo parts to the other oboe and a viola; the string body has the two violin sections and the violas doubled throughout, while the 'cellos and contrabasses play always in octaves. How many strings should you use? To some extent, that can reflect your situation, but you must be careful not to let the solo instruments be overpowered by the doubled sections. In the ideal circumstance, 7-6-4-4-3 might be the right string distribution. (A minimum might be 4-4-2-2-1.)

The quarter note carries the basic pulse here, but the most important metric factor is the Bach-like constant eighth note, unbroken from the beginning to the final measure. For a twentieth-century composition, the meter (in all three movements) is unusually consistent; only one $\frac{3}{4}$ bar (measure 25) interrupts the $\frac{4}{4}$ meter. The rhythms are somewhat complex: Although the individual parts are straightforward enough, the overlay of triplet sixteenths in the solo viola on the duple patterns of the other voices creates two-against-three relationships.

In assessing Hindemith's choice to give a viola this florid, rather virtuosic line, it is worth remembering that he was himself a fine violist. Approaching an instrument with the insight of an artist gives a composer a great advantage in writing for it.

Hindemith's palette of pitches is as great as that of the serialists; he uses all twelve tones of the chromatic scale (not counting repeated notes) within the first fifteen pitches (that is, within nine beats). There is much conjunct motion—the lines are not as jagged as in much music of the twentieth century—and some conservative melodic discipline: Observe that the minor seventh in the violins and violas from B-flat to the A-flat on the first beat of measure 2 "resolves by step in the opposite direction," the traditional Renaissance procedure. At the same time, however, all sorts of leaps are permitted to occur consecutively; note, for example, the initial notes of the solo viola (G–B–F–A), the last three reached by skips in the same direction. Perhaps the melodic interval he uses least is the tritone, which may be outlined metrically (see the G–D-flat relationship on the first and third beats of the violins-and-violas, bar 1); its appearance as a melodic interval is minimal here.

There is a clear tonal center for this movement: It is G-natural. It is heard in three octaves at the very beginning; its prominence is reinforced by its use as the closing of the first phrase of the string body in bar 3, and it returns to terminate the form (solo parts, measure 37). At the same time, in keeping with his theories, Hindemith emphasizes D, the pitch a perfect fifth above that G tonic. The first skip in the violins-and-violas is to D; the solo oboe first opens on D, and its first phrase ends there. The first of the three sections of the movement ends on D in measure 18, and (after a contrasting unit) the final section commences in bar 26 with a reprise of the opening string phrase, transposed to D. That phrase returns again on G in measure 32, on its way to the final cadence. Thus, Hindemith's design is a standard *ABA'*, with closed tonality.

In a sense, "line" seems to be more consequential here than "sonority." Any vertical interval, or any combination of intervals, can be used harmonically, but Hindemith controls the metric placement and the "resolution" of his tritones precisely.

In this melody-dominated process, all the textures he creates are contrapuntal. At the opening, we find a two-part fabric of the violins and violas against the 'cellos and basses. Next comes the two-part counterpoint between the two soloists, supported intermittently by the two voices of the string body. The *B* section is scored in three voices (the two soloists, plus the violins-and-violas). The *A'* unit brings the two-part string body back together as an underpinning for the solo instruments.

Conducting Hindemith's Spielmusik

The tempo markings here may seem strange to you, but they are typical of Hindemith. (You will find this sort of direction in *Requiem: When Lilacs Last in the Dooryard Bloom'd* and in his *Mass*.) The marking *Langsam schreitende Viertel* ("With a slow, striding quarter note") suggests a tempo in four at ♩ = 46–52. Keep in mind the triplet-sixteenths in the solo viola when you decide this. (You need not worry so much about the length of the oboe lines, for oboists can carry very long phrases.) Once the tempo is set, keep it steady, for the sake of those triplets.

The intervening markings give a sure impression of the atmosphere Hindemith wishes this movement to convey: *Immer ruhig* ("Always tranquil") at measure 18, *Beruhigen* ("Quietly") at bars 24–25, *Wie anfangs* ("As at the Beginning") at bar 26, *Ruhiger* ("Quieter") at measure 34, and *Immer langsamer* ("Ever slower") at measure 36, together with the *ruhig und gleichmäßig* indication for the solo viola in bar 3 ("tranquil and even"). His dynamic shifts are expressive and reflect a careful shaping of sound.

The conductor really is "accompanying" two solo instruments here, almost as in a concerto. Avoid controlling the unaccompanied solo spots with too firm a hand; it is enough to mark the pattern lightly, for the sake of the other players. Help the soloists as necessary in rehearsals, but do not hamper good people in performance. Be certain that your own sense of the rhythm of the soloists is exact in places like measure 20; don't lose your metric concentration at such points. You risk imprecision of beat that will cause the underlying half notes to lose their vitality, with the result that ensemble clarity will be lost also.

Observe these specific details.

1. Note the tenuto-with-dot articulation. These pitches, as you know, are longer than staccatos. Do not stop your beat, as you would do for a pure staccato; the forward motion must "stride," as Hindemith says, with longer notes; you could use an almost-subdivided gesture, however—a very slight break, but not a full one.
2. All Hindemith's dynamics should be shown in your stick.
3. Let the soloists manage the final ritard. Cue the oboe reassuringly in measure 36 if you must, but only if necessary.
4. A constant feeling of the subdivision is necessary. You may have to show your musicians the eighth note at certain points (particularly in difficult or risky passages) for the sake of precise ensemble work.

If you have the opportunity, compare this structure with the rest of Hindemith's *Spielmusik*. Learn the other two movements, as well, and come to view this one in that context. The whole work lasts only a few minutes, but it is clean-cut and charming.[11]

---

[11]You will find a list of additional twentieth-century instrumental music suitable for student conductors in Appendix B

CHAPTER 17

Planning, Programming, and Administration

You have gained from your studies thus far a comprehensive view of the processes of conducting choral and instrumental forces and of the techniques necessary to do so. Now it is time to test yourself against some of the greatest masterpieces. In each of Chapters 21–25, you can earn through study an encompassing understanding of one major, multimovement work, and prepare yourself to conduct it. Before you attempt all this, however, let us look in more detail at the fundamental functions of the conductor, onstage and off. In this chapter, our purpose is to look at the conductor as Strategist—that is, as planner and manager for a musical ensemble or institution.

MORE CONDUCTING THEORY
Planning

Which comes first: programming (that is, choosing which works you are going to perform) or study of ensemble literature? The answer is sometimes the one, and sometimes the other, for you must know something about a work before you can program it, and, on the other hand, you often will choose to schedule a work about which you do not yet know enough. The balance point between these two approaches is planning.

Any organization needs an overall developmental plan. Based on an assessment of the current state of the institution, such a plan compares it with a visionary image of where it could or should be a certain number of months or years from now. You can keep long-range goals realistic if you establish short-term tactical objectives in stages (periods of weeks, or months, or years, depending on how far ahead you are planning), measuring those objectives against the practical limitations of the situation. The whole process is rather like trying to plow across a wide valley in a perfectly straight line; you need to pick out interim milestones directly between you and the goal point, aiming for each of those objectives in its turn. In life, as in farming, it is too easy to get turned away from the real purpose by momentary incidents. A long-range plan is a means of maintaining perspective.

In musical terms, your goal may be to build an organization more capable in certain ways than it now is, and then to use that ensemble to present works of a specific sophistication. Your objectives, then, will enumerate specific skills you and your musicians must improve, abilities to be demonstrated in performances of increasingly difficult repertoire. In administrative terms—in secondary, supportive purposes, that is—you need to use personnel, budgets, public relations, your music library, and other such institutional aids to enable you and your ensemble(s) to reach toward your goals. In short, your overall plan must foresee artistic stages and administrative logistics, matters both of music and of management.

Making such plans takes time, thought, and experience. Get to know your situation well—be patient in so doing—and then proceed. If you lack experience (or even if you do not), ask good people for advice.

MATTERS OF MUSIC

Judging the Potential and the Needs of Your Ensemble

One of the more difficult things for a young professional (used to participating in a capable college-level ensemble) is to make realistic judgments about what students or amateurs can do in a high school band, a church choir, or a community orchestra. (We all have seen an unfulfilled Toscanini trying to turn a third-grade chorus into the Robert Shaw Chorale.) Many recent music graduates choose literature for their high school ensembles from the easier works they have been doing during their four years in college. This approach has both positive and negative aspects: It may be one reason some high schools are improving the quality of their repertoire markedly, but it also can result in some ill-suited programming.

Make an objective, precise, well-grounded assessment of the musicians in your organization. Hear them individually, by all means. Check their sight reading and their general musicianship. See what they have been performing. Gauge which of them are secure enough to be assigned solos. Recruit other strong people.

In determining what to program, then, there are three primary criteria.

1. What do your musicians *wish* to do? What do they like, and what is familiar to them? What do they think is "important" music?
2. What do *you* wish to do? What would be good experience for you, and good for your career? What do you do well? What do you like?
3. Far more significant than those two considerations, however, is the third: *Speaking as*

a trained professional, what music is important enough to be performed but still within the abilities of your musicians?

As a professional, you are being paid partly to make this judgment, not to share it with amateurs. You may wish—even need—to consider their likes and dislikes, but you are not employed to bow to the "least common denominator" within your ensemble.

One target you should aim for in programming is *balance*. **If you find that you continually avoid conducting the music of a particular style period, force yourself to address this shortcoming;** stretch yourself by actively searching for and programming works that fill this gap.

Whether you are conducting a great symphony orchestra or a junior high school band, the choices you make will be cyclic. You will want to look at the whole catalog of types of works, style periods, individual masters, soloists by medium, seasonal literature, and other categories. All these varieties of repertoire should be presented and, after a full cycle (four years, or whatever applies in your case), will begin to reappear (including some works so worthwhile that they deserve regular repetition).

By including in your repertoire music from long ago, you help to cross the chasm that separates us from the ideas of our ancestors. Each generation needs to be taught by the people of other times and other places, for all have something of value to tell us. As you have seen in earlier chapters, masterpieces of choral and instrumental music from at least the past five hundred years deserve your attention.

All of us try to find music that we have never performed (or even that no one has ever done). In the choral repertoire, this is relatively easy, for it is so vast; in band (especially) and orchestral literature, however, "standard" works tend to be repeated more frequently. Even so, resolve that you will discover *twice* as many pieces of music each year that are new to you as the number of familiar ones you repeat.

One critical need is *change*. No matter how distinguished the literature you are performing, rehearsals must vary and offer your musicians a blueprint for gradual development. The very finest players in the very best orchestras have limitations; they are not familiar with certain style periods, perhaps. Even senior members of these orchestras can grow if you approach the problem wisely and sensitively. Whoever your musicians are, the more they develop, the more you will have to plan for further evolution.

Assessing the Needs and Receptivity of Your Audience

Make the same careful judgments about the experience and *abilities* of your audiences as *listeners*. Look for talent in the box seats, as well. Challenge your audiences! Educate them.

The same three criteria discussed in the preceding section apply here: Consider the wishes of the listeners, and give weight to your own wishes and needs as an individual; tip the balance, however, toward your professional assessment of what repertoire is appropriate to the situation. This, again, is in the ultimate sense the reason you are assigned to your post.

Keep a sense of proportion in these decisions. We remember one church choir conductor who made regular efforts to subject his stodgy, conservative congregation to radical, new church music; his scheme was to sandwich a shocking anthem one Sunday between well-loved or traditional choices the weeks before and after; that way, the complainers could not justify *growing* indignation—only occasional wrath.[1]

In educational settings, your audience usually expects that some of the music you are performing is being done not to communicate with them but, rather, to instruct your students. In that context, they will accept music they personally find meaningless, dull, or even radical. In the professional concert hall, however, the listener regards almost everything as performed for her or him exclusively; ticket buyers give little thought to whether the literature performed for them is good experience for the performers or for the conductor.

Onstage excitement can be infectious, nevertheless. We find that if our ensembles are exhilarated about the performance of a difficult and perhaps controversial work, their enthusiasm often spreads to the audience, as well. Just don't confuse challenges for your ensemble with the need of your audience to find meaning in the music they hear.

We all set out when young to change the attitudes and musical appetites of the world of listeners. We can see so much that is but should not be, and so many things that are not but should be. We have our own favorites and are irritated to discover that not everyone shares our experience or our enthusiasms. In fact, it is only a little in our power to affect the attitudes of our audiences. Too many other influences reach them, and many should. Each of us does what he or she can.

Variety in repertoire may bring new faces to your audience. Remember that you are dealing with a rather small segment of the population. (The audience for major American orchestras, for example, once adjusted for population growth, apparently remained relatively stable for much of the twentieth century, in spite of energetic marketing efforts.[2]) You want to challenge the public, excite them, teach them, but *you also want to find ways to enlarge this audience pool*. It takes careful choices, cunningly programmed, to manage this metamorphosis.

Your listeners' expectations with respect to concert duration also must be considered, of course. We can say that orchestral audiences, in general, anticipate rather lengthy programs, whereas those who attend choral performances are ac-

[1]Henry Pleasants notes that most twentieth-century orchestra conductors have used this same approach, by "sneaking" contemporary music "into the concert hall under the coattails" of Beethoven and Brahms. See Henry Pleasants, *The Agony of Modern Music* (New York: Simon & Schuster, 1955), p. 7.

[2]See William J. Baumol and William G. Bowen, *Performing Arts: The Economic Dilemma* (New York: Twentieth Century Fund, 1966), beginning on p. 35, and especially pp. 60–63.

customed to shorter ones. Concert band (wind ensemble) audiences probably fall into a middle ground in this regard. (The authors believe, by the way, that educational institutions ought frequently to present more than one ensemble per concert. "Mixing and matching" large groups, chamber forces, and various genres onstage helps draw a larger audience and broadens the interests of those who favor a particular kind of music. Try one evening in which the entire orchestra, band, or choir never appears together, as we have done: This will give you a chance to program chamber works of all shapes and sizes within a traditional (large) aggregation, without using too large a force, and will bring real variety to your repertoire; it will give many of your people new challenges.)

Choosing Soloists

In a professional situation, soloists (concerto artists, and the like) are hired on the basis of reputation or by audition. In seeking new faces, a conductor may schedule private hearings in one or more cities, thus identifying individuals to be contracted for solo responsibilities.

In collegiate settings, soloists generally are chosen in competitive auditions. The conductor may hear them alone or may call together a committee of two or three colleagues to make the selections; the latter is the better choice whenever any appearance of favoritism constitutes a risk to the director. High school and college soloists usually are members of the ensemble with which they appear. Here, your experience in individual hearings and rehearsals may give you enough evidence to select soloists.

Understudies are essential in opera and musical theater for all major roles (the economic hazard of cancellation being too great otherwise), and may be appropriate in standard concert work, especially when you have more than one person capable of doing the part; this can be a way of giving inexperienced people a risk-free opportunity for growth.

Once you have chosen soloists, your next duty is to see that they are prepared. *Coaching* is important at any level of performance and should not be left to chance. (In great opera houses and symphony halls, it is done by assistant conductors.) This is the point at which a soloist, no matter how talented, learns to conform to the concepts of your planned interpretation. Do not fix in your ears too rigid an idea of the type of sound and the musical ideas you want from your soloists. If you have closed your mind, no performers are likely to be able to show you their real potential unless they happen to match exactly the qualities you already have in mind.

MATTERS OF MANAGEMENT

Finance

Money is an important consideration in the management of every musical organization, from the most modest volunteer choir to the greatest (and most expensive) opera company. You will have responsibility for some sort of financial planning and oversight, whatever your own situation. You may not have complete control of the funds, but, as conductor, you certainly will have a major voice in determining the priorities for their expenditure.

Know the budget! (Help draft it, if you can, and keep your own close watch over it.) *A budget is itself a planning document and thus gives you opportunities to shape and pursue your long-term goals and immediate objectives.* Study it carefully on both its income and its expense sides. If you have a business manager working for you or with you, do not leave the mysteries of this crucial document entirely to that individual. Make budget management a team effort in your situation, even if the responsibility is completely yours. Others who understand the financial picture (your musicians included) may have useful experience and may be able to help in certain valuable ways. Let them know the needs of the situation, and encourage them to help solve the problems.

Start by identifying your *realistic* needs. What must you have to achieve your objectives for the year to come? What about personnel (full-time or part-time)? What music must you purchase if you are to do as many new works as we have been recommending? What about advertising expenditures (in various media)? Do you have instruments that will need repairs and pianos that must be tuned? What about purchases of new instruments and equipment? Are you renting rehearsal space and concert halls?

On the other side of the ledger, examine what your income experience has been in recent years; institutional allocations and ticket prices tend to increase every year (generally modestly), so you probably can calculate some increment. There may be sources of additional income you can create: repeat performances on other sites, contributions and patronage from enthusiastic supporters, sales of peripheral items (specially designed concert posters, for example, or recordings). See what income can be obtained immediately, and, more important, put together a plan to develop resources over a period of years.

Does all this add up to a manageable balance of income and expenses? If your expenses are too great, look for items that can be postponed; just as income resources can be developed over a period of years, so can allocations. Which of your proposed expenditures can be delayed with the least effect? Be patient, and use your musical talents to prove that the costs you are generating are worth it to those who are paying the bills.

Library Resources

Institutions vary a great deal, and so do their budgetary situations, but every musical organization depends heavily on an adequate and growing library. You must acquire works you have not done before, for the sake of your musicians and your audience; you must obtain new and better editions of familiar works; you must replace damaged and missing parts; and you must purchase study scores. All this must stored adequately somewhere; that means that space, shelving, and storage boxes or envelopes are required, as you know.

Organization of the library is the first consideration, for music accumulates rapidly and, if it is not properly managed, becomes lost in heaps. Shelving is not enough. You must have some sort of cataloging process that can tell you where to find a particular item quickly.

In a smaller situation, this can be done with a pair of card files—one listing works by composer, the other listing them by title. Each work can be assigned an arbitrary number, and each can be shelved in that order.

In larger organizations, computerization is the answer these days. New software programs are appearing; a glance at a monitor can tell you where to find the piece of music you are seeking, and which parts, or how many copies, are available. More intricate cataloging like this allows you to "tab" works by the size and nature of the forces required (identifying music for brass ensemble, for instance, or for women's chorus); you can create rosters of seasonal music (Christmas, football marching band, or baccalaureate and commencement services); and you can categorize repertoire by difficulty (easy, moderately difficult, tough, almost impossible). Remember, too, that this library is not just for you. Others may use it now, and someday you will have a successor. Avoid cryptic abbreviations and undecipherable handwriting. A solid library is a lasting monument to judgment, organization, and good taste.

If you have a competent music librarian available to you, the catalog numbers you use can follow the Library of Congress ("LC") design. This has enormous advantages if your collection is a large one, for this method is systematic and detailed.

Circulation procedures are as important as cataloging. (If the music goes out and never returns, there is no reason to keep records!) Someone must check incoming parts and copies to see if they have been lost or damaged or have markings that need erasures.

If your library is small enough to be immediately adjacent to your rehearsal area, you may be able to use the English choir system, in which student librarians pull each envelope of music at the moment it is needed, distribute the parts, collect them immediately after use, and return them to the shelves while the next item is being issued. This approach keeps all the music neatly organized all the time.

Larger libraries must have their own rooms, however, and may be in another building. In such cases, more formal sign-out and check-in procedures are required. The ideal of immediate access remains the same.

You must have some system that holds the users of the parts responsible for their return in proper condition. If you do not, you will find yourself purchasing (literally) dozens of duplicate copies when you reuse an item.

How you view the marking of parts depends somewhat on your situation. After all, notation is only a set of incomplete instructions and cannot include all possible interpretations; if the printed music is to signal to the performers' eyes the intent of both the composer and the conductor, it must be edited before each rehearsal block or during these sessions. *Any rehearsal time that can be saved by advance editing is manna from heaven,* but not all marking can be done beforehand. All instrumental musicians must mark bowings, phrasings, and the like; most choir members probably should follow suit. Even if you are conducting a chorus that always memorizes everything, individual editings can serve as reminders from rehearsal to rehearsal of instructions you gave or mistakes the singer made; this makes your rehearsals more efficient. (The authors' practice is to *require* that students bring *pencils* [not pens] to every session. We encourage liberal, detailed marking of parts in rehearsals, so that each copy is personalized to the needs of that performer.)

Acquisition is the complex process of ordering, purchasing, receiving, cataloging, and shelving music you want to add to your library. Music orders must be coordinated with your budget. Obtaining them in a public institution generally must follow a regulated requisition system. Once they arrive, new purchases must be examined for completeness, stamped with identifying markings ("Rockville Community Orchestra"), assigned a number from your cataloging system, and (with choral music) given an individual copy number.

Your acquisitions in a given year should fit your overall developmental plan. Purchase what you need now, but also acquire music that fills in gaps in your library. Judge each order you place in the perspective of long-range value as well as immediate usefulness.

It may be best in some cases to rent music. This is appropriate particularly when an item you are unlikely to reuse soon is expensive. The cost may be one-quarter to one-third, or more, of the purchase price. (Rental parts must be cleaned up before their return, of course, and lost or damaged copies replaced.) You can gain income, too, by renting your own holdings at these same rates.

Public Relations

Another matter of significance is obtaining public attention for your program. You cannot assume that because you are doing important music well, people will come to hear it. Even in a school situation, you no longer can expect—as you could have in small-town America fifty years ago—that all the parents will attend. You have to publicize your activities.

Distinguish in your mind between publicity and advertising. *Advertising* costs money. Whether you buy time on radio or television (sold by the fraction of a minute), purchase "display ads" (sold by the column inch), design and produce posters, or print "flyers" (circulars for handout or mail distribution), your attempt to reach the public will require expenditures.

Publicity comes free. Press releases (written, double-spaced descriptions of coming events intended to serve as the basis for a newspaper or broadcast story) cost nothing but your time; the difficulty is to get them in print or on the air, for you are competing with the whole world for space and time, and editors decide what to use on the basis of its "newsworthiness." Radio and television stations are required by license regulations to broadcast public service announcements (PSAs) for community and nonprofit organizations, and they will often use short "releases" for this reason.

Although you may not think of them that way, concert programs are part of your public relations effort. Even in an uncomplicated school music situation, you should make every effort to have this "advertising" (for such it is) look as polished, positive, and professional as possible. Programs represent you and your efforts when parents or patrons carry them home with them after the performance; if they are well designed, with clean art (graphics and photographs), have wide, neat margins, are accurate and complete, and are free of "typos" (printing errors), then they represent you well. Try to find the funds to have your programs typeset and printed, or at least have them prepared on a letter-quality computer printer and reproduced on an offset machine. Don't let them look cheap! And get the names of your musicians right, exactly as they want them to appear!

For some organizations, by the way, the sale of advertising in their concert programs is an important source of additional revenues. After-concert restaurants, other music, theater, and fine arts groups, and businesses interested in reaching the same people who buy your tickets may want to purchase space in your attractive programs. (Just be sure the additional printing you must do to reproduce these ads is not so expensive as to eat up your apparent profits.)

To use public relations effectively, you need to have an annual operational blueprint for publicity, and this whole field should form part of your overall developmental plan. Try to decide exactly who your "market" is (that is, what segment of the public you especially are trying to reach). Then choose which of the media are likely to give you the best results for your money and work. Get acquainted with media staff members. Tell them what you are trying to accomplish, and ask for their advice and help.

Build these planned promotional activities into your annual budget. (For some organizations, public relations expenditures can represent 10 percent or more of total operational expenses.) Check to see whether the advertising you are buying is bringing in enough additional ticket sales to justify its cost. If it is not, then change approaches.

Personnel

With all this managerial work, how are you to find time for study and conducting? In most smaller programs (a standard one-rehearsal-per-week church choir, for instance), library matters, budgeting, public relations, and the like require few administrative hours. In larger organizations, where these burdens are made heavier by the very size of the operation, you must have additional staff to support you. Depending on the scale of the institution, here is the degree of assistance you are likely to need:

1. In even the simplest situation, you will want a librarian. The bigger the organization, the more professional she or he must be.
2. In a choral position, a skilled accompanist (a paid professional, if possible) is essential. With some instrumental groups (marching bands, some concert bands, jazz ensembles, and the like) and with vocal jazz groups or "show choirs," a capable arranger is essential.
3. If your choral program includes a Broadway-style group or a show choir, you will need a choreographer.
4. For large ensembles and multiensemble organizations, you will need one or more assistant conductors to run sectional rehearsals, sessions when you must be away, and segments of dress rehearsals (so you can listen out in the concert hall). Assistants coach soloists and perform such other duties as you find appropriate. If you operate your own performance hall, a stage manager, a house manager, a box-office staff, ushers, and a technical crew may be required.
5. For sophisticated programs of this size, a secretary becomes a necessity (for correspondence, bookkeeping, telephone coverage, and other office activities).
6. In a major organization, a business manager, administrative assistants, a public relations specialist, a professional music librarian, and other officers should take over budgetary, promotional, and other support functions, leaving you relatively free to oversee the administration and to prepare yourself to conduct.

The point at which any one of these people moves from part-time to full-time status depends, of course, on the institution and the success of your program. More employees will mean more responsibility for you. Keep your priorities clear in your own mind, and maintain them; the first of these surely continues to be your wish to program and present great music as well as you can perform it.

CHAPTER 18

Interpretation: Expression as an Outgrowth of Style Study

Once you have decided what it is you wish to program, you must prepare to conduct it. In Chapters 10–12 and 14–16, we led you step by step through this sort of preparation several times, but the process is not really that simple. Much of the historical background and theoretical character of each work was given to you in those earlier passages; in real life, however, you must find all that material and make that examination on your own. This chapter is intended to define in detail the stages in such important groundwork, and then to relate those results to the formulation of your interpretations.

MORE CONDUCTING THEORY
The Changing Basis for Interpretation

A few years ago a famed composer is said to have remarked, "You don't really like that early music—before Bach—do you? It's so . . . incomplete!" Schooled in the later years of the nineteenth century, when the unspoken assumption was that Art, like Technology, was progressive (that the artists of each new generation, and each unfolding century, were creating a more complex and sophisticated aesthetic expression than those who had come before them), he believed almost unthinkingly that he was "more advanced" than his predecessors (except, perhaps, Bach). He was condescending, in short, to all the geniuses of all the centuries leading up to his own. If a phrase of chant lacked meter, it seemed "primitive" to him. If Josquin's chord lacked a third, it sounded "incomplete." This, bluntly put, is "cultural bias."

Today it is generally believed that each artistic style is a legitimate outgrowth of its own time and that, as such, it is not an improvement over forerunners—it is only different. One should not assume, for example, that the Architecture that was the perfect expression of the religious faith and aspirations of the eleventh and twelfth centuries—the Gothic cathedral of stone—somehow is inferior aesthetically to the skyscrapers of the steel-and-glass-bound twentieth century. The Gothic world expressed itself in its Art, and so does our age.

Your ears should be open to the music of each era, and your mind should be seeking, through that music, to understand the inhabitants of long-dead centuries, striving to learn from them (just as you would seek knowledge of a visitor from a galaxy light-years away).

It is for this reason, then, that it is necessary for you to learn as much as you can about the background and indigenous qualities of each work before you conduct it. *You must seek to place yourself in the world of its composer, striving to think as he thought.* Then you will be better able to express the music he wrote.

Good jobs always are hard to get, and the successful candidate for an important position today must be very well balanced; she or he must have musical talent, analytic skills, historical comprehension, and a clear understanding of performance practice, period by period, through music history. There is much more of this scholarship for you to study today than ever before. (As detailed research comes out of the great university centers day after day, that last factor—experience with performance practice—becomes ever more important, and today's audiences are more aware than ever before of the ineffectiveness of, say, a Classical performance that is "too Romantic," or vice versa.)[1]

This commitment to musicology is obvious today in presentations of the great orchestral and choral repertoire. "Band literature" as we usually think of it does not extend back four, or five, or six centuries; the wind music of the Renaissance and the centuries since is there, nevertheless, and offers an enrichment to the repertoire of those who are learning how to perform it; conductors talk now, moreover, about "how Sousa interpreted his marches" a century ago, and Sousa's own performance practice is being researched. It may surprise you to learn that style study is becoming just as important in that most transient of all music—jazz: As "jazz classics" are recreated today in concert halls, colleges, and high schools, more and more emphasis is placed on accurate performance practices.

THE INFLUENCE OF MUSICAL STRUCTURE
ON INTERPRETATION

Any conductor is working (in essence) with sound stretched over time, from the articulation of a single eighth note to the unfolding of an hour-long symphony. She or he is continually balancing "vertical" sonorities (each isolated in a mo-

---

[1]This is true at every level: High school conductors who send audition tapes to the selection committees for national conferences are confronting a greater need to know and express something about the historical setting and performance practice of their repertoire.

ment of that time) but also is drawing out the continuity of those isolated chords over the "horizontal" flow; this is the whole structure of the work. One of the authors often says to his students, "Everyone can conduct from the beginning to the end of a piece of music. The interesting thing is 'how'—how to get from this point of the structure to that spot over there, and *how to do it in a unique and illuminating way* that justifies your having conducted again a work that many others have performed and will perform."

What do you see in that passage between "here" and "there"? What indications has the composer written that signal you *how* to proceed expressively through the form at hand? What do these combinations of sounds (in a purely acoustical sense) "mean"? **Your task is not to exhibit the music but to clarify it. The greatest conductors sometimes can find in the most complex and opaque forms the simplest answers—the essence of "meaning" in these works.**

The Historical Setting and the Internal Elements

To understand a form in these terms requires that you have studied it thoroughly, of course. It comes in the notated matrix we call a "score," as you know, but it is wrapped in a historical setting.

Do you remember our discussion of the "spiral study" in Chapter 1? The principle of this procedure was to begin with the work, find and read a basic background source about it or its composer, move on to three or four other sources (other texts on that composer, on other musicians of the period, on musical style within that era, on the music of that composer's predecessors, on the social values of his age and of the age before his), and from all these to others, until one had learned as much as one could about the environment in which that work was created.

The thoroughness required here may surprise you. Knowing a score means more than just "knowing the notes"; it requires of you a knowledge of what is inside—or, rather, *behind*—the notated approximation of the *music that was in its creator's mind*, and thus it leads to a *comprehension* of the work. In studying the environment of a composition, we are acquiring insights that will help us to answer our own questions about enigmas in the notation.

There is more "external evidence" to be gained from analyses of other music by the same composer, by musicians of the time, by those of earlier eras who are thought to have influenced him or his teacher, and so on through another spiral study.

Then there is the "internal evidence." This comes from an exhaustive theoretical analysis of the work itself, in every one of its parameters. Here we must beware of "prescriptive analysis"; in spite of everything we know and are learning about other music of the time, we must "let this work speak for itself." We must not prejudge its contents. Only when its elements are all clear to us can we begin to compare its totality with other such works.

Finally, there is the matter of "performance practice." Our research must include a careful examination of the evidence available to us about the ways in which this composer and his contemporaries "read" the notation (and "between the lines" of that notation) in their own era. In what sort of hall would this have been performed? What were its acoustical characteristics? How large a force would have performed the work? Would "modern" instruments, or "ancient" ones have been used? How would the audience have behaved? Were they focused on the music, or was it "background"? What do we know about tempos in the period? What about ornamentation? Dynamics? Expressive freedom with ritards, crescendos, and the like? How might all these considerations—and all the internal and external evidence collected—guide the interpretation we are seeking to form?[2]

Dissecting the Score

A theoretical analysis is like a physical examination: The doctor scrutinizes the entire body and carries out a series of laboratory tests, knowing that most of his procedures will produce nothing of interest, for the patient in most respects is healthy; only occasionally will something be found that must be treated. So it is in examining a piece of music; you must undertake many analytical operations, but only some of them will tell you something decisive or unique about the work before you and its overall structure. If the physician is careless, he may overlook the one life-threatening factor; similarly, if your analysis is lackadaisical, you may miss the one feature that would shape your interpretation.

The following parameters and details constitute a fundamental list of items you should consider (to which any given piece of music may suggest its own additions.

1. Forces (instruments, voices, or both) designated for use; timbral aspects (including unusual traditional or electronic instruments)
2. Overall tonal organization: tonality (where clear); modulations; temporary tonal shifts; chromatic variants; special devices like pedal points and pitch ostinatos (if present); editorial accidentals (if any)
3. Metric and rhythmic organization: meter(s) in use; rhythmic levels employed and their consistency; special devices like syncopation, hemiolas, rhythmic constants, and motor ostinatos (if present)
4. Harmonic relationships (including a complete harmonic analysis, unless inappropriate); use of dissonance; harmonic rhythm
5. Melodic organization: step-progressions (if present); proportions of skips to steps; types of leaps (harmonic or nonchordal); placement of dissonances; ranges and tessituras demanded of individual performers; ornamentation
6. Textural relationships: use of monophony, chordal homophony, melody/accompaniment, and polyphony

[2]If all this scholarly discipline seems a bit idealistic to you, ask yourself if you want your physician to undertake exactly this sort of "spiral study" when you go for treatment of a life-threatening illness. (And then ask yourself if you, as a professional, are less dedicated than is your physician.)

7. Text (if any): realization, including repetition of words or phrases; assignment to various parts; rhythmic placement of consonants; tessitural placement of vowels; filling-out of incomplete texts in older manuscripts

8. Compositional operations employed: developmental, variational, fugal/imitative, and additive procedures

9. Any special or unusual features

10. Structural summary: overall formal design[3] (taking into consideration all the features already itemized), including major sections, subsections, and phrasing; locations of important cadences; elisions; dynamics

This is the analytic matrix we suggest you use on any music you are preparing to conduct, and for studying works by other composers whose music you know to be related to the work at hand. Get to know this method (or some equivalent one) so well that you can use it by memory.

Gaining Supporting Perspectives

To give you a general sense of the background reading you should do in preparation to conduct a major work, we suggest the following kinds of sources.

1. The standard (most respected) biography of the "target" composer.

2. Other biographical writings, including especially those written during the composer's lifetime.

3. Books and articles analyzing the composer's musical style.

4. Biographical books and articles on the lives and musical styles of the target composer's teacher(s).

5. Equivalent sources on the lives and musical styles of both predecessors and contemporaries who influenced the target composer.

6. Books and articles providing political and economic overviews of the history of the period, beginning fifty years or so before the composer's birth.

7. Books and articles describing cultural and social features of the period, again beginning about fifty years beforehand.

8. Examples of the best work in the other arts during this era: painting, sculpture, theater, poetry, prose, and so on, *especially* architecture. (Look at pictures of the art and the buildings, read the literature, and see firsthand anything close enough to visit.)

9. Any other reading or viewing that your research makes relevant.

Perspectives about the work at hand are gained through analysis of other music. For example study the following:

1. Works by the target composer
   a. Of the same genre; using the same forces, or both
   b. From the same period of his or her life
   c. Written beforehand and directly influential

---

[3]In analysis, the most comprehensive deductions must be saved to be formed at the end. If you follow this outline in the order presented, you should find yourself ready to draw the necessary conclusions about the structure of the work.

    d. Written later and thought to have been affected directly by the work at hand

    e. Of less obvious significance (to the practical limit of time available to you)

  2. Works by the target composer's teacher(s), especially those in the same genre or otherwise thought to have been influential

  3. Works by predecessors or contemporaries, especially those known or thought to have been studied by the target composer

  4. Works of a similar genre by composers thought to have been more-or-less directly influenced by the work and the composer at hand[4]

As you continue in your profession, all this reading and research begins to snowball, of course. Every bit of understanding you gain is added to your overall perspective and then brought to the next work you conduct, so that your insights accumulate throughout your career. When you prepare to conduct another work by a composer whose music you have been performing, you need not read again every line you have read before about that individual and that era. You can use the time you save thereby to continue along the spiral to further enriching insights.

You should not immobilize yourself with endless extensions of these "spirals"; that is not the point. The more you can come to understand the setting in which the music was created, however, the more exciting and accurate your interpretation of that music is apt to be.

MORE CONDUCTING THEORY
Reassembling a Work: The Complete Structural Image

Dr. Johnson once remarked to Boswell:

> Sir, you may analyze this, and say what is there in in it? But that will avail you nothing, for it is a part of a general system. Pound St. Paul's church into atoms, and consider any single atom; it is, to be sure, good for nothing: but, put all these atoms together, and you have St. Paul's church.[5]

Sometimes conductors study carefully some piece of music, and then go on to a performance of it without first putting "everything back together" mentally into a consummate *concept* of the work. Having torn the music up into smaller and smaller pieces, they *conduct from problem to problem* (or from solution to solution), thus getting through the technical difficulties more-or-less successfully, without ever restoring in their minds, in the minds of the musicians, and thus, inevitably, *in the minds of their listeners* the whole shape, direction, and momentum of the work.

---

[4]This list of related works to be analyzed is reproduced for your convenience in Appendix C.

[5]James Boswell, *The Life of Samuel Johnson* (New York: Heritage Press, 1963), 1, 311.

It is surprising, in fact, how many musicians, both amateur and professional, are pleased with a given performance, not because of the whole aesthetic result, but because they have escaped disaster—have avoided all the obvious risks in getting (otherwise perfunctorily) through the music in a form of "damage control." **An ensemble is not successful in a performance simply because it conquers the hazards indigenous to the work, but also because it makes manifest to its listeners the whole shape, proportions, substance, and meaning of that music.**

This is the *complete structural image* of the work. This is ultimately what we are seeking to present when we perform. This conceives the music in terms of its consummate shape, as we interpret that shape in the light of everything we can learn about the historical environment, the musical style of the age, the abilities of the musicians, and the capacities of their instruments, as well as appropriate performance practices. And the "spiral study" applies here at one more level: For better (or worse, since sometimes fresh, youthful viewpoints can be the most exciting ones), your interpretation is configured partly by the experience of the last piece of music you conducted, and the three before that, and the twenty before that; after two or three years of such growth, you are bound to look at a work with significantly different eyes from those with which you would have seen it earlier.

Performance Practice and Conducting Decisions

Let us consider the decisions a conductor must make (once a substantial amount of research has been completed) as practical elements of the interpretation she or he is forming. (Bear in mind that any individual piece of music may contain special elements that must be assessed and placed in perspective.) Given what we are calling "the complete structural image" of the work;[6] address the following questions.

1. With the performance practice of the time in mind, and weighing what you know about the composer's instructions, the original performance(s), the size and acoustics of the halls in which this music was first presented, the customs of the audiences present, and all, what are the appropriate number and kinds of voices and instruments needed for your performance?
2. In what hall(s) will you perform? What are its (their) peculiar characteristics?

[6]Note that specific lists of criteria for decisions about tempos and dynamics are presented immediately hereafter.

Further, as implicit examples of this whole "spiral study" process, we provide for each of the major works studied in Chapters 21–25 suggestions as to writings of the kinds described as important here, other pertinent music, and contemporaneous artistic and cultural creations, as well as some characteristic features of the performance practice of the apposite style period. Once you have prepared each of these five masterpieces, you should understand precisely how to go about the interpretive process with most music literature.

3. What edition of the work is the best one for your purposes? Is it available within your time frame and budgetary situation?

4. Using this edition, how do you plan to arrange your forces in the hall(s) in which you will be performing?

5. In any piece of music, the structure makes some cadences more important than others. What is that hierarchy in this particular work?

6. Where are the climaxes in this design? How are they prepared, established, and left?

7. Are there cadenzas indicated; if so, where? Are there appropriate but unmarked opportunities for these important structural enhancements?

8. In the light of this whole structural hierarchy, what editing is appropriate with respect to such features as accelerandos, ritards, crescendos, diminuendos, and fermatas?

9. What are the individual phrase lengths present at each moment?

10. Which entrances are particularly important? How are combinations of voices, instruments, or both paired?

11. What types of articulation will make your interpretation more clear (within this historic style), and specifically where should each be employed? What bowings, tonguings, and vocal markings should be designated? What contrasts can be incorporated?

12. In view of these textural and articulatory factors, what and where are the inherent balance problems?

13. Weighing all the factors so far, including what you know of the composer's own intentions and practices, what tempo (or tempos) should be set?

14. What beat patterns are appropriate, and where? How do you plan to shift smoothly from one to another?

15. What editing of dynamics will make your interpretation clearer?

16. What editorial accidentals are to be honored, and what are the bases for these decisions? Are there other controversial elements in the edition you have chosen that require either objective or subjective choices to be made?

17. What about ornamentation? Is it appropriate here; if so, what types of embellishments fit what you have learned about the performance practices of the era? Where can such ornaments be employed?

18. What other elements of performance freedom are present to be enjoyed?

19. What individual soloists (if any are required) suit well all these considerations (either from your experience or on the basis of auditions you hold)?

20. What uncertainties do the limitations of your own knowledge and experience leave still present, and how should you proceed to neutralize or eliminate them?

Criteria for Choosing Tempos

With respect to choosing tempos rather specific considerations can be identified. Looking for *internal indicators*, take note especially of any of the following:

1. Time signature(s)
2. Tempo markings: Andante, Allegro, etc.
3. Expression markings: legato, espressivo, etc.
4. The pace of the very fastest rhythmic values
5. The pace of the very slowest *moving* rhythmic values

6. The harmonic rhythm
7. The lengths of phrases
8. Difficulties with the rapidity of the text (if any)
9. Tonguing problems for the winds (if any)
10. Danger of running out of breath or out of bow (if any)
11. Relationships of each given structural unit to other sections within the movement
12. Relationships to the tempos of other movements within the work

Among the *external factors* you should ponder are both historic and contemporary ones.

1. The composer's original metronome markings (if any are on record). This *is* an external consideration, for experience teaches us that such indicators often are untrustworthy. (Some authorities think, given the impracticality of some of Beethoven's own symphonic M.M. signs, for instance, that the master's metronome was faulty.) Any composer's M.M. markings either are based on the use of a certain concert hall or fail to define what sort of hall was in his or her ear; composers are not always fine performers, and their judgment about tempos has been less dependable than most of their other insights. Tempo choices simply are less rigid than, for example, matters of precision like pitch and rhythm.
2. Far more reliable and authoritative are the influential indicators signaled by the composer in
   a. The size and nature of the original forces used
   b. The size, nature, and acoustics of the hall(s) in which the composer performed or heard this music at any point in his or her lifetime
   c. Contemporary reporting of the composer's reactions
   d. Any available information about later modifications the composer undertook as a result of early performances
   e. Indications gained from more-or-less similar passages written by the same individual
   f. Indications gained from other works written by the teacher(s) and contemporaries of the composer
3. The performance practices of the period, based on the writings of reliable *primary sources* (that is, musicians and theorists who were contemporaries of the composer)
4. The performance practices of the period, based on *secondary sources* (that is, reputable authorities who have written about this music subsequent to the style period involved)
5. The size and capabilities of your ensemble
6. The size and nature of the hall in which you will be performing
7. Relationships between the work at hand and the other repertoire on your program.

In general, very slow tempos are harder than very fast ones. To keep a flow of "line" through a phrase at a deliberate pace, you have to have "more ideas of things to do inside each eighth or quarter note," in a sense; you have to make the connections between each pitch and sonority vivid enough to counteract the unhurried motion. **Even slow tempos must maintain real, if tantalizing, momentum.** Remember, too, in making these judgments, that **fast tempos are not a**

proper means to cover up problems (even though some great conductors sometimes have used them for that purpose). Keep in mind, also, that good instrumentalists generally can play a virtuosic phrase faster than good singers can sing it. **When a tempo is the right one, the technical problems within the ensemble should be minimal, the phrases should have the right shape and feeling, and the music should flow with a convincing, almost weightless momentum.**

Editing Dynamics, Articulation, and Related Features

Additions and revisions to the notated dynamics are matters of fitting your ensemble's characteristics and balances to both the indications of the composer's wishes and your interpretation of the complete structural image of the work. Clarifying the overall formal design, building to and leading away from potent climaxes, shaping phrases and longer melodic lines, dealing with loud soprano or trumpet sections, reinforcing parts overpowered by the tessituras of the texture, and the like are justifications for your undertaking this editing.

Especially in fugal passages, it is often necessary for you to add dynamic markings. Composers frequently have left these complex polyphonic sections relatively unmarked or undermarked; yet, it is important that subjects and countersubjects be kept in perspective and balance partly through the careful placement of dynamic changes and modifications. Repeated segments of orchestral works are another instance in which additional markings may be necessary, to "freshen" or "redefine" a passage just heard. The authors find that their focusing on a change of dynamics often encourages a good ensemble to view a repetitive unit in a reinvigorated, sensitive way. The real point is this: *The musicians must know what their individual functions are—what role they are playing at every moment of a work—and good, thorough dynamic markings signal them how to proceed.*

These same guidelines apply in exactly the same ways to articulatory markings. Again, the purpose of good editing is to clarify the form and enhance the momentum.[7]

It is the same with stylistic ornamentation: Once you have established standards for a particular work or a given style, you should be able to trust good musicians to apply your principles sensibly.[8]

We know that great composers who have worked daily with the same fine musicians (Joseph Haydn with his Esterházy orchestra, for example) have employed few dynamic and articulatory markings, because the musicians have come to comprehend the style and performance practices as well as their master. In other words, this is a form of editing that really *teaches style;* it places on your colleagues the responsibility to share with you the evocation of your interpreta-

---

[7]General principles about vocal articulation, enunciation, and diction can be found in Chapters 9 and 10. Discussions of instrumental articulation, bowings, tonguing patterns, and related matters can be reviewed in Chapter 13.

[8]Ornamentation concepts were discussed especially in Chapter 11.

tion. Your function is not to mark every note but to encourage your musicians to handle every note in a way consistent with the interpretive matrix you and they are envisioning.

READINESS: GETTING AWAY FROM NOTE-TO-NOTE DEPENDENCE ON THE SCORE

Once you have prepared properly, your conductor's score should be available to you in rehearsals and performances *only* as a reminder of special things you want to do, a resource in sudden emergencies (an early or a late entrance by an ensemble member, for example), a protective device against the danger that you might suffer a memory lapse, and perhaps—as Robert Shaw is said to have remarked—a source of inspiration in performance! It is not there to be *read* anymore (not even in rehearsals). It is now merely a reference book to be consulted.

Once you have in mind the complete structural image of the work, together with your own concept of how to present it (that is, your interpretation), the score itself is no longer the music! (In fact, of course, it never was; it was only a shorthand approximation of the *composer's* view of that same music.) One may turn back, like Shaw, to that notation for fresh ideas from time to time, but more of the whole work is in the conductor's head by that time than is left on the page.

In a sense, of course, the ultimate preparation *is* memorization, and many fine conductors commit to memory virtually everything they do.[9] Memorizing a major work—knowing every entrance and doubling and dynamic marking—is not easy, but it is a skill, and, like other skills, it requires practice. It gets easier the oftener one does it, and harder the less frequently it is attempted.

Some people feel threatened without a score at hand, however, and remain uneasy. ("What if . . . ?") Others seemingly never really learn to avoid memory slips. Try memorizing small pieces of music, then move to longer ones, and finally attempt a major multimovement work. If you find memorization a beneficial discipline, use it; if not, you can always keep the score in front of you.

Get rid of it in one way or the other, however! *Free yourself* from the limitations of the notation to pursue the unabridged interpretation in your mind. With a comprehensive understanding of the theoretical and historical background established, with a clear view of the structure set, and with your forces chosen and your editing complete, you are ready to rehearse the work.

[9]One of the authors has seen Giuseppe Patanè conduct three full-length operas in six nights at the Vienna Staatsoper, all three from memory! Conductors like Patanè do this routinely.

CHAPTER 19

In the Rehearsal

More of the work of a conductor takes place in rehearsals than in performances. This crucial, costly time must be used wisely. **In the ideal that we set for ourselves, nothing in a rehearsal happens by chance; yet, miscalculations intrude and surprises occur. The professional conductor carefully designs for each such session a thorough and detailed plan, yet is so well prepared as to be able to take positive advantage of the unexpected.**

PLANNING FOR THE CONCERT HALL

Your program is chosen now, and your interpretations are formed, if not yet final in detail. You are leading your ensemble through a sequence of sessions in which you need to make clear to them your wishes with respect to an impending performance. Almost everything you do in those sessions should reflect directly your priorities for that event.

You need to imagine the music in that context. Visualize the concert taking place. "See" the ensemble onstage (perhaps in varying seatings). "Walk through" the performance in your mind, from the entrance of the ensemble members to the final bows. Try to think of everything that will contribute to this scenario, and thus attempt to foresee any logistical problems or any clumsy situations that might arise because of some choice you are making. Now is the time to make adjustments.

Which players will be onstage for the first number? Are they your full force? Will some need to leave before the second work? Are there soloists to bring on then? Should you not leave the stage, and reenter with them, rather than waiting for them beside the podium? Have you made arrangements about the retuning process? Do you want your wind ensemble to stand as you enter the first time? Or every time?

If a chorus is seated before the concert begins, what is their signal to stand? When do they bring up their music? If the first number is *a cappella*, how will they get the initial pitch? What is the planned order for the bows?

In the concert hall, everything that is not music is theater! Every detail in a public performance can detract from the smooth professionalism of that event if it is not handled gracefully. You cannot afford to be casual about these minutiae, even though they may seem secondary in importance to the music you are presenting; although they can add only a little to the artistry of what you and your ensemble may be able to do, they could take a lot away from its effect. Plan everything, and (to the extent possible) do so before the rehearsals begin.

MARKING YOUR SCORE

One of your most important prerehearsal duties is to prepare your score. It may already be full of markings as a result of the analysis you have done, but many of those research notes probably are no longer needed; you already know everything they would tell you. If they distract you, erase them. (If you can, particularly in the case of an inexpensive choral work, change to another copy.) The purpose of that *rehearsal* score (as distinguished from your analysis copy) is to enable you to run these sessions more efficiently and effectively. Anything you do not need that remains in the score is cluttering up a page and may draw your attention away from something important at a crucial moment.

Edit your rehearsal copy to include at least all of the following:

1. Measure numbers or rehearsal letters (the former are better) throughout. Be certain that they correspond to the parts, which, even in the same edition, is sometimes not the case.
2. The overall form of the movement, indicated by letters or symbols inserted at the beginning of each section and subsection.
3. Beat patterns you have chosen (at the point each begins), with transitional subdivisions indicated.
4. Major events in tonality and harmony, including modulations and temporary tonal cells.
5. Your phraseology. Mark the beginning and the end of every phrase (spanning them with arches, drawing "macrobar lines" down through the whole stave, or whatever). Take note of elisions, extensions, and other variants.
6. Important thematic materials: fugal subjects and countersubjects, themes and variations, *A* and *B* ideas, germ motives, ostinatos, and all.
7. Melodic step-progressions, specifying where they begin and end.
8. Cadenzas, including note by note the last few pitches that cue you and the ensemble to reenter.
9. Spots you expect might be troublesome or dangerous, including
   a. Potential balance problems
   b. Sections where you expect intonation to waver
   c. Other rhythmically or technically difficult passages
10. Clarifying markings you have chosen, including
   a. Exact rhythmic spots for releases and cutoffs
   b. Added fermatas, ritards, accelerandos, etc.

      c. Additional articulatory marks

      d. Needed dynamics

      e. Ornaments

      f. Breath marks, to the extent these spots are unclear

  11. Important commentary about the work that you want to the ensemble to know. This can be written at the point it occurs, on the back of the front cover, or on the back cover itself. (Commentary for your own reference—counsel from historians and musicologists, advice from other conductors, and the like—can go on these covers or at the extreme top or bottom of pages, if you wish, but keep it out of your line of sight when you are conducting.)

  12. The dates of your present rehearsal–performance cycle (on one of the covers) so that you can see later at a glance when you last performed this work.

  13. Exact indications of points at which you want to (or fear you will have to) restart the ensemble during rehearsal on account of some breakdown or because the musicians will need to run a passage more than once. (If your score has measure numbers, those will do; if rehearsal letters, then denote these points as "4 before E," or "22 after J.") Do not waste rehearsal time by failing to plan these workouts.

If you have done all this work thoughtfully, your rehearsal score can be an enormous support to you in tight situations.

PLANNING REHEARSALS

Student conductors—and all those who must pay overtime if a rehearsal runs too long—should *schedule everything by the minute*. Know exactly how long each movement runs at your tempos, and estimate how much start-and-restart time you are going to need for working out problems. Allow a minute between works and movements for the musicians to relax and look ahead at what is coming next. Allow time for necessary (*only* necessary) explanations. Plan to save optional and lower-priority items for the end so that you can delete or postpone them if the more important things take too long. As you gain experience, some of this detailed scheduling may become unnecessary (for you learn ways of recovering if something takes too long), but *it always will be best for you to plan precisely.*

Be aware exactly which players you really will be using at each moment. Make a chart of all the players needed for any work to be rehearsed, see what pattern emerges from it, and that will establish the order in which the music should be undertaken. In professional organizations, it is customary to call everyone for the beginning of the session; one schedules the work calling for the largest forces first, the second largest next, and so on, releasing unneeded personnel as they have completed their responsibilities. (In a dress rehearsal, however, one usually should choose to run the program in concert order, even if that causes players to sit unused for a while.)

It is not enough to schedule everything. Prepare yourself so that you know exactly how to respond efficiently to mistakes and problems. **Know the music better than any of your musicians.** Sing or play through every line so that you recognize where the difficulties lie, know what is right, and can correct anyone who gets it wrong. Play as much as you can at the piano, two or more parts at a time, working to increase your ability to hear the interplay of the counterpoint.

Familiarize yourself with all the C clefs, especially the alto and tenor clefs, for they are much in use in orchestral writing, as well as in older manuscripts. Do *not* attempt to "transpose" this music into the treble and bass clefs; just as you expect yourself to read those two clefs, you can learn rather quickly to read with assurance in the alto and tenor (and even the soprano and mezzo soprano) systems.

Above all, learn to know exactly where you must spend the time you have. Most of the hazards are at the "seams," the transition points and structural divisions, and these need special attention. Continuity is important, and your musicians must hear the work through; nevertheless, you should not unnecessarily allow them to "enjoy playing beautiful music" just for their satisfaction.

See that your librarian does everything possible to help each session run without hitches. The right music must be marked and issued (or ready to issue), missing parts replaced, damaged copies repaired, rehearsal measures or letters added as necessary, and your special editing inserted (including bowings, where strings are present).

Arrange, also, to have any special instruments and equipment in place—the podium you want, unusual percussion items, and the like. See that chairs and music stands match your seating chart. If, in a school situation, you must have extra woodwind reeds and replacement strings available, be sure your stock is kept adequate.

Have ready any handout paperwork you want distributed—schedules of upcoming rehearsals and performances, corrections you want entered in the parts (if your librarian cannot do all that), and such items—and plan when you will have them issued, so that no time will be wasted. (Any device or procedure that minimizes announcements is worthwhile.)

PACING A REHEARSAL

The impression you want to create right from the moment your musicians walk in the door of the rehearsal room is that *this is a place of dedication*, that "in this hall we have no time to lose, for what we are doing here is very important, and we must be ready for the approaching performance." We mentioned in Chapter 9 that some fine school choir directors have the pianist begin playing a familiar chorale as the students enter the room; each singer moves, already singing, immediately to her or his place in the room, with no time wasted for greetings or chatter. Band and orchestra players cannot do this (for they must assemble their instruments and tune first), but the principle can be applied in other ways; try to begin every rehearsal (at any level) in a routine, formal way. Professional musicians realize (or should) that the rehearsal hall is a place of business, for their careers are at stake there; amateurs and students need an aura of commitment there too.

Make certain your musicians know what to expect in each rehearsal. To the extent possible, end each session by telling them what you plan to do next time so they can focus their own practice accordingly. You probably should have the day's repertoire written in sequence on a blackboard or an easel at the front of the room so that they can begin looking at the first number as they warm up.

For school ensembles, you should establish some sort of standard musical warm-up. Scales, sustained notes, vocalises, and tuning exercises all may be used, depending on the type and level of group. Once the musicians are physically and mentally ready, you can undertake the day's repertoire.

Discipline yourself to stay on schedule. If you stop too often, you condition your musicians to short-term concentration. They have too many such influences in their lives already—10-second TV commercials and television news programs using 45-second spots have affected all human discourse—and they have to learn to maintain concentration over longer spans; help them to do so. Don't be distracted yourself by minor problems. Don't lose perspective, spending time working today on matters you planned to tackle next week. Don't lose your own concentration, continuing further with one work than you intended. Above all, *don't talk*—don't say a single unnecessary word![1]

Learn to speak exactly to the point. As quickly as you finish a cutoff, say quickly, "Again! And listen for the oboe this time. Bar 112!" Freeze just a split second to let them find the place, and give them the "prep" beat. Music is a non-verbal art. Keep it as much that way as possible.

Keep pushing. Athletes are accustomed to being physically fatigued at the end of practice sessions, but many students do not think of school this way. **If your musicians are not genuinely tired, mentally and physically, after a rehearsal with you, they probably have not been concentrating hard enough.** The authors believe **even school ensembles can be essentially free of behavioral problems providing the work atmosphere is kept as intense and productive as it should be.**

Learn to gauge when a mixture of physical wear and tear and lapses of concentration are signaling you that your musicians are temporarily tired. Expect to deliberately relax them from time to time. Most of these breaks can be momentary. Don't lose their attention; instead, lower your arms, make a funny remark (in other words, use "comic relief"), or say, "Yes! That's really going well!" Do something that lets them take a breath and realize they really are accomplishing something. Then say, "Letter C," raise your arms, and go right back to work.

At the end of a movement or a major period of drilling a difficult passage, say something like, "Okay. Better. Relax a moment, *and look ahead to Letter G.*"

---

[1]When your musicians are playing or singing, they are active. When you stop them to talk, you begin doing all the work. Inevitably, they relax and lose at least some concentration; students may be tempted to talk among themselves. At the very best, this time is less efficiently used.

Or, "We'll take the Holst *Suite* next." The point is this: Except in long rehearsals, when you routinely take a five- or ten-minute break, *never completely lose command of the moment.* Keep at least slackened attention all the time, even when you are intentionally giving your people either a few seconds or a minute to loosen up.

Real rehearsal breaks for adults and professionals should come after an hour or so (depending on union rules, of course) and should give everyone time to get "offstage" mentally, if not physically, for a few minutes. Have some standard procedure—a bell, a clapping of hands, or the theater's "Places, ladies and gentlemen, if you please"—for calling them back, not just to the rehearsal room, but to the dedicated atmosphere, as well. You need them to reestablish their concentration quickly (and you will find that this is not an automatic process). Efficiency is lost briefly, at least, after every intermission. Calculate how to minimize this—don't leave it to chance!

MORE CONDUCTING THEORY
Attitude and Productivity

Learn gradually to sense when a given ensemble will be ready to give you its best concentration and work. Save the most crucial, most demanding, most difficult passages for that block of time. You can manufacture some such occasions by inspiriting them; usually you cannot do so with negativism, for eventually (as if you were a loud, constant noise) they will begin not to hear you. Positive approaches, on the other hand, put the burden on them.

Often for amateurs or students you can have planned an inspirational remark or vignette of some sort, ready to be used when you need it most. With professional musicians, as with paid athletes, on the other hand, "pep talks" have little real effect.

We spoke in Chapter 9 of the importance of the individual voice within the choir, and cautioned that "the absence of a single singer from a rehearsal changes the sound and character not just of that section but of the choir as a whole." The same is the case for instrumentalists, many of whom have *solo* responsibility for important musical passages. Work with your musicians to build a deep sense of interdependence that can assure you of their loyal attendance, solid concentration, careful preparation, and dependability.

INTRODUCING AN UNFAMILIAR WORK

"New" pieces of music present a special set of problems and opportunities. They freshen a rehearsal when an ensemble has been drilling familiar works for some time. They can broaden the repertoire, can stir certain members of the group who have been insufficiently challenged for a while, can reassure an orchestra that has been tackling more difficult works, or can humble a chorus that has been singing only easier music.

Whatever level you are conducting, try to let the music introduce itself as much as possible. Give your ensemble a chance to do some good sight reading, uninterrupted by your comments. Try to keep going, avoiding a complete breakdown, even if many things are going wrong. Give the musicians an overall look at the movement, as a start.[2]

Once an ensemble has been through the music once, a work begins to become an "old piece." Point out the quick adjustments needed, and go back to work for as long as you can. Make enough progress the first time that your people can recognize at least *some* good qualities in the music.

SAVING REHEARSAL TIME

In a sense, we have been talking about economizing your rehearsal time throughout this chapter. There are some specific procedures you can use that can help even more.

1. Each ensemble has its own personality (separate from that of each member); you need to sense that identity and make use of it. Learn to "read" your ensembles.

2. With better players, try to work in longer segments rather than stopping for each mistake. Wait for five or six problems to accumulate (or, with professionals, go through the entire movement); your tendency will be to halt every time you hear something you want changed, but *you need to stretch your memory*—retaining a list of corrections—so that the number of restarts is minimized. See how many things you and they can fix at once! (Some mistakes are repetitive, too; by waiting longer, you can respond to more of them at once.)

3. Give your musicians a chance to fix their own mistakes. The better they are, the more likely it is that they already know about most of the errors you heard, and will avoid making them next time. If they fail to respond as you want them to the second time, you can still point out the problem. What you really want from your musicians is *an atmosphere of personal responsibility.*[3]

4. Try to do whole things, then—whole phrases, whole sections, whole movements, whole works—whatever the unit you are rehearsing.

5. Be very demanding—be "picky"—in the early rehearsals so that your musicians understand how much you expect of them. Then, after their concentration is working for you, let them have more "rope."

6. Keep separating "repairing" from "continuity" in your mind, and work for the one or the other. In detail work, cut from problem to problem, and don't overdo the secure spots.

---

[2]In a school situation, you may need to give them a concise verbal (or verbal and musical) introduction if this music is written in a completely unfamiliar style. With professionals, this should be unnecessary.

[3]In some of the English choir schools, it is the practice to expect the boy sopranos to hold up a hand, without stopping, whenever they know they have erred. That makes it unnecessary for the master to take time to call those mistakes to their attention.

7. Demand that ensemble members retain what they have rehearsed before. Remind them of this responsibility: Without telling them the answer, ask them, "Remember what I asked for here last time?" Over the longer term they should need fewer and fewer reminders, for they gradually come to understand that using your instructions to build a shared conception of the work is part of their duty and discipline. (The interval between rehearsals is important in this respect; most church choirs rehearse just once per week, for example, and church choirmasters often find their singers have trouble retaining ideas over the span to Sunday. Repetition helps. Work more than just a week ahead.[4])

8. Consider imitating Robert Shaw's practice of writing explanatory and instructional letters to your ensemble members periodically.[5] Use those letters to reinforce your praises and criticisms of their work, and to address matters of diction, phrasing, articulation, dynamics, and the like. Any instruction you can get to them outside of rehearsal saves valuable time.

9. Watch your incidental rehearsal habits; for example, don't count several beats before you start each time; just give the "prep" beat. You can waste two or three total minutes per rehearsal counting "free bars," and that can add up to fifteen minutes per week, an hour per month, ten hours per year.

10. Set up a video tape recorder and camera from time to time, and aim it at yourself! Check on the timing, clarity, and efficiency of what you do in rehearsal.

REHEARSING WITH SOLOISTS

Very little has been written or taught so far about the psychology of the relationships between one soloist, other soloists, the ensemble, and the conductor. Once you have chosen these special artists, you need to come to mutual understandings about how the music is to be performed, either before the rehearsals (the best way) or during them. If there are to be disagreements, you do not want them during the performance!

If the soloist is a peer of yours, that individual deserves a full share in the decisions to be taken about the music making. A piano concertist of stature presumably has been invited to appear because he or she has something exceptional to bring to your performance of this work. Contact the artist well before you begin orchestra rehearsals—visit together, if possible—and talk out a mutual conception of the concerto.

If, on the other hand, the soloist is not a peer—is a student, perhaps—then it is in order for you to instruct the young artist clearly with respect to your interpretation. Make sure he or she understands how to prepare, how to function in your rehearsals, how to work out any difficulties that arise, and what will happen in the performance (including entrances and bows).

[4]Try something like this five-week system with a church choir: The full rehearsal attacks five works; the first is read at sight, the next is seen for the second time, the third and fourth are spot-drilled for problems, and the fifth is rehearsed for continuity. (It is the one to be sung next Sunday, and the choir has had five weeks to become familiar with it.)

[5]See Joseph A. Musselman, *Dear People . . . Robert Shaw* (Bloomington: Indiana University Press, 1979), beginning on p. 51. One of the authors has done this for his university ensemble, mailing the letters on a Friday so that they would be received at the beginning of the next rehearsal week.

It is the practice of the authors to introduce soloists formally to the ensemble at the time of their first rehearsal together (even if the artist is a member of that group). Mutual respect is important.

IMITATING THE PERFORMANCE ENVIRONMENT IN REHEARSAL

In Chapter 8, the authors recommended that you create a quasi performance near the end of each rehearsal, as a way both of making concrete the accomplishments of that session and of reminding the musicians of the ultimate purpose to which this labor will be put. The better this goes, the better the eventual performance is likely to be, for "practice concerts" tell you how good you are on any given day, and that gives you and your musicians a yardstick with which to measure the distance yet to go to reach a secure performance.

Come as close to the genuine performance feeling as you can, by every device you can use. Take your musicians from the rehearsal room to the concert hall occasionally, if you can. Invite visitors sometimes. Use nonstop run-throughs of the music. Insist on performance routines for sitting and standing, giving pitches, and taking bows.

One discipline you can demand of them as part of every reading of a work is that of stage presence. Tell them you expect them not to move around in introductions, transitions, silences, endings, and other passages where distracting gestures, scratching of (more-or-less imaginary) itches, and similar movements distract listeners from the atmosphere of the moment. Ask them to "Freeze!" just as they will have to do in concert. Once they acquire this habit, they will not thoughtlessly detract from the ensemble's bearing onstage.

PLANNING AND PACING THE DRESS REHEARSAL

The successful dress rehearsal accomplishes everything musical you believe must be achieved, reassures the performers, and readies everyone for the concert itself. The term *dress rehearsal* comes to us from the theater, where actors attend in full costume and makeup—that is, in performance "dress." These days, in most cases, it is a misnomer, for the majority of "dress rehearsals" take place with the musicians in street clothes. It is a special event, however, for it is the last chance to "get things right" before the concert. Try to point your musicians toward it, aiming for it as if it were the public performance; if they are prepared for it, then they will find it easier to be ready for the concert that follows it.

This final practice session is a time to stretch every second of every minute to the last extreme of efficiency. Lay out a schedule that calculates exactly how much time will be needed for each work, for resetting the stage between numbers, and all, and then stick to it. Know where you want to be at every minute of the dress rehearsal; then keep a copy of that firm, detailed plan on your music stand.

Some conductors keep track of time in dress rehearsals by hanging a large wall clock beside or behind their ensemble—a clock they can see every time they look toward the first clarinets or first violins or sopranos. However you do it, you have to assure yourself that time will not slip away from you.

And some conductors really treat the dress rehearsal as an uninterrupted run-through of the entire concert. They rarely stop for anything, assuming that if mistakes occur at this point, the musicians will know and will try to correct them themselves.

At least try to take the program in the order you will do it in the concert. That lets your musicians hear the continuity of the whole performance. Above all, *give them your performance tempos, momentum, and every other aspect of your interpretation.*

Plan to save three or four minutes *at the end* of each work to repair a couple of spots, quickly, in detail. Then you can go on to your run-through of the next work.

The newest element in their rehearsal experience with you may be the hall. Assume that it will take part of your precious rehearsal time to acclimate your musicians to a new room. Give them a chance at first to adjust to that; then go out into the hall to listen yourself while your assistant takes part of a movement. Once you know how the ensemble really sounds, work for the best aural result you can get.

If you attend the rehearsals of a great symphony orchestra, you will find that famous conductors spend an enormous share of their rehearsal time (which is in their performance hall, of course) working for precise articulation and distinct dynamics; so it is that they get excellent balance and transparent textures. You hear that transparency when you attend their concerts. Imitate in this regard: Ask your musicians for precision in these tiny details, and your ensemble will perform in its hall with all the clarity and power you want it to have.

Practice Exercise 19-1   *Designing a Schedule for a Final Dress Rehearsal*

Choose a program about seventy-five minutes in length (plus a fifteen-minute intermission), and—knowing the timings of works and movements—lay out a schedule for a two-hour dress rehearsal (minus ten minutes somewhere near the middle for a break). Allocate time as you think best, but take into consideration each of the factors described in this chapter.

CHAPTER *20*

The Performance

In music, the purpose of all the plans, research, and rehearsals is the public performance. This transfiguring event (almost unique among productive human activities) is so sharply defined against a threshold of time that once it is scheduled for a certain day and hour, it must begin then, even if the musicians are not ready, even if no substantial audience is present, even if a handicapping mischance transpires. The pressure-filled sequence of next month–next week–tomorrow–*now* is a recurring challenge for you.

PREPARING THE CONDUCTING SCORE FOR PERFORMANCE

We have discussed the use of the conducting score for analysis (in which it becomes a record of your ideas about the music and of commentary you have gained from other sources) and for rehearsing (when it becomes a script for your management of those sessions). For the public performance, it has quite a different purpose: Here it simply represents a blueprint of your interpretation—incomplete, as a map is incomplete, but with sufficient shape to remind you of your intentions and of the options among which you will choose at the moment you confront them.

Thus, it may be completely blank, for you may need nothing but the composer's own notations to remind you of "the complete structural image" you have come to recognize; it may be absent, in fact, for you may have memorized that image so thoroughly that it seems better to you to visualize everything in your mind only. It may, on the other hand, contain a rather elaborate set of special markings—related to some of those in the rehearsal version, perhaps—that remind you of structural and technical features you want to remember at certain moments. You may choose one approach one time and a different one on another occasion. If you do use the score in concert, remember that it is there for reminders, and not for reading!

Since you know the music so well and are so intent on your communication with your ensemble, in later rehearsals and in the performance you may not turn every page at exactly the moment you finish it. This can get clumsy, for precisely at the point you do need to glance quickly at the notes, the score may be on the wrong page; you may have forgotten to turn it. Stick a strip of ribbon or some other marker between the pages at each spot where you need to look at the notes.

There are other aspects of the performance that you must manage *during* the concert (the order of final bows, for example, or reminders about retuning), and these relate to the score, as well. Such details can be written on a separate page, for safety's sake, and taken onstage with you. (The order of bows, for example, can be stuck into the back of your score or left under your score on the music stand; consult it right after the final cutoff.)

MAINTAINING CONCENTRATION IN PERFORMANCE

Chapter 19 offered a discussion of the importance of concentration and of ways of maintaining it in the members of your ensemble. These concerns matter even more in performance, where nervousness can distract your musicians.

In general, the younger your people, the shorter the attention span. If you have built a "tradition of concentration"—of focused, disciplined *ensemble*—in your rehearsals, you have already solved part of this special problem of concert stress before the event itself. With that discipline established, it may be that all you have to do, even with students, is to remind them in your warm-up of the need to "concentrate." Watch for indications of wandering minds—wandering or staring eyes—during the performance, and try to call those people back to their responsibilities with a glance or a gesture. The more you work at this, the easier it gets.

Don't let *yourself* be distracted by anything (not even by the thought that "everything is going well so far"). Don't focus too much on details, either, but keep your perspective of the whole structure you are trying to portray.

One risk is that you may become overtired. As one nears a public performance, one naturally feels some tension (some of which is good, for it focuses one's attention). You may work too hard to prepare yourself conscientiously. The authors suggest that you study and work in the morning, before a performance, and then avoid looking at the score again until curtain time. Plan deliberately to relax with some other project, perhaps some hobby, during the intervening hours.[1] Many conductors concentrate so hard on reviewing the score, right up to the moment of conducting, that—fatigued—they have trouble keeping their concentration during the performance itself.

---

[1] For longer works (especially opera), this is a particularly helpful approach to performance-day preparation.

MORE CONDUCTING THEORY
Cultural Traditions of Performance in the West

One might assume that the set of customs that surround and influence the behavior of performers and listeners in the concert hall is ageless. In fact, of course, many of these traditions are comparatively recent developments.

The earliest public concerts are said to have taken place late in the seventeenth century; "performances" before that time (limited almost entirely to the houses of the nobility, save for religious services) could hardly be called "public." There was no need for "box offices" and "tickets" so long as princely palaces and churches were the principal sites for hearing music. In such circumstances, those who were favored (that is, invited) were "given" the music by the host.

It was when the European middle class began to be understood as a new economic base from which professional musicians could profit that the business systems with which we are familiar began to evolve: advertising, the reservation and sale of admission tickets, duplicate performances, and the rest. (The whole system was still fairly new when Johann Peter Salomon invited Franz Joseph Haydn to London for the famous series of public concerts in 1791–92, for example.)

This evolution offered a new source of income to composers, as well as to performers. It began to assure successful men (like Haydn) new financial benefits. Composers who in an earlier age would have written a piece of music for a single use could now look forward to substantial fees for the printing of works that would find concert uses in halls all over the continent. Audience members, on the other hand, could hope to hear acclaimed works in future performances.

The new conditions in the concert hall demanded some practical adjustments on the part of the musicians. Courtly ensembles had relatively stable rosters of personnel, led by a *kapellmeister* who had the advantage of working with the same musicians day after day; their performances generally took place in palace rooms of state of rather modest size. The Baroque tradition had tended to place the *kapellmeister* at the continuo keyboard, from which he did any necessary conducting. (The amount of daily contact he had with his musicians meant that relatively little such direction was needed.)

But the developing concert opportunities led to more flexible careers for singers and players. "Free-lancing" became an alternative for musicians, and this meant that the orchestras playing public concerts—and the singers and other soloists appearing with them—were not fixed in personnel, as the palace bands had been; performers had to become accustomed to working with a kaleidoscope of colleagues. Gradually, larger auditoriums (built in response to increasing public enthusiasm) implied—in an age without microphones or loudspeakers—correspondingly larger ensembles. By the middle of the nineteenth century, then, the increased difficulties produced by size and distance were encouraging the use of conductors with batons.[2]

This new atmosphere in the concert hall prompted an evolution in the etiquette of the listener, as well. Instead of being part of the background (choir members in a religious service or instrumentalists playing at a courtly dinner), the performers in a public concert were the center of attention—the reason for which people had paid for tickets. They were there to be seen and heard, and this imposed new social responsibilities on the audience. One had to be quiet, for example. Decorum became a duty, particularly in an age without artificial amplification.[3]

One extension of this set of developing social understandings is the "Bayreuth hush" (the general silence just before the music begins, from the time the houselights go down to the actual beginning of the sounds). As the name Bayreuth implies, this behavior (which might be thought to have been an ages-old form of consideration for the music and the performers) actually was first remarked on by audience members attending Wagner's operas in his new hall in the nineteenth century. Many formal traditions with respect to applause, bows, and the like also are relatively recent, and subject to constant change, as the physical and social circumstances of concert life continue to evolve.

PRACTICAL PERFORMANCE ARRANGEMENTS

Let us suppose here a hypothetical choral–orchestral concert, imagining the sequence of procedures and actions—before, between, and after the pieces of music themselves—that enable the concert to go smoothly. What follows is a checklist for that sample performance.

1. If you are dealing with students or amateurs, you may want to schedule a brief brushup session (either onstage or in your rehearsal room) an hour or so before curtain time. With professionals, this should not be necessary.
2. You have agreed with your stage manager on a "lighting script" for the event. For a standard performance in a concert hall, that probably means that you will have "house lighting" set for the audience beforehand, with the stage lit only well enough for the players to warm up.
3. Ten to fifteen minutes before curtain time, the stage manager should cue your players to move on stage. In general, band and orchestra musicians do not "process onto the stage" formally. They individually and casually take their seats, get their instruments and music settled, and begin to warm up, playing exercises or passages help-

---

[2]As late as the premieres of his early operas, Verdi stood inactive beside the violins, in front of the "pit," while the cast and orchestra performed with only sporadic leadership from the concertmaster.

[3]The ready availability of high-decibel reinforcement for the popular music of the late twentieth century is changing this common viewpoint. Making noise is becoming socially acceptable again in "rock" audiences.

ful to them. (Either a player, the librarian, or the stage manager should place your own music on the conductor's stand.)

4. Five minutes or less before curtain time, the orchestra should begin to tune. This process traditionally is managed by the concertmaster (who may, in fact, not come onstage until this time). For technical reasons, it has become the standard practice that the (first) oboe give the tuning pitch; if no oboe is needed onstage, the concert-master gives the pitch or designates some other instrument to do so. When the next work to be performed is a keyboard concerto, or when a keyboard instrument is in use in the ensemble, it is used to define the pitch, since it cannot be "tuned." The common current practice in orchestras is for the tuning pitch to be offered at least three times: first for the woodwinds, then for the brass, and last for the strings. (Bands usually tune one section at a time, led by the solo clarinet.) Orchestras tune to the A-natural at or about A-440. Most bands employ the B-flat a half step higher, called Concert B-flat to indicate that it is an untransposed pitch—the same, that is, as the "written C-natural" played by the "Trumpets and Clarinets in B-flat."[4]

5. The choir can be cued to enter either before or after the orchestral tuning, as you think more graceful. You may have their processional come single file, from one side of the stage, or—divided backstage—from both sides.

6. Make sure each choir member holds her or his music (if any), which may be covered with a folder of some sort, in the same hand and at the same angle. The "line" of music across the stage is very obvious to those watching.

7. Once all have reached their places, facing downstage, you may—if there are chairs—have them seat themselves (on a cue from the center of the front row or by some other means). If they are to sing at the very beginning of the work, you may prefer to keep them standing.

8. If the choir must start singing without an instrumental introduction or prelude of any sort, they may need to be given a pitch, either as part of the tuning process or by tones especially directed to them.

9. Once the ensembles are in place and the tuning process is completed, it is time for (a) the houselights to come down, (b) the stagelights to come up, and (c) the soloists (if any) to move to their places.[5] You may want the stage manager to "flare" the stagelights somewhat (that is, to take them up to "full" and then drop them a notch—to normal performance level—after your entrance). This can bring the audience a heightened sense of anticipation and excitement.

10. You may follow the soloists immediately, or you may wait for a moment for them to seat themselves. If the choir is already seated, you may wish them to stand as you enter. (Some professional conductors expect their band or orchestra to rise at this point, as well.)

11. It works well to use the moment of your stepping onto the podium as the cue for the singers to raise their music and the players to raise their instruments.

---

[4]There are exceptions to these routines. The Vienna Philharmonic, for instance, never tunes on-stage. They do so offstage and then walk on to play. Their warm-up exercises occur offstage, too, so that the first sound the audience hears is the real thing.

Controversy often surrounds the exact tuning pitch chosen. Some orchestras have used an A-natural as high as or higher than A-450. Although higher tunings may sound "brighter" to the strings, this tessitura can cause trouble, of course, for singers and wind players.

[5]As a general rule, women always lead men onstage, and men cross behind women when they must pass each other onstage. Women also lead men offstage. Soloists are first on- and offstage, with the conductor following last.

12. In a major work, you should have cues established if you wish the soloists and choir to stand and seat themselves at various points during the music.

13. Be careful not to cause applause between movements of a work by any gesture or mannerism of your own. (Keep at least one of your hands raised, for example, if you fear the audience will begin to clap. With more experienced listeners in major concert halls, this should not be necessary, of course.) To put the matter another way, it is part of your role to *know when you want the audience to applaud,* and to consciously guide them to do so at the most appropriate times.

14. In some circumstances (between works or movements), it may be necessary for an orchestra or a band to retune. It usually is necessary for only a single pitch to be given, probably with the concertmaster remaining seated.

15. Bows follow each work (and will be discussed in some detail later in this chapter).

16. Plan precisely who will leave the stage at the end of each piece of music. You probably should exit whenever soloists do, at the end of a major work, or after any complete group of pieces of music.

17. Manage intermissions in the same way as the original curtain with respect to entrances, tuning, lighting, and all.

18. Try to keep the atmosphere from seeming lethargic or indifferent. At the same time, avoid any frenetic or abrupt gestures or actions. Let the audience see that what you are doing is important and that they should be happy to be present for it.

DEALING WITH EMERGENCIES

One of the competencies for which you are being paid to conduct is the ability to coolly and effectively handle emergencies. All sorts of things can go wrong: There can be serious and disruptive musical mistakes, and technical problems can occur (lights and equipment can fail to work, electrical lines can become disconnected, stagehands can miss cues, and the like). Performers can become ill during a concert. Music can fall off stands (or, during outdoor concerts, can be blown away). In audiences, babies can cry at crucial moments and other untimely noises can interfere.

Here again the key is *concentration.* The first thing you and your musicians must fight to maintain is a clear focus on the music at hand. Your worst enemy in a crisis is distraction. **When one realizes that one is facing an emergency, one's tendency is to hurry to a solution. Don't let that happen. Take time!** The second priority is *flexibility.* Almost any emergency (even in performance) can be survived if you keep your composure, take your time, and *think what are your real requirements—the absolute essentials of the music.* Maintain those.[6]

There are some specific principles to follow.

1. Some emergencies can be prevented. Ideally, no performance should be held hostage by a single individual; well before the concert, consider what you would do if any given individual should become ill. Who would cover for your soloist, your concertmaster, your accompanist, your best tenor? Include yourself: Who would

---

[6]See the discussion of concentration in Chapter 19.

conduct should you be absent? Try to identify (or arrange) substitutes and understudies. Don't wait until you already need someone.

2. Similarly, try to prevent inanimate things from interrupting your music. Draw up a list of your requirements—piano, music stands, riser units, chairs, special instruments, and all—for your stage manager. Work up a checklist, and use it to be certain that all the things you need are both available and in good repair.

3. If you are touring, use that same checklist to ensure that all these requirements actually reach the hall and the stage.

4. See that your musicians protect themselves. Warn your singers, for example, not to "lock their knees" (not to stand rigidly) under hot lights. (Many people who do so faint onstage.) Remind all of them that stages are inherently dangerous places; they should keep their minds on their purposes, and move carefully.

5. Some emergencies cannot be prevented. **Prepare your musicians to deal calmly with surprises by the way you handle emergencies in rehearsals,** and especially in your dress rehearsal. Condition them to have confidence in themselves and in you.

6. One way you can work toward this level of mutual respect is to *avoid stopping* every time something goes wrong in a practice session. Force the musicians to get through trouble without a complete halt. Let them see that with your help they can recover, and then they will know that they can do so in the real public situation.

7. **Probably the most hazardous musical crisis is the early attack.** You have the means, with your own cues, to prevent late entrances, but early attacks are almost always a surprise. Sometimes you can cut off the offender, signal a point for a fresh attack and cue it. Sometimes it is best simply to hold together all those who are right, and wait for the conflict to end. Sometimes there are other choices. Which one to make depends on your experience, your judgment, and, above all, your own composure.

At the moment it happens, a musical crisis in a public performance is no fun! After you have dealt with it, nevertheless, it can be very satisfying to realize you have successfully used your professional experience and skills to carry yourself, like Odysseus, past rocks, whirlpools, and potential disaster into quieter waters.

APPLAUSE AND BOWS

When the music ends, you should continue to manage the performance, which is not over so long as the lights are "up" on the performers. Your planning should include each of the following considerations.

1. Know how long you want to maintain the silence between your release of the last note and the beginning of the listeners' reaction. (Silence is music, too.) If you would like instantaneous applause in a given case, let the crowd see a big cutoff. If you prefer a long silence in another, hide your final release from them by keeping it screened in front of your body.

2. Decide whether you will control the bows from the podium or from a spot (still in the lights) beside it.

3. Plan the order in which you will acknowledge your colleagues. Keep them all in the lighted areas! A standard order would be:

    a. Soloists (if any)
    b. Featured choral members (if any)
    c. Featured orchestra members
    d. The choir in general (by gesturing to them)
    e. The orchestra in general (by having them stand)
    f. The concertmaster (shaking hands with her or him, and moving then, perhaps, to the other string principals, to shake hands with them, as well)

4. Once all these have been recognized, it is time for you to acknowledge the audience's applause by bowing yourself. After you do so, you (and the soloists, if any) can exit backstage. (Plan whether you will leave your baton on your stand or carry it with you.)
5. As soon as you pass behind the curtains, be ready to return for further bows.
6. If the applause seems sufficient to justify (and cover) your return, go back to the stage to accept it as many times as proves viable. If your stage manager has been "flaring" the stagelights for your entrances (at the beginning and after the intermission), he or she should continue to do so each time you return for a bow.
7. During these extra bows, you may repeat any or all of the individual acknowledgments just listed, saving the soloists for last. You and they may bow simultaneously now, side by side, if you like.
8. If your soloist is a distinguished one, you may wish to send her or him on for a solo bow, rejoining the artist yourself the next time (the final time, perhaps).
9. The general practice is that string players may applaud soloists by lightly tapping their bows on their stands, if they wish, *but choristers and wind players do not clap.*
10. For concerts without orchestra, some conductors recognize the choir from the side of the stage, but it is just as appropriate for you to move to the center for this gesture.
11. With bands and wind ensembles, it is the solo clarinet (like the orchestra's concert master) with whom you shake hands.
12. In the case of the jazz ensemble, the usual practice is for the leader to acknowledge each soloist (by name and instrument, over the microphone) after each number.

Practice accepting applause. Many young musicians are uncomfortable doing this, and so they feel (and look) stiff and unnatural. Men bow. Women may bow or curtsy, as they prefer. Working in front of a mirror, practice this procedure again and again until you feel and appear at ease.

As you continue to acknowledge the applause, consciously look toward every area of the auditorium. Give each audience member the sense that you have glanced directly at him or her. All your listeners want to feel that you know how much they personally enjoyed your performance.

A SPECIAL ELECTRICITY

The world of the performance is a soul-stirring, extraordinary state. At best, it is a kind of "natural high." There is a powerful sense of lively awareness, of focus, of dedication.

No matter how effectively you emulate performance circumstances in your rehearsals, you cannot reproduce this atmosphere. At a performance, the audience really is out there! All—musicians and listeners—are hearing the work complete and uninterrupted. Rehearsals are over; in a sense, there is "no tomorrow." It is like diving off the "high board."

Real artists are better in concert than in rehearsal. Good ensembles become more flexible, pliable, and precise; they are able to reach new heights in a performance, levels of accomplishment they could not achieve in practice sessions. Properly trained beforehand, they can "stretch" toward the best, most perceptive presentation they have imagined up to now. For a conductor, *it is like playing a different instrument.* The smallest gesture is recognized in this heightened concentration, and the musicians respond to it with enormous empathy.

The relationship of conductor to ensemble is reinvigorated here. These empathetic feelings are an increased sensitivity to each other's ideas and actions. The outcome can be a much deeper realization of the music: Having led the musicians in defining an interpretation, the conductor can treat them here as *trusted partners,* turning over to them responsibility both for the rearticulation of that interpretation in the terms it has been rehearsed and the enhancing and enlarging of that commonly held view of the work. *Inviting* the players and singers to respond in this manner inspires them to reach further within their own insights and abilities to give you and the audience their very best.

In one sense, the conductor is loosening control over the musicians, rather like a parent who must let a growing child face error and danger as a part of maturation. At certain points in the performance, the ensemble members can be "freed" in this way; at other times, to maintain a unified momentum and shape for the evolving aural structure, the conductor has to impose a firmer dominance (during transition passages and in the establishment of new tempos, for example). **The result of this sharing of responsibility can be a perfect Platonic balance of authority and service in an atmosphere of exploration, of seeking after an ideal vision.** The mutual feeling of fellowship with capable colleagues leaves one both proud and humble.

Once one has been for a time in that special world, one is always trying to recreate those moments. This is much of what artists live for, this sense of fresh focus and potent communication—this clarifying vision of life and truth. It makes all the technical discipline, scholarship, thoughtful preparation, hard work, and courageous risk-taking meaningful.

CHAPTER 21

Style and Performance: Conducting a Major Baroque Work

Before the colossus that is Johann Sebastian Bach one stands silent. Then memories of the music he has written sound in the ear, and the almost unfathomable genius comes to life again. The achievement was so great—the talent so formidable and the conceptions so profound—that only the chords, the rhythms, the melodies themselves can enable us to reach the man behind them.

To read about this life and to guess the rest (the diffidence of the burghers, the shallowness of the listeners, the squalling children, the lawsuits, and everything else common and trivial) explains so little. To learn what people of his own time said about him—contrasting Bach himself more-or-less unfavorably with Telemann, and with others whose names are recalled now only because of their proximity to his career—is to wonder from what blindnesses we of this modern age suffer and what talents of today go unseen and unheard.

We can repay him in part for the indifference of his contemporaries by performing his works, and doing so with integrity. To conduct Bach is a great responsibility, for one can be certain one is performing a part of the greatest music of the human heritage. And you are about to do so.

J. S. Bach: Cantata No. 4, *Christ lag in Todesbanden*

Studying Cantata No. 4

Thus we turn to one of Bach's most remarkable works, his Cantata No. 4, based on the chorale "Christ Lay in the Bonds of Death." A sinfonia, six movements alternating soloists and chorus, and a final chorale present you with many of the analysis and conducting problems of the Baroque era.[1]

Earlier in this volume, you were led through a series of conducting analyses. You should know now how to proceed in preparing to conduct the major forms that appear in this chapter and the four that follow it. This time, the responsibility of pursuing our "spiral study" is yours.

Certainly, you will want to look at works by such scholars as David and Mendel,[2] Dürr,[3] Neumann,[4] and others. Those writings will lead you to other sources if you let them do so. For a broad discussion of the liturgical practices of the churches in which Bach was serving, look at the work of Stiller.[5]

Look at several of the other Bach choral cantatas. Among the ones we recommend (they all are beautiful) are Nos. 80, 140, and 182. Look, too, at movements in the other major choral works by the master. To gain a broader assessment of Bach's orchestral writing, look at the *Brandenburg* concertos.

Move on to examine at least one or two choral cantatas by composers before Bach, particularly Germans like Buxtehude. This will give you an image of both the technical mastery and the creative brilliance of Bach. How old was he at the time? The dating of this cantata is controversial; see, for example, Herz's discussion of the origins of Cantata No. 4 (pp. 21–23).

Give attention to the environment in which this music was created. What do you know about the German Lutheran world in which Bach worked? What was the political system? What was the assumed relationship between church and state? Was this a time of peace or war in Leipzig? What was Bach's position in this church–state structure?

What about the visual art Bach saw? What did Thomaskirche look like, inside and out? What do you know about German wood carving and the other forms of religious art in Bach's world?

Ultimately, you want to gain a sense of the juxtaposition of Bach and these influences: Was he revolutionary, or stolidly traditional, or something else? Was he a man of faith, or a doubter? Was he a searcher, or was his music a synthesis of its time? Was he the beginning or the culmination of an era?

No young student can answer all these questions in an initial study of a

---

[1]As of this writing, we recommend that you obtain for your study the following edition: Johann Sebastian Bach, Cantata No. 4, *Christ lag in Todesbanden*, ed. Gerhard Herz (New York: W. W. Norton & Co., Inc., 1967). The Herz edition is prefaced with three brief essays on the Bach cantatas, the dating of Cantata No. 4, and the chorale text/tune; then, after the score itself, there is an analysis of the work, movement by movement, and a section of passages of commentary about this cantata by eight other great musicologists.

[2]H. David and A. Mendel, *The Bach Reader* (New York: W. W. Norton & Co., Inc., 1945).

[3]Alfred Dürr, "Performance Practice of Bach's Cantatas," *American Choral Review*, 16, No. 2 (April 1974), 1–33.

[4]Werner Neumann, *Handbook of Joh. Seb. Bach's Cantatas* (Leipzig: Breitkopf & Härtel, 1947).

[5]Günther Stiller, *Johann Sebastian Bach and the Liturgical Life in Leipzig*, ed. Robin A. Leaver, trans. Herbert J. A. Bouman, Daniel F. Poellot, and Hilton C. Oswald (St. Louis: Concordia, 1984).

major work. You can form ideas now, however, and many of them will be right. Subtlety and elaboration can come later, as you move on to other research. **Never pretend (by just going blindly through the music) that the time and the setting in which the composer and his musicians worked are not part of the fabric and the character of the music itself. This perspective—this consummate conception of the work in its world—is the proper basis for your interpretation.**[6]

You should compare the Herz edition, of course, with the great *Gesamtausgabe* sources[7] and with the performing editions that are available.[8]

Your musical analysis of the cantata should follow the general processes displayed in the analyses we have done in earlier chapters of this volume. The same parameters should be examined; that is, as well as the historical setting, you should consider

> The forces needed
> Tonality and cadence aspects
> Meter and rhythm
> Harmonic factors and dissonance
> Melodic factors
> Textural aspects
> The text, in structure and meaning
> Miscellaneous features and peculiarities
> The overall structure

This elaborate examination will begin to prepare you to make choices among the various performance options open to you.

One large consideration, which you should not miss, is the part played here by the cantus firmus—by the chorale tune itself and by the text associated with that cantus firmus.[9]

You should complete this analysis before proceeding further with your technical preparation to conduct the cantata.

---

[6]As a convenience for your later use, the authors include in Appendix B a summary of style and performance practice for music from the Baroque era. You may want to review that at this time. You may wish also to refer to the historical and stylistic background for this era discussed in Chapter 11.

[7]Johann Sebastian Bach, *Christ lag in Todesbanden*, in *Werke* (Leipzig: Bach-Gesellschaft, 1855–1899 and 1926), 1, 97; also in *Neue Ausgabe sämtlicher Werke* (Kassel and Leipzig: Bärenreiter Verlag, 1954), 1, ix. See also the miniature score edited by Arnold Schering (New York: Edition Eulenberg, 1932); this last was used by Herz for the Norton Critical Scores edition already cited.

[8]The best performance edition of Cantata No. 4 may well be the Bärenreiter version based on the *Neue Ausgabe sämtlicher Werke*. See also the score edited by Reinhold Kubik (Stuttgart: Carus, 1981), and the Kalmus reprint of the original Bach-Gesellschaft edition.

[9]A transcription of the cantus firmus can be found on p. 81 of the Herz edition, and the text is presented by Herz in detail, movement by movement. The opening of the Eulenberg edition shows a text breakdown syllable by syllable in German with an English translation underneath.

Performance Forces

Let us speak of the forces appropriate for the performance of this cantata, and when we do so, let us aim, at first, for an ideal. We can compromise later.

We have good evidence that the choir singers Bach used on Sunday morning often numbered fewer than twenty. This SATB cantata could be performed with sixteen well-chosen, technically capable singers. Today's concert halls are substantially bigger and less reverberant than were the churches in which Bach served, however, so an ensemble of thirty singers may be a good choice for you. (Today's *churches* are not bigger than Thomaskirche, by the way, although present-day acoustics generally are drier.) The four soloists are included in that total, incidentally; the concertists were choir members at Leipzig.

For the orchestra, given a chorus of thirty, one might seat ten violins (divided six and four between the two parts) and six violas (divided three and three), with three or four 'cellos; add a string bass assigned to the continuo line. Either organ or harpsichord would be appropriate for the sinfonia and the choruses; consider, however, that it can be very effective to use harpsichord for the continuo parts in the arias and the duets, shifting to organ for the choral movements; the contrast between organ and harpsichord is striking. (Note that in the full-score editions now available, the keyboard part is not written out.)

Cornetto (you can use a trumpet, but keep its production light and bright) is shown doubled with the sopranos in some movements, and three trombones are doubled with the lower voice parts. (The older, small-bore trombones would be better in balance and character.) It is possible to perform the cantata without the *colla parte* instruments (especially since Bach may have added them later), but the sound is quite different. (Actually, the brass doublings work quite well if the players are skilled. If they are clumsy, all sorts of problems emerge.)

Remember that the characteristic sound for which you are striving is not dominated by the voices. What *is* appropriate is a more homogenized fabric of vocal and instrumental timbres (including the special flavor produced from the keyboard) that you will come to remember as a "Baroque sound," in much the same way that you have learned to remember the pungent odor of orange peel.

Textual Aspects

There is good evidence, in great and small ways, of Bach's devotion to, and sensitivity to, his texts. To recognize this, one need only recall the *Magnificat,* with its closing "Sicut erat in principio" ("As it was in the beginning") sung to the subject of the opening chorus.

Text-painting instances (what would be called madrigalisms in earlier centuries) are common. Sometimes they are obvious—as in the "Crucifixus" of the B Minor Mass, when the sopranos descend stepwise into the "grave" on the words "passus et sepultus est" ("died and was buried"). Sometimes they are subtler; to choose an instance at random from this cantata, note the vigorous, melismatic activity set to the word "Leben" ("life") in measures 26–35 of Versus I; or look at the repeated cascades of gaiety on "fröhlich" ("joyful") in bars 39–45 of the same chorus. This sort of analysis of the text can be very instructive for you.

Look at the other aspects of the text, too. Observe the part the rhyme scheme of each verse plays in influencing the cadential structure. Look for such peculiarities as the "hocketlike" setting of "Hallelujah" in measures 58–66 of Versus I.

When you have examined the text in detail, it is time for you to consider how Bach—setting that text to music—makes clear his own philosophical-theological interpretation of those words. Then you will be ready to express the words with the music.

Structure and Continuity

The sophistication of Renaissance polyphony limited to trained musicians its performance in liturgies. The original virtue of the "chorale," on the other hand, as it emerged in the sixteenth century, was that its simplicity permitted common folk to join in vocal praise of God.

The complexities of Bach's fugal writing again overreached the abilities of the congregation, of course, and from the cantata's Sinfonia through its verses—one by one—the *Volk* worshipped silently. The liturgy had not forgotten them, however; the last movement of the cantata provided a simple, chordal, straightforward setting of the final verse of the text, and here all those standing before the altar—clergy, musicians, and laypeople—joined together in a synthesis of worship symbolic for them of the union of Christ and His Church.

In Cantata No. 4, this marvelous liturgical conception is complemented by Bach's overall structural plan. There is a deliberate symmetry in the layout of the movements, with media arranged in parallels around the central Versus IV.[10] This arch form is similar to Bach's plan in other works.

Once you understand the overall design of the work, you need to turn your attention to *continuity*. Connections of all kinds are your concerns: how to approach one note from the last one, how to get from bar 4 to bar 5, and—ultimately—how to get from measure 1 of the Sinfonia to the end of Versus VII.

Choosing Tempos

We discussed in Chapter 18 the issues that influence choices of tempo. Here we must add that in a multimovement work, it is important that each movement fit into an overall tempo plan.

Considering the musical and external circumstances, we recommend that

---

[10]For an outline of this plan, see the Herz edition, pp. 83–86.

you consider taking the Sinfonia at a tempo a bit slower than the *tempo ordinarium*. Then relate the movements that follow to that opening pace.

Sinfonia	♩ = 42
Versus I	♩ = 84
Alla breve	♩ = 60–66
Versus II	♩ = 56
Versus III	♩ = 72
Adagio	♩ = 36 (half speed)
Allegro	♩ = 72 (*a tempo*)
Versus IV	♩ = 76
Versus V	♩ = 84
Versus VI	♩ = 84
Chorale	♩ = 60 (between 56 and 66)

Several of these tempos use the same metronome marking. Bach's rhythmic motion brings variety to the pace, however; compare the three movements we have marked ♩ = 84. Versus I moves in four with quarters, eighths, and sixteenths. Versus V is in triple meter and moves in quarters and eighths, with almost no sixteenths. Versus VI is back in four, employing quarters and a dotted rhythm.

Technical Considerations

The descending melodic half step (which is indigenous to the Chorale itself, of course) is featured all over the Sinfonia, and then throughout the cantata, as you will have seen by now. Bach passes the half steps from voice to voice and uses them dramatically in movement after movement. In all these cases—and especially in exposed circumstances, like the first violin lines in the Sinfonia, bars 1–5—give careful thought to the articulation, the weight, and every aspect of the presentation of this focal melodic interval.

For the Sinfonia, note the clear statement of the cantus firmus in bar 5. The peak comes at the end of measure 7, and then retrenchment begins; the descending step progression from bar 8 to bar 12 contributes much to the feel of this. You could stretch measures 12 and 13 a bit, subdividing to allow for the sixteenths.

The Sinfonia is quite chromatic, as you see. All twelve tones occur in bars 5–8. Do not underestimate this apparently simple movement; in its gravity, it balances all the rest of the work.

Versus I is a chorale fantasia, with each phrase preceded by a set of imitative fugal entrances (based on the cantus firmus) in the lower three voices, supporting a direct statement of the chorale melody in the soprano/cornetto. Try a marked, clearly articulated approach here to keep the texture clean.

The seam between the opening section and the *Alla breve* "Hallelujah" can be difficult for a young conductor. Try taking a *tiny* ritard in measure 67, unsettling the original tempo just enough to make clear your establishment of the new pace at the *Alla breve*. We suspect Bach wanted the closing section taken in two (hence "Alla breve"), but not at a naive doubling of the starting tempo. You could start this new section in four, and then shift to two, however; in any event, your downbeat at bar 68 must show exactly the new pace.

At the final ritard, it is of critical importance that you think the subdivision before you have to begin delivering it. That is always the case.

Proceed in similar ways with the remaining movements. The descending half step is often the key to phraseology. Look to see where it occurs, and where the cantus firmus appears. Watch the setting of the text.

Varieties of Baroque style appear. Versus III has a Buxtehude-like figuration in the violin line in what is a trio sonata texture. Versus IV is thought old-fashioned by some; another hocketlike passage occurs at measures 35–36. In Versus VI, the voices trade places back and forth, alternating as leader.

Don't forget about ornamentation! Look for places to decorate the lines, especially near cadences. (One example, taken at random: What about a trill on the D-sharp in the violin line of Versus III, bar 36?)

In Versus III, the Adagio starts on the pickup "denn" in bar 26; the motion shifts to eighth notes at half tempo and then doubles back to the original tempo at the Allegro. (Note, by the way, the tone-painting here: the descending line through bars 24–26 to "Tods Gestalt"—"the Figure of Death.")

Versus IV can be sung by a solo quartet, as some authorities recommend, or it can be performed by the whole choir. Watch the balance against the alto line in measures 39–41.

Balance is an issue in Versus V, too. Keep the violins in proportion to the solo bass voice. Check for ornamentation opportunities in this wonderful aria.[11]

If it is feasible, marshal the audience for the final chorale (Versus VII). That will bring your performance, whether in church or in the concert hall, closer to Bach.[12]

A Final Word

Closer to Bach? What a dream! We think it an honor merely to study and conduct this work. The debt for all the beauty, the power, the serenity—most of all, the reassurance—is too great to be paid, and was not paid in his lifetime. Remember, however, that Bach never intended we purchase his music; it was not created to be sold at public concerts and in music shops. He did not write it for us. Rather, he dedicated it *(Deo soli gloria)*.

Just so, in preparing to perform his music, and other great masterworks, we should offer up our talents—we should dedicate ourselves—not in payment to Bach for his music, but in gratitude for his life, his genius, and his dedication. In so doing, we rejoice in art that was, and is, and ever shall be.

[11]Note the debate about the G in bar 70, Herz edition, p. 76.
[12]See our discussion of a Bach chorale in Chapter 6.

CHAPTER 22

Style and Performance: Conducting a Major Viennese Classical Work

In 1794 Franz Joseph Haydn, at that moment the most famous living musician in all Europe, made his second trip to England. His first visit, in 1791–92, had been glorious; accolades, decorations, and admiration had come from the Prince of Wales, from the peers of the realm, from the professors of Oxford, and from purchasers of seats in the concert halls. The first six of his English "Grand Overtures" (as the "London Symphonies" were first christened) had been enthusiastically received. With a newfound recognition of his own identity—with a sure sense of himself as something far more than an Esterházy servant—Haydn returned in 1792 to the dominions of his Hungarian prince.

He must have felt joy in 1794 at the prospect of this second stay in England. Certainly, he found the esteem of the Londoners undiminished as he introduced them to the six new symphonic works commissioned for this tour.

Mozart had been in his unmarked grave more than two years, and Beethoven was still unknown at the time Haydn composed these six symphonies. Haydn was at the height of his powers, and these would be the last such works he would write. They would come to represent the Viennese Classical style on concert programs down through the ages, and their influence would resonate in the ears of Beethoven and generations of his successors.

Franz Joseph Haydn: Symphony in D Major, No. 101

Studying the Symphony in D Major

It is one of these six masterpieces that will provide for you a case study for the preparation and conducting of a major Classical work. Haydn premiered the four-movement "Clock Symphony" (so called because of the tick-tock effect produced by the pizzicatos in its second movement) in London in May 1794, and the work has remained justly famous. We believe you will find it an archetype of the style.[1] As has become your practice, you will want to look particularly at the analytic parameters. (See Chapters 18 and 21.) Your appreciation of these aspects will begin to direct you toward appropriate interpretive choices.

Beyond the work itself, there are wonderful opportunities for your "spiral study." Especially, you should become familiar with the scholarship of Landon, whose seminal work on the Haydn symphonies was one of the triggers of the wave of Haydn studies seen in recent years.[2] There is a respected modern biography by Geiringer,[3] as well as a pair of translations by Gotwals[4] of very early works of this master. You may find that the collection of letters Landon assembled is also of interest to you.[5]

As you read about Haydn, you should be analyzing other works of his. A couple of other symphonies (perhaps an early one and another late example) are essential.

You would do well to study two or three of the famous string quartets. All through his life, Haydn seems to have used the quartets as a sprawling compositional laboratory in which he could try out new ideas. Structural innovations, new tonal relationships, and, above all, the process we now call "thematic development" appear in the quartets over four decades of creative work; the earliest quartets predate, and the final ones follow, the whole roster of symphonies. Examine, for example, one of the Opus 17 quartets, in which the texture is dominated by the first violin, and compare it with the Opus 33 works—perhaps the famous No. 2, with its last-movement "Joke"—in which the new developmental process appears, tied to relative equality among the quartet members; go on, then, to a masterful late work like either of the two Opus 77 quartets.

And what about the piano sonatas? A glance at two or three of the late ones would prove beneficial.

Much of what we now call the Viennese Classical style was made concrete by Joseph Haydn, who combined and refined elements of the older Baroque tradition with the rudimentary experiments of transitional figures like Stamitz,

---

[1] As a convenience for your later use, the authors include in Appendix B a summary of style and performance practice for music from the Classical era. You may want to review that at this time. You may wish also to refer to the historical and stylistic background for this era discussed in Chapter 11.

[2] H. C. Robbins Landon, *The Symphonies of Joseph Haydn* (London: Universal Edition and Rockliff Publishing, 1955); and *Haydn: Chronicle and Works*, 5 vols. (Bloomington: Indiana University Press, 1976–1980).

[3] Karl Geiringer, *Haydn: A Creative Life in Music* (Berkeley and Los Angeles: University of California Press, 1968).

[4] Vernon Gotwals, *Joseph Haydn: Eighteenth Century Gentleman and Genius* (Madison: University of Wisconsin Press, 1963).

[5] H. C. Robbins Landon, *The Collected Correspondence and London Notebooks of Joseph Haydn* (London: Barrie and Rockliff, 1959).

Monn, and C.P.E. Bach (for whose music Haydn evinced great respect). You can trace the innovative work Haydn did by comparing their efforts with his own.

Of those whom Haydn himself influenced, the list is endless, but it begins with Mozart (who had great, if lesser, effect on Haydn) and Beethoven. Mozart spent his last ten years near Haydn in Vienna, and they frequently played for each other their newest manuscripts. Look at one or two of the late Mozart symphonies, not just to see the cross-influences, but particularly to spot the great differences between the two men. Consider also the obvious use of Haydn's structural processes in one of the earlier Beethoven symphonies or quartets.

Haydn was very much a child of his era. What do you know about the Habsburg Empire within which he served, and of the Hungarian potentates, the Princes Esterházy, by whom he was employed? Maria Theresa, the great Habsburg empress, was the center of the state in his youth, and the liberal reformer Joseph sat upon the imperial throne during the middle of Haydn's career. The Napoleonic Wars disrupted Austrian life in his last decade, bringing with them the revolutionary fervor that was to inspire Beethoven. All this influenced him, as did his devotion to the Roman Catholic church.

Where was his music performed? What were the physical and acoustical characteristics of the concert halls and churches in which he worked? (Certainly the Haydnsaal at Eisenstadt is one of the finest performing venues in the world, and he is said to have made it so by persuading the prince to lay a wooden floor on top of the ornate marble already there. The wood remains in place today.)

Editions and Performance Forces

The current edition we recommend most highly is the one prepared by Landon.[6] It has the benefits of the latest and best scholarship.

There are older editions around in libraries. Generally speaking, they are marred by out-of-date articulation markings, inaccurate bowings, and the like. In recent years, for example, a great deal of work has clarified the use of wedges (as opposed to staccato dots) in Haydn's music; you want to follow Haydn's wishes in that regard, of course. It is possible to edit corrections into an older, less accurate edition; this is time-consuming and tedious, however, and there is always the risk of further error.

The orchestration for Symphony No. 101 is standard. Haydn asks for woodwinds in pairs, two horns, two trumpets, timpani, and strings; for the strings, a minimum of 4-4-2-2-1 would be in keeping with the style, providing the hall you are using resembles the ones in which Haydn performed. In a large auditorium with less-than-ideal acoustics, you may want to go as high as 8-7-5-6-3 in the strings. *Balance and transparency must be a primal concern in performing works like this one.* Remember, it is quite possible that Haydn conducted the pre-

---

[6]Franz Joseph Haydn, Symphony No. 101 in D Major, ed. H. C. Robbins Landon (Haydn Mozart Presse, Universal Edition 182, 1967).

miere of Symphony No. 101 from the harpsichord, for we know he did so on occasion; there is no extant keyboard part, but that proves nothing (since he would not have needed one). Modern performances, at any rate, are done without harpsichord.

Structure and Continuity

In Haydn's youth, the four-movement design that became the standard for the Classical symphony and string quartet was not yet defined. His earliest string quartets, in fact, written in the late 1750s, employ *five* movements: an opening Allegro, a minuet, a slow movement, a second minuet, and a finale. During the writing of his long roster of quartets, Haydn experimented with movement order, first deleting the extra minuet, and then trading the remaining minuet back and forth with the slow movement; first one of them would appear as the second movement, and then the other. He also tried a variety of musical forms; the finales of the quartets, for example, range from sonata allegros and rondos to fugues, variations, and hybrid types of all sorts. (Haydn invented the sonata-rondo structure that was to prove so useful to Beethoven.)

In observing this engineering process, we can deduce that Haydn's interest in the internal structure of each movement and its place in the continuity that became the four-movement symphony was a vivid one. That implies that we must give careful attention to the possibilities he offers us to make of each of his works a coherent, cohesive whole. Symphony No. 101 is not a medley, a hodgepodge of four unrelated pieces, but, rather, a continuity of related and contrasting forms and materials, each one a carefully balanced architecture in itself.

Choosing Tempos

With respect to the opening Adagio in $\frac{3}{4}$, the current sense among those who are performing these works in Austria is that tempos for these slow introductions should not be as extreme, even lethargic, as those some well-known conductors have chosen in years past. We recommend that you ask your players to "feel this section in quarters, not eighths." The tempo here could be ♩ = 52–56; with a very good orchestra, playing with an excellent sense of "line," this could be stretched to ♩ = 48.

The Presto that follows should be approximately twice as fast as the Adagio, or even a bit faster—something approaching ♪. = 120. When Haydn uses a word like "Presto," he means it.

For the celebrated Andante in $\frac{2}{4}$, the basis of motion is the eighth note (even though we suggest that the players should try to think in two). Traditional tempos for this movement range from ♪ = 88 to ♪ = 100. We suggest ♪ = 92 as a starting point for you.

The third movement is no Mozart minuet. Not courtly in manner, this is a spirited (almost flamboyant) peasant dance. Coarser and heavier in character than the Viennese minuet of its time, it reflects the color and excitement of Eisenstadt and the Hungarian border more than the superciliousness and courtliness of the Imperial court in Vienna. Taken in an emphatic three, it is suited to ♩ = 128–136.

For the finale, the tempo depends on the ability of your string players. You may prefer to take this movement in one; whether you can do so depends on what you discover during rehearsals. In one, with professional players, we recommend something close to 𝅝 = 68. You may have to slow down slightly, and take it in two, perhaps at ♩ = 128; this will have two effects: The slower tempo will help, and the extra beat per bar will keep the orchestra from trying to rush.

Technical Considerations

The slow introduction to the first movement is uncomplicated. At this tempo, the cutoffs in bars 4 and 12 are also preparatory beats (unless your hall is very reverberant). Note the differences (in articulation and bowings, measures 7–11, for example) between the first violins and the lower strings. Make certain you have a concept of phrasing for these spots. Know what you want for spacing between figures. The wonderful set of sforzatos in measures 18–20 and the *p/pp* markings in measures 21–22 deserve careful preparation.

To begin the Presto, it might be safer to show more than one pulse. Here the cutoff (of the last note of the introduction) should *not* be a preparatory beat, since the silence needs to be longer than that would permit; release the fermata, freeze for a moment, and give the preparatory beat(s) for the Presto. Whether you give one beat or two, be certain that your tempo is clear and exact so that you will not encourage the musicians to rush.

The Presto begins with five-bar phrases, and Haydn's developmental procedures begin almost immediately. The *A* materials are truncated—shortened to only two bars at measure 72, *impelling the motion forward* but keeping hidden from the audience the exact proportions of the structure until each successive cadence displays them. This is the excitement and the humor of Haydn. It is heightened by the thematic simplicity of his materials; the *B* theme is rhythmically close in character to the *A* material and then becomes the basis for the Development section.

Note the ways Haydn freshens our ears; the legato passage he inserts in measures 92–96 is characteristic, for he loves to slide through an augmented-sixth chord legato, and at *piano*.

What about the first ending here? The movement could be played without repeats, but so doing would constitute a radical revision of Haydn's structure.

The Development section itself is like a labyrinth, with deliberate and temporary wrong turns. Tell your players: "You know what is coming next, but play as though you do not!" You can help with this; your body language can be as influential as the music itself in focusing the audience. And you need a full range of articulatory gestures—a variety of preparatory beats—to provide the surprises that hide here.

There are more surprises in the Recapitulation—the D minor section, for example. Begin the Recap by taking time for the structure to "sound" at bar 217; it is our view that whenever Haydn writes a fermata over a rest (as he does here), he means that he wants a lengthened, dramatic silence. That is made especially effective at this spot by the shift from the previous *fortissimo*.

There is another delightful moment at measure 329—the deft, hushed, staccato entrance of the flute, followed four bars later by a dramatic tutti marked *forte*. Listeners should go away from such movements chortling at Haydn's skill and wit.

For the second movement's Andante, it might be best to use a subdivided-two beat pattern. We prefer that the players keep a feeling of two, but you can make the fabric cleaner if you show in your beat the relevant eighth notes.

This is a perpetual-motion movement, with changes of momentum written in. Insist on good sound quality for the pizzicato notes, and work carefully on the phrasing of the first violin melody. Be precise about spacing, and honor the sudden dynamic changes, as you did in the first movement.

Repeats can be done differently, varying dynamics the second time (reversing a crescendo–diminuendo pattern, for example, or inserting a subito). This adds life to the movement, especially a movement as well known as this one.

Keep checking balances (at the powerful *forte* in bar 34, for example). Sometimes this is a matter of the priorities you display in your conducting. Beginning at bar 64, for example, the winds are still staccato; yet, the first violins are legato. Which should you show in your beat? (Which needs help at a given moment? Which is more important? Which do you want the audience to hear? Can you switch back and forth?)

The "clock" stops in bar 97. We recommend that you count the measure of rest metronomically (but don't let the audience see any beat).

At the end of this movement, some conductors choose to let "the clock run down" by making a gradual ritard in the Coda from measure 140 or so. One suspects that Haydn is asking for this: Note his handling of the triplet sixteenths and the *pianissimo* ending.

The heavy-footed minuet is clearly marked. How about the length of the opening pickup note, and the parallel pickup in measure 4? How long do you want these to be, here and throughout the movement? There are wonderful details here: Note the changing string-and-woodwind patterns in bars 18–19, the metric shifts in bars 20–27, the timpani accompanying the violins (all alone) in measures 29–34. Call attention to these spots. Plan what can be done differently in the repeated sections.

Haydn finales may sound effortless, but they are never easy for the players. Taking the Vivace movement in two will help prevent rushing, especially in bars 3 and 7—a very real danger here. Know exactly how many measures until the next change of material, motion, dynamics, and so on. Be prepared to show everything clearly.

The final fugal development, starting at measure 189, is tough for the strings. Look at the asymmetry of bar groupings here, and help them all you can. What a virtuosic piece this is for the first violins! Remember that Haydn was accustomed to working with fine players at Eisenstadt and Eszterháza, long before he went to London. (We can tell from the difficulty of the symphony and quartet parts, for instance, that his concertmaster in the prince's orchestra—Tomasini—was a masterful player.)

A Final Word

Haydn was "showing off" in these London Symphonies—especially so, perhaps, in the finales. He was at the peak of his career, and he knew how good he was. Sure of himself in his orchestration, confident of his imagination, proud of the wit of his musical rhetoric, he displayed in these works the adroit command of forms and materials he had earned over a lifetime.

A conductor *must* show energy in a work like this, and particularly in the finale. You must be the image of the spirit and excitement you want your players to convey.

The potential balance problems between woodwinds, brass, and strings are quite different from those encountered in the Baroque texture of the Bach cantata you studied in the previous chapter. Look carefully at Haydn's orchestration: What can you ascertain from the choices he made in assigning specific materials to given instruments? What does that tell you about the overall sonority he sought?

Haydn was a child of the Age of Reason. His ideal listener is one who strives to follow logically the turns and twists—the ambiguities and confirmations—he wrote into the music. **You know what is coming next, but the audience does not!** Surprise them! Keep the "contents" of Haydn's "package" hidden, and let the players gradually unfold the shapes in front of the listeners. That will delight them. They will find that the music of the Viennese Classical era is quite as sophisticated and exciting as they could hope.

CHAPTER 23

Style and Performance: Conducting a Concerto for Violin and Orchestra

Bright, talented, and highly educated, Felix Mendelssohn caught the attention of the musicians of Berlin before the young pianist had as many years as fingers. By his sixteenth birthday, he was known across Europe as a young composer of great promise. Before he had reached the age of twenty-one, he had conducted the performance of the *St. Matthew Passion* that restored the music of Bach to public esteem. Before he turned thirty, he had revived the Handelian oratorio and carried it to the land of Handel's greatest successes.

So brave a beginning—worthy of Mozart—promised a radiant maturity, and thus it transpired: the *Midsummer Night's Dream* music, the *Italian* Symphony, and *Elijah*, spread over three decades, confirmed that promise; his stewardship of the Leipzig Gewandhaus orchestra and his impact on audiences across Europe and Britain had as much impact as his compositions. Unfortunately, the Mozart metaphor proved too apt, for Mendelssohn was to die at thirty-seven, having been granted only two years more of life than his Austrian predecessor.

Born of a sophisticated family, and shaped by conversations with such geniuses as Goethe and Hegel, the youthful Mendelssohn brought a Classical education together with a temperament influenced by the ideas of the emerging Romantic era. His was a transitional period in music; Mendelssohn was thinking as a Classical composer but living in a time when limits were being stretched. Rhythms were growing more complex; the bar line was becoming mobile and the pulse less regular. Song—accompanied melody—was beginning to dominate texture; composers were turning into tunesmiths. Both melody and harmony were increasingly affected by chromaticism. Tonal shifts to more distant keys were becoming common. New instruments and larger numbers of players were joining the orchestra. In the spatial dimensions, forms and tessituras were moving toward the extremes.[1]

In many respects, Mendelssohn himself was to remain conservative, but an increased obviousness of sentiment was part of his world, and part of him, as well. The Classical style *had* been expressive—all Art is expressive—but the newer Romantic mood tended toward the melodramatic. The Age of Reason had died in the streets of Paris, and a new preoccupation with passion now characterized the times.

The Concerto for Violin and Orchestra in E Minor, Op. 64, with "Allegro molto appassionato" designating the tempo of its first movement, is a product of those times. The last major orchestral work Mendelssohn was to write (don't let the confused roster of his opus numbers mislead you), the concerto was completed in 1844 and first performed in Leipzig the following March. It looks and sounds like a Romantic work by a Classical composer: Caught on the border between the two styles, it offers many more opportunities for rubatos and other expressive liberties than, say, the Bach you studied two chapters back.

The Concerto Soloist

Before you begin your study of this concerto, however, it is necessary that you give thought to the solo artist on which the work depends. (That is, in fact, the order in which things happen in the professional world: A "guest artist" is chosen and contracted, and then by direct negotiation a particular concerto is scheduled.)

First, it is important that you become well acquainted with the prospective soloist. What kind of musician is she or he? How good is her technic? How does he handle difficult passages, transitions, and the like? We recommend that (well before the first rehearsal) you sit down for a conference with the artist, asking what his or her ideas are about the shape and pace of the work. Agree on tempos then, rather than foraging for them in rehearsal. Ask where the soloist needs more time for a fermata, a ritard, or whatever. Make it clear where the difficult orchestra spots are, too.

Although any great concerto is an artistic whole, and the orchestra is an equal in that circumstance, the soloist is the central figure—and the guest! Treat the artist hospitably, acceding to her or his musical wishes wherever possible.[2]

---

[1]As a convenience for your later use, the authors include in Appendix B summaries of style and performance practice for music from the Classical and Romantic eras. You may want to review that at this time. You may wish also to refer to the historical and stylistic background for this era discussed in Chapter 12.

[2]In a famous incident, well reported in the newspapers at the time, one of the most prominent American conductors stepped to the front of the stage just before a concerto, announcing to the audience that although he believed the tempos in the imminent performance to be unjustifiably lethargic, the stature of the guest artist was so great he had decided to cooperate so that the concertist's interpretation could be heard and judged by others.

To say it another way, consider yourself in this circumstance an *accompanist*. To be a fine accompanist as a conductor is a great skill, as it is with pianists. Learn, as excellent accompanists do, to "get inside the soloist's mind." Know what the artist is going to do before he or she does it; then communicate that anticipation to your orchestra players.

Felix Mendelssohn: Concerto for Violin and Orchestra in E Minor, Op. 64

Studying the Violin Concerto in E Minor

Reacquaint yourself with the overture to *A Midsummer Night's Dream*, Op. 21; completed before Mendelssohn was eighteen, it is nevertheless, like this concerto, a genuine masterwork. Note the almost naive directness and clarity of expression. Look also at the *Songs without Words*, Op. 19. Here is the ideal of songlike melody that enchanted the Romantics.

Examine carefully the *Italian* Symphony, Op. 90, written a decade before this concerto, particularly noting the delicacy and the meticulous balancing of the woodwind parts at the very beginning. (Someone once said that if Mendelssohn had miscalculated the orchestration of the repeated chords, this spot would "sound like a chickenyard"—in an asylum, at that.) Glance at one of the piano concertos, as well.

It is essential that you study at least a couple of the Mozart concertos (perhaps one for violin and one for piano). Mozart was the master who brought the Baroque concerto form to what would be the modern world. Don't fail to compare the Mendelssohn also with at least two other great nineteenth-century violin concertos, those by Beethoven and Brahms.

In addition to biographical sources on Mendelssohn, give some time to writings about the concerto form, including such works as those by Lang[3] and Tovey.[4]

You can gain a sense of the spirit of the time by reading some of the poetry of Keats and Wordsworth, or a novel by Sir Walter Scott. Look at paintings ranging from Constable to Delacroix to Turner, or at David's "Napoleon Crossing the Alps." Or—to get a clear image of the sentimental—read Dickens.

Just so, in Mendelssohn's *Elijah*, one finds that all is filled with drama, poignancy, and alternations of passion with despair. Be careful not to condescend! These were brilliant people, from whose view of their world we still can learn something about ours.

---

[3]Paul Henry Lang, *The Concerto 1800–1900* (New York: W. W. Norton & Co., Inc., 1969).

[4]Donald Francis Tovey, *Essays in Musical Analysis, Volume III: Concertos* (London: Oxford University Press, 1939).

Editions and Performance Forces

At the present time, there are at least three published editions of this concerto. The authors use the Breitkopf & Härtel version,[5] of which the Kalmus[6] is a reprint; a Peters edition is also available. For study purposes, the miniature score printed by Norton is inexpensive and useful, and it contains a brief commentary on the nineteenth-century concertos already mentioned.[7]

Mendelssohn's ensemble is still the basic Classical orchestra. Woodwinds in pairs, two horns, two trumpets, timpani, and strings are required (the same instrumentation as that needed for the Haydn symphony in the previous chapter). At a minimum, the string body might be 6-6-4-4-2; we suggest a somewhat larger group, however: Perhaps 10-9-7-8-4 would be ideal.

Structure and Continuity

The Italian Baroque forerunner of the form we are studying typically employed in its first movement a ritornello design in which four or more tutti statements of the orchestral material alternated with solo (or soli) sections. The latter generally emphasized figuration, and the technical demands for the solo players became more virtuosic as the eighteenth century began. By the time of Torelli, this concerto likely would have three movements (fast–slow–fast); the soloists would be members of the orchestra—first-desk players—who would join in the tutti passages, as well.

The characteristic features of the Classical sonata allegro design penetrated this Baroque ritornello structure as the years passed. In Mozart's splendid first movements, the Italian tuttis still can be seen, but the orchestral material belongs to the soloist, as well; commonly, the orchestra presents the first theme, and then the soloist reprises it. This so-called double-exposition design substitutes for the repeated exposition of the Classical sonata/symphony structure. The alternation of tutti and soloist continues through the development and recapitulation; near the end comes a cadenza for the soloist, and then a brief final tutti closes the movement. This is the structure you should find in your analyses of Mozart's opening movements.

Beethoven's concerto forms were rather conservative—typically Classical in character—but he did assign the soloist the opening phrase (see his Concerto No. 4, in G Major, Op. 58, first movement), and in his own Violin Concerto in D Major, Op. 61 (as in the late piano concertos), he wrote a connecting passage to link the second and third movements.

[5]Felix Mendelssohn-Bartholdy, Concerto for Violin and Orchestra in E Minor, Op. 64, ed. Julius Rietz, in *Werke* (Leipzig: Breitkopf & Härtel, 1877). A Broude Brothers edition (New York, no date) also is available.

[6]As of this writing, there are miniature score editions and piano reduction versions available for study purposes. Consult the Bibliography.

[7]Mendelssohn, Concerto for Violin and Orchestra in E Minor, Op. 64, in Lang, *The Concerto*, already cited.

Mendelssohn's splendid violin concerto can claim to be the finest between Beethoven and Brahms, and indeed deserves to stand next to those two masterworks. He has followed along on Beethoven's path: There is no orchestral exposition here, and all three movements are linked. Everywhere, the soloist and the orchestra share thematic materials. The work is not long, but there is no interval; consider what that means for your orchestra and your audience. How will you and they maintain concentration throughout the three movements, and how will you and the soloist handle the two great transitions?

Choosing Tempos

In choosing the pace for each of these movements, remember that any seasoned soloist has a right to cast the majority vote! The opening Allegro molto appassionato generally is taken in two at about ♩ = 100–108. The "Presto" at 493 should be in *one*; that means you need to plan to increase the tempo gradually from bar 473 through the "Sempre più presto" at 481 to arrive at the pace you and the soloist have agreed upon at measure 493.

The aria-like slow movement needs to be taken in a flexible six pattern— one in which you can signal on various beats the accents, crescendos, and other rhythmic effects. We recommend ♪ = 84, although some conductors do it a bit slower. (One may choose to arrive gradually at this tempo, by the way, decelerating out of the previous movement so that the Andante tempo is actually confirmed by measure 7.)

The Allegretto non troppo is a bridge into the finale. We prefer it to move at about ♩ = 100–108, near the tempo of the first movement.

The finale ultimately should be conducted in two at about ♩ = 92. It may be best to take the opening of the movement in four, however, switching over to the two pattern at measure 9.

Technical Considerations

There are two vital concerns for you at the beginning of the first movement: balance and the motor rhythm.

The orchestration is well calculated, but balance between soloist and orchestra is a constant issue in every concerto. (Look, for example, at the passage beginning at measure 101, with the soloist now in the low register and next in the high range.) For the opening bars, you need just enough of the four woodwinds to get a homogenized sound from the orchestra over which the soloist can ride. Have someone you can trust listening to balance out in the hall.

The "sewing machine" figures played by the strings must be metrically rock-solid. The pizzicatos in the 'cellos and basses help to set the rhythm and hold the tempo. Be precise and entirely clear.

In spots where only the soloist is playing (see bars 26–32, for example), it is best for you to use a smaller beat so that you are just marking the pulses for the orchestra. (You want to keep the orchestra "in rhythm" so they can catch the soloist cleanly on the last half of the second beat in bar 28.) A strong second stroke in bar 28 (and at the parallel point in bar 32) is the preparation beat for the tutti entrances. The same sort of situation comes in bars 41–43, but this time, since the tutti attack comes *on* the second pulse, your prep beat is *one*, of course. Similar circumstances occur throughout the work.

Remember that you and the soloist are a team. At bar 47, the tutti attack on the A theme is a spot for the conductor to "take charge"—to stop accompanying for a time. With the soloist tacet until bar 76, the responsibility is solely that of the conductor, and the music is being produced by the orchestra. In concertos, this trading back and forth is part of the nature of the form.

Many conductors—taking a Romantic approach to this work—begin a rallentando at about bar 121, arriving at a substantially slower tempo for the new *tranquillo* theme at 131, in which case Tempo I does not return until bars 172–173. These forty measures can move only slightly below the opening pace, or as slowly as $\quarternote = 72$, for example. Here is one case where you and the soloist should have worked out an understanding in your prerehearsal conference.

After the fermata in bar 165, time your second beat to meet the third quarter in the violin part.

Many performers choose to take a ritard at measures 208–209. In the "seam" at 224–226, be careful to time your ritard (and the trills in flutes and violins) against the soloist, and then set the motor rhythm again at measure 226, as a pace for the clarinets and bassoons. And do not permit the orchestral *forte* in measures 257–261 to cover the rather difficult solo passage there.

In concertos, the cadenzas always are dangerous times. The orchestra tends to relax, losing some alertness. They are inactive for a time, and then must be brought back into action, often in a tricky attack. The conductor's role in general is to stand at rest, baton down, until some point at which the orchestra knows his or her conducting will resume.

The example at measure 299 is Mendelssohn's own cadenza, and he has marked an *a tempo* at bar 323; in this case, you might start conducting with a small beat—marking the pulse for the orchestra—in measure 332 (three and a half bars before the flute–oboe–violin I entrance at measure 335); cue these instruments with your eyes and left hand, throwing a full preparatory beat for the rest of the orchestra on the second pulse of measure 335. In such spots, always make certain that in rehearsal you have shown the orchestra exactly what to expect!

If you took a slower tempo at bar 131, structural balance requires that you do the same thing at 377, returning then to the original pace about 414. Do not let the players rush the separate pizzicatos at 428 (a common risk). Hold the tempo steady. Finally, watch the balance at the tutti in 453.

The Andante is a lovely movement, with a singing A theme. Maintain flexibility at spots like bars 23–25, where a small ritard can allow room and respect for the woodwind echo.

The *B* theme, which appears at bar 52, might move *slightly* faster. Once again, the conductor is in charge here, if only briefly; the entire *B* section resembles a conversation between the soloist and the orchestra, with the conductor and the ensemble responsible for providing an underlying pulse for the solo line. Be certain the timpani and the basses furnish a precise, clean pulse in thin, fragile spots like measures 69–70.

We have already spoken about the transition from the slow movement through the brief Allegretto to the finale. This is a flashy, yet rather delicate work taken at almost a breakneck pace. Getting clean ensemble from both soloist and orchestra may require as much rehearsal as the first two movements combined. Demanding for the guest artist, it is touchy for the orchestra, too, for they must play crisply, with immaculate rhythm throughout; if they do not, then at the very least they will cause the movement to sound sluggish; at worst, it will fall apart.

The wind attacks at the opening of the movement must be sharply articulated. Fresh, exciting energy is needed for the big tutti at bar 55. Structural ritards are appropriate at measures 78–80, at 163–167 (where the *a tempo* falls on the downbeat of bar 168), and finally at 220–221 (as a means of highlighting the final passage); this last ritard should be modest so that the culminative momentum is not lost.

A Final Word

Although *all* music needs to be performed expressively, this style period tends to take every sensitive opportunity. You must make that happen. Insist on subtle dynamic differences. Mark all the accents, tenutos, and special designations ("scherzando" in measure 2 of the finale, for example). Exaggerate the "hairpins" (the crescendo–diminuendo pairings) in the middle of measures, and so on. Do not underestimate the value of these precautions. You cannot count on even a professional orchestra to do these things automatically.[8]

Be certain that the orchestra really plays with *line*—with thoughtful shaping of phrases—when they are accompanying. Their music should be made interesting enough that it is worth listening to *alone*, without the soloist. Many orchestras simply don't rehearse concertos enough before the soloist arrives on the scene; then, thinking of themselves as secondary to the guest artist, they undervalue what they are doing. The result, too often, is a flaccid sound. Work instead to get the players to regard themselves and the music they play as genuinely worthy.

There is, as you will recall from Chapter 20, a special etiquette with respect to bows after a concerto performance, and it involves the concertmaster, at least, as well as the soloist and you yourself. Review those practices so that you can use them gracefully.

---

[8]The authors cherish a remark made to one of them by a member of one of the world's greatest orchestras. "How sorry I feel for conductors!" he said. "They must spend their entire careers forcing professionals to play the markings they should be observing anyway!"

CHAPTER 24

Style and Performance: Conducting a Major Work for Concert Band

Before you take up your examination of the featured work in this chapter, it seems a good moment to review the all-important physical basis for your work. Recent chapters have focused on musical and intellectual issues, but the control and the coordination you gained early in this process of development remain vital.

MORE CONDUCTING THEORY
Conducting as an Ongoing Relationship to the Body

Each conductor is an individual, with unique qualities and characteristics that reflect his or her background, physical makeup, and personality. Some of this uniqueness may be manifested in unattractive mannerisms; it is the province of your teacher (and good friends) to warn you of those and help you get rid of them. Other personal traits, however, may define you as special and talented, and those should be cultivated. A certain way you develop of addressing a musical situation may express your ideas to your ensemble in a different, better way than any other conductor. Honor the features that make you distinctive, even incomparable, and build on them.

Having said that, we urge you to constantly reevaluate yourself, to be certain that you are not developing bad habits. Check your posture. Be certain that the basic stance and approach you take in front of the ensemble has a solid foundation, that you have good balance, that you can relax within that basic stance, and that the whole ensemble is included in the presentation of your gestures.

Your upper arms should be flexible. Especially now, as you grow more confident in yourself as a conductor, there should be a complete lack of rigidity, and that for three reasons: because rigidity limits your ability to communicate your ideas, because it tires you, and because it affects others, particularly by inhibiting them and making them hesitant.

Be certain your conducting gestures are precise and efficient. Never let yourself become careless and lax with the baton. Check yourself occasionally against the conducting frames you used early on. Discipline your technic, and keep improving it.

Here are three more ways of enhancing your physical foundation as a conductor: (1) Videotape yourself in working rehearsals (as we have said before), and be stiffly self-critical when you audit those tapes. (2) Take a class in ballet or in dance movement of some sort, as many fine athletes do, to gain a better sense of your whole body as a dynamic, integrated instrument of communication. (3) Learn and practice relaxation techniques so that you can keep yourself on an even keel in stressful rehearsals and performances.

Only if your body is a balanced and facile mechanism can you move on to the level where what you do as a conductor becomes interpretation, in the fullest sense, rather than technic. That is the goal. If you can make your body fully responsive, then every gesture you make will be expressive, and every gesture of expressiveness will serve the purpose of the music itself. Free yourself! Let your physical gestures represent the music so clearly that your musicians themselves are freed to play and sing their very best.

They should get past technic themselves, of course, and go on to this level of interpretation. Listen constantly to good musicians. Find their limits (of technic, imagination, and flexibility), and seek ways to boost the musicians who are working with you to and beyond those same limits into a new freedom of their own. That is an ideal toward which you can strive for a lifetime.[1]

Gustav Holst: Second Suite in F for Military Band, Op. 28, No. 2

Studying the Holst Second Suite

Let us turn now to a magnificent suite for concert band. It comes from a tradition that produced the best wind-band writing of the first half of the twentieth century.

Gustav Holst was one of a school of English composers—Benjamin Britten, Ralph Vaughan Williams, Gerald Finzi, and Martin Shaw, among others—who took an active interest in the English folk song and carol about the turn of the twentieth century. In new works, they used these melodies as canti firmi and composed new tunes whose modal character and phraseology close-

---

[1]Conducting posture and relaxation techniques were discussed in Chapter 2. The concept of the conducting frame was a central feature of Chapter 3.

ly resembled the folk song. Out of this viewpoint were to come *The Oxford Book of Carols,* Britten's *Folk Songs of the British Isles,* and a large body of English music.

At the same time, both in England and in America, the band (symphonic band, military band, wind ensemble, and so on) was in vogue. Patrick Gilmore and John Philip Sousa in the United States had formed famous touring ensembles during the last half of the nineteenth century, and the "march," like the minuet and the waltz before it, had been stylized into a concert work. Of the school of English composers active near the turn of the new century, Holst, especially, undertook a synthesis of the English "military band" and this body of folk songs.

Raised in beautiful Cheltenham, on the fringe of the Cotswolds, Holst became a student at the Royal College of Music, and was much influenced by Wagner, by Indian literature, and by his good friend Vaughan Williams. A professional trombonist for a time, he turned to teaching in an effort to gain more time for writing. As a composer, Holst sought a natural, open, efficient means of musical expression, generally with a strong rhythmic basis. Those attitudes show through clearly in his most famous work, *The Planets,* and in his very best writing, of which the suite at hand is an example.

His gift as a composer for winds relates, of course, to his experience as a trombonist. The suites he wrote for band stand at the heart of the twentieth-century wind ensemble repertoire;[2] they have encouraged other composers, especially British and American writers, to add to that repertoire, thus enriching the literature for band far beyond the body of orchestral and organ transcriptions that were once its main staples.

Look at the other Holst works for band. Since writing for winds and for voices is similar in certain technical respects, examine some of Holst's choral writing, as well.[3] Get acquainted with *The Planets* and at least one or two other major works of his, including perhaps *Egdon Heath,* which is highly regarded by many.

The biography written by his daughter Imogen is a standard source.[4] (See also her biography of Benjamin Britten.) There are also useful essays by the composers Vaughan Williams[5] and Rubbra,[6] among other items. You certainly should familiarize yourself, at the same time, with some of the music of Vaughan Williams himself, and of others of Holst's English contemporaries. This will help

---

[2]There are four such major works: the First Suite in E-Flat, the Second Suite in F, *Hammersmith* (all three for "military band"), and *A Moorside Suite* for brass band.

[3]There is another setting of "Song of the Blacksmith" in his *Six Choral Folk Songs,* Op. 36b, for example.

[4]Imogen Holst, *Gustav Holst, A Biography* (Oxford and New York: Oxford University Press, 1988).

[5]Ralph Vaughan Williams, *Heirs and Rebels* (London and New York: Oxford University Press, 1959).

[6]Edmund Rubbra, *Gustav Holst* (London: Triad Press, 1974).

you draw comparisons between this English school and the other idioms current in music during the first half of the twentieth century.[7]

For perspective on the folk song and carol traditions in England, familiarity with the collections of Cecil Sharp, particularly his great two-volume work on English texts and tunes borne to America,[8] is essential. *The Oxford Book of Carols*[9] is another distinguished source.

Editions and Performance Forces

Written in 1911, the suite was premiered in 1922, at the time its score and parts were first published. The revision made for American bands in 1948 has become the standard edition;[10] the holograph exists, however, and recent work (especially affecting doublings, and so on) has resulted in a newly edited version.[11]

The instrumentation is typical of the concert band, and the ideal ensemble described in Chapter 13 would be appropriate for performance purposes. It could be presented equally well, however, by a select wind ensemble of forty or so, with two players per stand in the B-flat clarinets, cornets, and tubas, and generally one per stand elsewhere. Remember, by the way, that when Holst calls for cornets *and* trumpets here, he really means it. The wonderful timbre of the cornet is unique, and that tone quality is one of the essential elements of the overall sound of the band.

The third movement of the suite, in a reference to the "blacksmith" of the title, calls for "anvil." Speak with your percussion principal (or a percussion teacher, if yours is a school situation) about an appropriate instrument. The ideal, of course, is a genuine hammer and anvil.

Structure and Continuity

Cast in four movements, the Second Suite begins with a March (the First Suite ends with one) and goes on to an Andante, a craggy, syncopated Moderato, and a giguelike finale. Like its E-flat counterpart, the work is dominated by four- and eight-bar phraseology. This is typical of Holst; there is a formal simplicity and a

---

[7]As a convenience for your later use, the authors include in Appendix B a summary of style and performance practice for music from the contemporary era. You may want to review that at this time. You may wish also to refer to the historical and stylistic background for this era discussed in Chapter 12.

[8]Cecil Sharp, *English Folk Songs from the Southern Appalachians*. 2 vols. (London and New York: Oxford University Press, 1952).

[9]Percy Dearmer, Ralph Vaughan Williams, and Martin Shaw, *The Oxford Book of Carols* (London: Oxford University Press, 1964).

[10]Gustav Holst, *Second Suite in F for Military Band*, Op. 28, No. 2 (New York: Boosey & Hawkes, Inc., 1948).

[11]Gustav Holst, *Second Suite in F for Military Band*, Op. 28, No. 2, ed. Colin Matthews (New York: Boosey & Hawkes, Inc., 1984).

melodic candor here that is characteristic of his overall style and that defined him as a conservative among some of his twentieth-century peers.

Folk songs are used for most of the themes (although—as with Josquin, Ives, and others—one can never be certain whether Holst is using a cantus firmus or a composed melody unless one can recognize the tune itself). The $\frac{6}{8}$ theme in the first movement, the song in the Andante, and the "Blacksmith Song" in the third are all identified by Holst. The finale is something of a quodlibet; the "Dargason" is used as an ostinato,[12] while a variant of "Greensleeves" appears as a counterpoint to it in two sections.

Thus, we can draw a link between the regular, square shapes of Holst's phrases and his evident use of folk songs. The phrase durations in these canti firmi predetermine the structure of the music, we might say; we should recall, however, that Holst *chose* these particular tunes, and may have done so on the basis of their regular design. Either way, he has elected to build symmetrical structures.

The very predictability of these shapes frees the listener to focus on other parameters—timbre, for instance—and this in turn calls attention to the wide variety of tone colors (with the saxophones, the cornets, the secondary clarinets, and all) that constitute the band.

Choosing Tempos

The March, we suggest, should be taken in two at something between ♩ = 108 and ♩ = 120 (depending on the abilities present in your ensemble and on the acoustics of your hall). The brighter tempo is better, all things considered, for it will encourage lighter, crisper playing. No change in tempo is needed for the $\frac{6}{8}$ middle section; this is simply a change from duple to triple subdivision (♩ = ♩.).

For the "Song without Words," your choice could range from ♩ = 60 to ♩ = 66 or so. Here the slower pace may be the better one, provided your players can maintain a firm sense of "line." Ask them to "sing!" We would move up to ♩ = 104–108 for the third movement.

At spots in the finale, Holst has specified that you are to use "one beat . . ." or "two beats in a bar," and that you are to "keep the same pace as before." These shifts are necessary so that the "Dargason" (which is a compound duple melody) and "Greensleeves" (which is triple) can be superimposed on each other; the "Greensleeves" tune's sets of three quarter notes equal two "Dargason" dotted quarters. Holst has managed this harmonic and metric mating skillfully.

Depending, again, on acoustics and on your players' talents, this Allegro moderato could range from ♩ = 128 to ♩. = 144. Some conductors boost the pace slightly at measure 145 to heighten the excitement of the ending; if you want to

---

[12]For a review of the history of this famous tune, see *The New Grove Dictionary of Music and Musicians*, ed. Stanley Sadie (London: Macmillan, 1980), 5, 41.

do that, it may be more effective to take a slightly slower tempo at the beginning, thus "leaving room" for that sort of *Poco più mosso* at bar 145.

Technical Considerations

In the March, crisp articulation is the first priority. The staccatos Holst has marked imply lightness—deftness—and elegance of rhythmic presentation.

Balance is the next issue. The first cornet has the melody at measure 3, and the other parts are accompanimental; as the texture changes, then, watch carefully to maintain a transparency like that of the first ten bars. In the B-flat minor section at measure 111, the melody is in the clarinets and saxes at *mezzo forte;* the accompaniment in the lower voices is marked only *piano;* the tutti that follows at bar 135 is *piano* and *pianissimo,* not *forte!* (This sets up one of Holst's few crescendos, from bar 146 to the *fortissimo* at 151.) *The band comprises even more instrumental timbres than the orchestra; honor them all by giving them equality within the whole fabric of sound.*

The third principal need here is a "singing style," particularly because of the emphasis on melody. Sing the tunes yourself, and gauge the problems—breath support, and so on—the wind players will have. Teach them to conceive these lines as lyric and vocal.

Do not let them rush the first five-note motive. That is always a risk because it is quick and scalewise.

The "Song without Words" is a setting of a folk song also employed by Vaughan Williams. Again the texture is melody-with-accompaniment, and all the phraseology (save the first two and last three bars) is made up of four-bar units.

There is a doubling question starting with the pickup to bar 3. We prefer oboe *or* clarinet, but not both, for at least eight measures, and perhaps sixteen; some conductors employ both.

A constant flow of eighth notes begins at bar 18. Note that there is no break in that flow (save for the fermata at bar 32) until the final measure. Make certain the players are aware of that interchange of eighths from part to part.

Require that those playing the accompanimental lines work for "line," playing toward peak points, and tapering the ends of phrases. Just as in the Mendelssohn concerto (see Chapter 23), the whole ensemble needs to play with a sense of direction.

The *ad libitum* marking in measure 30 is (in this instance) a rubato indication. You may want to ritard the approach to the fermata. Remember the effect this will have on the constant eighths.

Next comes the "Song of the Blacksmith." This robust melody[13] has been given a rambunctious setting, full of emphatic rhythms and sharp staccatos. Note

---

[13]The distinguished conductor Frederick Fennell recalls that this blacksmithing tune is one he learned as a boy in a family shop in Cleveland. Frederick Fennell, "Gustav Holst's Second Suite in F for Military Band," *The Instrumentalist,* 32, No. 4 (November 1977), 48–49.

the beginning: What sort of preparatory beat does one give when *no one* is playing on the downbeat? You have essentially two choices: Start with the stick up (at the top of the first beat) and drop it straight down; or, give quite a small fourth beat as a preparation, and then start; the latter choice is probably simpler and has the advantage of showing the tempo.

When *everything* is syncopated, inexperienced players will tend to rush! Try having them sing their lines, adding an extra note *on* the beat and accenting the "real" notes so that they get the feel of the rhythm. This should give them security.

After the opening, check the balance again in bars 6–7 as the theme enters. And note the solo for *second* cornet at measure 10; this is somewhat unusual, but the reason becomes obvious when Holst passes the line to the first cornet at 14. The tenuto on the third beat of bar 13 really makes the phrase work, by the way; do not ignore it.

Evaluate the sound you are getting from the "anvil" starting at bar 19. A slight ritard at measure 23 helps communicate the structure and adds weight to the *fff* attack, but it is somewhat dangerous because of the syncopations. You *and* the players should *think* the subdivision here if you are going to ritard. Actually conducting the subdivision would go too far in inhibiting the flow.

The ending is brilliant. The major triad, complete with cymbal crash and *fff*, is well calculated and exciting.

The final movement is really a set of ostinato variations on the "Dargason" tune, with the variant on "Greensleeves" laid into the texture as a kind of contrapuntal obbligato. Momentum comes from the addition of voices to the ostinato, an accretion of accompanimental figures, and a gradual increase in the dynamic level to the peak. Well played, the movement sounds deceptively easy. It is not that simple.

Choose one pattern of articulations for the eight bars of the "Dargason" melody, and insist that everyone consistently use that interpretation. The charm here lies with what the accompanying voices do: Again, as in the second movement, the accompanying figures—even long notes, like those in the alto clarinet and saxes in measures 9–16—must have direction to them. That will help maintain good ensemble with those playing the "Dargason," just as in the finale of the Mendelssohn concerto (see Chapter 23).

At bar 41, for example, the risk is that the lower voices will lag behind, or at least fail to match exactly the metric drive of the ostinato. The greatest danger is with the voices that have rests on the downbeat of each bar. (This same texture recurs at measure 105, but without the downbeat rests.)

At measure 57, again, the real difficulty is not with the "Dargason," or with the juxtaposition of the triple-meter "Greensleeves" counterpoint, but, rather, with the lines having the two-bar tied notes. These must have shape and direction. Here, and once more beginning at bar 145, it is important that those playing the "Greensleeves" tune maintain a real legato line; this will help sustain the identifiability—the aural integrity—of this obbligato. At the same time, the crispness and aural shape of the "Dargason" must be preserved. (For young players, this is a wonderful exercise to develop rhythmic skills.)

One more rhythmic variant: Do not underestimate the importance and power of the accented duplets in measures 117–120.

We think the ending—the final eleven measures—is more sharply drawn using only the piccolo and the solo tuba on the eighth-note lines. Keep the muted cornets as soft as they are marked! These last measures *must* be clearly in two, for the sake of security in the two-against-three rhythms. And make sure everyone knows exactly how long the "stinger" (the last note) is to be!

A Final Word

If the ostinato is kept fresh and clean, the other voices have sufficient shape, balance is maintained, and the overall dynamic arch is patiently configured, this makes a witty, breathtaking movement. Remember that the forward motion—the momentum—really hangs on voices *other* than those playing the ostinato.

CHAPTER 25

Style and Performance: Conducting a Twentieth-Century Opera

Many conductors find performing opera the greatest technical and musical challenge they confront.

The music of opera is lengthy and complicated, demanding great flexibility from the conductor and the musicians. Passages of recitative, exchanges of dialogue, abrupt dramatic interruptions, and virtuosic, dangerous showpieces follow one another through an opera score. Some of this requires superb technical skill from a conductor: the lively interjections of the scene between Tamino and the Priest in *The Magic Flute,* for example, with all the changes of tempo (contrasting the manners of the two principals), or the fluid metamorphoses within the acts of *Madama Butterfly,* so basic to Puccini's way of structuring a scene.

The forces employed tend to be large and cumbersome, too. The "Kromy Forest" scene of *Boris Godunov* fills the stage with a large chorus of Russian peasants, and then passes through them solo voices, monks, nobles, the pretender to the throne (often on horseback!), and an invading army. The opening scene of *Tosca* mixes together lovers, conspirators, priests, and a religious procession. The last act of *Der Rosenkavalier* has singers literally popping up through the floor.

All this music must be coordinated with the theatrical aspects of the work so that the music and the action (sometimes languid, sometimes frenetic) dovetail exactly. Timing is everything here. Yet the conductor is at the disadvantage of being placed in the orchestra "pit"; at best, the singers have some difficulty seeing the conductor, and at worst, they may be too busy with violent actions to even look for the baton. Lights go up and down, losing the conductor in darkness at one moment and hiding him behind an impenetrable screen of dazzling spotlights the next. And the singers, above the pit and often quite far away, must be kept together with the orchestral players, whose heads are at the height of the conductor's hips, or below.

There is also the matter of stamina. A standard three-act opera may require two and a half hours, and some last almost twice that long. It is no light task to maintain your concentration—moment by moment—for so long, and it is even harder to keep a clear perspective about musical relationships over such a long span.

Finally, there is the expense. The comprehensive costs of opera, more perhaps than any other artistic medium, can be backbreaking; that means there are relatively few opportunities for one to conduct it. These are the reasons we come to this medium last in our sequence of study.

Conducting from the Orchestra Pit

An orchestra pit is by its nature a critically different acoustical environment from the standard theater stage. It can be difficult to hear the performers onstage, to hear instruments in certain areas of the pit itself, to hear offstage singers and players, and to equalize all those forces. The "balance" as it sounds in the ears of the conductor is often quite different from the "balance" the audience hears; yet, the conductor stands responsible for them both.

The conductor should play a central role in the selection of the singers, of course. Know exactly what ideal voices you want to hear in each role, and match those ideals with the auditionees. Consider diction, musical flexibility, and, especially, stamina in these hearings.

When working in a pit, have an assistant take frequent stretches of rehearsals so that you can go listen to balance in the house. Compare that with your aural experience in the pit itself so you know how to "discount" some of what you hear there in favor of what you believe (on the basis of your sound checks in the hall) the audience is actually hearing.

Rehearsals for opera productions are elaborate. You will need to "coach" (or have someone thus prepare) the singers. You will have traditional rehearsals with your orchestra, and you or your chorus master will handle musical preparation of the choral ensemble. There will be piano rehearsals with the singers, and finally all the musical preparation will come together in the *Sitzprobe*, a concert-style run-through of the whole score.

The singers also will undergo "blocking rehearsals," in which staging will be established by the director. As things proceed, your piano rehearsals and the stage director's scenes can be combined, act by act. The stage manager, lighting staff, and stage crew will have one or more "technical rehearsals." Last of all, about the same time as the *sitzprobe*, come the costumed "dress rehearsals." Expect pressure. The stress of bringing together an opera production can be substantial.

On the concert stage, some may take the visual considerations for granted. (They should not do so, as we have said.) Especially in musical theater productions, however, you must evaluate every aspect of the "sightline" problem. Placing yourself in the pit, you must judge how high your podium must be for singers in the far corners of the stage to see you clearly; at the same time, your players must be able to see you *and* their music simultaneously, so you cannot use a podium so high that you lose contact with the orchestra.

If there are to be offstage musicians, you must plan from what angle (probably through an offstage assistant) they will follow you. If there are to be singers in the pit at some point (as in the last act of *Rigoletto*, for example), save room for them and plan that sightline, too.

The singer onstage looks out into bright spotlights and—moving about as an actor—often has difficulty glimpsing the conductor to follow the beat or to catch an important cue. *Check the background against which you stand.* Since you will probably be clothed in dark garb, it will help if the pit wall behind you is white. Hang a bedsheet centered there if necessary. (Some use a lighted baton in these circumstances, but such models can be badly balanced and clumsy; in any case, it is best for you to use the baton familiar to you, particularly in a situation involving long hours and stamina.)

Especially for offstage choruses, a backstage video monitor—providing all the wiring is secure—is much to be preferred to the old technique of peering through the curtains. A video camera placed in the pit can be aimed directly at you, and you can cue "it" directly at the proper moments; thus, the offstage personnel have a sense that you are looking precisely at them. Monitors placed high on the proscenium arch, or in the wings, can serve for distantly placed onstage singers, too.

Be certain your beat pattern is big enough and high enough to be seen from the stage. Be sure your cues are clear and prominent. Most of your players are seeing your beat in a side view from one direction or the other. This means that they are seeing a relatively flat, two-dimensional image. It may be helpful to turn out the extremes of your sideways beats (counts two and four in $\frac{4}{4}$, for instance). Do anything you can to clarify that image.

Communication with the stage manager is usually managed through one or more signal lights placed on or beside your music stand. A green light coming on, or a red light going off, may signal you that a set change is finished and that you may start the next scene.

Finally, we should mention some performance conventions in opera. Normally, the sequence is this: (1) The orchestra tunes before the conductor enters the pit; (2) the houselights dim, at least to "half"; (3) the conductor enters the pit (from the side of the house or from under the stage); (4) if there is applause when the conductor steps onto the podium, he or she bows; (5) the music begins; and (6) the houselights go off, and—on the planned cue—the curtain opens.

The conductor's bow from the pit before the last act is customarily an important one. Even though the players cannot be seen, you may ask them to stand. After the final scene, then, it is appropriate for you to go quickly from the pit for an onstage bow. The typical routine is for you to move to center stage after the principals have had their first bow, stand with the leads, and gesture for the pit orchestra to stand; your bow acknowledges the applause. If the bows are taken in front of a closed curtain, then you make your entrance (in some cases with the stage director and the chorus master) with the principals or alone.

Now let us turn to an important one-act opera and consider how to prepare and perform it.

Gian Carlo Menotti: *Amahl and the Night Visitors*

Gian Carlo Menotti was born in Italy in 1911, and—even though he moved to America, studied at Philadelphia's Curtis Institute, and remained here—he retained his Italian citizenship. Those details can serve as the first signals to guide your study of his 1951 opera *Amahl and the Night Visitors:* The great tradition of Italian music (and especially opera) was part of his heritage; the time at Curtis introduced him to Samuel Barber, and important cross-influences between them shaped the writing of both throughout their lives.

Review the nature of Italian opera, and look at some specific masterpieces from that tradition, including perhaps works by Rossini, Verdi, and Puccini. Go as far as you possibly can into our usual "spiral study." Look at contemporary operas by non-Italians (Benjamin Britten, Carlisle Floyd, and others). Look to see if there are other major works written specifically for television production, as *Amahl* was.

Trace Menotti's career, seeking to understand him and his background. Develop a list of other major works, placing *Amahl* in that context. Consult at least a sampling of those (you will find that the bulk of his catalog is opera), and begin building an inventory of style features; compare his stylistic approaches with those of his twentieth-century peers.[1]

In starting your examination of Menotti's score,[2] note the information printed in the preliminary pages, including the "Production Notes" written by the composer himself. Then study the music, following our usual format.[3]

As you develop a view of the overall structure of this opera, be particularly careful to note the smaller units hidden within: There are recitatives, arias, trios, choruses, and the like. All those forms have traditional applications and significances in the history of opera, of course, and you need to see in what ways, if any, Menotti's procedures are traditional or unique.

Who wrote the libretto for *Amahl*? Is that unusual in your experience? Remember that the librettist paints the characters of the story as much as the com-

---

[1]As a convenience for your later use, the authors include in Appendix B a summary of style and performance practice for music from the contemporary era. You may want to review that at this time. You may wish also to refer to the historical and stylistic background for this era discussed in Chapter 12.

[2]Both the full score and the vocal score are published by G. Schirmer, Inc., New York. You should consult both.

[3]Review Chapter 18 if necessary.

poser does. If a composer serves also as librettist, there can be no tension between the poetic and musical images of a character. (There have been major composers in the past who have written their own librettos, notably Wagner; perhaps you can learn from parallel approaches to this sort of process.)

In any case, the text is of the greatest importance here. Study it in great detail, and fit your reading of it to the musical settings. How does Menotti handle metric accent? What vowels does he use for high notes? Does he take choices that make diction—intelligibility—easier or more difficult? Is intelligibility crucial to this work?

The orchestration is standard in most respects, though the use of piano is not common. (By the way, the listing of instrumentation on the copyright page of the score does not mention that the flute doubles the piccolo, nor does it itemize the percussion; both B-flat and A clarinets are needed—watch for the changes.)

The work can be played successfully with strings distributed 8-6-5-6-3, although either fewer or more can be employed; taken together with the winds, harp, piano, and percussion, that would mean an orchestra of about forty, including the bulky piano and percussion instruments, to be fitted into the pit. Various arrangements can be used, depending on your preferences and on the size and shape of the pit in question.

Play through the work for continuity—at first using the vocal score if your keyboard skills are limited. Then go to the orchestra score, playing parts and singing some roles, too. Consider the use Menotti makes of his various thematic and textural materials, including repetitions and variations. This should prepare you for all the cueing that opera requires—cues to single singers, to ensembles onstage, to the orchestral players, and all. You must be prepared in the dangerous environment of live opera performance to provide security and clarity to your forces, and, beyond that, to "hold things together in an emergency."

Specific Features in the Work

We are not going to suggest tempos to you for *Amahl*. It is time you chose your own. In doing so, you should give thought to the special impact that staging and movement have on the performances of singers (and dancers).

As the production effort proceeds, friction can develop between the stage director, the designers, and the conductor. Singers can be placed ("blocked") facing upstage, so they cannot see the conductor; embraces, struggles, and other events can encumber both the voice and the body. Vocal projection can be hampered. Yet opera is a *dramatic* medium, as well as a musical one, and staging is a cardinal aspect. It must have its place, as must the music.

Some conductors (von Karajan comes immediately to mind) have tried to do both jobs—to conduct and to stage-direct. That permits a unified approach, certainly, but it is unusual to find an individual equally capable of both responsibilities.

The key is this: The score is primary, and all policy choices should rest finally on it. Anything that impedes the directions present in that score is suspect, and anything that facilitates the image presented in that score is helpful. Although the score is only a template, and interpretive choices must be inferred from it, in any disagreement about a production it must be the basis for final decisions.

Among the technical difficulties here, perhaps the most prominent is the matter of the recitatives. Orchestral entrances in recitatives can be especially risky, and clear, clean cueing of both singers and players is of the utmost importance. The preparation beats, which may fall on any pulse, must be precise. Your handling of fermatas, and your resuming motion after them, must be skilled, as well.

Some effectively use the left hand for cueing the singers, and the right hand—with the baton—for the beat and the players. That is appropriate, but it is not the only possibility, and (depending on the musical circumstances at hand) it is still the best policy to show as much in the baton as you can.

Let us look at several *Amahl* recitatives. First, note the one at the *più mosso* just before rehearsal number 14. There are nine beats in the "bar" and the meter is suspended. *Within the recitative, different pacings can be employed on a beat-to-beat basis.* Here, after the downbeat, you "waste" the second pulse (that is, quickly and lightly show a minimal beat); after the soprano's "Stop bothering me!" you throw (as the third pulse) a prep beat—perhaps quicker than the *più mosso*—to get a quick, emphatic pair of staccatos from the players. Then give a circular "fifth beat," and wait for the soprano; at the word "day," you should be ready with the prep beat for the *a tempo* at number 14.

A more complex case occurs at number 38. Here, the recitative is barred. In the first measure, the "wasted beat" is a circular one; at Amahl's "Mother," your downbeat is a prep beat for the three pizzicato eighths in the next bar. Again, a "soft" downbeat for the next bar is followed by a prep beat for the next three pizzicatos. Two quick "wasted" downbeats "release" the orchestra for the span up to number 39. Remember that none of this is necessarily metric. Amahl himself can take extra time for "There is a King with a crown." Your prep beat at that point sets up the *non troppo presto.*

You can begin to apply these principles yourself to other situations. Look at number 15: After the first bar, there are six pulses for Amahl's first phrase; your responsibility is to set with an appropriate prep beat the woodwind interjection in the third bar, to show a "soft downbeat," and again to time a prep beat against Mother's "Amahl" to set up the metric *a tempo* at number 16. Or look just before number 35: Here, one can cue the singers with the left hand, holding the baton until time for the prep beat that establishes the $\frac{6}{8}$ Allegro at number 35. Finally, a more extended such case follows number 124; there at Mother's " . . . you can't, you can't," you cue the violin tremolo and hold for another prep beat to initiate number 125.

In these brief discussions, you have seen a series of tempo situations—here an Allegro, or a *più mosso*, then an *a tempo*, and perhaps a Prestissimo. All this demands from you a sure sense of the pacing of each passage. *You must hold in your memory—and instantaneously recall—each such tempo setting, triggering it precisely at its moment.* That requires a consummate image of the continuity of the work.

There are a number of dangerous offstage entrances in *Amahl*. At number 25, the entrance of the Three Kings is set to a chordal accompaniment from harp, piano, and percussion, to which winds and strings are added later. The woodwind lines are quite rhythmic, and it is crucial that clean ensemble be maintained in spite of distance and sightline problems.

At number 84, the Shepherd's Chorus begins offstage, but since it is *a cappella*, there is less risk. The orchestral entrance at number 85 comes after the chorus stops. Near the end, at number 132, the chorus is again unaccompanied. (Remember that a video camera and monitors can be very helpful in such circumstances.)

Here in *Amahl* is the first situation we have seen in this volume in which you must conduct dancers. The Shepherd's Dance (number 91) offers you that experience. For dancers, *exact tempos are absolutely essential.* You must land on precisely the tempos you agreed on in rehearsal. Note that the Dance itself is a transition from Lento to Allegro vivace to *più presto* to *sempre animando* to Prestissimo. That sequence is a very demanding set of transitions between tempos that must be strictly observed, for the sake of the dancers' coordination.

With all the transitions that occur in *Amahl*, you will be tempted to use *subdivided beats* in a great many spots. The best rule is to do so only when absolutely necessary.

Let us look at a couple of examples. At number 76, you may want to allow Melchior a little extra time at the end of each phrase. In the second bar after number 76, the *con sordino* figure in the violins will be cleaner if you subdivide pulses three and four; similar choices offer themselves throughout the developing Quartet that begins here. Or see number 131: At the Adagio, Menotti himself has indicated that the tempo is set in eighths. You should subdivide here but should return to simple beats at the measure before number 132.

Flexibility on your part is of ultimate importance in opera. You must expect emergencies, and they may occur at any moment. A door may stick, a singer may have a memory slip, the chorus may begin to rush, another singer may miss a cue. Your best defense against disaster is your ability to concentrate and to respond flexibly.

Prepare your orchestra to respond flexibly, too. Train them with hypothetical situations in your rehearsals so that they will react effectively to sudden cutoffs, extended fermatas, whispered instructions, and the like.

Know the work completely. A sure knowledge of "what comes next," a solid technique, good concentration, and flexibility are all you have to protect yourself in emergencies. Given the number of tempos and transitions and entrances and all in *Amahl*, that is no small task. And *Amahl* is only a one-act opera; imagine what it will be like when you conduct, say, *Tristan und Isolde*!

A Final Word

Amahl and the Night Visitors may be only an hour or thereabouts in duration (remember it was written for television), but it is a little gem, and it gives you a vehicle with which you can demonstrate to yourself and to others all the technical skills you have acquired during this study of conducting. It lets you use those technical skills to express your considered, balanced musical interpretation of a radiant masterwork. That is your special responsibility here, as it is with all the great music you now are prepared to conduct.

APPENDIX A

Coaching a Typical English Madrigal

Madrigal singing, in concept and in history, is a form of chamber music. The earliest of these works were intended for impromptu songfests at home, rather like parlor games; in practice, then, we believe, one should not conduct madrigal singers. In this repertoire your singers can develop the independence, interdependence, and confidence of chamber players.

There is a role here for you, nevertheless: In contemporary circumstances the "conductor" works with the ensemble as a coach, teaching about the madrigal itself and overseeing the rehearsal process. Once you have checked the pitches and rhythms, and have arrived with the singers at concepts of tempo, form, and phraseology, you send them onstage to perform without you.

Audiences traditionally love the interplay of madrigal singers, by the way, and enjoy for its own sake the repertoire they perform.

STUDYING A MORLEY MADRIGAL

If you are working from a library in a university, or even a large high school, you are likely to find one or more versions of Thomas Morley's wonderful *April Is in My Mistress' Face* already on the shelves. Many works of this genre have been overedited in years past; even if it means you must purchase another edition, look for one with few editorial marks, so that you and your singers can make your own informed decisions about interpretation.[1]

There are four vocal lines here; they can be sung with one on a part, or two, or three. (Generally, one does not speak of "madrigal groups" of more than three

---

[1] As opposite extremes, the authors point to the heavily marked version in *The A Cappella Singer* anthology, edited by H. Clough Leighter (Boston: E. C. Schirmer Music, 1933), with its dynamics, crescendos, dashes, ritards, and all; contrast this to an essentially unmarked version published in New York (Arista Music Co., 1983).

voices per part.) In choosing singers, one always is concerned with tone quality and diction. With an ensemble you will not conduct, pitch stability, rhythmic precision, and balance are especially important; the ideal, by the way, is *not* to have "twelve voices that sound as one"; it is to have an ensemble of beautiful voices that maintain balance in every register.

In contemporary terms, we would say the Morley is set in G minor. Although the first sounds hint ambivalently at B-flat major, the cadences in measures 3, 6, and 9 reinforce G clearly. Beginning with the F-natural in bar 10, the tonal center shifts temporarily (note the E-naturals in measure 12, too) to B-flat, and remains somewhat unsettled for a time. Bars 28–30 are decisive, however; the cadence on G *major* there, reinforced by the repetitive texture of bars 30–38, gives us a sure tonal footing. (The shift to major managed by the B-naturals is part of a historic tradition extending all the way from medieval *musica ficta* on past Bach.) The tonal organization we see in this G minor/B-flat major ambivalence is mature and deft, by the way, signaling that Morley was a great craftsman.

Note carefully, too, another sort of ambivalence: This is no rigid four-beat meter. Our bar lines can clutter our minds. Each phrase has its span, so that sometimes our modern downbeat seems most important, and other times other points in our measures.

The vertical sonorities are mostly major and minor triads. There are beautiful suspensions, but relatively few other dissonances. Harmonic thirds are important between melodic lines from the first measure to the end. Step-progressions abound in this imitative counterpoint. (Note, for example, the soprano line over bars 23–28.)

Morley begins with two voices for one phrase, then three, and finally four for the last two counts of measure 7. This coupling of parts (like that in Josquin) continues throughout the madrigal, ending in the four-voice imitative entrances from bar 23 to the end. The ranges and tessituras are modest in modern terms; the sopranos and tenors have high F-naturals, and the basses nothing below G.

The courtly romance of the text is bound into four lines, two of eight syllables and two of nine. The rhyme scheme is *aabb*. Morley saves the first ironic appearance of the word "heart" for a whole note on high F at the peak of the dramatic soprano line in measures 23–24.

The sopranos' melodic line in bars 1–2 is never repeated exactly (although the tenors come close in bars 6–7). The real motif here is the coupling of thirds that we see in the opening bars; this parallelism is carried throughout, and probably its gracefulness has much to do with the popularity of this madrigal.

We suggest you read first the articles on the "madrigal" and about "Thomas Morley" in a good reference source.[2] Go on to readings on England and

---

[2]See, for example, the articles in the *New Grove Dictionary of Music and Musicians*, ed. Stanley Sadie (London: Macmillan, 1980), vol. 11, pp. 461–482, and vol. 12, pp. 579–585.

English vocal style in Morley's time, and on his contemporaries, especially Byrd, Weelkes, Gibbons, and Wilbye.

Then look at a number of madrigals by Morley and these same masters, comparing them with Italian madrigals of the period 1550–1600 or so. In the works of de Rore, di Lasso, Marenzio, and their peers, you will recognize Italian musical influences on this English school a generation later.

COACHING MORLEY'S APRIL IS IN MY MISTRESS' FACE

Madrigal singers may perform sitting or standing, as you prefer. You may arrange your personnel in any effective grouping; originally, they sat 'round a table, or in a circle, and this is still the best way for them to hear each other.

There are no difficult conducting problems here. The *alla breve* sign recommends to us a broad two, and leads us to suggest a tempo of ♩ = 54 to 60. Be careful, however, not to let the bar lines become audible; rhythms should be precise, but the linear flow is the important thing. (Our contemporary "sense of syncopation" has no place in this music.) The soprano and alto lines in bars 10–12 have a triple ($\frac{3}{2}$) feeling, for example; the soprano-and-alto cadence on "place" in bar 11 feels musically like a downbeat, yet it occurs a half note before the unequivocal metric accent in the bass line on "eyes" (measure 12). Let each part find its own "meters."

As you prepare to rehearse Morley's madrigal, try out in your mind a variety of interpretive choices. Should the first measure start quietly, or full-voiced? Should the phrases adopt an arched shape, or not? Should certain lines be emphasized?

The final phrases (measure 23 to the end) are beautifully succinct, and offer a glimpse of the refined loveliness of the English madrigal at its best. Decide whether you want your singers to ritard into the final cadence, and (if so) how much? Modest ornamentation is possible here, too.

In all that you do to prepare your singers, remember that you are working to free them from your direction. In rehearsal, have one of the ensemble give the pitch, starting the group with a subtle nod. All should breathe together at the start. Teach them to listen closely to intonation, especially where there are perfect intervals between lines. Teach them also to watch each other, and to think of this genre as a sophisticated conversation. You will not cue their entrances; they will pass musical ideas back and forth, from one to another, in the wonderful atmosphere of sharing that is chamber music.

APPENDIX B

Guidelines for Style and Performance Practice

These stylistic summaries are intended as quick and general reminders of performance practice in the various eras approached in this volume, and refer to more detailed discussions in the preceding chapters. They should not be accepted dogmatically; rather, each should be examined in the context of the work at hand, since a given work is the best counsel as to its performance.

GREGORIAN CHANT

- The Solesmes approach has come to be regarded as the orthodox performance tradition in Gregorian chant.
- Remember that chant was part of the oral tradition, which means that, in general, the monks sang from memory. Your singers should know this music that well, so that they can bring to it the flexibility the monks could have.
- The most important quality of Gregorian rhythm is flow.
- Although a constant pulse flows through this music, we need to suspend our modern sense of meter.
- Chant should make the text more accessible to listeners.
- Our modern 1-beat probably comes closest to creating the feeling we want to convey.
- Work to shape the line (the only line you have), with its upward and downward sweeps. Do not let it become humdrum and square.
- Your singers must avoid audible breaths.
- The four-line staff, the neumes, the bar lines that represent phrase structure, and the special symbols used for chant must be understood thoroughly.
- Chant gives a great deal of freedom to the conductor. Find a personal way of conducting it that is clear to your ensemble, allows you a certain amount of freedom, and gives you a basis for a lyric approach to all sorts of music. Then return to chant whenever you need to remind yourself of that lyricism (in contemporary music, for example).

For further practice, we suggest the following passages of chant. (See *Chants of the Church*, cited in Chapter 10.)

Ave Maria
Ave maris stella
Ave Regina
Ave verum (corpus)
Magnificat (Tone 8 G, the reciting-tone chant)
Pange lingua
Salve Regina
Victimae paschali laudes

RENAISSANCE MUSIC

- In the sacred music of this era, the mystical, prayerful beauty of the rhythmically sophisticated counterpoint must be achieved.
- The long, arching lines must have rhythmic interest and vitality, yet maintain their restraint and dignity.
- The feeling of flow found in Gregorian chant should guide your judgments about pace, meter, and rhythm. Remember that bar lines were not yet in use and that early time signatures signal the subdivisions within longer note values, rather than an insistent meter.
- Study especially the placement of dissonances.
- The (somewhat imprecise) *tactus* is the basis for tempo.
- The secular music of the period generally emphasizes rhythm even more and can approach the feeling of constantly changing meters. Avoid creating any feeling of syncopation and any sense of "bar line."
- Works tend to begin and end with assurance, but internal phrases may feel rather upbeat.
- Assume some separation as the standard articulation in the secular and instrumental works. Skips, at least, will naturally provoke separation. If you use modern instruments, remember to discourage their players from automatically using a "symphonic" legato.
- Accent here comes from duration. Long notes are (by their nature) emphasized. If a short note must have a feeling of emphasis, the previous note must be sung or played shorter.
- In most circumstances, early instruments can be substituted for some or all of the voices in both sacred and secular works. You can make very interesting, effective choices of strings, winds, and percussion for this period, particularly if you have access to authentic instruments of the period. Experiment with doublings, balances, and the like.
- Especially in the instrumental passages, it appears that ornaments began to be improvised into these textures by the last part of the sixteenth century, if not earlier.
- Remember that the churches and halls in which performances of this music occurred had very long reverberation times! This should affect your choices of tempos, of articulation, and of durations. In the cathedrals, echoes could last six seconds or more!

For further practice, we suggest the following choral and instrumental works from this period.

> Josquin des Prez: Mass movements and motets, including
> especially the *Ave Maria* motet and other works using the
> Gregorian chants you have learned
>
> Flemish, Italian, and English works suitably voiced for
> winds, strings, or both (remembering that you may
> substitute instruments for voices in almost any
> Renaissance chanson, canzona, and so forth)
>
> Dance movements by Susato, Gervaise, and others
>
> Byrd: *Ave verum corpus*
>
> Victoria: Masses and motets, including especially the *Ave
> Maria* motet
>
> Palestrina and Morales: Masses and motets
>
> Venetian choral/instrumental works, such as Giovanni
> Gabrieli's *In ecclesiis*
>
> Madrigals (Italian and English) by de Rore, di Lasso, Byrd,
> Morley, Weelkes, and Marenzio, including the radical
> works of Gesualdo

THE BAROQUE ERA

- The template for much of the Baroque repertoire is a single expressive melodic line superimposed on an instrumental bass, with a keyboard mechanism (as a bridge between these two) assigned to fill out what we would now call the harmonies. The keyboard instrument and the bass constitute the *basso continuo.*
- Consciousness of meter and tonality emerge through the period, and bar lines begin to signal metric accent.
- The characteristic timbre of the Baroque tends to be an aural homogenization of voices and instruments, in which neither color dominates.
- This is the era in which "functional harmony" *begins* to appear.
- The nature of dissonance shifts significantly in the Baroque; unprepared clashes, tritones resolved by skip, and other dramatic sounds not found in Palestrina occur commonly in this style.
- Ornamentation (which you must study in detail) is used to increase interest in lines, to focus attention on certain dissonances, and to bring to these lines an extra element of virtuosity. It is obligatory in Baroque style, and can be improvised in performance. (Do not assume your performers understand much about it. Teach them.)
- Each complete work or movement should have its own character, its own image. The Baroque composers regarded each one as a unique mixture of tempo, dynamics, and materials, all in motion (hence the word *movement*).
- Separation (nonlegato) is the standard articulation in this style.
- In setting tempos, depend on performance practice commentary by Baroque musicians themselves. Consider all the rhythmic levels involved, as well as key, mode, meter, dissonance, the hall, and the mood of the work. Keep your choices somewhat moderate.

- Look for sharply drawn contrasts: between concertist and the tutti, between *piano* and *forte*, between fast and slow. Little develops gradually in a Baroque work; things tend to happen suddenly, without crescendos, accelerandos, and the like.
- Think of dynamic levels in blocks: A *p* for a soloist is softer than a *p* for the tutti, which is softer than the soloist's *f*, which is itself still softer than the full ensemble's *f*; thus you have at least four levels of loudness available just with two simple markings.
- Give each subject and countersubject its own distinct aural signature by varying dynamics and articulation.
- Musical instruments gradually were assigned more and more idiomatic responsibilities through this era. The pizzicato and a variety of other special techniques were introduced, and "instrumental melodic style" began to appear. Vocal virtuosity hit a peak in this style.
- Consider carefully any cadenza opportunities for either voice or instrument.

For further practice, we suggest the following works from this period.

Purcell: The overture and the recitative-aria-chorus segment "Thy hand, Belinda" through "With drooping wings" from the opera *Dido and Aeneas;* the entire *Come, Ye Sons of Art*

Bach: "Sicut locutus est" from *Magnificat* in D Major, BWV 243

Kuhnau: *Tristis est anima mea*

Lully: The overtures to *Alceste* and *Armida*

Hammerschmidt: The cantata *Therefore Watch that Ye Be Ready*

Corelli: Any of the *Concerti grossi,* Op. 6

Vivaldi: Concerto in A Minor, Op. 3, No. 8.

Handel: Wind band transcriptions of Handel's *Water Music* and *Royal Fireworks Music;* "And believed the Lord" from *Israel in Egypt;* the "Pastoral Symphony" and many of the arias and choruses of *Messiah*

THE VIENNESE CLASSICAL PERIOD

- Instead of the rhythmic regularity of the Baroque, look for mixed and broken rhythms at the beginning of some movements, followed by a shift to faster rhythmic levels as an important cadence is approached.
- Note and enjoy the varieties of phrase length here.
- Tempos can cover a bit more range here than in the Baroque, but study the sources and avoid extremes.
- Some elements of the Baroque (monothematicism and *fortspinnung,* for example) were carried by Haydn and others into this style. Other features—development is an instance—are innovations.
- Work for drama; here, as in the Baroque, things tend to change suddenly, not gradually. Make the most of the best spots, but don't overdo them.
- Remember that the silences in this music are wonderful opportunities to hold your audiences spellbound.

- As with the Baroque, honor possible cadenzas.
- Work for clarity but not simplicity in this music; avoid naivete and childishness, above all. The passions here lie just under a veneer of courtly grace. Make this music sound important.
- Take time. Let the music breathe.
- Early in the nineteenth century, melody gains prominence in the music of Schubert and others, but that does not mean that the extremes of late Romantic style are appropriate. Continue to look for a Viennese Classical aesthetic in these works (constant rhythmic elements, for example, and block-style dynamics).

For further practice, we suggest the following works from this period.

Haydn: *Die Beredsamkeit* ("Freunde, Wasser macht man stumm"); "Gloria in excelsis Deo" from the *Nelsonmesse* (the "Lord Nelson Mass"); the Kyrie of the *Harmoniemesse;* other symphony movements; Concerto in E-flat for Trumpet, any movement

Mozart: Any movement(s) from *Eine kleine Nachtmusik;* any movement of the Requiem; other symphony movements; Piano Concerto No. 21 in C Major, first movement

Beethoven: Symphony No. 1, in C Minor, first movement; Symphony No. 7, in A Major, second movement; Violin Concerto in D, second movement; *Choral Fantasia* from the first Allegro to the end

Schubert: Any of the movements of Mass in G Major; Symphony No. 8, in B Minor *(Unfinished),* second movement

THE ROMANTIC STYLE

- The tonal palette of the Romantic composer is more elaborate. Often, the same basic harmonies are present, separated by long chromatic transitional passages. Look for these "real" tonal landmarks and connect them with your phrases.
- Similarly, the metric/rhythmic relationships in this style are more complex; yet, sharply defined time structures still must be communicated to listeners.
- The music is much more heavily annotated than that of earlier times, and the sheer number of markings tends to intimidate performers. Try to see through the notation (in *any* style) to the overall conception of the composer that lies behind the printing.
- Some aspects here *evolve* more subtly; accelerandos, crescendos, and other processes move gradually from one level or station to another.
- The normal articulation in many cases will be a full-blown Romantic legato.
- Often, the focus in this century is on extramusical influences; forms arise out of literary, mythological, nationalistic, and other sources. Those generally should have only limited impact on your own decisions, which still should be musical in nature. You may choose to do picturesque things, but pitch, rhythmic clarity, balance, line, and all remain at the center of your concerns.
- The expansive attitudes of the period led composers to reach for extremes. Miniatures and giant works, enormous technical demands, huge ensembles, and other

such extravagances can be found in the period. Look always for legitimacy, whatever the scope of the work.

For further practice, we suggest the following works from this period.

> Schubert: Choral settings of "Ständchen," D.920 (for women's voices); "Widerspruch" (for men); other such works
>
> Mendelssohn: "Cast Thy Burden Upon the Lord" and the aria-recitative-trio-chorus segment "It Is Enough" through "He Watching Over Israel," all from *Elijah; Military Overture* (for band)
>
> Rossini: Overture to *La Gazza ladra;* other opera overtures
>
> Berlioz: *Roman Carnival Overture* (orchestra; see also the transcription for band)
>
> von Weber: Overture to *Der Freischütz*
>
> Brahms: *Alto Rhapsody; Schicksalslied*
>
> Fauré: *Cantique de Jean Racine;* "Agnus Dei" from the Requiem
>
> Wagner-Caillet: "Elsa's Procession to the Cathedral" from *Lohengrin;* other Verdi and Wagner transcriptions for band
>
> Tchaikovsky: Symphony No. 6 *(Pathetique),* second and third movements

TWENTIETH-CENTURY STYLE

- The tendency of the nineteenth century to pursue extremes of one kind or another continued into the twentieth century in many respects. So did the concept of "freedom," by which generally was meant the license to use any combination of pitches, rhythmic units, instruments, or whatever.
- As they discarded traditional structures, some composers looked for other matrices that could serve as foundations for their works. (Serial technique, ethnomusicological relationships, new theoretical formulations, and other rationales served as experimental approaches.) By the end of the century, all were in doubt.
- Probably the most important parameter of the nineteenth century had been melody. In the twentieth century, it became timbre.
- Jagged melodic lines and extremely complex rhythms are typical; extreme tessituras and strange harmonies abound, although many more moderate stylistic usages can be observed.
- A strong strand of eclecticism can be identified in many composers.
- Most twentieth-century music (in spite of Schoenberg and his followers) remains clearly tonal (in a broader sense than the word would have been defined in earlier times). The same possibilities for communicating the feeling of "returning home" to tonic are present here as were in the music of Bach and Beethoven.

For further practice, we suggest the following works from this period.

B. Britten: "Concord" and "Concord and Time" from *Choral Dances from Gloriana*; "Let Nimrod, the mighty hunter" and the "Hallelujah" finale from the cantata *Rejoice in the Lamb*

Ives: *Serenity*; Symphony No. 4, slow movement; *Psalm 90*

Barber: Adagio for Orchestra; "Mary Hynes" and "The Coolin" from *Reincarnations*

H. Wood: *Mannin Veen* (for band)

Holst: Suite No. 1, in E-flat (for band)

Kodály: *Jesus and the Traders*

Stravinsky: *Symphony of Psalms*, first movement

Debussy: *Trois Nocturnes*, third movement

Vaughan Williams: *English Folk Song Suite* (for band); the opera *Riders to the Sea*

Persichetti, *Divertimento* (for band)

Bibliography

Items listed here are categorized as musical scores, reference works (including diction guides for choral works), and textual sources.

TEXTUAL SOURCES

APEL, WILLI, *Gregorian Chant*. Bloomington: Indiana University Press, 1957.

BABITZ, SOL, "Concerning the Time that Every Note Must Be Held," *Music Review* 28 (February 1967), 21–37.

BACH, CARL PHILIPP EMANUEL, *Versuch über die wahre Art das Clavier zu Spielen*, trans. W. J. Mitchell. New York: W. W. Norton & Co., Inc., 1949.

BAUMOL, WILLIAM J., AND WILLIAM G. BOWEN, *Performing Arts: The Economic Dilemma*. New York: Twentieth Century Fund, 1966.

BOSWELL, JAMES, *The Life of Samuel Johnson*. 3 vols. New York: Heritage Press, 1963.

CARDINE, DOM EUGÉNE, *Gregorian Semiology*, trans. Robert M. Fowells. Solesmes: Abbaye Saint-Pierre de Solesmes, 1983.

DAVID, HANS T., AND ARTHUR MENDEL, *The Bach Reader* (rev. ed.). New York: W. W. Norton & Co., Inc., 1965.

DEMAREE, ROBERT W., JR., *The Structural Proportions of the Haydn Quartets*. Ph.D. diss., Indiana University. Ann Arbor: University Microfilms, 1973.

DOLMETSCH, ARNOLD, *The Interpretation of the Music of the Seventeenth and Eighteenth Centuries*. Seattle: University of Washington Press, 1980.

DONINGTON, ROBERT, *A Performer's Guide to Baroque Music*. New York: Scribner's, 1973.

DÜRR, ALFRED, "Performance Practice of Bach's Cantatas," *American Choral Review* 16, no. 2 (April 1974), 1–33.

EHMANN, WILHELM, "Concertisten und Ripienisten in Bach's H-Moll Messe," *Musik und Kirche* 30, 2–6.

FENNELL, FREDERICK, "Gustav Holst's Second Suite in F for Military Band," *The Instrumentalist* 32, no. 4 (November 1977), 42–52.

FREY, HERMANN WALTER, *Die Diarien der Sixtinischen Kapelle in Rom der Jahre 1560 und 1561* (Diaries from the Archives of the Sistine Chapel Choir, Rome, 1560–1561). Düsseldorf: Musikverlag Schwann, 1959.

FUX, JOHANN JOSEPH, *Gradus ad Parnassum*. Vienna, 1725.

GAJARD, JOSEPH, *The Rhythm of Plainsong According to the Solesmes School*, trans. Dom Aldhelm Dean. New York: Fischer & Bros., 1945.

GEIRINGER, KARL, *Haydn: A Creative Life in Music*. Berkeley and Los Angeles: University of California Press, 1968.

GLAREANUS, HENRICUS, *Dodecachordon*, trans. C. A. Miller, *Musicological Studies and Documents* 2 (1965), 232.

GOTWALS, VERNON, *Joseph Haydn: Eighteenth Century Gentleman and Genius* (translation of early biographies by G. A. Griesinger and A. C. Dies). Madison: University of Wisconsin Press, 1963.

GRASSINOT, JAMES, *Musical Dictionary*. London, 1740.

HILLIS, MARGARET, *At Rehearsals* (instructions for the Chicago Symphony Chorus). Barrington, Ill.: American Choral Foundation, 1969.

HOLST, IMOGEN, *Gustav Holst, A Biography* (2nd ed.). Oxford and New York: Oxford University Press, 1988.

JONES, ANN HOWARD, *An Examination of Expressive Rhythm and Articulation Practices in the Baroque Period with Suggestions for Their Application to the Duet Choruses of Messiah*. Ph.D. diss., University of Iowa, 1984.

KIRNBERGER, JOHANN PHILIPP, *The Art of Strict Musical Composition*, trans. David Beach and Jurgen Thym. New Haven and London: Yale University Press, 1983.

LANDON, H. C. ROBBINS, *The Collected Correspondence and London Notebooks of Joseph Haydn*. London: Barrie and Rockliff, 1959.

————, *Haydn. Chronicle and Works*. 5 vols. Bloomington: Indiana University Press, 1976–1980.

————, *The Symphonies of Joseph Haydn*. London: Universal Edition and Rockliff Publishing, 1955. See also the *Supplement to the Symphonies of Joseph Haydn*. London: Barrie and Rockliff, 1961.

LANG, PAUL HENRY, *The Concerto 1800–1900*. New York: W. W. Norton & Co., Inc., 1969.

LANGER, SUZANNE K., *Feeling and Form*. New York: Scribner's, 1953.

————, *Philosophy in a New Key*. Cambridge: Harvard University Press, 1957.

LEINSDORF, ERICH, *The Composer's Advocate: A Radical Orthodoxy for Conductors*. New Haven: Yale University Press, 1981.

MARPURG, FRIEDRICH WILHELM, *Anleitung zum Klavierspielen*, trans. Elizabeth Loretta Hays. Ann Arbor: University Microfilms, 1976.

MATTHESON, JOHANN, *Der vollkommene Capellmeister*, trans. Ernest C. Harriss. Ann Arbor: University Microfilms, 1981.

MEYER, LEONARD B., *Emotion and Meaning in Music*. Chicago: University of Chicago Press, 1956.

————, *Music, the Arts, and Ideas*. Chicago: University of Chicago Press, 1967.

MOROSAN, VLADIMIR, *Choral Performance in Pre-Revolutionary Russia*. Ann Arbor: UMI Research Press, 1986.

MOSES, DON V, ROBERT W. DEMAREE, JR., AND ALLEN F. OHMES, *Face to Face with an Orchestra*. Princeton, N.J.: Prestige Publications, 1987.

MOZART, LEOPOLD, *Versuch einer gründlichen Violinschule*, trans. Editha Knocker. London: Oxford University Press, 1951.

MUSSELMAN, JOSEPH A., *Dear People . . . Robert Shaw*. Bloomington: Indiana University Press, 1979.

NEUMANN, FREDERICK, "External Evidence and Uneven Notes," *Musical Quarterly* 52 (October 1966), 448–464.

NEUMANN, WERNER, *Handbook of Joh. Seb. Bach's Cantatas*. Leipzig: Breitkopf & Härtel, 1947.

PLEASANTS, HENRY, *The Agony of Modern Music*. New York: Simon & Schuster, 1955.

QUANTZ, JOHANN JOACHIM, *Versuch einer Anweisung die Flöte traversiere zu spielen*, trans. Edward R. Reilly. London: Faber and Faber, 1958.

REESE, GUSTAVE, *Music in the Renaissance* (rev. ed.). New York: W. W. Norton & Co., Inc., 1959.

ROUSSEAU, JEAN-JACQUES, *Dictionnaire de musique*. Paris, 1768.

RUBBRA, EDMUND, *Gustav Holst,* collected essays ed. Stephen Lloyd and Edmund Rubbra. London: Triad Press, 1974.

SACHS, CURT, *Rhythm and Tempo.* New York: W. W. Norton & Co., Inc., 1953.

SANFORD, SALLY ALLIS, *Seventeenth and Eighteenth Century Vocal Style and Technique.* Ann Arbor: University Microfilms, 1979.

SCHROCK, DENNIS, "Aspects of Performance Practice During the Classic Era," in *Five Centuries of Choral Music: Essays in Honor of Howard Swan,* ed. Gordon Paine, pp. 281–323. Stuyvesant, N.Y.: Pendragon Press, 1988.

STILLER, GÜNTHER, *Johann Sebastian Bach and the Liturgical Life in Leipzig,* ed. Robin A. Leaver, trans. Herbert J. A. Bouman, Daniel F. Poellot, and Hilton C. Oswald *(Johann Sebastian Bach und das Leipziger gottesdienstliche Leben seiner Zeit).* St. Louis: Concordia, 1984.

STRAVINSKY, IGOR, *Poetics of Music.* Taken from the Charles Eliot Norton Lectures at Harvard University, 1939–1940. New York: Vintage Books, 1956.

TOLSTOY, LEO, *War and Peace,* trans. Louise Maude and Aylmer Maude. New York: Simon & Schuster, 1942.

TOVEY, DONALD FRANCIS, *Essays in Musical Analysis.* Vol. 3, *Concertos.* London: Oxford University Press, 1939.

TÜRK, DANIEL GOTTLIEB, *School of Clavier Playing,* trans. Raymond H. Haggh; music autography Helen M. Jenner. Lincoln: University of Nebraska Press, 1982.

VAUGHAN WILLIAMS, Ralph, *Heirs and Rebels. Letters Written to Each Other and Occasional Writings on Music,* ed. Ursula Vaughan Williams and Imogen Holst. London and New York: Oxford University Press, 1959.

VEILHAN, JEAN-CLAUDE, *The Rules of Musical Interpretation in the Baroque Era,* trans. John Lambert. Paris: Alphonse Leduc, 1979.

REFERENCE WORKS
AND SUPPLEMENTARY TECHNICAL GUIDES

ANGELIS, MICHAEL DE, *Correct Pronunciation of Latin according to Roman Usage,* ed. Nicola A. Montani. Philadelphia: St. Gregory Guild, 1937.

APEL, WILLI, *Harvard Dictionary of Music* (2nd ed.). Cambridge: Harvard University Press, 1969.

APPELMAN, D. RALPH, *The Science of Vocal Pedagogy.* Bloomington: Indiana University Press, 1967.

Band Music Guide (9th ed.). Northfield, Ill.: *The Instrumentalist,* 1989.

CARSE, ADAM, *The History of Orchestration.* New York: Dover Publications, 1964.

COLORNI, EVALINA, *The Singer's Italian: A Manual of Diction and Phonetics.* New York: G. Schirmer, Inc., 1970.

COOK, GARY, *Teaching Percussion.* New York: Schirmer Books, 1988.

DANIELS, DAVID, *Orchestral Music: A Handbook.* Metuchen, N.J.: Scarecrow Press, 1982.

EATON, QUAINTANCE, *Opera Production I.* New York: Da Capo Press, 1974.

GALAMIAN, IVAN, *The Principles of Violin Playing and Teaching* (2nd ed.). Englewood Cliffs, N.J.: Prentice Hall, 1985.

GRUBB, THOMAS, *The Singing of French.* New York: G. Schirmer, Inc., 1979.

HINES, JEROME, *Great Singers on Great Singing.* Garden City, N.Y.: Doubleday, 1982.

KENNAN, KENT, AND DONALD GRANTHAM, *The Technique of Orchestration* (4th ed.). Englewood Cliffs, N.J.: Prentice-Hall, 1990.

MARSHALL, MADELEINE, *The Singer's Manual of English Diction.* New York: G. Schirmer, Inc., 1953.

MORIARTY, JOHN, *The Sounds and 81 Exercises for Singing Them*. Boston: E. C. Schirmer Music Co., 1975.

The New Grove Dictionary of Music and Musicians, ed. Stanley Sadie. 20 vols. London: Macmillan, 1980.

ODOM, WILLIAM, *German for Singers*. New York: G. Schirmer, Inc., 1981.

OTTMAN, ROBERT, *Music for Sight Singing* (3rd ed.). Englewood Cliffs, N.J.: Prentice-Hall, 1986.

PISTON, WALTER, *Orchestration*. New York: W. W. Norton & Co., Inc., 1955.

RIMSKY-KORSAKOV, NICHOLAI, *Principles of Orchestration*, ed. Maximilian Steinberg, trans. Edward Agate. New York: Dover Publications, 1964.

SCHEIL, RICHARD F., *A Manual of Foreign Language Diction for Singers*. Fredonia, N.Y.: Palladian Co., 1975.

VENNARD, WILLIAM, *Singing, the Mechanism and the Technic* (5th ed.). New York: C. Fischer, 1968.

MUSICAL SCORES

BACH, JOHANN SEBASTIAN, *Christ lag in Todesbanden*, in *Werke*, 1, 97. Leipzig: Bach-Gesellschaft, 1855–1899 and 1926.

_____, *Christ lag in Todesbanden*, ed. Alfred Dürr, in *Neue Ausgabe sämtlicher Werke*, 1, ix. Kassel and Leipzig: Bärenreiter Verlag for the Johann Sebastian Bach Institut, Göttingen, and the Bach-Archiv, Leipzig, 1954–.

_____, *Christ lag in Todesbanden*, ed. Arnold Schering (miniature score). New York: Edition Eulenberg, 1932.

_____, *Christ lag in Todesbanden*, in the Edition Eulenberg miniature score version, ed. Arnold Schering, with analysis and editorial comments by Gerhard Herz. Norton Critical Scores. New York: W. W. Norton & Co., Inc., 1967.

_____, *Christ lag in Todesbanden*, ed. Reinhold Kubik. Stuttgart: Carus-Verlag, 1981.

_____, *Christ lag in Todesbanden*. Reprint of the Bach-Gesellschaft edition (above). New York: Edwin F. Kalmus.

_____, *The St. John Passion*, ed. Arthur Mendel. New York: G. Schirmer, Inc., 1951.

BARBER, SAMUEL, "Sure on this shining night." New York: G. Schirmer, Inc., 1961.

_____, *Reincarnations*: "Anthony O Daly." New York: G. Schirmer, Inc., 1942.

BRAHMS, JOHANNES, *Schaffe in mir, Gott, ein rein Herz*, Op. 29, No. 2. Leipzig: Breitkopf & Härtel, 1980.

Chants of the Church (The Monks of Solesmes). Toledo, Ohio: Gregorian Institute of America, 1962.

DAVISON, ARCHIBALD T., AND WILLI APEL, *Historical Anthology of Music*. 2 vols. Cambridge: Harvard University Press, 1962.

DEARMER, PERCY, MARTIN SHAW, AND RALPH VAUGHAN WILLIAMS, *The Oxford Book of Carols*. London: Oxford University Press, 1964.

GABRIELI, GIOVANNI, *Sonata pian' e forte*. See Davison and Apel, *Historical Anthology of Music*, 1, 198–200.

_____, *Sonata pian e forte*, ed. Fritz Stein (brass instruments). New York: C. F. Peters, 1932.

_____, *Sonata pian e forte*, ed. Douglas Moore (eight violoncellos). Williamstown, Mass.: D. Moore, 1988.

_____, *Sonata pian e forte*, ed. Richard Charteris (mixed instruments). Redcroft, Huntingdon, Cambridgeshire: King's Music, 1990.

HANDEL, GEORGE FRIDERIC, *Messiah*, in *George Frideric Handel Werke*, ed. F. W. Chrysander, vol 45. (Vol. 96 is a facsimile of the autograph itself.) Leipzig: Breitkopf & Härtel for the Deutschen Händelgesellschaft, 1858–1894.

_____, *Messiah, a Sacred Oratorio*, ed. Watkins Shaw. London: Novello, 1965.

_____, *Messiah, an Oratorio*, ed. Alfred Mann. 3 vols. New York: Dover, 1989 (reprint of editions by ABI/Alexander Broude, Inc., (vol. 1), Jerona Music Corp. (vols. 2–3), and Rutgers University Press, 1959–83.

HAYDN, FRANZ JOSEPH, Symphony No. 88, in G Major, ed. H. C. Robbins Landon. Salzburg: Haydn-Mozart Presse, Universal Edition, 1964.

_____, Symphony No. 101, in D Major, ed. H. C. Robbins Landon. Salzburg: Haydn-Mozart Presse, Universal Edition, 1967.

HINDEMITH, PAUL, *Spielmusik*, Op. 43, No. 1. Mainz: B. Schott's Söhne, Mainz, 1927.

HOLST, GUSTAV, Second Suite in F for Military Band, Op. 28, No. 2. New York: Boosey & Co., 1948.

_____, Second Suite in F for Military Band, Op. 28, No. 2, ed. Colin Matthews. New York: Boosey & Hawkes, 1984.

JOSQUIN DES PRES, *Misse Pange lingua*, ed. Friedrich Blume, in *Das Chorwerk*, vol. 1. Wolfenbüttel: Moseler Verlag, 1929.

_____, *Misse Pange lingua*, in *Werken van Josquin des Prez*, ed. Albert Smijers, vol. 33. Amsterdam: G. Alspach, 1952.

_____, *Misse Pange lingua*, ed. Thomas Warburton. Chapel Hill: University of North Carolina Press, 1977.

LEIDZÈN, ERIK W. G., *Pictures at an Exhibition*. See Mussorgsky-Leidzèn.

MENDELSSOHN (-BARTHOLDY), FELIX, Violinkonzert, Op. 64, ed. Julius Rietz, in *Werke*. Leipzig: Breitkopf & Härtel, 1874–1877.

_____, Konzert in E moll für Violine und Orchester, Op. 64. Leipzig: N. Simrock, 1905.

_____, Konzert in E moll für Violine und Orchester, Op. 64. New York: Broude Brothers.

_____, Concerto for Violin and Orchestra in E Minor, Op. 64, ed. Leopold Auer (piano reduction). New York: C. Fischer, 1917.

_____, Concerto for Violin and Orchestra in E Minor, Op. 64, ed. Carl Flesch (piano reduction). New York: C. F. Peters, 1927.

_____, Concerto for Violin and Orchestra in E Minor, Op. 64 (miniature score). London and New York: Edition Eulenberg, 1951.

_____, Concerto for Violin and Orchestra in E Minor, Op. 64 (piano reduction). New York: International Music Co., 1967.

_____, Concerto for Violin and Orchestra in E Minor, Op. 64 (miniature score based on the Breitkopf & Härtel edition above). New York: Edwin F. Kalmus.

_____, Violinkonzert, Op. 64. See Lang, *The Concerto*.

MENOTTI, GIAN CARLO, *Amahl and the Night Visitors. An Opera in One Act*. New York: G. Schirmer, Inc., 1952.

_____, *Amahl and the Night Visitors. An Opera in One Act* (piano reduction). New York: G. Schirmer, Inc., 1952.

MONTEVERDI, CLAUDIO, Overture (Toccata and first Ritornello) to *Orfeo*, in *Tutti le Opera di Claudio Monteverdi*, vol. 11, ed. G. Francesco Malipiero. Vienna: Universal Edition, 1926.

MORLEY, THOMAS, *April Is in My Mistress' Face*, in *The A Cappella Singer*, ed. H. Clough-Leighter (heavily edited). Boston: E. C. Schirmer Music Co., 1933.

_____, *April Is in My Mistress' Face* (no editorial markings). New York: Arista Music Co., 1983.

MOZART, WOLFGANG AMADEUS, *Ave verum corpus*, kv 618, ed. Ernst Tittel. Wien, Graz, and Köln: Musik Verlag Styria, 1952.

_____, *Ave verum corpus*, kv 618, in Ser. 1, 3, *Kleinere Kirchenwerke* of *Neue Ausgabe sämtlicher Werke*. Kassel and New York: Bärenreiter, 1963.

_____, *Ave verum corpus*, kv 618. New York: Edwin F. Kalmus.

Mussorgsky, Modest, *Pictures at an Exhibition*. The piano version in *Complete Works*, vol. 17, ed. Paul Lamm. New York: Edwin F. Kalmus.

Mussorgsky-Leidzèn, *Pictures at an Exhibition*. The concert band version. New York: Carl Fischer, 1941.

Mussorgsky-Ravel, *Pictures at an Exhibition*. The orchestral version. New York: Boosey & Hawkes, 1929.

_____, *Pictures at an Exhibition*. The orchestral version (miniature score). New York: Edition Eulenberg, 1929.

Purcell, Henry, *Come, Ye Sons of Art*, ed. William Herrmann. New York: G. Schirmer, Inc., 1974.

Ravel, Maurice, *Tableaux d'une exposition*. See Mussorgsky-Ravel.

Schubert, Franz, Mass in G Major, D.167, ed. Eusebius Mandyczewski, in *Franz Schubert's Werke*, Ser. 13, vol. 1, 2. Leipzig: Breitkopf & Härtel, 1884–1897. Reprinted as *Franz Schubert Complete Works*, vol. 6, pp. 121–156. New York: Dover Publications, 1964.

_____, Mass in G Major, D.167, ed. W. Durr, A. Feil, C. Landon, and others, in *Neue Ausgabe sämtliche Werke*, Ser. I, vol. 1b. Kassel: Bärenreiter, 1964–.

_____, Mass in G Major, D.167, ed. Willi Schulze. Stuttgart: Carus-Verlag, 1984.

_____, Mass in G Major, D.167, ed. Robert Shaw and Alice Parker (piano reduction). New York, G. Shirmer, Inc., 1954.

_____, Mass in G Major, D.167, ed. Berthold Tours (piano reduction). New York: H. W. Gray.

_____, Mass in G Major, D.167 (miniature score). New York: Edwin F. Kalmus.

Sharp, Cecil, *English Folk Songs from the Southern Appalachians*, ed. Maud Karpeles. London and New York: Oxford University Press, 1952.

Vivaldi, Antonio, *Gloria*, ed. (and "elaborated") Alfredo Casella. Milan and New York: Ricordi and Franco Columbo, 1941 and 1958.

_____, *Gloria*, ed. Mason Martens. New York: Walton Music Corp., 1961.

_____, *Gloria*, ed. Clayton Westerman. New York: Edwin F. Kalmus, 1967.

Index

Conducting axioms: These basic precepts are highlighted in bold type throughout the text. Conducting theory: These extended explanations of underlying concepts of conducting processes and traditions begin on the following pages: 9, 13, 30, 40, 47, 67, 69, 83, 99, 101, 107, 116, 125, 128, 132, 143, 184, 257, 393, 403, 408, 426, 454.